THE GOD WHO REJOICES

THE GOD WHO REJOICES

Joy, Despair, and the Vicarious Humanity of Christ

Christian D. Kettler

CASCADE *Books* • Eugene, Oregon

THE GOD WHO REJOICES
Joy, Despair, and the Vicarious Humanity of Christ

Copyright © 2010 Christian D. Kettler. All rights reserved. Except for brief quotations in critical publications or reviews, no part of this book may be reproduced in any manner without prior written permission from the publisher. Write: Permissions, Wipf and Stock Publishers, 199 W. 8th Ave., Suite 3, Eugene, OR 97401.

Cascade Books
An Imprint of Wipf and Stock Publishers
199 W. 8th Ave., Suite 3
Eugene, OR 97401

www.wipfandstock.com

ISBN 13: 978-1-60608-857-9

Scripture quotations are from the New Revised Standard Version of the Bible, copyright © 1989 the National Council of the Churches of Christ in the USA. Used by permission. All rights reserved.

Cataloging-in-Publication data:

Kettler, Christian D., 1954–

The God who rejoices : joy despair, and the vicarious humanity of Christ / Christian D. Kettler.

xxvi + 328 p. ; 23 cm. — Includes bibliographical references and index(es).

ISBN 13: 978-1-60608-857-9

1. Joy—Religious aspects. 2. Despair—Religious aspects—Christianity. 3. Jesus Christ—Person and offices. I. Title.

BT772 .K48 2010

Manufactured in the U.S.A.

In grateful memory of my teachers:

Ray S. Anderson

Geoffrey W. Bromiley

Robert W. Myers

James B. Torrance

Thomas F. Torrance

theologians of joy

Contents

Preface • ix
Abbreviations • xxvi

PART ONE
Despair: The "Grand Inquisitor" of Our Souls and the Vicarious Despair of Christ

CHAPTER ONE — The Sources of Despair • 3
CHAPTER TWO — Despair over Something • 20
CHAPTER THREE — Is Despair from God? • 44
CHAPTER FOUR — Despair as Meaninglessness • 62
CHAPTER FIVE — The Resolution of Despair? • 83

PART TWO
Can Joy Live with Despair? And the Vicarious Joy of Christ

CHAPTER SIX — The Problem of Joy • 105
CHAPTER SEVEN — Can We Live with Both Joy and Despair? • 134
CHAPTER EIGHT — Joy as Gift, Grace, and Gratitude . . . and Its Enemies • 182
CHAPTER NINE — The Joy That Comes from Struggle • 209
CHAPTER TEN — Joy as the Yes of God • 230
CHAPTER ELEVEN — Joy as the Yes of Humanity • 251

Subject Index • 297
Name Index • 311
Scripture Index • 319

Preface

It is joy unspeakable and full of glory,
Full of glory, full of glory,
It is joy unspeakable and full of glory,
Oh, the half has never yet been told.
—Barney E. Warren, "Joy Unspeakable" (1900)

Oh, Mama, can this really be the end . . .
—Bob Dylan, "Stuck Inside of Mobile with
the Memphis Blues Again" (1966)

I am not a normally joyful person. I'll be honest with you. I can identify with the "Underground Man" in Dostoevsky's classic story of existential angst: "I am a sick man . . . I am a wicked man. An unattractive man. I think my liver hurts . . ."[1] Well, maybe I'm not *that* bad (most of the time)! I remember well the angst of my teenage years, spending most of the day in the Southeast High School library with my headphones on playing incessantly Bob Dylan's song "Stuck Inside of Mobile with the Memphis Blues Again." Not really much different than any other adolescent, but not less significant! Despair, sorrow, or depression in my life has not been greater than anyone else. In fact, I have lived a relatively uneventful life, mostly teaching at a college on the prairies of Kansas. Yet that does not mean I am without despair. I do not mean that to say that I am constantly morose, but I am not a portrait of the glad-handing pastor whose glistening white-teeth smile seems to be an expectation of his parishioners, portraying a sad lack of sincerity. Christian "joy" can be very superficial. "Joy unspeakable"? Maybe. But perhaps not in a positive way! Fortunately, my early Christian experience involved someone who lived with both joy

1. Fyodor Dostoevsky, *Notes from the Underground*, trans. Richard Pevear and Larissa Volokhonsky (New York: Vintage, 1993) 3.

and despair, but not as equals. My first pastor was a man so crippled by arthritis that every joint, knuckles, knees, and elbows, had been replaced by plastic ones. I so vividly remember Bob Myers of Faith Presbyterian Church in Wichita, Kansas, bent over, hobbling around with his Bible. Yet what a Bible teacher and what a pastor he was! For Bob Myers, theology and ministry were always wedded together. What a surprise to find that was not true for all pastors! Bob did not appear to be "joyful." Yet he was one of the most joyful Christians I have ever known, despite his intense physical suffering. I am offended by those who "demand" Christians to be joyful. I remember one day on campus being reprimanded (or so I felt) by a young student: "Be happy!" "Rejoice!" or a word to the effect. What if I had just lost a loved one, or a job, or just had a traffic accident even? Life is full of despair. Can one really be joyful in the midst of despair? And where is Jesus Christ in this? This is the basic, gut-level, question of this book.

Despair can be both a synonym and also distinct from other words, such as depression, sorrow, melancholy, or pain. I am restricting depression to the clinical disease often treated by medication. Despair, as I see it, can include the clinically depressed, but it is a much wider phenomenon. It can come from a loss, such as the loss of a loved one, or a lack, the gnawing feeling that life has not given something to you for which you were entitled, or even in Kierkegaard's analysis, a "unconscious" despair (not knowing that you are in despair). Hope is sometimes viewed as the opposite of despair. This definition is a more "final" meaning of despair, the kind of despair that may lead to suicide. Again, my definition of despair is broader, but certainly has relevance to those in "final" despair.

Joy, likewise, can be a synonym and distinct from other words, such as happiness, gladness, and delight. Happiness can often be used as synonym for joy, but I believe the biblical accounts of joy, and particularly the joy of Jesus, speak of a distinct emotional action, whereas happiness may be more of a state, e.g., "the pursuit of happiness." Joy seems to have a richness that happiness does not possess. Gladness and delight can more easily be seen as synonyms.

The Scottish theologians Thomas F. Torrance and his brother James B. Torrance in recent years have been the foremost proponents of what they have called the vicarious *humanity* of Christ.[2] Different from speak-

---

2. The most important writings on the vicarious humanity of Christ are found in T. F. Torrance, *The Mediation of Christ*, rev. ed. (Colorado Springs: Helmers &

ing of simply the vicarious *death* Christ, this proposal seeks to present an integration between Christology and the doctrine of the atonement that stresses the radical nature of the substitutionary atonement, not restricting substitution only to Christ paying the penalty for our sin.

The vicarious humanity of Christ is found in the New Testament testimony about Jesus. The New Testament scholar Dale Allison can speak of the historical Jesus at the least as one who trusted in God. The parables of Jesus represent Jesus's "confessions" of faith: in "the righteousness and compassion of Israel's God," in his power, and in "the goodness of creation: the God who dresses the lilies of the field will not abandon the world but redeem it, for everything that God has made is very good."[3] Jesus confesses that he knows the limitations of human beings as well, that they are of little faith and are evil and that human inadequacy means that we should pray for God's will to be done on earth as it is in heaven.[4] In the New Testament Jesus can do nothing "of himself" (John 5:19, 30; 12:49), speak "of himself" (John 7:17; 12:49; 14:19), or desire to do his own will instead of the Father's (John 5:20; 6:28) because he is the Son of the Father who did not come of himself (John 8:42).[5] Jesus lived under the providence of the Father so that even in response to the tempter in the wilderness he can say, "Man shall not live by bread alone" but by the Word of God (Matt 4:4).

Theologically the Christian community knows that it must confess its faith. But that confession is based on the prior confession by Jesus Christ

---

Howard, 1992); T. F. Torrance, "The Word of God and the Response of Man," in *God and Rationality* (Oxford: Oxford University Press, 1971) 133–64; James B. Torrance, "The Vicarious Humanity of Christ," *The Incarnation: Ecumenical Studies in the Nicene-Constantinopolitan Creed*, ed. T. F. Torrance (Edinburgh: Handsel, 1981) 127–47; James B. Torrance, *Worship, Community and the Triune God of Grace* (Downers Grove, IL: InterVarsity, 1996); Thomas F. Torrance, James B. Torrance, and David W. Torrance, *A Passion for Christ: The Vision That Ignites Ministry* (Edinburgh: Hansel, 1999); and Thomas F. Torrance, *Incarnation: The Person and Life of Christ*, ed. by Robert T. Walker (Downers Grove, IL: InterVarsity, 2008). This volume of Torrance's Edinburgh lectures will be followed with another on *Atonement* in 2010. Elmer M. Colyer provides a helpful survey of the vicarious humanity of Christ in Torrance's thought in *How to Read T. F. Torrance: Understanding His Trinitarian and Scientific Theology* (Downers Grove, IL: InterVarsity, 2001) 97–126.

3. Dale C. Allison Jr., in Robert J. Miller, ed., *The Apocalyptic Jesus: A Debate* (Santa Rosa, CA: Polebridge, 2001) 150.

4. Ibid.

5. Karl Barth, *Church Dogmatics* (cited afterwards as *CD*) III/2, ed. Geoffrey W. Bromiley and T. F. Torrance (Edinburgh: T. & T. Clark, 1936–69) 62–63.

who made "the good confession" before Pontius Pilate (1 Tim 6:13). T. F. Torrance puts it frankly: "To partake of that salvation is to share with Christ Jesus in the confession which he himself made, for it is to be yoked together with him in the very exigencies and conditions of our human life which he came to assume and in assuming to heal and save."[6] The Christian confession is "a grateful response to the fact that first and supremely Jesus Christ has confessed it, does confess it, and will continually do so . . ."[7] He is the living Subject that continues to confess his faith in the Father even to the present day.[8] Christ the last Adam "recapitulates" (Irenaeus), or in David Bentley Hart's phrase, "retells" the story of humanity without sin.[9] As such, his response to the Father reflects the being of God as Trinity, as seen in the baptism of Jesus (Matt 3:13–17; Mark 1:9–11; Luke 3:21–22; John 1:29–34). The baptism of Jesus in the Orthodox tradition, David Bentley Hart claims, "is a disclosure of the Trinity itself, not an allegory, revealing the intra-divine relations . . . Christ's emergence from the waters is at once his resurrection, his ascent and return of all creation to the Father as a pure offering, and also his eternal 'response' to the Father as the Father's everlasting Word."[10] Hart puts it bluntly: "God both addresses and responds."[11] Hart rightly critiques the Catholic theologian Karl Rahner, otherwise well-known for his trinitarian theology, for denying that there is "a reciprocal Thou" in God.[12] For Karl Barth, this address and response of God is made manifest in the work of salvation:

> God is now not only the electing Creator, but the elect creature. He is not only the giver, but also the recipient of grace. He is not only the One who commands but the One who is called and

---

6. T. F. Torrance, "Immortality and Light," in *Transformation and Convergence in the Framework of Knowledge* (Grand Rapids: Eerdmans, 1984) 344.

7. Barth, *CD* IV/3.2, 790.

8. Ibid., 790–91.

9. David Bentley Hart, *The Beauty of the Infinite: The Aesthetics of Christian Truth* (Grand Rapids: Eerdmans, 2003) 325.

10. Ibid., 168.

11. Ibid.

12. Ibid., Hart might be going too far in criticizing social trinitarianism when it speaks of the Trinity's "responsiveness" as encompassing "another utterance." Why not? Would this not express the freedom of God? See Karl Rahner's view in Karl Rahner, *The Trinity*, trans. Joseph Donceel (New York: Crossroad, 1997): "The Logos is not the one who utters, but the one who is uttered. And there is properly no *mutual love* between Father and Son, for this would presuppose two acts," 106; cf. 62.

pledged to obedience. He does not merely go into lowliness, into the far country, to be Himself there, as he did in His turning to Israel. But now He Himself becomes lowly. He Himself is the man who is His Son. He Himself has become a stranger in Him.[13]

Christ confesses because not only *is* he the Word of God, but he has also *heard* the Word of God. Christ is "the one Word of God and its one Hearer, Witness and Guarantor in advance of all others."[14] "It was and is His royal freedom to be as man the perfect hearer of God, the One who knows God perfectly, and therefore the perfect servant and witness and teacher of God; the light shining in the world for us . . ."[15] Hearing the Word of God he then responds by offering himself to the Father for the sake of humanity, the element of sacrifice in the doctrine of the atonement. Jesus is not "a private person," Barth argues, for "this One, this Individual, this First-born, this Lord and Head, He has taken the place of all others, to die for them and to live for them, to live for them as the One who dies for them. No one can alter the fact that he, too, is a brother of this One, and that this One lives for him."[16] So Ephesians can say that "Christ loved us and gave himself up for us, a fragrant offering and sacrifice to God" (Eph 5:2).[17] In other words, sacrifice is not first something *we* offer to God but that Christ does. As he did, we are to "be imitators of God" by "living in love" (Eph 5:2). In this sacrifice he is the "first born off all creation," with cosmic consequences (Col 1:15, 20).

Part of Christ's response in hearing is in worship as the "liturgist" or "minister in the sanctuary" spoken of in the Epistle to the Hebrews (Heb 8:2), an emphasis in both worship and theology that James Torrance gives renewed emphasis.[18] This was essential in the devotional life of none other than Dietrich Bonhoeffer in the last book published during his lifetime, *Psalms: The Prayer Book of the Bible*. How are the Psalms, admittedly human prayers to God, also the Word of God? Bonhoeffer

---

13. Barth, *CD* IV/1, 170.
14. Barth, *CD* IV/3.2, 831.
15. Barth, *CD* IV/2, 409.
16. Ibid., 383.
17. Colin E. Gunton, *The Actuality of the Atonement: A Study of Metaphor, Rationality and the Christian Tradition* (Grand Rapids: Eerdmans, 1989) 125.
18. James B. Torrance, *Worship, Community, and the Triune God of Grace* (Downers Grove, IL: InterVarsity, 1997); "The Place of Jesus Christ in Worship," in *Theological Foundations for Ministry*, ed. Ray S. Anderson (Grand Rapids: Eerdmans, 1979) 348–69.

asks.[19] "We grasp it only when we remember that we can learn true prayer only from Jesus Christ, from the word of the Son of God, who lives with us men, to God the Father, who lives in eternity."[20] These prayers are all encompassing, concerning every aspect of life, including our needs and joys. "Jesus Christ has brought every need, every joy, every gratitude, every hope of men before God. In his mouth the word of man becomes the Word of God, and if we pray his prayer with him, the Word of God becomes once again the word of man."[21] He prays for us, knowing our needs, so that our prayers become his prayers. "It is really our prayer, but since he knows us better than we know ourselves and since he himself was true man for our sakes, it is also really his prayer, and it can become our prayer only because it was his prayer."[22] Karl Barth reminds us that John Calvin, in his Geneva Catechism (1541), speaks of us praying by the "mouth" of Christ because he intercedes for us.[23] Barth comments: "Thus, fundamentally, our prayer is already made even before we formulate it. When we pray, we can only return to that prayer which was uttered in the person of Jesus Christ and which is constantly repeated because God is not without humankind."[24]

This *leitourgos,* Ray Anderson contends, should not be restricted to the sanctuary, however. "He is the liturgist, who chooses the fields, the shops, and the streets as his sanctuary in which to render service to God. As the incarnate Son of God, he takes humanity and brings it back to its appropriate serviceableness to the Creator."[25] Athanasius in the fourth century classically speaks of Christ "having become Mediator between God and men, He might minister the things of God to us, and ours to God."[26] This includes ethics, as Barth comments: "The true basis of the

19. Dietrich Bonhoeffer, *Psalms: The Prayer Book of the Bible,* trans. James H. Burtness (Minneapolis: Augsburg, 1970) 13.

20. Ibid., 13-14.

21. Ibid., 14.

22. Ibid., 20.

23. Karl Barth, *Prayer,* ed. Don E. Saliers, 50th anniv. ed. (Louisville: Westminster John Knox, 2002) 14; John Calvin, "Calvin's Geneva Catechism, 1541," in *The School of Faith: The Catechisms of the Reformed Church,* ed. by T. F. Torrance (London: James Clarke, 1959) 44.

24. Barth, *Prayer,* 14.

25. Ray S. Anderson, *On Being Human: Essays in Theological Anthropology* (Grand Rapids: Eerdmans, 1982) 181.

26. Athanasius, *Four Discourses Against the Arians,* 4.6-7, NPNF, second series, 435.

command to serve is that the Lord Himself goes ahead not merely in command but also in original fulfillment of the command," because he assumed the form of a slave (Phil 2:7).[27]

A theology of the incarnation makes manifest that God is involved in both revelation and reconciliation.[28] The incarnation is not simply the revelation of the Word of God but also the responding act of reconciliation. In other words, reconciliation is not to be left up to our faith first of all, but to the obedient faith of the Son in response to the Father. The pastoral consolations of this are immense. In the words of T. F. Torrance, the incarnate Word of God

> came to share our lost and contradictory existence in order to save and reconcile us to God, and to regenerate and restore us through union with himself in his vicarious humanity as true sons and daughters of the heavenly Father who hear him, love him and obey him. Divine revelation and divine reconciliation are the obverse of each other.[29]

The vicarious humanity of Christ is one aspect, the second movement of the double movement of the incarnation that begins from God to humanity (the deity of Christ) but then proceeds from humanity to God (the humanity of Christ). Christ's humanity is not simply that which we imitate (*imitatio Christi*) but is vicarious, on our behalf and in our place. T. F. Torrance again makes this plain: "It is thus that Jesus Christ is himself God and Man, the Word of God become man in the fullest sense, for he is the Word of God not only spoken to man, but the Word of God faithfully heard by man and uttered by man in response to God."[30] Torrance can even dare to say, "Jesus Christ *is* our human response to God. Thus we appear before God and are accepted by him as those who are inseparably united to Jesus Christ our great High Priest in his eternal self-representation to the Father."[31] As the human response to God, Christ intervenes in the middle of our sinful responses and broken fellowship with God. "Christ is

---

Cf. T. F. Torrance, *The Trinitarian Faith: The Evangelical Theology of the Ancient Catholic Church* (Edinburgh: T. & T. Clark, 1988) 154.

27. Barth, *CD* III/4, 662.

28. T. F. Torrance, *The Christian Doctrine of God: One Being, Three Persons* (Edinburgh: T. & T. Clark, 1996) 41.

29. Ibid.

30. Ibid.

31. T. F. Torrance, *Mediation of Christ*, 80.

at once the Word of God to man and for the first time a real word of man to God . . . Here we have One who steps into the midst of our religious estrangement from God which rests upon a perversion of both Scripture and priesthood and calls scribe and priest alike to account."[32] Christ is both the giver and the one who is "the gift of fulfillment."[33] Bringing the things of God to humanity so that the things of humanity may be brought to God (Athanasius), God affects a "wonderful exchange" (*The Epistle to Diognetus* 9; cf. 2 Cor 8:9).[34] This is at the heart of Paul's doctrine of the Christian life, as seen in a favorite verse of T. F. Torrance's, Gal 2:20-21: ". . . and it is no longer I who live, but Christ who lives I me. And the life I live in the flesh I live by the faith in (or the alternative translation, "of") the Son of God . . ."

> "The faith of the Son of God" is to be understood here not just as my faith in him, but as the faith of Christ himself, for it refers primarily to Christ's unswerving faithfulness, his vicarious and substitutionary faith which embraces and undergirds us, such that when we believe we must say with Paul "not I but Christ," even in our act of faith.[35]

Barth interprets Phil 1:21 ("For to me, living is Christ and dying is gain") in a vicarious sense. "Christ lives vicariously for me, as it could be summed up."[36] In fact, according to Barth, "the life of Paul" has been "checkmated, so to speak (although it is still there on the board) by *another* life. This other life is Christ himself."[37] Even Reinhold Niebuhr can speak of the significance of Christ as the "second Adam": "The same Christ who is accepted by faith as the revelation of the character of God is also regarded as the revelation of the true character of man."[38] We may be all too used to

---

32. T. F. Torrance, *Royal Priesthood*, rev. ed. (Edinburgh: T. & T. Clark, 1993) 8.

33. Barth, *CD* IV/1, 13-14.

34. *The Epistle to Diognetus* 9, ANF, 28; cf. T. F. Torrance, *Trinitarian Faith*, 4.

35. T. F. Torrance, "Preaching Jesus Christ," in Thomas F. Torrance, James B. Torrance, and David W. Torrance, *Passion for Christ*, 24-25. See also the on-going discussion about "the faith of Christ" among New Testament scholars, such as in Richard B. Hays, *The Faith of Jesus Christ: The Narrative Substructure of Galatians 3:1-4:11*, 2nd ed. (Grand Rapids: Eerdmans, 2002).

36. Karl Barth, *Epistle to the Philippians, 40th Anniversary Edition*, trans. James W. Leitch (Louisville: Westminster John Knox, 2002) 37.

37. Ibid.

38. Reinhold Niebuhr, *The Nature and Destiny of Man*, vol. 1 (New York: Scribner's, 1946) 146.

viewing grace as "God's part" and faith as "our part" and end up bypassing the vicarious humanity of Christ, regardless of how orthodox we say our Christology is.

Why the need for the vicarious humanity of Christ? Because of our inadequacy, in knowing God as well as being able to save ourselves. Yes, even in thanking God. The Orthodox theologian Alexander Schmemann writes that to speak of Christ as "the new Adam" is to speak of him as the One who is perfectly thankful to the Father, "for He Himself was the perfect Eucharist" (thanksgiving). "He offered Himself in total obedience, love and thanksgiving to God. God was His very life."[39] This offering, we will see, includes an offering of joy in the midst of despair. "It is our Eucharist. It is the movement that Adam failed to perform, and that in Christ has become the very life of man: a movement of adoration and praise in which all joy and suffering, all beauty and all frustration, all hunger and all satisfaction are referred to their ultimate End and become finally meaningful."[40]

In like manner, the lack of the vicarious humanity of Christ in the church's pastoral theology, particularly as reflected in the often neglected priesthood of Christ, can have disastrous effects in the ministry of church, as Andrew Purves points out. "In particular, it is the failure to think of pastoral theology out of a center in the priesthood of Christ that has cast pastoral ministry back upon programs of its own devising. The effect has been to replace the vicarious humanity of Christ with the ministry of the pastor and his or her skills."[41] Whereas some traditions might be accused of the temptation of replacing the vicarious humanity of Christ with the vicarious humanity of Mary or the saints, Protestants suffer the same temptation: the vicarious humanity of *the pastor* or the individual, solitary Christian, often under the disguise of Luther's doctrine of "the priesthood of all believers."[42] None of us are guiltless here. Some have suggested that in Dietrich Bonhoeffer's concept of Christ as *Stellvertretung* (translated "deputyship" or "vicarious representative action") we find

---

39. Alexander Schmemann, *For the Life of the World: Sacraments and Orthodoxy* (Crestwood, NY: St. Vladimir's Seminary Press, 2002) 34–35.

40. Ibid., 34; cf. 60–61.

41. Andrew Purves, *Reconstructing Pastoral Theology: A Christological Foundation* (Louisville: Westminster John Knox) 96.

42. James B. Torrance, *Worship, Community, and the Triune God of Grace*, 18, 23; Purves, *Reconstructing Pastoral Theology*, 99.

"the theological foundation for connecting Christology, ecclesiology, and ethics."[43] This may even be the theological foundation for the justification of Bonhoeffer's participation in his conspiratorial activities.[44]

Often the objection is raised, If Christ has believed for us, of what use is our faith? The Holy Spirit as God bringing us into the relationship between the Father and the Son should not be ignored on this issue. Through the Holy Spirit, "we live as Jesus lives," in Karl Barth's memorable words.[45] "In Him, in spite of all appearances to the contrary, we are the new and true and exalted man."[46] There is not a causal or mechanical relation between our humanity and the Spirit but always a mystery (John 3:8). The result of the work of the Spirit, however, is a new humanity. "The Holy Spirit does not create the ghost of a man standing in decision, but the reality of the man concerning whom decision has already been made in the existence of the man Jesus."[47] It may be instructive that the Gospel of Luke, in one of the few mentions of Jesus possessing joy, says that he "rejoiced in the Holy Spirit" as he prayed to the Father (Luke 10:21). Jesus's faith must certainly be involved in his prayers and even he did not rejoice without the Holy Spirit. Joy itself, in terms of the joy of Jesus, may be mysterious as the relationship between the grace of God and the human response. What the vicarious humanity of Christ is saying is that we should not forget about the humanity of Christ when considering that perennial problem. "It is good to be with Jesus and not elsewhere," Barth movingly remarks. "This is good because it is there that God Himself is good for us."[48] The "elsewhere" may be lonely and isolated in our often powerless faith where joy can rarely be found and despair is often the only companion. Faith itself should not be seen as a support apart from the object of faith. So that to say "Jesus Christ lives" is to say something about

---

43. Joachim von Soosten, "Editor's Afterword to the German Edition," Dietrich Bonhoeffer, *Sanctorum Communio: A Theological Study of the Sociology of the Church*, ed. Clifford J. Green, trans. Reinhold Krauss and Nancy Lukens, Dietrich Bonhoeffer Works 1 (Minneapolis: Fortress, 1998) 303; cf. 155ff.; 293ff. Cf. Dietrich Bonhoeffer, *Ethics*, ed. Clifford J. Green, trans. Reinhold Krauss, Charles C. West, and Douglas W. Stott, Dietrich Bonhoeffer Works 6 (Minneapolis: Fortress, 2005) 231–59.

44. Soosten, "Editor's Afterword to the German Edition"; Bonhoeffer, *Sanctorum Communio*, 305.

45. Barth, *CD* IV/2, 363.
46. Ibid.
47. Ibid.
48. Barth, *CD* II/2, 570.

his humanity, his faith, yes, his joy and despair, as well as his deity, and how that humanity and faith relates to our humanity. To say "Jesus Christ lives" is to abandon all other support, including our faith and religion.⁴⁹ My former professor Geoffrey Bromiley used to say that evangelicals speaking of only "penal" substitution (Christ paying the penalty for our sin) do not believe in substitutionary atonement enough! Christ takes on the whole of our lives so that we may partake of the whole of his life. T. F. Torrance states it bluntly:

> That Jesus Christ really took our place in the human responses of knowing, believing and worshipping God, of repenting, obeying, laying hold of eternal life or bearing testimony, is something that many people find extremely hard to accept, ready as they may be to accept that God acts on their behalf in Jesus Christ, for somehow they want to reserve what they conceive to be an element of their own independence or freedom for themselves.⁵⁰

The issue for Torrance is our unwillingness to step out of the way instead of stubbornly demanding, particularly when it comes to religion (as Karl Barth saw so clearly).

> But are they not thereby substituting their own faith and their own personal response in the place of Christ's which he offered to the Father on our behalf, and is that not a way of finally setting the Man Christ Jesus in his saving mediation aside, and indeed of declining to let him take our place completely and unreservedly?⁵¹

C. S. Lewis expresses the caution of many who fear that an Augustinian-Calvinistic determinism means that God overrides the human will. "Merely to override a human will . . . would be for Him useless. He cannot ravish. He can only woo . . . He wants them to learn to walk and must therefore take away His hand . . ."⁵² Certainly God's action in Jesus Christ is not coercive, God does not "ravish," but do we want to say with Lewis

---

49. Barth, *CD* IV/3.1, 39.

50. T. F. Torrance, "Immortality and Light," in *Transformation and Convergence in the Framework of Knowledge*, 345.

51. Ibid.

52. C. S. Lewis, *The Screwtape Letters and Screwtape Proposes a Toast* (New York: Macmillan, 1962) 38. Lewis in another place suggests a soteriology of the vicarious humanity of Christ in terms of Christ as "The Perfect Penitent," in *Mere Christianity* (New York: Macmillan, 1960) 56–61.

that God "takes away" his hand, a kind of implicit deism? Is God only a wimpy cosmic lover, trying to "woo" us? (C. S. Lewis and process theology coming together?) Can this result in a kind of a "reverse" or "bizarro" vicarious humanity, ironically and sadly enough, in which we try to take the place of Christ? We think we are expressing our freedom but instead still act in bondage, as T. F. Torrance reminds us:

> All this, of course, is not to detract in any way from the freedom he gives us or the obedient response he demands of us as his children, but to give them their full value, for it is only within his all-embracing and undergirding faithfulness in giving himself unreservedly for us in the totality of our human being and life that we are genuinely and spontaneously free in our response, for then they are rendered unconditionally in answer to unconditional grace.[53]

True freedom comes when freedom is given to us, Barth eloquently adds:

> Our faith, love and hope and we ourselves—however strong may be our faith, hope and love – live only by that which we cannot create, posit, awaken or deserve. And although our believing, loving and hoping themselves and such are in us, they are not of us, but of their object, basis and content, of God, who in that one man not only answers for us but answers for Himself with us, who gives to us in freedom that we may believe, love and hope...[54]

Not only does God give us "freedom that we may believe, love and hope," but in Christ he also exalts us with him (Phil 2:5–11), so that

> the glory of our own being, life and activity is still His, and can be valued, and exalted and respected by us only as His; but all in such a way that in and with His glory we too are really exalted, because in the depth, where we can only give Him the glory, we find our true and proper place. It is in this way and in this sense that the Christian community proclaims "We with God" when it proclaims "God with us."[55]

---

53. T. F. Torrance, "Immortality and Light," in *Transformation and Convergence in the Framework of Knowledge*, 345.

54. Barth, *CD* IV/1, 15.

55. Ibid., 15–16.

Out of that relationship with him, then, comes a new faith, a new religion, and a new freedom. This is what the doctrine of the vicarious humanity of Christ is all about.

All of this is to suggest that foundations of the doctrine of the vicarious humanity of Christ are found in the Christian tradition, founded upon the biblical witness, from Athanasius and Irenaeus to Barth and Bonhoeffer, and even Orthodox theologians such as Alexander Schmemann and David Bentley Hart.

This book is a continuing exploration of the doctrine of the vicarious humanity, building upon previous studies I have done.[56] As the latest, *The God Who Believes*, dealt with faith and doubt, this one looks at joy and despair.

My conviction is that the radical implications of the vicarious humanity of Christ go beyond theological observations into implications for existential human existence and the ministry of the church, posing the question, "How can we have joy in the midst of despair?"

My approach is to first look at the phenomenon of despair, defined personally and theologically, how it attaches itself to us, its distinction from and relationship to depression, and its sources. Does despair come from sin, sickness, or God? Why does despair come in the form of meaningless, both in the context of tragedy and even masked by our lack of awareness, what Kierkegaard calls "unconscious despair"? What then is the path to the resolution of despair? The vicarious despair and the vicarious joy of Christ are introduced as two foci of the one gospel. Joy presents a problem in a world of despair. Yet the Bible speaks much of joy, particular in terms of song and music. In the Bible joy is a gift that demands a response of gratitude. The lack of joy among Christians, Nietzsche claims,

---

56. Christian D. Kettler, *The Vicarious Humanity of Christ and the Reality of Salvation* (Lanham, MD: University Press of America, 1991); "The Atonement as the Life of God in the Ministry of the Church," in *Incarnational Ministry: The Presence of Christ in Church, Society, and Family: Essays in Honor of Ray S. Anderson*, ed. Christian D. Kettler and Todd H. Speidell (Colorado Springs: Helmers & Howard, 1990) 58–78; "For I Do Not Do the Good I Want . . . and I'm Tired of Trying: Weakness and the Vicarious Humanity of Christ," in *On Being Christian . . . and Human: Essays in Celebration of Ray S. Anderson*, ed. Todd H. Speidell (Eugene, OR: Wipf & Stock, 2002) 51–69; "He Takes Back the Ticket . . . for Us: Providence, Evil, Suffering, and the Vicarious Humanity of Christ," *Journal of Christian Theological Research* 8 (2003) 35–55; *The God Who Believes: Faith, Doubt, and the Vicarious Humanity of Christ* (Eugene, OR: Cascade Books, 2005); "The Vicarious Beauty of Christ: The Aesthetics of the Atonement," *Theology Today* 64 (2007) 14–24; and "Advocate and Judge: The Vicarious Humanity of Christ and the 'Ideal' Self," *Edification: Journal of the Society for Christian Psychology* 1:2 (2007) 49–55.

is the greatest indictment of Christianity. In turn, we are often lured by "pseudo-joys" that promise much but deliver less than we think. The tendency is to try to live for joy without despair. The vicarious joy of Christ, however, is never without despair, including the struggle. Still the ultimate reality of joy is the joy of God that becomes the joy of humanity in the vicarious joy of Christ.

This is a theological look at joy and despair. The social and behavioral sciences, particularly, have great interest in this human phenomenon. What I am doing is unapologetically theological, not because I believe that the only genuine knowledge is theological, but because the theological work needs to be done first before there is any attempt at "integration" with other arts and sciences. Too often, as my friend Todd Speidell points out, integration is proposed that does not have much of a "theology" with which to integrate! I welcome the interaction with social and behavioral scientists and believe that they can benefit the most from a strictly theological presentation. In doing so I will at times offer points of intersection but that will not be my main thrust. In a sense this is a "pre-integration" study that I hope would serve those who seek to pursue the integration of a thoughtful theology with the social and behavioral sciences, but this is not a work of integration in itself.

This work is also not a "popular" work that is, written at the simplest possible level for the widest possible audience. This is certainly a place for that kind of book. Theology should not just remain for the theologians! But the themes of joy and despair often lend themselves to popular treatments that are unfortunately often shallow and superficial. I am seeking to push the envelope theologically and see how far we can open up the doctrine of the vicarious humanity of Christ to new implications, pastorally, practically, and existentially.

Theologians tend to avoid the personal, existential issues. Sometimes because of theological reasons: Do not personal issues create an anthropocentric theology? Karl Barth, one who does not tend to embrace an "experience-centered" theology, can nonetheless speak of the place of personal angst in theology, "that only on the lips of a man who is himself afflicted, seized and committed, controlled and nourished, unsettled and settled, comforted and alarmed by it, can the intrinsically true witness of the act and revelation of God in Jesus Christ have the ring and authority of truth which applies to other men."[57] Also, our answers will always

---

57. Barth, *CD* IV/3.2, 657.

be fragmentary and incomplete, not lending themselves to the kind of certitude that both the academy and the church often demand. Certitude, however, can often degenerate into positivism, a kind of resignation that, as Kierkegaard would remind us, is the opposite of faith. So, we press ahead, as one of my favorite early rockers, Rick Nelson used to sing, "fools rush in, where angels fear to tread . . ." But it that not the glory and risk of theology?

Because joy and despair are not just academic issues, I am compelled to bring my personal joys (and despairs!) at times, from the novels of Tarzan's creator, Edgar Rice Burroughs, to Golden Age comic books of the 1940s, from the lyrics of Bob Dylan to the darkness of the *film noir* genre in movies, not because am I trying to "communicate" or be "relevant," but because these things are parts of who I am. I cringe when anyone says that my passions, as inconsequential as they are to other people, are only "pop culture." Quite the contrary, this is part of who I am, regardless of whether or not Bob Dylan is popular at this time in culture! That kind of attitude would only diminish my joys. But I believe that often academic theology denies the importance of its personal (and therefore pastoral) nature if the personality of theologian, including one's passions, does not shine through (even if you could care less about The Flash and Green Lantern!). I would add that this goes for preaching as well (as the long-suffering congregation at the Church of the Savior in Wichita, where I regularly preach, would point out!).

Some may suggest that like the previous book, *The God Who Believes*, there is a problem with considering *The God Who Rejoices*: Does not this just accentuate the problem of an anthropomorphic God, a God who is spoken of in terms of human characteristics and emotions? Can we meaningfully say that God "rejoices"? And can we meaningfully rejoice with him?

This book has experienced the ebb and flow of despair and joy itself. Should I be surprised? Are not we plagued by being surprised that joy and despair can dwell together? But there have been times when joy has come upon me, when I have experienced the goodness and grace of the moment given by God, when I have been able to rejoice with Jesus.

Many times I would go to Ray Anderson's theology classes during my days at Fuller Seminary not just for information but desperate for grace. Southern California, where Fuller is located, as Raymond Chandler's *noir* mystery novels remind us, is busy and wide but full of despair and desperation. We are all desperate for grace. And I would find it in Anderson's lectures because of the kind of theologian Anderson was. His recent passing deprives the church of a wonderful spirit. But you can still find that spirit in his many books. Anderson is unique in his existential wrestling and christocentric theology. This book is written for people who are desperate for grace yet open to a radical yet orthodox christological reconstruction.

It might be strange to read about joy and despair in a theology that takes very seriously the revolution in theology brought about by Karl Barth: We have genuine though not exhaustive knowledge of God by God's grace in Jesus Christ. As the theologian Cynthia Rigby puts it, we do not know God exhaustively but we do know God *truly*. Most existential theologies, indebted to Paul Tillich and others, begin with the phenomenological wresting of the restless human spirit, or so such language. I do not ignore that wrestling. But I am not helped by either intellectual narcissism or fundamentalist platitudes. If you are that kind of person then this book may be for you. I am helped, however, by the intellectually satisfying and spiritually edifying Christian tradition that says boldly, unapologetically, but therefore always self-critically, that God has revealed himself in Jesus Christ (the gender-specific reflexive pronoun cannot be avoided without depersonalizing God, I'm afraid. To those offended by this, it's time to get over it).

On the other hand, as my former professor Lewis Smedes once said, Karl Barth is one of the few theologians who takes joy seriously.[58] I have found this to be true as well, as seen from the wealth of insights cited in this work. I make no apology for this. I only wish more theologians would take joy (and despair) as seriously as Barth does! "Evangelical theology is concerned with Immanuel, God with us!" Barth reminds us. "Having God for its object, it can be nothing else but the most thankful and *happy* science!"[59] In a letter Barth wrote,

> In all circumstances theology is a fine and joyful task . . . when I began it as a young man I was often troubled and saddened by it. Later I could see that if one understands theology properly, it takes one to a place which—for all the difficulties, all the labo-

---

58. Lewis B. Smedes, *Mere Morality: What God Expects from Ordinary People* (Grand Rapids: Eerdmans, 1983) 117. Cf. T. F. Torrance, *Karl Barth: An Introduction to His Early Theology, 1910–1931* (London: SCM, 1961) 23–25.

59. Karl Barth, *Evangelical Theology: An Introduction*, translated by Grover Foley (New York: Holt, Rinehart & Winston, 1963) 12.

rious work that is required—is a happy one, where a man can *live* and long for the time when he will see "face to face" (1 Cor 13:13): for himself *and* for others.[60]

Barth, as much as he was confident of God's self-revelation, never forgot that theology is a very human task, full of laughter, humor, and joy.[61] Barth himself suggested the headline for a newspaper article about him: "a joyful partisan of the good God."[62] He notices that in one characteristic of the music of his beloved Mozart was a turning "in which joy overtakes sorrow without extinguishing it."[63] That is a fitting conclusion for what we found in the implications of the vicarious humanity of Christ for joy and despair!

Many friends have contributed to this book: Joe Barthell, Michael Beardslee, Greg Belew, Marcia Dillon, Ryan Mackey, Derek Maris, Leigh Anne Petersen, Randy Powell, Wilma Hollaway. What a gift that these former students are now friends and colleagues of mine in the ministry of theology. May we all seek to live God's joy in the midst of the despairs of life.

Many thanks are due to Charlie Collier, Halden Doerge, Kristen Bareman, and the staff of Cascade Books and Wipf and Stock.

I am grateful to the trustees and administration of Friends University in providing a sabbatical for the spring 2009 semester in order to complete this work.

Assistance provided by my assistants, Audrey Wade and Kara Yuza, and the staff of Edmond Stanley Library at Friends University was much appreciated.

This book is dedicated to the memories of my beloved teachers who have gone home to the Lord: Ray S. Anderson, Geoffrey W. Bromiley, Robert W. Myers, James B. Torrance, and Thomas F. Torrance. Like Karl Barth who went before them, in the content of their theology and the living of their lives they were faithful witnesses of the joy of Jesus Christ in a broken world. As the Orthodox would say, *Memory eternal*!

60 Karl Barth, "An meine Freunde in Japan," cited in Eberhard Busch, *Karl Barth: His Life from Letters and Autobiograhical Texts*, trans. John Bowden (Philadelphia: Fortress, 1976) 418.

61. Bernard Ramm, *After Fundamentalism: The Future of Evangelical Theology* (San Francisco: Harper & Row, 1983) 194.

62. Busch, *Karl Barth*, 440.

63. Karl Barth, *Wolfgang Amadeus Mozart*, trans. Clarence K. Pott (Grand Rapids: Eerdmans, 1986) 55.

Abbreviations

ANF	*Ante-Nicene Fathers.*
CD	Karl Barth, *Church Dogmatics.* Edited by Geoffrey W. Bromiley and T. F. Torrance. Edinburgh: T. & T. Clark, 1936–69.
Calvin, *Institutes*	John Calvin, *Institutes of the Christian Religion.* Edited by John T. McNeill. Translated by Ford Lewis Battles. Philadelphia: Westminster, 1960.
NIDNTT	*The New International Dictionary of New Testament Theology.* Edited by Colin Brown. 3 vols. Grand Rapids: Zondervan. 1975–78.
NPNF	*Nicene and Post-Nicene Fathers*, Series 1 and 2.
TDNT	*Theological Dictionary of the New Testament.* Edited by Gerhard Kittel and Gerhard Friedrich. Translated by Geoffrey W. Bromiley. 10 vols. Grand Rapids: Eerdmans. 1964–74.

PART ONE

Despair: The "Grand Inquisitor" of Our Souls and the Vicarious Despair of Christ

CHAPTER ONE

The Sources of Despair

Been Down So Long That It Looks Like Up To Me. I've never read this book, an obscure title out of the sixties by a folk musician named Richard Fariña.¹ But I remember the title. I cannot help but remember the title. And it becomes more meaningful to me as I grow older. Despair. How long have I lived with it? When I was younger, it seemed that all I needed to do to rid myself of despair was a certain relationship; a certain educational goal reached, a certain job, a certain Christian experience. But these things pass and despair is still there. *Been Down So Long That It Looks Like Up To Me.* No, this does not mean that one lives in a constant despair, creating paralysis of action (although that too may be able to come with frightening regularity). But despair does seem to have made its home. It has almost become a friend. I have to laugh in order to live with it. David Frost speaks of the man who turned his life around. He used to be depressed and miserable. Now he's miserable and depressed.² Is that the extent of change in my life anymore? Is despair my real marriage partner, one that I better get used to living with for the rest of my life? Like the character in the Dostoevsky novel, is despair the "Grand Inquisitor" of our souls that exposes who we really are?

I love the notorious "E. C." comic books of the 1950s. Criticized as harmful for children by a plethora of parents, psychiatrists, and pastors, along their crime and horror comics, "E. C." was proudest of their science fiction line, boasting stories by Ray Bradbury and other noted science fiction writers. One of their stories tells of a popular television kid's show

---

1. Richard Fariña, *Been Down So Long That It Looks Like Up to Me* (New York: Penguin, 1966).

2. David Frost in *The Penguin Dictionary of Modern Humorous Quotations*, ed. Fred Metcalf (London: Penguin, 1986) 73.

starring a puppeteer and his puppet (borrowed from the real life fifties show, "Kukla, Fran, and Ollie"), an "alligator" named Alexander (Alley) K. Gator.[3] The presidential elections are approaching, and, as usual, the public is dissatisfied with the choices. Someone suggests that they might as well write in the name of the popular Alley Gator for president. He would do just as well as the bozos nominated by the political parties. The idea mushrooms and grabs the public's fancy! What a joke, but also, what a message to send to Washington. Alley Gator, however, is an alien who has attached himself to the puppeteer's arm, like a parasite! And other aliens are now doing the same throughout the country. The motion is made to nullify the election of Alexander K. Gator. But it is defeated. It is too late. Every hand raised in the Congress is a hand with a gator attached to it . . . a gator just like Alley.

THE ATTACHMENT OF DESPAIR

Do my beloved E. C. comics have an insight here? Does despair have that kind of attachment, that kind of hold of us? Is it now virtually a part of who we are, like another arm, or appendage, which is just as much a part of us as our arms and legs? When Christians speak of the doctrines of creation and humanity, can they ignore how thoroughly despair seems to capture who we are, even if we are creations of God's? What does it mean to be human? Must I answer candidly: I am a creature in despair, despair over my finitude, despair over dashed hopes, despair over the absurdity of a world that would have kittens run over by automobiles (an argument against the existence of God by the cartoonist Matt Groening!). I despair over a life that seems to promise so much, have so much potential for love, adventure, meaning, and purpose, yet seems to deliver so little. The sweetness of birds singing outside my office on a spring day is quickly soured by the thought that an innocent teenager was killed the other night in a drive-by shooting at an amusement center. The tragedy of the World Trade Center needs no further comment from me. Is God an underachiever, as Woody Allen suggests? *Been Down So Long That It Seems Like Up To Me.* Seems like it.

The terror of life can be almost overwhelming to the point that all we can do is cling to what we know. We sometimes can lack the courage to the extent, Kierkegaard suggests, we would rather hang on to

---

3. *Weird Science* #16, November–December, 1952.

"the darkness of quiet despair" than to let it go.⁴ The very nature of our humanity is called into question: Who are we, the active creature who investigates and is investigated, the creature who possesses activities, purposes, and goals, or a fearful creature, lonely and rejected, negotiating desperately in a world hostile with fellow-humans and nature? Is not the latter the reality and the former the luxury? As Bob Dylan sings in his song, "Dignity," one can be searching everywhere asking, "Have you seen dignity?"⁵ Authorities and religion both wind up clueless in answer in the song.

We recoil against the attachment of despair. Are we not created by God to live in harmony and peace, so that struggle and pain are aberrations to be fought against? Or is Ray Anderson correct that this way of thinking betrays both an ideal God and an ideal humanity (the connection between the two is tantalizing to consider)? The abstractly good and powerful God can only regard the idealized perfect human being, free of pain.⁶ But I am not an abstract being . . . I am my pain . . . more than that, but not less, as Kierkegaard's typographical error reminds us: I may be only a typo, but don't erase me . . . this is the only existence I've got!⁷ Anderson tells of "Martin," who "demanded" of God that his mother be healed, thereby denying her mortality based on his belief in a certain abstract doctrine of God.⁸ In effect we cannot believe that God would love someone like us, as mortal as we are. As a counselor, Anderson responded to Martin by meeting him at the level of his feelings, not abstractions.

The philosopher Leibniz is not helpful when he simply accepts sorrow as a larger pattern to the great scheme of the universe, as simply a consequence of being a material being.⁹ As many would agree, imperfection is necessary for perfection. But at what price? Is the perfection worth

---

4. A sermon cited by Howard and Edna Hong in "Historical Introduction" to Søren Kierkegaard, *The Sickness Unto Death*, ed. and trans. Howard V. Hong and Edna H. Hong (Princeton: Princeton University Press, 1980) x–xi.

5. Bob Dylan, "Dignity," Online: http://bobdylan.com/moderntimes/songs/dignity.html.

6. Ray S. Anderson, *Spiritual Caregiving as Secular Sacrament: A Practical Theology for Professional Caregivers* (New York: Jessica Kingsley, 2003) 58–59.

7. Kierkegaard, *Sickness Unto Death*, 74. See also Anderson, *On Being Human*, 3.

8. Anderson, *Spiritual Caregiving as Secular Sacrament*, 46–60.

9. See the discussion in Barth, *CD* III/3, 316–19.

the price? Dostoevsky's Ivan asks in "the Grand Inquisitor" portion of *The Brothers Karamazov*.[10]

The pastoral ministry of the church is continually challenged at a gut level. Anderson puts it bluntly: "On what grounds could one convince a person for whom life appears to be unrelenting pain and meaningless frustration that he or she is the object of a Creator's love and as such 'of more value' than all other creatures?"[11] How dare we offer a gospel of a good God to someone in unspeakable despair? Perhaps at the heart of this anguish is our search for love. We can bear a great deal of suffering if we know that we are loved. So much of human endeavor seeks to fulfill that desire; in the pursuit for sexual gratification or in the acknowledgement of power, as two examples. Ministry has to beware that genuine despair is not placated by superficial spiritual platitudes.

To deny our attachment to despair is to deny the crucial role feelings play in our understanding of being human, in contrast to many theological anthropologies, but in harmony with the life of Jesus himself, who in "the days of Jesus' life on earth . . . offered up prayers and petitions, with loud cries and tears . . ." (Heb 5:7). For this reason, Georges Bernanos, in *The Diary of a Country Priest* dares to equate sadness and despair with the Spirit, not just as states of the Spirit.[12] We have to fight against a long tradition that disassociates God from the feelings, rather than seeing the reality of the incarnation in God's solidarity with us, including our feelings, as petty and potentially self-destructive they may be (cf. Rom 8:23). Feelings are more than sensations, Ray Anderson suggests, but "a more accurate indication of the state of the self than emotions."[13] If we are hit on the head with a baseball bat then we cannot deny the feelings of pain. Our emotions need to make a decision, of course, whether or not we were hit by accident or on purpose! But the feelings are the self and should not be denied. That includes despair.

Such an anesthetization against despair is common in our wider society of entitlement and victimization, where you have moral authority if you can claim that you have been victimized because of race, gender, dis-

---

10. Fyodor Dostoevsky, *The Brothers Karamazov*, trans. Richard Pevear and Larissa Volokhonsky (New York: Farrar, Strauss & Giroux, 1990) 246–64.

11. Anderson, *On Being Human*, 4.

12. Georges Bernanos, *The Diary of a Country Priest*, trans. Pamela Morris (New York: Carroll & Graf, 1965) 199.

13. Ray S. Anderson, *Self-Care: A Theology of Personal Empowerment and Spiritual Healing* (Wheaton, IL: Bridgepoint, 1995) 64, 67.

ability, etc. "Despair is big with friends I love," the poet William Meredith admits.[14] Both their "glands" and the "world" have treated them badly. "The stench of time and man's own smell" is "the smell of consequence" that nonetheless still stands with our saying, "I choose, I choose." In other words, get a life. This is the only world we have. Despair is an attachment that is inevitable. Don't be anxious to be involved with me romantically, Bob Dylan cautions a potential lover in his song, "Is Your Love in Vain?"[15] Is the lover willing to not only cook and sew but also "understand my pain" and take that risk? As self-absorbed as Dylan sounds here, he is realistic enough to admit the issue of his despair, rather than simply pretend he is something else.

The alternative to choosing to live in the midst of despair is to stay motionless, to give up as much as one practically can. One may continue to go through the motions of life: jobs, families, friends, but still be motionless. This is a kind of resignation to despair that at least sees virtue in its honesty. Our activist culture usually recoils against this. But Simone Weil suggests motionlessness may possess a virtue: "The only choice before man is whether he will or will not . . . stay motionless, without searching, waiting in immobility and without even trying to know what he waits . . ."[16] May motionlessness mean that there is a place for Christ to act in our place, the vicarious humanity of Christ in the midst of our despair? Weil adds, ". . . it is absolutely certain that God will come all the way to him."[17]

There is a long literary tradition of "heroic melancholy" (and Kierkegaard may be seen as a prime member). This took philosophical and even theological form with the descendents of Kierkegaard, existentialism, in mid-twentieth century. It was probably a healthy reaction to centuries long tradition in Roman Catholic theology viewing despair as a mortal sin.[18] Yet the obvious narcissism of this trend becomes disquieting

---

14. William Meredith, "Consequences I. Of Choice," in *Effort at Speech: New and Selected Poems* (Evanston, IL: Triquarterly, 1997) 90.

15. Bob Dylan, "Is Your Love in Vain?" Online: http://www.bobdylan.com/#/songs/your-love-vain.

16. Simone Weil, *On Science, Necessity and the Love of God*. Edited and translated by R. Rees (New York: Oxford University Press, 1968) 159, cited in Mary Jo Meadow, "The Dark Side of Mysticism: Depression and 'The Dark Night,'" in *Psychology of Religion*, ed. H. Newton Malony (Grand Rapids: Baker, 1991) 248.

17. Weil, cited in Meadow, "Dark Side of Mysticism" in *Psychology of Religion*, 248.

18. Joyce Carol Oates, "The One Unforgiveable Sin," *New York Times Book Review* (July 25, 1993) 73.

eventually. Is it really that cool to be depressed? asks the author of *Listening to Prozac*, Peter Kramer, questioning the entire "culture of depression" following the success of his book, in which medication became the knee-jerk solution to every problem.[19]

Does our Christology have a place for the neediness of Jesus, and neediness that then connects with our needs? This acute, personal way is how God shares in our broken and lost existence.[20] Barth makes it very clear that the vicarious life of Christ, that is, his unique life that nonetheless is in connection with ours, includes the life of feelings and emotions:

> No one who came to the Jordan was as laden and afflicted as He. No one was as needy. No one was so utterly human, because so wholly fellow-human. No one confessed His sins so sincerely, so truly as His own, without sideglances at others. He stands alone in this, He who was elected and ordained from all eternity to partake of the sin of all in His own person, bear its shame and curse in the place of all, to be the man responsible for all, and as such, wholly theirs, to live and act and suffer. This is what Jesus began to do when He had Himself baptized by John with all the others.[21]

The attachment of despair to us is so deep that only one who shares in our humanity but is still different from us can deal with that despair.

DESPAIR AND DEPRESSION

Despair, in our discussion, is not necessarily depression. Depression can have many causes of a medical kind. Hippocrates in the fifth century, BCE and Robert Burton in the seventeenth century, have been joined in recent years by those suggesting biological reasons for depression.[22] Clinical depression distinctly caused by physical reasons is a narrow yet important concern. Depression can affect the entirety of our being, and therefore, may be included within despair.[23] Clinical depression, such as

19. Peter D. Kramer, *Against Depression* (New York: Viking, 2005) 5ff.

20. T. F. Torrance, *Christian Doctrine of God*, 41–42.

21. Barth, *CD* IV/4, 59.

22. Mary Louise Bringle, *Despair: Sickness or Sin? Hopelessness and Healing in the Christian Life* (Nashville: Abingdon, 1990) 60, 120. A fine discussion of the implications of the gospel for those who suffer from bi-polar depression is offered by Kathryn Greene-McCreight, *Darkness Is My Only Companion: A Christian Response to Mental Illness* (Grand Rapids: Brazos, 2006).

23. Richard O'Connor, *Undoing Depression: What Therapy Doesn't Teach You and*

unipolar major depression, bi-polar depression, or obsessive-compulsive disorder, deserves specific attention beyond this book.[24] Despair, theologically speaking, is both a broader and deeper category. The despair of Jesus himself will be an indication of this.

There is cause, however, for caution in ascribing all despair and depression to biological sources. Findings in the *Archives of General Psychiatry* recently suggest that up to twenty-five percent of depression treated by psychiatrists and prescribing medication "may only be reacting normally to stressful events like divorce or losing a job."[25] In addition, the vested interest of a 12 billion dollars (!) a year market for antidepressant drugs must always be watched. Many have suggested that the descriptions of clinical depression in the DSM-IV, such as "depressed mood, loss of interest in usual activities, insomnia, lessened appetite, inability to concentrate," can be simply caused by life's problems, such a betrayal of a romantic partner, being passed over for a promotion, or discovering a life-threatening illness.[26]

There is also a temptation to mark a hard and fast line between sin and pathology. The result, Ray Anderson observes, is that the theologian resolves sin by grace and the psychologist uses therapy to deal with the pathology, but never the twain shall meet.[27] The implications this can have for personhood are profound, Anderson continues. Does this not encourage splitting the human person in two, promoting a dichotomous

---

Medications Can't Give You (New York: Berkley, 1993) 8. See the official psychiatric definitions of depressive disorders in American Psychiatric Association, *Diagnostic and Statistical Manual of Mental Disorders (DSM-IV)* (Washington, DC: American Psychiatric Association, 1994).

24. On unipolar major depression and against the culture of "heroic melancholy," see Kramer, *Against Depression*. See the excellent discussions of OCD by the psychiatrist Ian Osborn, *Can Christianity Cure Obsessive-Compulsive Disorder?* (Grand Rapids: Eerdmans, 2008) and *Tormenting Thoughts and Secret Rituals: The Hidden Epidemic of Obsessive-Compulsive Disorder* (New York: Dell, 1998).

25. Shankar Vedantam, "Study: Some Depression Isn't Illness," *The Wichita Eagle*, April 3, 2007. Cf. Sharon Begley, "Happiness: Enough Already," *Newsweek* (February 11, 2008) 50–53.

26. Allan V. Horowitz and Jerome C. Wakefield, *The Loss of Sadness: How Psychiatry Transformed Normal Sorrow into Depressive Disorder* (Oxford: Oxford University Press, 2007) 9.

27. Ray S. Anderson, "The Social Ecology of Human Personhood: Implications of Dietrich Bonhoeffer's Theology for Psychology," in *On Being A Person: A Multidisciplinary Approach to Personality Theories*, ed. Todd H. Speidell (Eugene, OR: Cascade Books, 2002) 168–69.

self-identity and lifestyle? Theologically, this views the human person as only having one part that is "spiritual," easily separated from the psychological and the physical. Care must be taken among any therapist not to ignore the spiritual issues and questions that a client may possess.[28] Separating the spiritual and psychological can lead to extremes taking over, such as the pastor who interprets every illness as demon possession, or the psychologist who recommends medication for every problem. It is very difficult (and rare) to be both an accomplished pastor and a qualified therapist, so one must always know when to do a referral, but also recognize theoretically that we are always ministering to a whole person. Theologically, the ministry of Jesus Christ for us and in our place is always that which addresses the whole person. The whole person is called by Jesus to "follow me" (Matt 4:19).

As much as sin and neurosis are parts of the one person, they are not two sides of the same coin, Anderson reminds us.[29] Sin affects both the physical and social elements of the human person but is not to be understood solely in a "religious" way. The grace of God in the humanity of Jesus, in his faithful obedience to the Father for our sake, exposes the absurdity of sin. It is a perversion that cannot and should not be explained away psychologically or religiously. Its meaning is found in its contrast to the person of Jesus Christ as portrayed in the Gospels, and who continues to live today through the Holy Spirit in the ministry of the church. "Perversity is more than a disease," Anderson contends, "it is a deliberate and intentional, though not always conscious, deviation from what is good, for the self and others."[30] Christ acted deliberately and intentionally throughout his ministry to be faithful to the Father. A stark contrast exists in human perversity, as demonstrated in Augustine's famous example of stealing the pears as an adolescent; not because he was hungry but for the sheer perversity of the act: "I became evil for no reason . . . I was seeking not to gain anything by shameful means, but shame for its own sake."[31]

There is much that human beings do because of that which has been thrust upon them by environment or biology. Despair involves those

28. See Ray S. Anderson, *Christians Who Counsel: The Vocation of Wholistic Therapy* (Grand Rapids: Zondervan, 1990).

29. Anderson, "The Social Ecology of Human Personhood . . . ," in *On Being a Person*, 169.

30. Ibid.

31. Augustine, *Confessions*, trans. Henry Chadwick (Oxford: Oxford University Press, 1992) 29.

predicaments, but expands beyond them. Since human beings are whole persons, however, biological problems are bound to be aggravated (but not caused) by the perversity of human sin.

The relationship between sin and sickness is not cause and effect, as Jesus taught concerning the man blind from birth: "His disciples asked him, 'Rabbi, who sinned, this man or his parents, that he was born blind?' Jesus answered, 'Neither this man nor his parents sinned; he was born blind so that God's works might be revealed in him'" (John 9:2-3; cf. Luke 13:1). Jesus heals the man, thereby declaring that God is the enemy of misery. God is against both sin and sickness. This is what we see the ministry of Jesus, in his human acts of faith and obedience that also display the character of God. We may not be able to understand our sickness, Stanley Hauerwas argues, if we do not understand our sin.[32] We are whole persons and Jesus addresses the whole person. And in doing so he brings pastor and therapist together in standing against both sin and sickness.

As Barth comments, the person whom Jesus ministers to is the needy one, the one who needs help. "It is the man with whom things are going badly; who is needy and frightened and harassed."[33] The Eastern Church has been better than the West, Barth adds, in recognizing that the needy are not just sinners but sufferers.[34] Those whom Jesus helps are not just viewed from their past but with a look to their future, so he desires for them to be healed and forgiven. The paralyzed man is both healed and forgiven by Jesus (Matt 9:1-8; Mark 2:1-12; Luke 5:17-26). So the essence of Jesus's ministry is always vicarious, on the behalf of and in place of another. So the essence of his humanity is always a vicarious humanity, not just a human Halloween costume of God or a demonstration of religious and moral purity. All of us at times are like *The Hunchback of Notre Dame* in the Victor Hugo novel and the Lon Chaney film: viewed as horribly deformed by society, maybe even functioning like a lonely bell ringer in a cathedral, hoping that at least God is listening as we swing from the bell rope.[35] We cry to Jesus as the sick and possessed did: "If you

---

32. Stanley Hauerwas, "Sinsick," in *Sin, Death, and the Devil*, ed. Carl E. Braaten and Robert W. Jenson (Grand Rapids: Eerdmans, 2000) 10.

33. Barth, *CD* IV/2, 221.

34. Ibid., 223.

35. Victor Hugo, *The Hunchback of Notre Dame*, trans. Catherine Liu (New York: Random House, 2007) and *The Hunchback of Notre Dame*, directed by Wallace Worsley, Universal Pictures, 1923.

choose, you can make me clean" (Mark 1:40); "Jesus, Son of David, have mercy on me!" (Mark 10:47).

Jesus does not rebuke us as those around us do (Mark 10:48) because he is the great physician (Mark 2:17) whose every action is always in response to human need. The New Testament sees the dynamic interrelation between sin and sickness when Matthew interprets Jesus' ministry of exorcism and healing as that which was spoken of by Isaiah 53:4: "He took our infirmities and born our diseases" (Matt 8:17). Isaiah 53 further adds the place of vicarious atonement in v. 5: "But he was wounded for our transgressions, crushed for our iniquities; upon him was the punishment that made us whole, and by his bruises we are healed." The one "struck down by God" (Isa 53:4) is the healer of both sin and sickness. Atonement is at the heart of God's opposition to that which "troubles and torments and disturbs man," for "He does not will his (humanity's) death, but life."[36] In fact, Barth adds, "His affirmation is joyful to the very core."[37] As much as God is joyful, however, "the sorrow which openly or secretly fills the heart of man is primarily in the heart of God."[38] God is sorrowful over the plight of humanity. This life includes the whole of the human being. This we know. The battle is God's. Does this answer the questions of why God allows suffering or why some are healed now but not others? No. But what we do know through the vicarious actions of Jesus is whose side God is on, and that his ministry is that of helping the needy in all ways, spiritually, emotionally, and physically. Both pastor and therapist can unite in that attitude because of the vicarious actions of Jesus that the church believes continues today.

Depression can be extremely dangerous when biological elements may well be involved. Unhappiness, as Garrison Keillor puts it, "is part of the human condition, along with itchiness and the common cold. If you're a living sensate being, you will experience gloominess and the vapors and the heebie-jeebies . . . but when the darkness gets a grip on you and you can't shake it, then you need to think about depression."[39] He then goes on to tell of the friend who one day unexpectedly put rocks in her jacket, went out to the lake, and threw herself over. Her friends had

36. Barth, CD IV/2, 225.
37. Ibid.
38. Ibid.
39. Garrison Keillor, Online: http://prairiehome.publicradio.org/features/ptth/2002/04.shtml.

no clue. "She needed help," Keillor concludes, "and none of us knew that." Pastors, therapists, physicians, and friends must all be involved with these tragic people.

THE SOURCES OF DESPAIR: SIN, SICKNESS, OR GOD?

If despair is more than depression, then from where does despair originate? Is it the result of sin, the fruit of self-love? Thomas Merton thinks so:

> Despair is the absolute extreme of self-love. It is reached when a man deliberately turns his back on all help from anyone else in order to taste the rotten luxury of knowing himself to be lost.[40]

How biting, even sarcastic, Merton is! Despair is a "rotten luxury" of those who want to feel sorry for themselves and therefore relieve themselves from any responsibility, even the responsibility of receiving help from another. Such a despair is "the too-little of responsibility," as pride is the "too-much," according to Wendell Berry.[41] "The shoddy work of despair, the pointless work of pride, equally betray creation. They are wastes of life . . . . For despair there is no forgiveness, and for pride none. Who in loneliness can forgive?"[42] Despair is a waste of life, of time, of creation that does not know forgiveness, and therefore, atonement. Ethics is unknown to despair because it is purely obsessed with itself and its condition. Even if ethics is defined as how to treat people, including ourselves, despair makes us blind to our true needs.[43] Responsibility goes by the wayside, forgiveness becomes irrelevant. "Doubt is thought's despair; despair is personality's doubt," remarks Kierkegaard.[44] Despair is not far from doubt, regardless of how one feels about doubt's virtue or vice. Despair is too close to our personality, but has a negative essence, the doubting side of our personality, doubting about life and creation.

---

40. Thomas Merton in Tony Castle, *The New Book of Christian Quotations* (New York: Crossroad, 1989) 61.

41. Wendell Berry, *What Are People For?* (New York: North Point, 1990) 10.

42. Ibid.

43. Lewis B. Smedes, *Choices: Making Right Decisions in a Complex World* (San Francisco: Harper & Row, 1986) 17.

44. Søren Kierkegaard, *Either/Or*, Part II, ed. and trans. Howard V. Hong and Edna H. Hong (Princeton: Princeton University Press, 1987) 211.

"Despair is the conclusion of fools," according to Benjamin Disraeli.[45] The implication is obvious. People in despair are not to be pitied, but to be reprimanded. Their "rotten luxury" is a manifestation of an obsessive self-love, the essence of sin. To some extent, this is hard to argue against. There is a sense of "coziness" or refuge found in our despair, when we can simply focus upon ourselves without regard for anyone else. Is this not sin? "I have my books and my poetry to protect me," Simon and Garfunkel sing in "I Am a Rock."[46] "I am a rock," despite the fact that I am in despair.

An ancient tradition suggests a demonic source of despair. For the Christian East, "There is no evil worse than melancholy" because "it breaks the will" (Chrysostom). "It attacks not only the flesh but the very soul . . . [It is] an unceasing executioner who saps the strength of the soul."[47] Such insidious work comes from "the noonday demon," often striking monks, first identified as the source of *acedia* by Evagrius of Pontus.[48] Kathleen Norris interprets *acedia* (or the Latin, *accidie*) as a combination of melancholy and sloth.[49] Interestingly enough, the demon works by leading the monk to reflect on how uncharitable other monks have been to him! Rejection is a key source for despair, especially rejection by those with whom one is in community.

Despair is the personality of doubt, as Kierkegaard says. Thus, despair is deeply connected to human beings as personal, and therefore, social beings, able to be deeply hurt, for example, by the rejection of our fellow brothers in the monastery. So spiritual formation should not be seen as disciplining one to "empty" oneself of the human for the sake of being filled with the divine.[50] This is a bare "imitation of Christ" without the vicarious humanity of Christ. Our temptation is to give into this religious impulse because we are, as Anderson puts it, in "double jeopardy":

---

45. Benjamin Disraeli in Sherwood Wirt and Karen Beckstrom, *Living Quotations for Christians* (New York: Harper & Row, 1974) 54.

46. Paul Simon, "I Am A Rock." Online: http://www.paulsimon.com/node/88.

47. John Chrysostom, *Lettres à Olympias* 10.2, SCh 13 bis; 246ff.; cited by Tomáš Špidlik, *The Spirituality of the Christian East*, trans. by Anthony P. Gythiel (Kalamazoo, MI: Cistercian, 1986) 251.

48. Evagrius, *Pratikos* 12, cited by Špidlik, *Spirituality of the Christian East*, 252–53.

49. Kathleen Norris, *Acedia and Me: A Marriage, Monks, and a Writer's Life* (New York: Riverhead, 2008).

50. Anderson, *Spiritual Caregiving as Secular Sacrament*, 64.

vulnerable because both our physical and spiritual natures are vulnerable.[51] The solution is not to empty ourselves of our humanity, but to seek an intentionality of community that is a participation in the intentionality of community sought by the Son with the Father. Vicariously, we participate in that community first of all, not the monastery. Out of this community comes the potential for intimacy, not seeking to perform acts, usually physical, that hope to create intimacy.[52] If community is sought through intimacy, only greater despair can result. Intimacy is a gift from the other, the result of a mutual relationship, not in using the other in order to satisfy a desire for intimacy.

The relationship of the Son to the Father is very instructive at this point, and perhaps helpful in understanding how the Son can suffer, and despair, and still trust the Father, even still have joy. The relationship of the Son to the Father is not simply that of "free will," but also of dependence. The despair he feels in the garden of Gethsemane and on the cross is because of a relationship of trust and dependence. The freedom of autonomy is unknown to Jesus because his joy is in doing the will of the Father. Anderson says it well:

> To esteem 'freedom of choice' as an expression of individual autonomy and the basis of human dignity and responsibility is to miss the point. The so-called freedom to be the 'master of my fate, the captain of my soul' is at bottom joyless and cheerless. For this is a freedom which denies dependence on the other as the source of one's own personhood.[53]

There is a "nightmare" of freedom of choice from which humanity must be awakened by Jesus Christ, Barth claims.

> There can be no more question of the pride and misery of unrestricted thought and aspiration. He has awakened from the dream or nightmare of a freedom of choice in which he might always in all respects do different things, loving, choosing, grasping and executing now one thing and now another according to fate or preference, chance or caprice. Called to be a witness of

---

51. Ibid., 66.
52. Ibid., 71–72.
53. Anderson, *On Being Human*, 82.

> Jesus Christ, he finds a Lord and becomes His Servant, and thus finds that he is given a definite task and definite orders.[54]

This is "not external constraint," however, "but his own freedom, which he owes to the grace of his Lord electing him in divine freedom, which prevents him from emancipating himself from his Lord."[55] To be called by Jesus Christ means that one's course is "already fixed" so that one "can be unfaithful to this direction, but he cannot reverse it. He has been deprived of all possibilities but one. He can only remember and never dream again that old dream of unlimited freedom of choice."[56] We may think that we are limiting our options but the opposite is the case. We really do not know the whole range of our capacities. Only God does.

> The capacity of each individual is in reality as incalculable and uncontrollable as he is in himself. It can be known and decided only by God. If a man says, "I cannot," he must remember that he might well be able to do to-day what he quite honestly thought he could not do yesterday. But if he says: "I can," he must consider that he might not be able to do to-day or ever again what he was confident he could do yesterday. In both he must perhaps make new discoveries, whether positive or negative, in relation to his capacity. In both the decision must be made in relation to the God who has created, sustains, guides and knows him.[57]

"Freedom of choice" is the nature of the fall of humanity, as Barth reminds us.[58] Such a choice apart from God means that we do not live "gladly," with joy, but despair in our relationships. Dependence upon someone else than God becomes an excuse for slavery and abuse in relationships.

The intentionality of the Son in relationship to the Father is an alternative to viewing the core of being human as a free choice of "emptying" one of the self. The Son is not a victim of the abuse of the Father but he goes to the cross willingly for the sake of others.[59] This expresses his faith in the Father, a faith that drives out demons through prayer (Mark 9:28–29) despite others that believe yet plead for help in unbelief (Mark

---

54. Barth, *CD* IV.3.2, 665.
55. Ibid.
56. Ibid.
57. Barth, *CD* III/4, 394.
58. Barth, *CD* III/2, 273.
59. Christina Baxter, "Jesus the Man and Woman's Salvation," in *Atonement Today*, ed. John Goldingay (London: SPCK, 1995) 133.

9:24).⁶⁰ In the Gospels only Jesus possesses a doubt-free faith (Matt 17:20; 21:21–22; Mark 11:22ff.; Luke 17:5–6).⁶¹

Self-denial for the Christian is not a matter of simply trying to be "like" Jesus. But self-denial does remind us that the vicarious work of Christ does not let us "off the hook." There is a union with the vicarious humanity of Christ which means that we will suffer. "The joy of discipleship," Bonhoeffer reminds us, will involve despair and sorrow.⁶² As Jesus was intentional in his faith in and obedience to the Father, so Christian suffering is intentional because of the Christian's allegiance to Christ. "The cross is neither misfortune nor harsh fate. Instead, it is that suffering which comes from allegiance to Jesus Christ alone. The cross is not random suffering but necessary suffering."⁶³ As necessary suffering, it also involves being rejected. A Christianity that accepts "cheap grace," Bonhoeffer adds, views suffering as just a part of natural existence including being rejected. "Being shunned, despised, and deserted by people, as in the Psalmist's unending lament, is an essential feature of the suffering of the cross, which cannot be comprehended by a Christianity that is unable to differentiate between a citizen's ordinary existence and Christian existence."⁶⁴ Bonhoeffer, however, understands the suffering and rejection of the Christian as a participation in the unique, vicarious suffering of Christ, not just imitating Christ. "The cross is suffering with Christ. Indeed, it is Christ-suffering. Only one who is bound so to Christ as this occurs in discipleship stands in seriousness under the cross."⁶⁵

"Suffering must be borne in order for it to pass."⁶⁶ With these remarkable words Bonhoeffer signals the necessity of suffering for the Christian that is not based on fatalism but on the vicarious life, death, and resurrection of Jesus. "God is a God who bears. The Son of God bore our flesh. He therefore bore the cross. He bore all our sins and attained

60. Ralph P. Martin, *Mark: Evangelist and Theologian* (Grand Rapids: Zondervan, 1973) 109.

61. Ian G. Wallis, *The Faith of Jesus Christ in Early Christian Traditions* (New York: Cambridge University Press, 1995) 12–13.

62. Dietrich Bonhoeffer, *Discipleship*, ed. Martin Kuske, Ilse Tödt, Geffrey B. Kelly, and John D. Godsey, trans. Barbara Green and Reinhard Krauss, Dietrich Bonhoeffer Works, vol. 4 (Minneapolis: Fortress, 2001) 86.

63. Ibid.

64. Ibid., 86–87.

65. Ibid., 87.

66. Ibid., 90.

reconciliation by his bearing. That is why disciples are called to bear what is put on them. Bearing constitutes being a Christian."[67] In this way he seeks to tie in the suffering of the world with the suffering born by Christ, and thereby, Christians. "Either the world must bear it and be crushed by it, or it falls on Christ and is overcome in him."[68]

Christ's suffering includes rejection by the world, but, ironically, it is only Christ who will be able to "bear" the suffering of the world. "This is how Christ suffers as vicarious representative for the world. Only his suffering brings salvation."[69] Because of the union of the church with Christ, it will not be able to avoid participating in bearing the suffering of the world with Christ. "But the church-community itself knows now that the world's suffering seeks a bearer. So in following Christ, this suffering falls upon it, and it bears the suffering while being borne by Christ. The community of Jesus Christ vicariously represents the world before God by following Christ under the cross."[70]

The critical question, however, is whether the church will be able to bear suffering without a sense of triumphalism in which Christ is displaced by the church's religious authority. The church can only do so in maintaining communion with Christ, as the Son maintains communion with the Father. "Just as Christ maintains his communion with the Father by bearing according to the Father's will, so the disciples' bearing constitutes their community with Christ."[71] Sharing in this communion is the only way for the church to experience joy in the midst of despair.

> Bearing the cross does not bring misery and despair. Rather, it provides refreshment and peace for our souls; it is our greatest joy. Here we are no longer laden with self-made laws and burdens, but with the yoke of him who knows us and who himself goes with us under the same yoke. Under his yoke we are assured off his nearness and communion.[72]

In the New Testament, Paul can certainly speak against "the sorrow of the world," although he will hasten to commend an alternative, a "godly sorrow" (2 Cor 7:10). Such a "worldly sorrow" is likewise condemned by

67. Ibid., 90–91.
68. Ibid., 90.
69. Ibid.
70. Ibid.
71. Ibid., 91.
72. Ibid.

Thomas Aquinas as the source for giving up on hope, which leads people to rush headlong into sin and be drawn away from good works.[73] But can despair come from God? Is this the same as saying that God is the author of evil and suffering, with all of the theological and personal questions that creates for the believer?

At least, do not the large majority of people believe that despair is a sin, a kind of moral failure? Is that not why we will go to practically any length to hide our despair? If not, people will no longer respect and think well of us, much less be our friends.

---

73. Thomas Aquinas, *Summa Theologica*, II of II, qu. 20, art. 3c; cited by Gaetano Benedetti and Ekkehard Starke, "Despair," in *The Encyclopedia of Christianity*, ed. Erwin Fahlbusch et al., trans. Geoffrey W. Bromiley (Grand Rapids: Eerdmans, 1999) 1:813. Cf. Edwin C. Hui, *At the Beginning of Life: Dilemmas in Theological Bioethics* (Downers Grove, IL: InterVarsity, 2002) 267.

CHAPTER TWO

Despair over Something

DESPAIR: A SICKNESS OF THE SPIRIT

Whereas many today will cringe from thinking of despair (or much of anything) as a sin, Kierkegaard was bold enough to view despair as both sin and sickness. In contrast to Lazarus's death (John 11:4), it is despair which is "the sickness unto death."[1] In fact, "Christianity has in turn discovered a miserable condition that man as such does not know exists" ... despair.[2]

"That man as such does not know exists." How can the Dane say such a thing? If there is one thing I know about myself, it is my despair. Dare I say it: "I despair, therefore I am!" It may be that Kierkegaard's insight comes from a christological source: Christ's vicarious humanity as the revelation, not just of God, but also of how little we know about ourselves, even our despair. While we may be troubled by depression, despair is much more total, a fact revealed by the vicarious humanity of Christ.

As despair involves the totality of our being, it reveals itself as "a sickness of the spirit."[3] Spirit is the self, but the self finds itself in a quandary. The human being is a synthesis of the finite and the infinite, of being godlike in creativity and reflection, but just another animal in its mortality. This relation between the two is not the self, but keeps the self from relation, thus causing despair. Out of this proceeds two forms of despair: unconscious and conscious. Within the latter, the conscious despair, exist two forms: "not to will to be oneself" and "to will to be oneself." Despair is

---

1. Kierkegaard, *The Sickness Unto Death*, 7.
2. Ibid., 8.
3. Ibid., 13.

more than either sadness or depression. Despair is different than depression, as devastating as that state can be.

Here is the state of the lostness of human beings. Dietrich Bonhoeffer observes that "melancholia" so overwhelms human beings that he dares to say "they are no longer human," so tortured are they by the "inner split" and "utter evil," where they have been laid hold of by "that which is utterly painful."[4] In the Book of Revelation, "no one in heaven or on earth or under the earth was able to open the scroll or to look into it" so John "began to weep bitterly" (Rev 5:3–4).[5]

"No longer human"! Dare we say this with Bonhoeffer? But do we risk underestimating sin if we do not recognize its all-pervasive aspects? The destruction of the human for the Christian is only the crying imperative for nothing less than the vicarious humanity of Christ, a humanity that literally has to take our place.

We might recoil from what may be conceived to be a hyper-Augustinian emphasis on the total depravity. Or we may see despair as a symptom of our total need. Is this not what is enacted in the event of baptism? Baptism is a communal affair, as Barth stresses, that hears "the sighing of the creature," acknowledging that this estranged, weakened (and maybe even "dead") human being as being welcomed in.[6] The community of Christ affects our humanity, for the sighing of the baptized one has been "heard already in Jesus Christ." Jesus Christ is the one who sighs as our representative, and in this case, representing the baptized one. "In each baptism, then, the church crosses its own frontiers into the territory of the people which walks in darkness."[7] This is humanity encompassed by despair. Here is the basis of the church's "freedom to wait" for its Lord.

We often restrict despair to what fate, God, or *necessity* lie upon or take away from us by genes, traffic accident, or to whom and where we have been born. No, Kierkegaard contends, despair is also *possibility*.[8] This proceeds from "the eternal," or the spiritual in humanity. So Jesus was tempted by the devil according to his possibilities, to throw himself

---

4. Dietrich Bonhoeffer, *Creation and Fall*, ed. Martin Rüter, Ilse Tödt, and John DeGruchy, trans. Douglas Stephen Bax, Dietrich Bonhoeffer Works 3 (Minneapolis: Fortress Press, 1997) 89.

5. T. F. Torrance, *The Christian Doctrine of God*, 255.

6. Barth, *CD* IV/4, 200.

7. Ibid.

8. Kierkegaard, *The Sickness Unto Death*, 17.

down from the parapet to be caught by angels, etc. (Matt 4:1–11; Luke 4:1–13). He refused in order to walk in the place of humanity and live a life vicariously for us and in our stead.[9] There is despair in the cross of Christ if there is no oneness between Christ and God, T. F. Torrance claims.[10] If God is not ontologically involved, the cross is the failure of God to rescue a godly and righteous man and a sad testament to the possibilities of humanity. We stumble over our possibility. Although initially intoxicated by it, we are inevitably frightened by our freedom. This can become a virtual torment for us, Kierkegaard concludes: the torment of, in Kierkegaard's Platonic view, an immortal soul that is unable to die.[11]

We are much more familiar with the despair which is *over something*.[12] What an individual does not usually acknowledge is that "in despairing over *something*, he really despaired over *himself*, and now he wants to be rid of himself."[13] This is the form of conscious despair that is despair at willing to be oneself since one has been rejected by the beloved. How common is this to the experience of humanity, and not uncommon to Jesus who "came to that which was his own, but his own did not receive him" (John 1:11). There is a despair of Jesus. Jesus despairs in our rejection of him, a rejection that continues through the sad history of Christendom's crusades up to a contemporary church's triviality and superficiality.

Such despair, like doubt, gives birth to anxiety. But what can we do, when Jesus says "do not worry about your life" (Matt 6:25) and Paul exhorts the Philippians, "Do not be anxious about anything . . ." (Phil 4:6)?

It is not enough, however, to say that despair is simply caused by what we have lost or what we lack. We may have lost the job or the woman, we may lack the brains or the brawn, but conscious despair is much deeper, according to Kierkegaard, and, I think, according to the vicarious humanity of Christ.

Kierkegaard divides conscious despair into a) "In Despair Not to Will to Be Oneself: Despair in Weakness" and b) "In Despair to Will to

---

9. Barth, *CD* IV/1, 261.

10. T. F. Torrance, "The Goodness and Dignity of Man in the Christian Tradition," *Modern Theology* 4:4 (1988) 316. Cf. T. F. Torrance, "The Goodness and Dignity of Man in the Christian Tradition" in *Christ in Our Place: The Humanity of God in Christ for the Reconciliation of the World: Essays Presented to James Torrance*, ed. Trevor Hart and Daniel Thimell. Princeton Theological Monograph Series 25 (Allison Park, PA: Pickwick, 1989) 369–87.

11. Kierkegaard, *The Sickness Unto Death*, 18.

12. Ibid., 19.

13. Ibid.

Be Oneself: Defiance." The first, the despair "not to will to be oneself" is further divided into two categories, 1) "Despair over the earthly or over something earthly" and 2) "Despair of the eternal or over oneself." As a synthesis, human beings can despair over the earthly, losing the woman or the job, even if one has rejected oneself, does not like oneself, and still dutifully attends church.[14] Worse yet, he may even seek to be "someone else, to wish for a new self."[15] He has lost any sense of belonging to the eternal (church going not necessarily connected with that!).

DESPAIRING OVER THE EARTHLY: LACK AND LOSS

Despairing over the "earthly" is an obvious despair. This is where we usually acknowledge our reality, where we usually experience our losses or lacks. Job, of course, is the paradigm of all of those who despair over something. In chapters three and seven, Job particularly laments over his very creation, even making a parody of the creation story in Genesis.[16] "Yes, let that night be barren; let no joyful cry be heard in it" (3:7). "Why did I not die at birth, come forth from the womb and expire?" (3:11). "I loathe my life," Job states bluntly (7:16). His only desire is to be left alone (7:19).

But Job only reveals the need he has for his humanity to be taken up, in all its misery, by Someone else. Even at the level of his very creation, Job needs God to take his place. Job wants be left alone, but God will not leave him alone. But in that despair is a genuine place for Christ to take Job's place. At least Job realizes he cannot bear the burden himself.

Like Bonhoeffer, Barth sees the "following" of Jesus to be more than imitation. Yes, the follower "takes the same road" as the one he follows, yet he also "respectfully walks behind a master or prince.... And in cases like this imitation is not only unnecessary but impossible."[17] To be a child of God is not to be a "second Christ" but to be "directed away to the one for whose sake and in whom he is a child of God."[18] Christ "replaces" us,

---

14. Ibid., 52.
15. Ibid., 53.
16. David J. A. Clines, *Job 1–20*. Word Biblical Commentary 17 (Dallas: Word, 1989) 84; Francis I. Andersen, *Job: An Introduction and Commentary*, Tyndale Old Testament Commentaries (Downers Grove, IL: InterVarsity, 1976) 138.
17. Barth, *CD* I/2, 277.
18. Ibid.

replacing our own standards, as our faith "consists in our recognizing and admitting and affirming and accepting the fact that everything has actually been done for us once and for all in Jesus Christ."[19] The "sweet" or "wonderful exchange" (*Epistle to Diognetus* 9; 2 Cor 5:19) means "an exchange of status between Him and us."[20] This "exchange" is not at a superficial level but deeply within the mystery of being human and the mystery of iniquity that manifests itself not the least in humanity's attempt to be religious. Barth makes this clear: "Sin is always unbelief. And unbelief is always man's faith in himself. And this faith invariably consists in the fact that man makes the mystery of this responsibility his own mystery, instead of accepting it as the mystery of God. It is this faith which is religion . . . This stamps religious as unbelief."[21] Job's friends do not see any mystery in humanity, and most of all, in Job. There is no mystery in his despair because there is no mystery in their God.

The toil of life brings despair, as Ecclesiastes remarks often: "So I turned and gave my heart to despair concerning all the toils of my labor under the sun," for life is short and one's toil will be enjoyed by the next generation who did not toil for it (Eccl 2:20). "This also is vanity and a great evil" (Eccl 2:21). The futility of life brings the kind of sorrow that can "melt away" the soul (Ps 119:28). Our mortality is a grim signpost of despair, when all that we have will be taken from us, or so it seems. Roy Hobbs, the baseball phenom in the novel *The Natural*, laments that after his failures in life, at winning a game as well as at love, "he fought his overwhelming self-hatred . . . I never did learn anything out of my past life, now I have to suffer again."[22] Likewise the story of the New Testament scholar George Eldon Ladd includes a lifetime of depression and despair fueled by deep-seated needs to prove himself to the academic community.[23] What we lack may often be the approval or love of others, but that can drive us to the pit of despair.

Is our problem again that we do not see the freedom in Someone taking our place, even taking our goods and things that we so highly value, most of all, our lives? Yes, perhaps the fruit of our labor is to be "enjoyed

19. Ibid., 308.
20. Ibid.
21. Ibid., 314.
22. Bernard Malamud, *The Natural* (New York: Farrar, Strauss & Giroux, 1952) 230.
23. John A. D'Elia, *A Place at the Table: George Eldon Ladd and the Rehabilitation of Evangelical Scholarship in America* (Oxford: Oxford University Press, 2008).

by another" (Eccl 2:21), but that One will live for the Many of whose labor is cut short by death and who cease to enjoy the fruit of that labor. In his enjoyment we will find the basis for our eternal enjoyment. Despair over something is deadly because we are mortal. The good news is that there is joy for us in that in which Christ will enjoy. And that joy is eternal.

Despair has the uncanny possibility, because it is despair over something, of closing us off to joy. The miseries of life can say that the only response we can give intellectually or emotionally is to say "No!" to joy. In fact, this can become our "highest duty and virtue."[24] This can be viewed as the only "mature" or "adult" approach. Adults often present this callous view towards life in the Narnia books by C. S. Lewis, in contrast to the children in the stories who more easily possess faith.[25] The fantasy writer Ray Bradbury is famous for exalting the importance of not growing up, for in the metaphor of the toy and the exercise of the imagination is reality.[26] Bitterness is that which can so easily characterize our growing older. The right to become bitter may be the final, most desperate right that we defend.[27] In this sense, Barth is arguing that despair, like in Augustine's definition of evil, is a privation of being—despair is a privation of joy—it has no life of its own but is dependent on joylessness. That certainly makes sense as we anticipate the joy of Jesus that is the indication of what it genuinely means to be human. He identifies with our sorrow, despair, and bitterness, but does not leave us in it, as we share in his vicarious life. Yet joy remains as anticipation, eschatological—we cannot "possess" joy—it is a gift of grace, always.

The miseries of life are very evident to the psalmist: "For my days pass away like smoke, and my bones burn like a furnace . . . Because of my loud groaning my bones cling to my skin . . . I am like a lonely bird on the housetop, All day long my enemies taunt me . . ." (Ps 102:3, 5, 7–8). For some reason, however, the psalmist is able to say, "But you, O Lord, are enthroned forever . . ." (Ps 102:12), and continue to exalt the God of history and creation. Our question is, How? How can he do this? Is he

---

24. Barth, *CD* III/4, 378.

25. Paul F. Ford, *Companion to Narnia*. Fourth Edition (San Francisco: Harper San Francisco, 1994) 1–2; Christian D. Kettler, "Joy and Logic in a Glad Embrace: The Theology of Narnia," in *C. S. Lewis's The Chronicles of Narnia: A Study Guide and Workbook for Groups and Individuals*, ed. Frank S. Kastor (Wichita, KS: St. Mark's) 97.

26. Ray Bradbury, *Yestermorrow: Obvious Answers to Impossible Futures* (Santa Barbara: Joshua Odell Editions, 1991) 3–15.

27. Barth, *CD* III/4, 378.

a fool or a possessor of faith only a few saints obtain? Either way, is the psalmist ultimately irrelevant to the ordinary person?

We can only speculate about Jesus praying this psalm: "Hear my prayer, O Lord; let my cry come to you. Do not hide your face from me in the day of distress" (Ps 102:1–2). But, knowing the Jesus of the Gospels, it takes little imagination to think of him doing so.

The miseries of life include the loss of those who are dear. It cannot be any more striking than to appeal to the story of Mary Magdalene weeping outside the tomb of the crucified Jesus (John 20:11–18). She has lost a beloved friend. The lostness is made even more stark by the fact that she does not even know where they have laid him (John 20:13). Mary has lost her Lord and what is more cutting, Jesus's body is lost itself. Despair can mean loss. As Indiana Jones' friend comments in the latest film of Indiana's adventures, twenty years after the last one takes place, that there comes a time when life takes away more than it gives.[28] But Mary's weeping is interrupted by Jesus: "Woman, why are you weeping?" (John 20:15). Despair over loss is interrupted by Jesus and by recognizing Jesus (John 20:16).

Even the joys of the earthly, such as enjoying beauty, can bring sadness, as Chesterton comments, because beauty is fleeting.[29] The video accompanying Bob Dylan's song, "When the Deal Goes Down" seems like an old home movie from the 1950's (with reference to Dylan's growing up in Minnesota and his early heroes, Hank Williams, Buddy Holly, and Woody Guthrie). The feature, however, is a young, beautiful girl played by Scarlett Johansson, invoking memories of relationships and times that are long past.[30] The brightly tinted old photos of the young beauty on the shiny, bright new car portray physical beauty that will change, much to our sadness and anguish. Why does this have to be so? Is this a cruel joke, to give us beauty in the world and then have it decay or disappear?

Despair can come over the things that we think would make us happy, such as fame. Bob Dylan recalls his early days of celebrity and how demeaning it felt to even sit in a restaurant, watching people gawking at

---

28. *Indiana Jones and the Kingdom of the Crystal Skull,* directed by Steven Spielberg, Lucasfilm, Ltd., 2008.

29. G. K. Chesterton, "On Gargoyles," cited by Ralph C. Wood, *Contending for the Faith: The Church's Engagement with Culture* (Waco, TX: Baylor University Press, 2003) 138.

30. Bob Dylan, "When the Deal Goes Down." Online: http://bobdylan.com/modern-times/songs/when the deal goes down.html.

him.³¹ There is no freedom there. George Reeves, the famous Superman TV star of the fifties, ended up dead; a suicide in despair over his acting career or the victim of a mob hit man.³² In the film, *Hollywoodland,* based on the events leading to Reeves' death, children are portrayed in deep despair because the impossible has happened: "Superman" has killed himself!³³ Did any children ever react this way? I don't know. But there is no doubt that George Reeves' portrayal of the defender of "Truth, Justice, and the American Way," brought a great deal of joy to children. (I know. I was one of them.) In the film, there is a memorable scene when Ben Affleck as Reeves is commiserating with a friend in a bar over being stuck in a kids' TV show. Then he hears little cheers out front. He turns to the window and sees a mob of little kids calling out, "Superman! Superman!" Affleck/Reeves stands straight up and gladly places his fists up to his the side of his waist, like in the TV show introduction. Reeves knew that he was bringing millions of children joy. Like when your favorite TV show is cancelled, there is despair because that which gave you joy is gone. Despair over something.

Despair over the earthly is also concretely portrayed in the despair of relationship. The self is an agent, the philosopher John Macmurray contends, that cannot be an isolated self.³⁴ An isolated self is a contradiction, for even the rejected self who has been excommunicated exists alone precisely in separation from the community. In 2 Cor 7:5–7, Paul is in despair because of external and internal pressures, "disputes without and fears within," but he is consoled by the arrival of Titus, who tells him of the Corinthians' "mourning" over him, "so that I rejoiced still more." There is no self, Macmurray boldly argues, apart from "a dynamic relation with the Other."³⁵ Despair over the earthly is created when I intentionally isolate myself from you, so that our relation becomes impersonal. An impersonal relationship creates despair. Not all intentions of isolation create despair. Not all of my students are in despair when they no longer have to take my courses! But the potential is there, certainly when even one's best

---

31. Bob Dylan, *Chronicles: Volume One* (New York: Simon & Schuster, 2004) 121.

32. Sam Kashner and Nancy Schoenberger, *Hollywood Kryptonite: The Bulldog, the Lady, and the Death of Superman* (New York: St. Martin's Press, 1996).

33. *Hollywoodland,* directed by Allen Coulter, Focus Features, 2006.

34. John Macmurray, *Persons in Relation* (London: Humanities Press, 1979) 17, 24, 28.

35. Ibid., 17.

friend can betray one: "Even my bosom friend in whom I trusted, who ate of my bread, has lifted the heel against me" (Ps 41:9). "The social basic category is the I-You relation," Bonhoeffer claims.[36] The separateness of persons in sociality is seen in the Trinity itself. The principle of "receptivity and activity" or "spirit in a person" is first of all in God himself, in the relationship between the Father, the Son, and the Holy Spirit.[37] The difference, of course, with human relationships is the potential for strife. "Will itself experiences resistance only in the will of a person who wills something different."[38] This means that we cannot ignore the social reality of the other, even (and maybe especially) the one who betrays us. "The individual becomes a person over and again through the other, in the 'moment.'"[39] The "collective person" for Bonhoeffer "is not as if many persons, gathered together, now add up to a collective person. Rather, the person comes into being only when embedded in sociality."[40] Therefore, we are not able to isolate that relation with the other person from our relationship with God. The other person presents us with the same challenge to our knowing as does God. "My real relationship to another person is oriented to my relationship to God."[41] How much despair is caused over the revelation that we really do not "know" the other person! It is not that God is so much more difficult to know. "But since I know God's 'I' only in the revelation of God's love, so too with the other person; here the concept of the church comes into play."[42] Here in the very structure of our humanity is that which cries out for the vicarious humanity of Christ, our humanity that does not exist apart from the necessity of Someone else's humanity: Jesus Christ. The "wonderful exchange" will include our broken relationships as Christ takes our prayers for those relationships as feeble as they are and makes them his prayers.[43] The despair that can be caused by despair over the earthly will not be able to be separated from the grace of Christ.

36. Bonhoeffer, *Sanctorum Communio*, 55.
37. Ibid., 67.
38. Ibid., 72.
39. Ibid., 55.
40. Ibid., 78.
41. Ibid., 55.
42. Ibid.
43. James B. Torrance, *Worship, Community, and the Triune God of Grace*, 15.

Like Mary, Peter, too, is found weeping because of his relationship with Jesus. But in this case, it is the sorrow of his own guilt over denying his Lord three times (Matt 26:75; Mark 14:72; Luke 22:62). Despair comes in the betrayal of a relationship. Even John Calvin counsels a grieving man after losing his father not "to shake off or suppress the love of a father, as not to experience grief on occasion of the loss of a son. Neither do I insist upon you laying aside all grief."[44] This is because we cannot "put off that common humanity with which God has endowed us, that, being human, we should be turned into stones," although he hastens to add that one should "set bounds" to the time of grief and that one should not "give way to senseless wailing." For Calvin, the importance of our humanity recognizes the place of grief over the loss of a loved one. Of course, this is profoundly christological, as witnessed by Jesus before the tomb of Lazarus: "Jesus began to weep" (John 11:35). Jesus had seen both Mary and the Jews weeping for Lazarus, and "he was greatly disturbed in spirit and deeply moved" (John 11:33). Many interpretations have been offered for Jesus's disturbance, from despair over sin and death to anger with Mary and the Jews for their lack of faith.[45] Jesus does not, however, just add his weeping to theirs, nor does he simply criticize Mary and the Jews, for he joins in weeping as well. His weeping is in solidarity with the grief over Lazarus, and for the sorrow that Mary and Martha possess, but the weeping is also vicarious, a unique, efficacious kind of weeping that is the foundation for the raising of Lazarus from the grave, as an answer to his prayer to the Father (John 11:41–43).

Despair as loss of a relationship is of course more stark in the death of a loved one. In Mary's weeping over Jesus, the relationship is over, even if no betrayal set it asunder. At the least the betrayal gave a reason! Death has no reason but only gives finality. The movie is over; leave the theatre. Yet is joy really left totally behind, for example, when one loses a parent? Is not the gift of the relationship, so often taken for granted, now accented in the bold relief of joy, like a brightened outdoors after a spring storm? The disciples certainly knew Jesus's value once he was gone, once they experienced despair. Somehow, joy can come out of despair. Again, Jesus

---

44. John Calvin, *Writings on Pastoral Piety*. The Classics of Western Spirituality, ed. Elsie Anne McKee (New York: Paulist, 2001) 300.

45. Edwyn Clement Hoskyns, *The Fourth Gospel* (London: Faber & Faber, 1947) 403–5.

has lived a life of sorrows (Isa 53:3), but his unique suffering is vicarious, and paves the way for resurrection and resurrection joy.

Despair is seen in the emptiness of relationships; relationships that are a shell of what they once were, a mockery of love that only gives pretense. Our relationship to our culture is seen to be the same thing in Ecclesiastes' eyes. He "sees the emptiness in homes filled with furniture. He sees the futility in overly-busy lives. He sees the lack of love between family members . . ."[46] Yes, he may conclude that all is "vanity," but, as Anderson observes, "seeing all of this, he becomes terribly wise, and terribly sad, for he sees too much that's crooked and cannot be straightened."[47] Aslan, the regal lion in C. S. Lewis's stories, can be powerful, yet also sad.[48] Yet through Ecclesiastes' sadness comes a wisdom of knowing the limits of being human. This becomes particularly evident when we reflect upon how tenuous our relationships often are, even though their value is the stuff of ballads and torch songs.

Relationships imply both sorrow and joy. Paul is well aware of this when he comments on the nature of the church as the body of Christ: "If one member suffers, all suffer together with it; if one member is honored, all rejoice together with it" (1 Cor 12:26). Is he simply arguing for a uniformity of value, a collectivism of humanity, denying the reality of the individual? That cannot be, for he recognizes that each member of the body has a different function (1 Cor 12:14f.). Despair and sorrow can happen, however, because we cannot avoid weeping with those who weep any more than we should avoid rejoicing with those who rejoice (Rom 12:15). Oneness bears fruit when despair is not just born by a suffering individual, but the entire body joins, *vicariously,* on behalf of, and maybe even in place of, the suffering of their sorrowful friend. The greatest sorrows are too difficult to be dealt with alone. A poignant moment from one of my favorite television shows of the sixties, *The Fugitive,* featured the portrayal of the loneliness of the hunted man, Richard Kimble, who goes from town to town, never able to bear the burden with anyone else of being hunted for a crime he did not commit. Being "the body of Christ"

---

46 Ray S. Anderson, *Exploration into God: Sermonic Meditations on the Book of Ecclesiastes* (Eugene, OR: Wipf & Stock, 2006) 29.

47. Ibid.

48. C. S. Lewis, *The Lion, the Witch and the Wardrobe* (New York: HarperTrophy, 1993) 164.

(1 Cor 12:27) is not simply an empty metaphor.[49] But despair voluntarily embraced is rare and difficult. Do we not see this in the incarnation most of all? We have all experienced a vicarious kind of sorrow when a good friend has sympathized with our pain.[50]

Despair over the earthly can cause us to seek to ignore, even escape the earthly. In Gethsemane, the disciples were found by Jesus "sleeping because of grief" (Luke 22:45). They were trying to escape the impending tragedy of Jesus by sleeping. We do not want to face the day, and in fact, may try to avoid it as long as possible by staying in bed. Escape may take many other forms for the workaholic, or through entertainment, or the arts. Comic books and other forms of popular culture were long derided as "escapism," a refusal to face reality. Perhaps they are. But look at how terrible this world can be! There is a good case to be made that children need fantastic imaginary monsters and comic book violence in order to deal with their fears.[51] The true escape may be the idealist who believes that this is "the best of all possible worlds," the foolish and silly *Candide* character in Voltaire's play, or *Goodman Beaver* in Harvey Kurtzman's comic strip, that refuses to admit to the terror of the world.[52] Perhaps escape is needed because the world can be so terrible and escape can even be a gracious provision of God. Sleeping is sometimes a very good thing. But obviously the kind of sleeping that the disciples represent can become a lack of faith, a refusal to face the future and trust God, which reflects our need for the vicarious faith of Christ.

The Old Testament, particularly in the Psalms, is filled with sorrow over approaching death. It is not something to look forward: "Remember how short my time is," the psalmist cries to God (Ps 89:47), where God's wonders are forgotten (Ps 88:10–12; 6:5). Yet, C. S. Lewis, in his study on the Psalms, relates the benefit of his own experience when he tried to believe and obey God without thinking of any future reward for an

---

49. C. K. Barrett, *The First Epistle to the Corinthians*. Harper's New Testament Commentaries (New York: Harper & Row, 1968) 292.

50. Murray J. Harris, *The Second Epistle to the Corinthians*. The New International Greek Testament (Grand Rapids: Eerdmans, 2005) 483.

51. Gerard Jones, *Killing Monsters: Why Children Need Fantasy, Super Heroes and Make-Believe Violence* (New York: Basic, 2009).

52. Harvey Kurtzman and Will Elder, *Goodman Beaver* (Princeton, WI: Kitchen Sink, 1984); Voltaire, *Candide*, 2nd ed., trans. Robert M. Adams (New York: Norton, 1991).

entire year.⁵³ He sees the same value for the Jews in their view of the afterlife reflected in the Old Testament. Hezekiah did remind God that "Sheol cannot thank you, death cannot praise you," in praying for his life to be extended (Isa 38:18). All one can do in death is "to cry and sob helplessly."⁵⁴ Yet Lewis was able to see benefit, perhaps, in an accentuated sense of his need. Despair can be used for the sake of joy. The disciples of Jesus, unfortunately, saw the grief caused by the forthcoming death of Jesus as only the occasion to repress their despair, rather than as an opportunity to sit with Jesus while he prays—a vicarious event if there ever was one (Matt 26:36; Mark 14:32)—and to "pray that you may not come into the time of trial" (Luke 22:40). The disciples lost the opportunity to "weep with those who weep" (Rom 12:15), an act of solidarity that becomes a vicarious act as one prays with Jesus.

Both joy and sorrow point beyond themselves, Barth argues, in commenting on Rom 12:15.⁵⁵ To react against joy and sorrow may be enmity with God, such as Michal's disgust with David's dancing or when the friends of Job criticize his cry of despair. Barth is here at his dialectical best:

> There is a laughter which represents life; and there is a weeping which signifies death. Both are pointing to the "One." All stoicism and moralism, all instruction, every attempt to interfere with human emotion or set one emotion against another, may dangerously upset their parabolic witness . . . The true protest against the world is, strangely enough, here brought about by affirming even the ecstasies of human joy and sorrow.⁵⁶

This is a protest against the form of the world, Barth contends, when "the unknowableness of the Son of God is apprehended," and the "other" can forget one's "otherness."⁵⁷ We are participating in one's sorrow along with Jesus just as we participate in one's joy along with Jesus, and only because of Jesus. Jesus can be troubled because of what he has to do one behalf of humanity (John 12:27). The mystery of Christ is known, yet maintained as mystery, as one we cannot control, when we weep and rejoice with one another, thereby joining them with his life. Otherwise, we are simply always

---

53. C. S. Lewis, *Reflections on the Psalms* (New York: Harcourt, Brace & World, 1958) 42.

54. Barth, *CD* III/2, 589–92.

55. Barth, *Epistle to the Romans*, 459–60.

56. Ibid., 460.

57. Ibid.

victims to that which we despair over; we have a new god. The mystery of Christ is found in the Lord who became the servant (Phil 2:5–11), and the reality of humility that he brings (Phil 2:2–4). In his later shorter commentary on Romans, Barth can say this:

> The Christian will always be found where God's grace in Jesus Christ has found him, in the humility of one who knows that, for time and eternity, he owes nothing to his own wisdom and strength in the lowliness of one—in whatever position he may be, in joy or in sorrow, in success or in failure, the majority or in a minority—who has been accepted, whom God has admitted to his way and his work. A Christian can always be found where man's humanity is stressed in contrast to any likeness to God (12:16).[58]

EARTHLY DESPAIR: LACK AS LONGING

Despair can be over the earthly longing that is not fulfilled. We may be longing to be parents, or for our parents to be grandparents, that which never comes. We have certain expectations out of life which each increasing year creates more disappointment. Despair seeps in. This is truly, however, despair over the earthly, not the kind of longing for eternity advocated by C. S. Lewis and others, such as F. LeRon Shults:

> The longing for unity with the divine that one finds in the various myths of world cultures, in the structures of human self-consciousness, and in philosophical reflection or metaphysics, is fulfilled in and through the spiritual regeneration of those who become "one spirit" with the Lord.[59]

Is this longing really separated, however it protests its spirituality, from a longing for something earthly? Is the religious or philosophical impulse any different from any other desire, even if it is defined by fulfilling that which is lacking in the earthly? Like defining God in terms of communicable attributes such as love or power, our temptation is to create a God who is more Superman than the God of the Bible, the *Deus ex machina* so criticized by Bonhoeffer as the God that the "world come of age" no

---

58. Karl Barth, *A Shorter Commentary on Romans* (Richmond: John Knox, 1959) 155–56.

59. F. LeRon Shults, *Reforming Theological Anthropology: After the Philosophical Turn to Relationality* (Grand Rapids: Eerdmans, 2003) 78–79.

longer needs.⁶⁰ The famous "cosmological arguments" of Thomas Aquinas and others, which seek to prove the existence of God by reason alone, are dependent upon logical deductions based on observation of contingent reality. This is still a despair over the earthly that will be interrupted by the longing of Jesus (not a longing *for* Jesus but the longing that *belongs to* Jesus): a longing for communion with the Father in the Spirit, a harmony that we do not know or have any analogy.

All mourning and all rejoicing in the end will be relativized, Paul claims, so "those who mourn" should be "as though they were not mourning," and "those who rejoice as though they were not rejoicing" (1 Cor 7:29–31). This is because "the present form of this world is passing away." Augustine characteristically sees Paul speaking of detaching oneself from the world and attaching oneself to love for God:

> While that which you must lose is still with you—and either during your life or when you die you will lose it, it cannot always be with you—while it is still with you, loosen your love for it, be prepared, by the will of God, to fasten your love upon God.⁶¹

What may first be perceived as just "warmed-over" Stoicism or Buddhist detachment may be seen in a vicarious sense, as Calvin puts it: "For the man who thinks of himself as an alien sojourner in the world, uses the things of the world as if they belong to Someone else; in other words, as things which are lent for the day only."⁶² "If they belong to someone else! Even rejoicing and weeping now belong to the vicarious humanity of Christ. If this is so, then the Christian is called upon to let them go to Christ and not jealously possess them. "For the present form of the world is passing away" (1 Cor 7:31). The eschatological Christ, "the last Adam" (1 Cor 15:45) is now the owner of our joy and our sorrow. They are no longer to be burdens upon us to maintain (joy) or endure (despair) but are wrapped up in Jesus Christ and his vicarious humanity. As C. K. Barrett comments, "The point is that neither laughter nor tears

---

60. Dietrich Bonhoeffer, *Letters and Papers from Prison*, ed. Eberhard Bethge and trans. Reginald H. Fuller, et al. (New York: Macmillan, 1972) 326.

61. Augustine in *The Church's Bible: I Corinthians, Interpreted by Early Christian Commentators*, translated and edited by Judith Kovacs (Grand Rapids: Eerdmans, 2005) 123.

62. John Calvin, *Calvin's New Testament Commentaries: I Corinthians*, ed. David W. Torrance and Thomas F. Torrance, trans. John W. Fraser (Grand Rapids: Eerdmans, 1960) 159–60.

is the last word; a man should never allow himself to be lost in either."[63] The basis for this is the vicarious joy and the vicarious despair of Christ, the last Adam.

Longings will eventually be interrupted by the day of the Lord. Jayber Crow, the humble barber in Wendell Berry's novel of the same name, also has a life long longing for the good wife with a nice church where he can be a pastor; longings never to be fulfilled but displaced by something else.[64] Here is another picture of the gracious displacement that takes place in the vicarious humanity of Christ, a radical substitutionary atonement that goes far beyond Christ paying the penalty for our sins. Paul can speak of the longing that even this bodily existence possesses: "For in this tent we groan, longing to be clothed with our heavenly dwelling . . ." (2 Cor 5:2). The "groaning" must be a distress because we have yet to possess the fullness of the eschatological joy.[65] Yes, there is wonderful anticipation and longed for joy here, but because something is missing there is indeed distress in this groaning. Paul tells us also that the creation "has been groaning in labor pains until now, and not only the creation, but we ourselves, who have the first fruits of the Spirit, groan inwardly while we wait for adoption, the redemption of our bodies" (Rom 8:22–23). In the meantime, "the Spirit intercedes with sighs too deep for words" even though "we do not know how to pray as we ought" (Rom 8:26). The Spirit helps us in our inability to connect us with the vicarious prayers of Jesus. Our inability is certainly an occasion for distress! But that inability and distress will lead to the joy we possess when we share in the joy of the Son through the power of the Spirit. Barth connects this with our ignorance of knowing what God knows. "Therefore it is precisely our not-knowing what God knows that is our temporal knowledge about God, our comfort, light, power, and knowledge of eternity."[66] We are not left in ignorance, however. "My final possibility is to groan—and to await the promise. Now, *adoption* means *the redemption of the body*, that is, the

---

63. Barrett, *The First Epistle to the Corinthians*, 178.

64. Wendell Berry, *Jayber Crow* (Washington, DC: Counterpoint, 2000).

65. Ralph P. Martin views this as an anticipation without distress in *2 Corinthians*. Word Biblical Commentary 40 (Waco, TX: Word, 1986) 104, in contrast to F. F. Bruce, who views the "groaning" as distress in *1 and 2 Corinthians*. New Century Bible (Grand Rapids: Eerdmans, 1980) 202.

66. Barth, *The Epistle to the Romans*, 310.

complete identification between Christ and me."[67] At present, we long for that joy. The anticipatory joy is longed for in the midst of sorrow, pain, suffering, and despair. So it was by "the man of sorrows who is also the prince of peace." There is one Jesus Christ who is both despair and joy. That is how deep the vicarious humanity of Christ exists.

"The man is sorrows who is also the prince of peace." This thought comes from a former PhD student at Fuller Seminary, who, while dying of cancer, started a blog, making this comment shortly before he died.[68]

DESPAIR OVER THE ETERNAL

The preceding may be *"despair in weakness,"* but the second form of despair in not willing to be oneself is a *"despair over his weakness."*[69] This is to despair over knowing the eternal, the kind of despair expressed, in Kierkegaard's example, of the person who rarely attends church "because he feels that most pastors really do not know what they are talking about."[70] Still, he regrets this spiritual laziness, and retreats to solitude, the loneliness that Kierkegaard says that nonetheless gives evidence that spirit still resides in such a person. In a way, we are again meeting doubt. Or such a despair over weakness may take the form of despairing over one's sin. Here is where weakness becomes not just an excuse for pity, but also an occasion for sin. "By sin, that is, by despairing over his sin, he has lost all relation to grace—and also to himself."[71] Despair is connected then with shame. Despair becomes shame, James Fowler contends, when it communicates unworthiness.[72] Kierkegaard, despite his sympathies with any opposition to "Christendom," does not let the person off the hook. Like the "despair in weakness," the "despair over his weakness" does not turn to faith, and is still sin.

Despair over one's weakness, in light of the vicarious humanity of Christ, is seeing the brightness of the new day that brings the judgment of enlightening everything that was obscured by the night. Not simply a

---

67. Ibid., 312–13.

68. Scott Becker, "Con Patienti." Online: http://aufhebung1.blogspot.com/2007/06/con-patienti.html.

69. Kierkegaard, *The Sickness Unto Death*, 61.

70. Ibid., 64.

71. Ibid., 110.

72. James Fowler, "Foreword" in Bringle, *Despair: Sickness or Sin?* 14.

moral exhortation nor a forensic acquittal of sin, the vicarious humanity of Christ is an ontological reality in which humanity is both justified and delivered at its very core; in simplest terms, genuinely helped. It was not guilt over the Law that brought Saul to his knees but meeting Jesus Christ.[73] The accusation is the accusation of grace. "No Pharisee or moralist can accuse him as soberly and straightforwardly and totally and comprehensively as this."[74] As James Torrance reminds us, when the only priesthood is our priesthood, of the Catholic or Orthodox priest but also the Protestant "priesthood of all believers," "the only offering" becomes "our offering, the only intercessions our intercessions," and this only creates weariness in worship and the entire Christian life.[75]

Such despair is found in the laments of the pious one who suffers while others mock him with taunts of God's absence: "My tears have been my food day and night, while people say to me continually, 'Where is your God?'" (Ps 42:3). Tragedies of natural catastrophe in needless waste and the suffering of innocents create a despair about the eternal among even the most religious. Where is the eternal in my present, very earthly suffering? I want to be fed by God but the "tears" are my only food and drink. The cry of Jesus from the cross is not far from this.

The despair over the eternal can take a decidedly malevolent turn as seen in Judas's betrayal of Jesus. Not only did he betray Jesus and receive money for it, his guilt was so great that he ended his own life (Matt 27:3–5). Peter will also betray Jesus (Matt 26:69–75), providing the question of how does he differ from the icon of treachery, Judas? Peter did "weep bitterly" and the fact that we have no record of Judas weeping is only an argument from silence. Both have a despair over the eternal. Peter and Judas should not be so easily separated. Perhaps it is our despair over the eternal that wants to keep Peter "religious" and assign Judas to perdition. The difference is that Judas kills himself. He is not able to live with himself, and Peter was. Did Judas try to take himself out of grace? Was that his greatest sin? Ray Anderson suggests this in imagining a post-mortem conversation between Judas and Jesus.[76]

---

73. Barth, *CD*, III/2, 604–5.

74. Ibid., 605.

75. James B. Torrance, *Worship, Community, and the Triune God of Grace*, 20.

76. Ray S. Anderson, *The Gospel according to Judas* (Colorado Springs: Helmers and Howard, 1991); rev. ed. (Colorado Springs: Navpress, 1994) and Ray S. Anderson, *Judas and Jesus: Amazing Grace for the Wounded Soul* (Eugene, OR: Cascade Books, 2005).

This same kind of despair is found in other religious headliners such as Jonah and Elijah. Jonah is disquieted that God will not judge the Ninevites as Jonah thinks he should. So he responds, "It is better for me to die than to live" (Jonah 4:8). Elijah is distraught by the challenge of Jezebel. He asks that he, too, might die (1 Kgs 19:4). Elijah expects the Lord to be victorious over Jezebel. The word of the Lord comes to Elijah but not in a natural way; not in the wind or the fire (1 Kgs 19:11–12). The word of God comes in the silence. It is not just silence, it is a word, but comes by the grace of silence so that God can speak: "Yet I will leave seven thousand in Israel, all the knees that have not bowed to Baal, and every mouth that has not kissed him" (1 Kgs 19:18). Elijah's despair does bring him hope. Barth's comments on this passage are interesting:

> Man is always and everywhere involved in suffering and death, conflict and guilt. But it is far from obvious, nor is there any compelling reason to suppose, that it is such crises which really bring man into relation with the wholly other, and lead him to an existence which embodies the meaning of this relation . . . Fire, drought, earthquake, war, pestilence, the darkening of the sun and similar phenomena are not the things to plunge us into real anguish, and therefore to give us real peace. The Lord was not in the storm, the earthquake or the fire (1 Kgs 19:11f.). He really was not.[77]

Here is a caution: As much as we may experience joy coming out of despair, we must steadfastly refuse to see a necessity for despair in order to have joy. The joy of Jesus will demand this.

The grace of God is that which gives both prophets hope. Their despair is real, and it is a despair over religious things and religious goals, a despair over the eternal in contrast to one's weakness. Even the religious mantle proves to be a burden that no one can eventually wear.

This despair does not necessarily come directly from God (That is a despair we will deal with next). We are close to it. But this kind of despair is more indirect yet is still a sense of being abandoned by God. Left loose to be victims of one enemies, the despair over weakness is real. The religious guarantee over life seems to have failed. The classic text, of course is Ps 22:1: "My God, my God, why have you forsaken me," cried by Jesus from the cross (Mark 15:34; Matt 27:46). Immediately we are thrust into the reality of the incarnation in which the Son takes upon our

---

77. Barth, *CD*, III/2, 114–15.

humanity at the furthest point of estrangement.[78] Despair over the eternal is something the Son experienced, something that God has experienced. The Son cries out, nonetheless, "my" God, affirming even in terror the filial relationship between the Son and the Father.[79] We have here, as John McLeod Campbell puts it, "a trial of the faith of sonship."[80] The implications of this are profound and will be explore much more later on. But we do see that despair ought not to be foreign to Christology.

If God has abandoned one, according to the Psalms, one does not have the resources to continue: "For my soul is full of troubles and my life draws near to Sheol . . ." (Ps 88:3); "Vindicate me, O God, and defend my cause against an ungodly people; from those who are deceitful and unjust deliver me! For you are the God in whom I take refuge; why have you cast me off?" (Ps 43:1-2). The psalmist continues, "Why are you cast down O my soul, and why are you disquieted within me?" (Ps 43:5). The answer is to "Hope in God; for I shall again praise him, my help and my God" (Ps 43:5). But how easy is this to do?

Such a despair over one's weakness can take the form of what Bonhoeffer calls an "infinite thirst" in human beings.[81] This is the thirst that causes despair because it is a bridge between despair over the earthly and despair over the eternal. Its source is portrayed in Adam's desire to live out of his own resources, resources that are finite and can never satisfy; despair quickly follows. This is a manifestation of the prophesied consequence of the fall: human beings, in trying to become like God (*sicut Deus*), find they are woefully short of the resources to do so. A kind of "solitude" is created, Bonhoeffer suggests, that produces the "infinite thirst," a thirst that inevitably leads to death. An infinite thirst is only fulfilled by the One who is infinite. The weakness of even the religious person is exposed by the grace of God. God speaks through Hosea, "They do not cry to me from the heart, but they wail upon their beds, they gash themselves for grain and wine; they rebel against me" (Hos 7:14).

---

78. See Ray S. Anderson, *Historical Transcendence and the Reality of God* (Grand Rapids: Eerdmans, 1975).

79. John Calvin, *Calvin's New Testament Commentaries: A Harmony of the Gospels: Matthew, Mark and Luke*, ed. David W. Torrance and Thomas F. Torrance, trans. A. W. Morrison (Grand Rapids: Eerdmans, 1972) 359.

80. John McLeod Campbell, *The Nature of the Atonement* (Grand Rapids: Eerdmans, 1996) 204.

81. Bonhoeffer, *Creation and Fall*, 143.

A kind of despair over one's weakness may be seen in Karl Barth's suggestion that joy itself can bring despair. Despair is so insidious, so all pervasive, that it can be created by joy. This is the perhaps paradoxical transcendent joy of *eros*, a joy that lifts us out of ourselves, which nonetheless may be the despair over one's weakness. One becomes vulnerable because the joy of one's love inevitably leads to disappointment and hurt. As Anderson suggests, animals mate but it is human beings who meet.[82] More is involved with us than just mating. "Eternally" pledging love to one another often does not work out because finite (and sinful) beings that have to deal with the complexity of intimacy with another human being are involved. As Barth remarks, "The well-known cycle of *eros*, with its alteration of possession and loss, intoxication and soberness, enthusiasm and disillusionment, is a tragic and therefore melancholy business."[83] Andre Dubus, in his story, "A Father's Story," relates that what causes despair is "the imagination that pretends there is a future and insists on predicting millions of moments, thousands of days, and so drains you that you cannot live the moment at hand."[84] This use of imagination describes much of our experience of joy. Despair descends on the imagination that flees from the present and the past and its traditions of institutions, values, and order for the unknown yet frantically expectant future. This is one aspect, Barth contends, of how we deal with the problem of identity: "What guarantee is there that I am really the same to-day as I was in the past?"[85]

"Is memory better for joyful impressions?" Dietrich Bonhoeffer asks from prison.[86] "A past grief stands under the sign of its being *overcome*, only griefs that have not been overcome (unforgiven sin) are always fresh and tormenting to the memory." Joy is born in the overcoming of past griefs, so that memory is made of the stuff of joy that is birthed by despair.

Yet Bonhoeffer also reflects on the effects of a night's bombing. It has the result of shattering memory, creating an absence of memory, giving ruin to "all obligations of love, marriage, friendship, and loyalty."[87]

---

82. Anderson, *On Being Human*, 53.

83. Barth, *CD* IV/2, 788.

84. Andre Dubus, "A Father's Story" in *God's Stories*, ed. C. Michael Curtis (Boston: Houghton Mifflin, 1998) 42.

85. Barth, *CD* III/2, 533–35.

86. Bonhoeffer, *Letters and Papers from Prison*, 35.

87. Ibid., 203.

"Nothing sticks fast, nothing holds firm; everything is here today and gone tomorrow." This is in contrast to "the good things of life—truth, justice, and beauty—all great accomplishments need time, constancy, and "memory," or they degenerate." Truth, justice, and beauty are the transcendent things of joy that are now gone. There is no longer a place for responsibility, for one's identity has been shattered, as it were, by the bombs. This is what Kierkegaard calls "despair of the eternal or over oneself." Note how the eternal is linked to personal identity. How temporal and tangential is memory in personal identity then?

"Rejoice in hope, be patient in suffering, persevere in prayer . . ." the apostle exhorts the Romans (Rom 12:12). Joy dares to come out of despair if we dare to hope. In fact, Barth contends, hope is only an ethical behavior when we rejoice.[88] Hope can be silly wishful thinking in the midst of real despair, but it becomes an ethical action when one rejoices in the midst of sorrow or suffering. This argues against the ultimate value of present possessions, which is the opposite of hope. Hope means that one is in despair. We boast (the word can also be translated "rejoice") "in our hope of sharing the glory of God," although this includes "sufferings" (Rom 5:3). Despair raises the question of the ethics of hope. In spite of Kant, is it right to hope in a desperate situation? What does it mean for Jesus to be confronted by the ethics of hope? Is he the only one who can take the risk before the Father and really live Kierkegaard's "teleological suspension of the ethical" when he must trust the Father despite all the circumstances to the contrary?[89] Is this our only hope? Barth continues: "To *rejoice in hope* means to know God in hope without seeing Him, and to be satisfied that it should be so. This is what makes hope an ethical action; for to hope in God turns hope into a joyful act which cannot be brought to naught."[90] Paul lives this kind of dialectical existence himself:

> We are treated as imposters, and yet are true; as unknown, and yet are well known; as dying, and see – we are alive; as punished, and yet not killed; as sorrowful, yet always rejoicing; as poor, yet making many rich; as having nothing, and yet possessing everything (2 Cor 6:8–10).

88. Barth, *Epistle to the Romans*, 457.

89. Kierkegaard, *Fear and Trembling* in *Fear and Trembling/Repetition*, ed. and trans. Howard V. Hong and Edna H. Hong (Princeton: Princeton University Press, 1983) 54–67.

90. Barth, *Epistle to the Romans*, 457.

"As sorrowful, yet always rejoicing!" Paul does not deny that he is viewed as sorrowful. His circumstances made that obvious. Yet joy is going to live with sorrow, just as the unknowable God is made known through a cross. The man of sorrows is also the prince of peace.

Barth contends that in resorting to "oblivion" we reject all tradition for the sake of "the spirit of the age."[91] The opposite response is to enshrine "memory" of the past as a certain golden age to be recovered. Both alternatives, however, involve despair over something: over the future that really never changes things (the hippies of the sixties and their expectations) or the impossibility of ever repeating the past. Both create despair by our inability to maintain continuity, a psychologically horrible threat that is only a prelude to death. The only alternative, Barth concludes, is the action of God. Both the joy of nostalgia, or trying to repeat the past, or the joy of fantasy, investing oneself completely in a future that never comes, can become forms of despair.

The joy of beauty can be bittersweet, Walker Percy suggests in one of his novels. In *The Moviegoer,* Binx Bolling is hiking in the mountains, and the comradeship with his friends and the beauty of the smoky blue valleys "instead of giving us joy, became heartbreaking" and Binx "sank into a deep melancholy."[92]

Why heartbreaking? Is this simply ingratitude towards God, self absorption, an underdeveloped aesthetic appreciation, or what? Perhaps that it can be all of these demonstrates the power of beauty and the tragic experience of joy. Experiencing joy does not destroy despair; it may increase it, or even create it. What will this mean for the despair and joy of Jesus?

The joy in loving is paramount, Barth argues, regardless of whether or not that love is returned. (This is certainly true with God.) In this the lover is imitating God, based on the fact that one is loved by God. Here is peace and joy. "This is a reason for laughing even when our eyes swim with tears."[93] The despair is caused by the freedom to love in a gratuitous way, "unsought, unplanned, and undesired" and made free by God. This is where the joy exists, in this freedom to love.

But one might ask Barth, Does not God's love yet desire a response? "I will be your God and you will be my people," Yahweh pledges uncondi-

---

91. Barth, *CD* III/2, 534ff.
92. Walker Percy, *The Moviegoer* (New York: Vintage International, 1998) 41.
93. Barth, *CD* IV/2, 789.

tionally to Israel, and because of that, desires their obedience to his law. A response to God is deserved, yet the Old Testament narrative is certainly the story of how Israel was unable to respond in faith and obedience to Yahweh. The need for the *vicarious response of Christ* is apparent. Dare we say that without an obedient and faithful response to God, a cosmic catastrophe would occur, an ontological absurdity, with sin at its impossible core? More particularly, a *vicarious joy* will be needed.

THE DESPAIR OF DEFIANCE

The more obvious sinful kind of despair, for Kierkegaard, is the "despair to will to be oneself: defiance."[94] We have spent less time on this despair because its deadly consequences are much more obvious. This second kind of conscious despair is the self-seeking to be its own master, to refuse the "relational" nature of the self, with God, and others, "rebelling against all existence."[95] The error which slips into the writer's story, in Kierkegaard's parable, is in this kind of despair because he refused to be corrected. "I will stand as witness against you, a witness that you are a second-rate author."[96] The error "despairs," yet refuses to be "erased," and continues to be defiant, much like, in a much more serious vein, the monster in the original *Frankenstein* novel in which at the end of the story the very articulate monster seeks to kill Dr. Frankenstein for bringing the monster to life. The monster so much despairs of life that he wants to kill his maker (an obvious parable of modern, secular humanity and God).[97] This is the kind of despair that still stands defiantly in its "error," no matter what. The dwarfs in C. S. Lewis' fantasy, *The Last Battle,* are a good illustration of this. In the last days, Narnia has been transformed, but they are so cynical, so bitter, that the new, wonderful world they are living in only appears to them as a smelly stable.[98] Can one conceive of a better picture of hell?

---

94. Kierkegaard, *Sickness Unto Death*, 69.
95. Ibid., 73.
96. Ibid., 74.
97. Mary Shelley, *Frankenstein* (New York: Bantam, 1991).
98. C. S. Lewis, *The Last Battle* (New York: HarperTrophy, 1994) 171–86.

CHAPTER THREE

Is Despair from God?

Dare we speak of despair coming from God? Is that the same as saying that God is the author of evil, suffering, and sin? Much of the Christian tradition does not hesitate to see the origin of despair (or at least certain manifestations) in God. Isaac of Nineveh (ca. 700) offers comfort that the darkness is not troubling when one realizes that it has been given "by God's providence for reasons known to him alone."[1] Although "the soul is utterly deprived of hope in God and the consolation of faith" and "entirely filled with perplexity and anguish," God never allows the soul to remain in that state for a whole day, but allows it "to emerge very soon from the darkness." Like Barth speaking of joy creating despair, Isaac believes that "after grace, the trial returns." Isaac may be interpreted in light of Ecclesiastes: "For everything there is a season . . . a time to weep, a time to laugh; a time to mourn, and a time to dance . . ." (Eccl 3:1, 4). Calvin is even more explicit: Gratitude is the only attitude we should have, even for sorrows.[2] Creation should be enjoyed, yet not with an "excessive joy."[3] "But we must always come back to this consolation: The Lord planned our sorrows, so let us summit to his will."[4] How hard it is to hear these words: "The Lord planned our sorrows"! Yet, for many, there is great comfort in believing that God is control of every minute event in one's life, including sorrows. Is there any alternative, however, to such language?

---

1. Isaac of Nineveh, *Ascetic Treaties* 57 (Spanos, 231–233) cited by Olivier Clément, *The Roots of Christian Mysticism: Texts from the Patristic Era with Commentary*, trans. Theodore Berkeley, O.C.S.O. and Jeremy Hummerstone (Hyde Park, NY: New City, 1995) 188.

2. John Calvin, *The Golden Booklet of the True Christian Life*, trans. Henry J. Van Andel (Grand Rapids: Eerdmans, 2004) 73.

3. Ibid., 73, 87.

4. Ibid., 64.

DESPAIR IN THE ABSENCE OF GOD

It is hard for the Psalmist to accept the abandonment that he eventually cannot but see as from the hand of God: "I cry aloud to God, aloud to God, that he may hear me. In the day of trouble I seek the Lord . . ." (Ps 77:1-2). His conclusion is stark: "I think of God and I moan" (Ps 77:3). How different is this from the pop theology that can very glibly in its youthful immaturity shout, "Everything is spiritual!"[5] If everything is spiritual, is there any place for the human, and especially the suffering human being? Scripture itself does not promote such a "theology of glory" without taking seriously the "theology of the cross" first. The Psalmist genuinely wrestles and moans with despair coming from God. The Psalmist of Psalm 102 likewise is in deep despair: "Hear my prayer, O Lord; Let my cry come to you. Do not hide your face from me in the day of distress . . . For my days pass away like smoke, and my bones burn like a furnace . . . " (Ps 102:1-3). "My bones burn like a furnace"! What pain! Like the Psalmist in Psalm 77 (vv. 11-12), the Psalmist will look to the promises of God (Ps 102:12f.), but not before he wrestles with the presence of God in the midst of despair. Job has a longer, more difficult route it seems. He begins by practically mocking the grandeur of the creation narrative: "Let the day perish in which I was born . . . Let that day be darkness! May God above not seek it, or light shine on it . . ." (Job 3:3-4).[6] There is no place for joy in this darkness: "Yes, let that night be barren; let no joyful cry be heard in it" (Job 3:7). The readers know, additionally, that God is at least allowing the adversary to send this suffering upon Job (Job 1). Do we feel more like the ancient Greeks of Greek mythology than we want to admit; at the hands of capricious gods?

Can we really speak of God as being "absent," however? Is God truly God if his omnipresence can cease? Is it not better to speak of the "hiddenness" of God, as Paul Fiddes does, than to surrender the traditional doctrine of God's omnipresence?[7] Certainly God can feel absent to us and not really be absent. Yet if we are going to take the despair of Jesus seriously—and this means his suffering, death, and burial—will it be sufficient to speak of Jesus just "feeling" abandoned by God? Hiddenness can

---

5. "Looking Everywhere Seeing the Divine," *Fuller Focus* (Spring, 2008) 12-14.

6. Clines, *Job 1-20*, 84.

7. Paul Fiddes, *The Creative Suffering of God* (Oxford: Oxford University Press, 1988) 192.

too easily convey that God is merely play acting. No, there is a genuine absence in the cry of abandonment, "My God, my God, why you forsaken me?" (Matt 27:46) that reflects the Son taking up the deepest of our despairs. Paul can speak in a very "Platonic" way of our earthly existence as being "away from the Lord" (2 Cor 5:6). To be in Christ is not the same as being with Christ, as Harris points out.[8] For Paul, his desire "is to desire and be with Christ, for that is far better . . ." (Phil 1:23) than to stay in this earthly life. For him, "our citizenship is in heaven" (Phil 3:20). Certainly an aspect of the "exile" of this earthly existence that Calvin speaks of involves being vulnerable to vicissitudes of the bodily frame so that being "absent from the Lord" does bring about despair.[9]

DESPAIR, SIN, AND GRACE

Is despair necessary in order for God to be gracious? Is law necessary in order for there to be grace? Is evil necessary in order for there to be good? What is it in the cosmos, or even in God, that makes this necessary? Is there another way to interpret this, to interpret despair and joy? John Sanders tells his own story in the preface to his book, *The God Who Risks: A Theology of Providence,* of his anguish as a young boy when his brother was killed. The theology he was taught was that God causes all things to happen. His only thought could be, "Why, God, did you kill my brother?"[10] Is this the God of Jesus Christ, the Father that he trusted?

Despair that comes from God is not just restricted to the results of the Fall. The creation of Eve out of Adam is the story of God acknowledging that without the corresponding voice, Adam is in despair and loneliness.[11] There is an innate despair in Adam without the corresponding "co-humanity," a possibility not found in the rest of creation. We cannot avoid the opposite gender without despair. They are a part of our humanity. The ontological impossibility of this is a despair within the human

---

8. Harris, *Second Epistle to the Corinthians,* 395.

9. John Calvin, *Calvin's New Testament Commentaries: The Second Epistle of Paul to the Corinthians and the Epistles of Timothy, Titus and Philemon,* ed. David W. Torrance and Thomas F. Torrance, trans. T. A. Smail (Grand Rapids: Eerdmans, 1964) 69.

10. John Sanders, *The God Who Risks: A Theology of Providence* (Downers Grove, IL: InterVarsity, 1998) 9.

11. Anderson, *On Being Human,* 81.

being given by God. That is why estrangement between the sexes is particularly devastating.

Certainly the Fall brings in a new kind of despair from God. For in being estranged from God, not just other human beings, humanity experiences genuine and devastating *lostness*. The cryptic billboard that reads "Call 1-800-THE LOST" is not just a reflection on the quirkiness of our culture, but an ironic sign of our genuine situation of both societal abuse of children and even more our estrangement from God and ourselves.

The Fall means that humanity has become shamed before God. Shame was the first evidence of the Fall to Adam and Eve (Gen 3:7). Could despair not fail to follow, a despair ultimately from God (see Cain in 4:13)?[12] For it is when humanity is confronted by God that the deepest despair comes, as in the parable of the Pharisee and the publican (Luke 18:9f.; cf. Peter in Luke 5:8; 22:61-62; John 21:17). The Pharisee thinks that he is different from other people. The publican knows otherwise and therefore exclaims, "God be merciful to me, a sinner!" Barth concludes, "The basic and total shaming which we cannot avoid is either from God or it does not take place at all."[13] But there is bad shame and good shame. Bad shame makes us create scenarios that make us ashamed of who we are. Unfortunately, the church can easily try to "motivate" people by this kind of shame.[14] Good shame is found in being confronted by the grace of God. In this we find out something about God: He does not want us to live in our lostness. "A God who is God only in and for Himself is not the true God," Barth interestingly remarks.[15] In other words, the God of Jesus Christ is *vicarious in himself*, not only in the economy of salvation, or only in how he appears to us. God is not lost or lonely within himself because he exists as One God in Three Persons of love: Father, Son, and Holy Spirit. There is an "Other" in God. It is sinful humanity that lives for themselves because of the Fall.

Despair from God in the Bible is most concretely in the form of the difficult phenomenon of his wrath. Generations continue to ask if a God of love can be also a wrathful God. The wrath of God in the Old Testament cannot be ignored: The Psalmist cries, "O God, the nations

12. Barth, *CD* II/1, 412.
13. Barth, *CD* IV/2, 385.
14. Lewis B. Smedes, *Shame and Grace: Healing the Shame We Don't Deserve* (San Francisco: HarperSanFrancisco, 1993).
15. Barth, *CD* IV/2, 385.

have come into your inheritance; they have defiled your holy temple . . . How long, O Lord? Will you be angry forever?" (Ps 79:1, 5; cf. Ps 77). The desolation of Jerusalem shook the Hebrews at their core. They are the elect people of God . . . How could this happen (Amos 9:10)?[16] Joy can be taken away by Yahweh, even with the right to mourn and weep: "Mortal, with one blow I am about to take away from you the delight of your eyes [cf. v. 25]; yet you shall not mourn or weep, nor shall your tears run down . . . you shall not mourn or weep, but you shall pine away in your iniquities and groan to one another" (Ezek 24:15–16, 23). Groaning is all that will be left to the elect of Israel. Ezekiel is sad-eyed in this passage, the literary critic Christopher Ricks remarks, like the "Sad-Eyed Lady of the Lowlands" in Bob Dylan's epic testimony in song to melancholy love.[17] He is particularly sad-eyed because he is forbidden to weep. What a terrible place to be at when one is forbidden (or not able?) to weep. There are more results from the destruction of Jerusalem: "The joy of our hearts has ceased; our dancing has been turned into mourning" (Lam 5:15). God brings despair in his wrath. And this is not just an Old Testament theme (see Rom 1:18–32). Eschatological wailing of the people is typical of the apocalyptic denouement in the New Testament: "Then the sign of the Son of Man will appear in heaven, and then all the tribes of the earth will mourn, and they will see 'the Son of Man coming on the clouds of heaven' with power and great glory" (Matt 24:30). "Look! He is coming with the clouds; every eye will see him, even those who pierced him; and on his account all the tribes of the earth will wail" (Rev 1:7; cf. Zech 12:10).

Yet there is often the promise that the judgment will not last; compassion will eschatologically arrive one day: "For the Lord will not reject forever. Although he causes grief, he will have compassion according to the abundance of his steadfast love" (Lam 3:31–32). Still, God is the one who "causes grief." Can we bear to say that in postmodern America? Politicians since the events of 9/11 have been reckless in attributing the wrath of God as the causation for personal evil as well as natural disaster. (Hurricane Katrina was also said to be punishment for a homosexual parade in New Orleans.) For most Americans, these voices are from the lunatic fringe of religion. Yet, according to Lamentations, God "causes grief." Should this be our good-bye to biblical religion?

16. Marvin E. Tate, *Psalms 51–100*, Word Biblical Commentary 20 (Dallas: Word, 1990) 302.

17. Christopher Ricks, *Dylan's Vision of Sin* (New York: Ecco, 2004) 104.

DESPAIR, REPENTANCE, AND WEEPING

God sends a message to us in Jesus Christ that we are indeed lost, for in Jesus Christ God stands before us as our Creator and Redeemer.[18] This is much more than existential angst and alienation, but qualitatively different when Christ takes our place in our angst and despair. For on the cross the Son indeed realizes that this despair comes from God. Our attempts to "let God off the hook" by appealing to his self-limitation (which is true) or his distinction from our creatureliness (which is also true) should not blind us to acknowledging that our lostness is proclaimed and sent by God in the very one who redeems us. This is genuine despair. *Weeping* should be our only response. The tradition of "compunction" in the Christian East comes to mind. John Cassian, the monk, describes "saving compunction" emerging "as an unspeakable joy and a liveliness of soul, as it bursts out in joy, "bringing to a neighboring cell the word of our heart's gladness and of the mightiness of our exultation."[19] "Sometimes the soul lies low," Cassian continues, "hidden in the depth of silence. The stunning onset of sudden light takes all sound of voice away," pouring out its longing to God. Or "sometimes it fills up with such sorrow and grief that it can only shake it off by melting into tears." The medieval classic, *Dark Night of the Soul*, by John of the Cross sees God not the sinner as the action in the purgation of "the dark night."[20]

As Barth comments, the twin errors of false pride or pretending there is no misery of life are not good alternatives. Worse yet is to try to combine joy and sorrow in a "painless mingling" that ends up taking neither joy nor sorrow seriously.[21] Because we have known the joy of Jesus we are in despair, but we are not to remain in despair, as Calvin reminds us, thinking of Peter after his denial of Christ: "After we have despaired in ourselves, let us come to taste His grace, let us receive it and accept it by faith."[22] Anderson interprets Ecclesiastes' despair as a despair from God that brings health: "The sadness of life is its health, and we have

---

18. Barth, *CD* III/1, 373.

19. John Cassian, "Conference 9" in *Conferences*, trans. Colin Luibheid, Classics of Western Spirituality (New York: Paulist, 1985) 117.

20. St. John of the Cross, *Dark Night of the Soul*, trans. and ed. E. Allison Peers (New York: Image, 1990) 60.

21. Barth, *CD* III/1, 373.

22. Calvin, "Passion Week" in *Writings on Pastoral Piety*, 118.

learned that life has greater meaning which cries out to be discovered."[23] Perhaps our interpretation of the cry of Jesus from the cross should be seen as the cry from our side that acknowledges our limitations, not just a cry that speaks of losing hope. If so, Christ's vicarious work is not just limited to his death, but includes the cry leading up to the death as a part of his vicarious humanity. What can that mean but that our cries are not foreign to God?

Because of the grace of God in Jesus Christ, repentance becomes the fruit of that grace. For Paul it is the difference between "worldly grief" that "produces death," and "godly grief" ("sorrow," NIV) (2 Cor 7:10). In fact Paul "rejoices" that the Corinthians were brought to this "godly sorrow," for it leads to "repentance" (2 Cor 7:9). This "leads to salvation" (2 Cor 7:10). "The humility of faith," Barth reminds us, "is a comforted despair."[24] Yes, it is sent by God, but it is neither despair without comfort, nor comfort without despair. The man of sorrows is also the prince of peace. It is also, Barth continues, "the humility of obedience," a genuine obedience because "it is laid upon" the believer.[25] It is a despair that comes from God, so this obedience is not simply the believer's choice, but a despair that brings guilt from Another. This kind of despair is not something that one wants to rid oneself, for it leads to weeping and repentance. Not "a wild and desperate despair," it is "a comforted despair," Luther's *desperatio fiducialis*.[26] Thus "the humility of faith is the humility of obedience" (cf. "the obedience of faith" of Paul in Rom 1:5 and 16:26).[27] Here is the heart of the doctrine of justification by faith, the "humble obedience" based on the "alien righteousness" of Jesus Christ.[28] This means an end to reliance upon ourselves and instead a reliance on the vicarious righteousness of Christ. Despair from God is a comforted despair that brings relief from the anxiety of fallen humanity. However, to be "in Christ" is more than to be in "analogy" with Christ in his humility, in Barth's words.[29] "To believe and to realize that He lives for us means (without any claim but quite

---

23. Anderson, *Exploration into God*, 23.
24. Barth, *CD* IV/1, 620.
25. Ibid.
26. Ibid., 620–21.
27. Ibid., 621.
28. Ibid., 633.
29. Ibid., 636.

unquestioningly) to live with Him."[30] I would want to add, "*in* him," in the Pauline sense of being "in Christ," an ontological relationship and reality: "It is no longer I who live, but it is Christ who lives in me. And the life I now live in the flesh I live by faith in [or "of"] the Son of God who loved me and gave himself for me" (Gal 2:20). Barth rightly speaks of the "poverty" of faith, but this includes even the poverty of an analogy. A vicarious reality has been created by God, the same God who in his grace brings the despair, the "godly sorrow" that leads to repentance and salvation. Something has done for us and in us, creating a "poverty" that is despairing but healing. There is a genuine "renunciation" here, Barth continues, that does not even allow faith to glory in its "poverty": "It is not faith if it does not renounce all such glory and merit and even the brightness of its poverty."[31]

EDUCATIVE DESPAIR?

Diadochus of Photike (fifth century) represents the belief of many in what he calls "educative desolation":

> Educative desolation brings to the soul humiliation, grief, and proper despair in order that the part of the soul that seeks glory and is easily exalted may return to humility. But it leads the heart immediately to the fear of God, to tears, and to a keen desire for the beauty of silence.[32]

Instead of fighting against despair, or even viewing trials as "educative desolation," can we speak as Bernanos does of sadness, anguish, and despair as not "only states of the Spirit," but as "the Spirit itself"?[33] That is, does God in the incarnation identify so closely with our despair that we can no longer speak of the Spirit except where the Spirit meets our spirit in despair (yet not to be identified with our spirit, as Barth reminds us)?[34] Taking upon our humanity to the point of ontological unity, for the sake of a vicarious relationship, Christ mediates the Spirit who is not afraid to

---

30. Ibid.

31. Ibid.

32. Diadochus of Photike, *Gnostic Chapters* 87 (SC 5 bis, 146–147) cited by Clément, *The Roots of Christian Mysticism*, 190.

33. Bernanos, *Diary of a Country Priest*, 199.

34. Karl Barth, *Dogmatics in Outline*, trans. G. T. Thomson (New York: Philosophical Library, 1949) 140.

"groan" on our behalf (Rom 8:23. See also the Spirit who can be "grieved" in Eph 4:30). So Bernanos is even bold enough to conclude: "I believe that ever since his fall, man's condition is such that neither around him nor within him can he perceive anything except in the form of agony."[35]

Agony? "Various trials," 1 Peter 1:6–7 writes, are the occasion for "rejoicing." The educative function is that of proving "the genuineness of your faith." Yet trials can also prove how weak I am, what little faith I have. Can this educative function simply result in "bad" shaming? But the goal, Peter continues, "may be found to result in praise and glory and honor when Jesus Christ is revealed." It is an eschatological goal. We may not see the vindication in this life. But it is centered on Jesus Christ being revealed. He will reveal the "poverty" of our faith, in Barth's words.[36] The trials will seek to make us confess our poverty, but since the goal is "praise and glory and honor when Jesus Christ is revealed" (certainly not praise and glory and honor to us, but to God), the revelation will be of God's good purpose for us. He is not a tormentor. "Blessed is anyone who endures temptation," writes James (Jas 1:12). But "no one, when tempted, should say, I am tempted by God'; for God cannot be tempted by evil and he himself tempts no one" (Jas 1:13). We are tempted, instead by our own desires (Jas 1:14). Can despair come from God, then? Only in the sense that Christ is our *telos,* our goal.

CHRIST THE COMPANION OF DESPAIR

God never sends despair apart from Christ and his vicarious despair. He is the revelation of the Father's heart (John McLeod Campbell).[37] Because Jesus revealed God as his Father he then could reveal him as our Father.[38] We are "hidden with Christ in God" (Col 3:3), not hidden in our sin, Barth adds.[39] Barth makes this plain: "As Jesus acts in His commission and power, it is clear that God does not will that which troubles and torments and disturbs and destroys man . . . He does not will his death, but life."[40] At the center of this is the joy of Jesus: "And as His affirmation is

---

35. Bernanos, *Diary of a Country Priest,* 199.
36. Barth, *CD* IV/1, 636.
37. Campbell, *The Nature of the Atonement,* 137.
38. T. F. Torrance, *Christian Doctrine of God,* 57.
39. Barth, *CD* IV/2, 289.
40. Ibid., 225.

joyful to the very core, His negation is in every sense unwilling and vexed and wrathful."[41] God does not send sorrow apart from also sending the Son (Luke 20:13; John 17:8; 20:21; Acts 3:20). This solidarity of the Son with human sorrow is that which demonstrates that human sorrow does not have its source in the "Cosmic Sadist," the divine vivisectionist that C. S. Lewis contemplated as he mourned the loss of his wife.[42] Barth adds, "The sorrow which openly or secretly fills the heart of man is primarily in the heart of God . . . God Himself engages the nothingness which aims to destroy man."[43] Lewis concludes, after much struggle, "It was allowed to One, we are told, and I find I can now believe again, that He has done vicariously whatever can be so done. He replies to our babble, 'You cannot and you dare not. I could and dared.'"[44] C. S. Lewis, in his personal grief, clings to the vicarious humanity of Christ. The goal is Christ, yet that is concealed to us in all of its fullness; we are "hidden with Christ in God" (Col 3:3). This may be "a necessary and perhaps even a decisive, element in the work of His grace."[45]

Bernanos' point remains, however. The human condition being what it is, we cannot perceive anything except from agony. This "agony," however, is not to be seen apart from the summons of humanity by the Word of God. There is no knowledge of humanity through Jesus Christ apart from humanity as summoned by the Word of God, for Jesus Christ, whatever else we care to say about him, is the man summoned by the Word of God. Humanity is awakened by the Word.[46] In this awakening humanity is called of itself, a painful experience that causes despair. We are used to our self-containment and self-satisfaction. We are comfortable with this. But to be "in the Word of God" is to be in despair, as with Peter to Jesus: "Go away from me, Lord, for I am a sinful man!" (Luke 5:8; cf. Exod 3:6; Judg 6:22; Isa 6:5). Jesus says to the disciples, "But because I have said these things to you, sorrow has filled your hearts" (John 16:6). This is different, however, from simply despairing of oneself because of failure or finitude.[47] God's Word is powerful enough to awaken faith in

---

41. Ibid.
42. C.S. Lewis, *A Grief Observed* (New York: Bantam, 1976) 33, 43, 49.
43. Barth, *CD* IV/2, 225.
44. Lewis, *Grief Observed*, 51.
45. Barth, *CD* IV/2, 289.
46. Barth, *CD* III/2, 165–66.
47. Ibid., 166.

the midst of that despair, powerful enough, having created that faith in the vicarious faith of Jesus Christ as the foundation for our faith. This is a free act of God that does not leave us in despair. Thus, one must be careful not to speak of God "creating" despair because all of what God creates is "very good" (Genesis 1). God is not the author of evil or of suffering. God is not only to be found in the darkness. "We must not fondly imagine that we have to seek Him only in the shadow."[48] God does not exist in only "His silence, No and judgment." That is not the God of the Bible. That would make God the author of evil and suffering. Yet he is *free* to use that darkness in order to bring us his joy. The passion of Jesus Christ is the archetype of all such joy that comes out of darkness, a vicarious joy that comes from a vicarious despair. Yes, "God . . . brings darkness upon us" (Barth) but does not create that darkness as in a mechanical doctrine in which God is foremost and above all sovereign and his love secondary. A subtle distinction? Yes, but one which we must maintain.

There is no doubt that one can be humbled by despair, and even obtain "a keen desire for the beauty of silence," but are we to conclude that every source of despair comes from God because he seeks to test and discipline us? Hebrews does speak clearly: "Endure trials for the sake of discipline. God is treating you as children; for what child is there whom a parent does not discipline?" (Heb 12:7; cf. Prov 6:23; 2 Macc 6:12–17; 2 Cor 6:10). Is God then the source of all despair? Or do we despair because we do not see the trials as discipline? Or perhaps we forget the christological context of Hebrews: "Looking to Jesus the pioneer and perfecter of our faith, who for the joy that was set before him endured the cross . . . " (Heb 12:2). Despair, yes, can be from God, and, yes, it can lead to joy afterwards, but the christological critique must not be forgotten: Jesus's faith is the basis for our faith. *Only in union with him can we accept despair from God.* We can certainly plunge ourselves into despair, but that is different, Barth reminds us, from "the saving and blessed despair" in which we seek refuge only in God (Ps 123:2–3). "God plunges us into despair," Barth is even bold enough to say, but if there is a "cause" to despair, it is caused by joy, the joy of the incarnation, of the Word made flesh and the kindling of our faith by the Holy Spirit.[49] We cannot place ourselves in this position. In fact, when it comes down to it, only Christ and faith can dare accept despair from God—the despair of a Holocaust, or other

---

48. Barth, *CD* III/1, 374.
49. Barth, *CD* I/2, 372–73.

innocent and needless suffering, of John Sanders' brother's death—if we really believe in a God of love.

It seems so poignant and strange to hear of the early disciples rejoicing in being persecuted: "As they left the council, they rejoiced that they were considered worthy to suffer dishonor for the sake of the name" (Acts 5:41). Where was the source of such an attitude? Perhaps Gethsemane provides a clue. In Gethsemane, Jesus "began to be grieved and agitated. Then he said to them, 'I am deeply grieved, even to death; remain here, and stay awake with me'" (Matt 26:37). But they did not stay awake for him. Jesus asks for the vicarious humanity of the church to help and they fail miserably![50] This is the stark reminder of their total need for his vicarious humanity. James and John had told Jesus that "we are able" to drink of the cup that Jesus was to drink (Matt 20:20). But they are not. We are not. Religious martyrs of all sorts of religions testify to the power of religious courage. But the cup that Jesus is to drink is different. In the book of Acts, to rejoice in being able to suffer for the name is different than the rejoicing that depends upon Jesus receiving the despair from God yet responding with joy. James and John are not able to share of the cup but because of the vicarious humanity of Christ they will indeed share in that cup (Matt 26:26–39), sharing in his death and resurrection, his despair and his joy. We follow Christ in suffering because Christ precedes us, Kierkegaard writes. This can include sharing in the loneliness of Christ.[51]

Jesus's anguish is genuine anguish before God: "In his anguish he prayed more earnestly, and his sweat became like great drops of blood falling down on the ground" (Luke 22:44). Jesus prayed, and he prayed loudly: "In the days of his flesh, Jesus offered up prayers and supplications, with loud cries and tears, to the one who was able to save him from death, and he was heard because of his reverent submission" (Heb 5:7). He was heard, but interesting enough, he still underwent death. Yet his death will not be the end. Jesus anguishes because he knows that there is to be a despair from God but not caused by God. Like John in the apocalypse, sorrow and joy are mixed together: "So I went to the angel and told him to give me the little scroll; and he said to me, 'Take it, and eat; it will be bitter to your stomach, but sweet as honey in your mouth'" (Rev 10:9).

---

50. Stanley Hauerwas, *Matthew*, Brazos Theological Commentary on the Bible (Grand Rapids: Brazos, 2006) 178.

51. Søren Kierkegaard, *Gospel of Sufferings*, trans. A. S. Aldworth and W. Ferrie (Cambridge: James Clarke, 1982) 19, 23.

This reflects Ezekiel's directions in accepting the prophetic calling (Ezek 2:8–3:3), except that the bitterness in the stomach is added by the angel in the Apocalypse. The Book of Revelation is all too aware of tribulations in the end times (Rev 6:8–18).

Alan Lewis, in his poignant and powerful book, *Between Cross and Resurrection: A Theology of Holy Saturday*, observes that the "godforsakeness" of Jesus on the cross leads one frankly to say, "Here at least, there can be no place for God."[52] It is that way in our own despair. Eberhard Jüngel can even say, "God's identification with the dead Jesus implies a self-differentiation on God's part."[53] But is this trinitarian event between the Son and the Father, that "which took place between God and God," as Moltmann puts it, imply a struggle within God?[54] We see in the cross God himself becoming "a servant Lord, a guilty judge, a wounded healer."[55] So Christ's "descent into hell" should be viewed as nothing less than an action of his vicarious humanity; he goes into the midst of *our* hell, for us and in our place.[56] Jesus cried out (with despair?), "I have a baptism to be baptized with; and how I am constrained until it is accomplished" (Luke 12:50). Paul makes sure the Romans understand their relationship to Christ's baptism: "Do you not know that all of us who have been baptized into Christ Jesus were baptized into his death?" We were buried therefore with him by baptism into death" (Rom 6:3, 4a). Lewis says it well:

> Christ's painful, bloody baptism in human sin reaches its nadir in the suffering and death of Golgotha; and his guiltless repentance as a sinner is perfected, its price now full paid, as he lies in the baptism of hell on Easter Saturday, buried among the wicked and stricken for the sins of many, although he had done no violence and there was no deceit in his mouth (Isa 53:9).[57]

---

52. Alan E. Lewis, *Between Cross and Resurrection: A Theology of Holy Saturday* (Grand Rapids: Eerdmans, 2001) 92. Cf. Hans Urs von Balthasar, *Mysterium Paschale: The Mystery of Easter*, trans. Aidan Nichols (San Francisco: Ignatius, 1990) and the criticism by David Bentley Hart in *Beauty of the Infinite*, 373.

53. Eberhard Jüngel, *God as the Mystery of the World: On the Foundation of the Theology of the Crucified One in the Dispute between Theism and Atheism*, trans. Darrell L. Guder (Grand Rapids: Eerdmans, 198) 363.

54. Jürgen Moltmann, *The Crucified God*, trans. R. A. Wilson and John Bowden (New York: Harper & Row, 1974).

55. Alan E. Lewis, *Between Cross and Resurrection*, 91.

56. Ibid., 39 n. 43.

57. Ibid., 447.

Despair comes from God in the sense that it does not come apart from God. It is God himself who goes even into the depths of hell for us, the meaning of Holy Saturday, the second day which we often ignored while rushing from the cross to the resurrection. Yet this is no triumphalistic display of deity. God seems to have failed Jesus.[58] Still from this death will come life, a "presence—amid—absence." That which becomes the greatest stumbling block to unbelief—the crucified messiah—is now the source of hope.[59] Despair from God? Yes, but not apart from the despair, the vicarious despair, of Jesus.

Despair comes from the God whom Jesus responds to by emptying and humbling himself (Phil 2:7f.), giving himself (Gal 1:4; 1 Tim 2:6), offering himself (Gal 2:20; Eph 5:2), and sacrificing himself (Heb 7:27; 9:14).[60] In his prayers he acknowledges the expression of the kingdom of God in the will of God for him, and therefore, for all humanity.[61] This is Christ's "election for suffering," the rejected who is nonetheless also the elect, "both priest and victim."[62] He is "handed over" in "powerlessness" to "strange and hostile overwhelming power," deprived of his "freedom."[63] It may appear that it was Judas' act that robbed Jesus of his freedom but it was actually the power of God, a despair given by God, if you will. As Barth remarks, "The freedom of which Jesus was robbed by Judas is clearly only a pale reflection of the divine freedom of which God robbed Him, of which he robbed Himself."[64]

Yes, Jesus is not "a mere puppet," as Barth reminds us, but the fact that he prays to the Father and obeys the Father speaks in some sense of a despair given by God.[65] Jesus is the "elected man" in whom "God's eternal will has as its end the life of this man of prayer."[66] Despair comes from God, not in an arbitrary way, but in the election of this praying man Jesus. But what does it mean for Jesus to be a man of prayer? It means that he

58. Ibid., 54.
59. Ibid., 91.
60. Barth, *CD* II/2, 106.
61. On Christ as "pray-er" to God see John C. McDowell, "'Openness to the World': Karl Barth's Evangelical Theology of Christ as Pray-er," *Modern Theology* 25:2 (2009) 253–83.
62. Barth, *CD* II/2, 126.
63. Ibid., 490.
64. Ibid.
65. Ibid., 178.
66. Ibid., 180.

first prays to the Father in order to do the Father's will and in doing so he takes us into his prayer in the midst of despair, vicariously.

What has happened to Christ, being robbed of his freedom by God, being given the despair of the Passion, is a vicarious act of God, "that in Christ God stands in our place and is for us as the owner and Lord of our life, as the Head of His Church, ruling and determining us. If we want it otherwise, we can only be against ourselves, working against ourselves and at the same time resisting God."[67]

A VICARIOUS COMMUNITY OF TEARS

If the church is to pray the Psalms along with Jesus, as Dietrich Bonhoeffer suggests, then what are the implications of these words for us: "Hear my prayer, O Lord, and give ear to my cry; do not hold your peace at my tears. For I am your passing guest, or alien, like all my forebears. Turn your gaze away from me, that I may smile again, before I depart and am no more" (Ps 39:12–13)? The Jesus of Gethsemane and Golgotha prays these words; and we pray with him, with fear and trembling, *a despair from God but not caused by God*. In this way we are truly "hid with Christ in God" (Col 3:3), only able to admit a despair that comes from God as we pray with Jesus in the garden through his vicarious humanity. Our life is not merely "hid with Christ," Barth reminds us, but "hid with Christ in God."[68] Jesus did pray, "My God, my God, why have you forsaken me?" (Mark 15:39; Matt 27:46; cf. Ps 22:1), but he prayed it for us and on our behalf. "Of first importance," Paul will say, is that "Christ died for our sins" (1 Cor 15:3). In this way we can understand that Christ was given despair from God, for our sakes, and therefore God did not "cause" the despair. Jesus still believes, but in our pain, "for our sins." As Davies and Allison comment on Matt 27:46, "This does not express a loss of faith—certainly the soldiers who soon confess Jesus the Son of God have seen no such loss—but is instead a cry of pain in circumstance . . . in which God has not shown himself to be God."[69] Yet, we do not pray the "cry of abandonment" alone. We pray with Jesus.

---

67. Ibid., 494.

68. Barth, *CD* IV/2, 289.

69. W. D. Davies and Dale C. Allison, Jr., *A Critical and Exegetical Commentary on the Gospel According to Saint Matthew*, vol. 3 International Critical Commentary. (Edinburgh: T. & T. Clark, 1997) 625.

We pray with Jesus but this will not be always comfortable. In praying with Jesus he takes our place yet that cannot help but involve what Barth calls "a total disturbance of my being, a radical decision in relation to my situation . . ."[70] Bonhoeffer reminds us that "because Christ has suffered for the sin of the world, because the whole burden of guilt fell on him, and because Jesus Christ passes on the fruit of his suffering to those who follow him, temptation and sin fall also onto his disciples."[71] This is a part of union of Christ. "The cross is neither misfortune nor harsh fate. Instead, it is that suffering which comes from our allegiance to Jesus Christ alone. The cross is not random suffering, but necessary suffering."[72] This is the meaning of discipleship. "The cross is suffering with Christ. Indeed, it is Christ-suffering. Only one who is bound to Christ as this occurs in discipleship stands in seriousness under the cross."[73]

Jesus is the object of despair from God, but it is a despair for the sake of others, a vicarious suffering. As such, the early church interpreted their lives as continually involved with the One who suffers for others. Paul can even say, "I am now rejoicing in my sufferings *for your sake*, and in my flesh I am completing what is lacking in Christ's afflictions *for the sake* of his body, that is, the church" (Col 1:24, emphasis mine). The church now saw itself living a life conformed to the image of God's Son (Rom 8:29), meaning living *a vicarious lifestyle*, living on the behalf of others.[74] The puzzling language of "what is lacking in Christ's afflictions" makes more sense when we see that as language of participating in the ongoing vicarious life of Christ in his body, the church. The portrait of Isaiah 53, the "despised" and "rejected" "man of suffering," who "has borne our infirmities and carried our diseases," yes, the one who was "struck down by God" (!) therefore, was never far away from the early church and its own identity (Isa 53:3–4; cf. Acts 8:32–33). The church is to live a vicarious life.

The vicarious life of the church is the life of those who live with the Rejected One, the one who was rejected in their place. In this way they

---

70. Barth, *CD* IV/1, 766–67.
71. Bonhoeffer, *Discipleship*, 88.
72. Ibid., 86.
73. Ibid., 87.
74. See the relationship between the "vicarious representative action" *(Stellvertretung)* of Christ as "he represents the whole history of humanity in his historical life" and the implications for the church as community in Bonhoeffer, *Santorum Communio*, 147ff. Cf. Christine Schliesser, *Everyone Who Acts Responsibly Becomes Guilty: Bonhoeffer's Concept of Accepting Guilt* (Louisville: Westminster John Knox, 2008).

also participate in their election. This is one of the great insights in Barth's remarkable reworking of the doctrine of election. We know ourselves now in Christ, the rejected who has taken the place of all.[75] Christ takes upon himself for all, vicariously, the despair of rejection, a despair that comes from God. "Jesus Christ is *the* Rejected of God, for God makes Himself rejected in Him, and has Himself alone tasted to the depths all that rejection means and necessarily involves."[76] Christ's suffering is unique so the sufferings of Christians should never be seen apart from Christ's unique suffering. They cannot duplicate it. But they cannot tear themselves away from suffering. Like Barth states concerning the judgment of God, judgment has now become pardon in Christ but Israel, the church, and the world now stand "in the shadow of divine judgment."[77] "The afflictions of Israel, the church, the world and ourselves are all announcements and echoes of the reality of the divine judgment."[78] To speak of "shadows" may be a bit cryptic, but Barth is trying to maintain the uniqueness of the cross while never forgetting our union with Christ. Substitutionary atonement does not mean that we no longer suffer in any way, the objection of the Orthodox theologian Kallistos Ware, but that every aspect of our humanity is taken up by Jesus Christ.[79] We may no longer suffer the penalty for sin but we can say that we do endure the despair that Christ continues to feel. If Christ is just our representative, he can only represent the despair we now experience. As our substitute, he will eventually take away that as despair is eschatologically replaced by joy, the joy of Jesus. Despair does not live without the goal of joy.

What is it that God wills? Jesus taught his disciples to pray, "Your will be done . . . " (Matt 6:10). The faith of Jesus is a key to doing the will of God. And that leads us to the goal of joy: "looking to Jesus the pioneer and perfecter of our faith, who for the sake of the joy that was set before him endured the cross, despising the shame . . . " (Heb 12:2). The cross is still involved. As Barth remarks, sickness is to be endured with "quiet patience," because God is present as Lord and Victor, so that even that illness is to be borne "because it comes from Him."[80] Yet we can only say

75. Barth, *CD* II/2, 451.

76. Ibid., 496.

77. Barth, *CD* II/1, 405.

78. Ibid., 406.

79. Kallistos Ware, *The Orthodox Way* (Crestwood, NY: St. Vladimir's Seminary Press, 1979) 82.

80. Barth, *CD* III/4, 374.

that because of "the joy that was set before him." Suffering is never caused by God for the sake of suffering. Joy is the christological goal for every human being. In our hearts we all seek for joy: "The will for life is also the will for joy," as much as we seek for this to be satisfied by that which does not satisfy, a joy different from the joy that Jesus sought.[81] Even our high minded moral, religious, and aesthetic obedience should not refuse joy.

Despair may come from God, but not without the goal of joy. Barth is clear about what God wills: God

> does not will that which troubles and torments and disturbs and destroys man. He does not will the entanglement and humiliation and distress and shame that the being of man in the cosmos and as a cosmic being means for man. He does not will the destruction of man, but his salvation . . . He does not will his death, but life.[82]

Sorrow exists, yet it mysteriously exists first of all in the heart of God that we see made manifest in "the man of sorrows" (Isa 53:3, NIV), Jesus Christ. This is the one who also endures the cross for the sake of joy. "The sorrow which openly or secretly fills the heart of man is primarily in the heart of God."[83] God is on both sides. The man of sorrows is also the prince of peace.

Can we live with despair caused by God? No, but we can live with Jesus and his despair from God. It is through him that we see another side of God, the side in which God is on our side, the side of Jesus. Susie, the student of Ray Anderson's with cerebral palsy from birth, was able to "forgive God" for creating her the way she was.[84] I suspect that was God from the side of Jesus. As Anderson often dares to remark, pastoral counseling is not trying to defend God to the afflicted, but to take up the side of the afflicted, even before God! The faith of Jesus is able to do that. That is being on the side of the human Jesus, which we discover means that God is on both sides.

---

81. Ibid., 374–75.
82. Barth, *CD* IV/2, 225.
83. Ibid.
84. Ray S. Anderson, *The Seasons of Hope: Empowering Faith through the Practice of Hope* (Eugene, OR: Wipf & Stock, 2008) 135.

CHAPTER FOUR

Despair as Meaninglessness

Apart from sin, are there other sources of despair? Ecclesiastes is well known for his understanding of one source of despair: the vanity of life:

> So I turned and gave my heart to despair concerning all the toil of my labors under the sun, because sometimes one who has toiled with wisdom and knowledge and skill must leave all to be enjoyed by another who did not toil for it. This also is vanity and a great evil. (Eccl 2:20–21)

Life seems purposeless, meaningless, and an endless cycle of work that often does not bear any substantial or long-lasting fruit. Despair oozes in and works its influence over our minds. There is the fear that something must be done because life might be wasted, as when the "Un-man" in C. S. Lewis' interplanetary novel, *Perelandra,* tempts the Green Lady with "a 'now or never' (and) began to play on a fear which the Lady apparently shared with the women of earth—the fear that life might be wasted, some great opportunity let slip."[1]

Still, why work? Why strive? Why have aspirations? None of them will last. Human life seems to be that meaningless. Alexander the Great conquered the known world. But, as Shakespeare says, his bones have now become the dust which is part of an ordinary house.[2] Alexander, the conqueror of the world, now keeps the wind out. The endless protestations, ambitions, and ideals of humanity seem like nothing but "the sound and the fury, signifying nothing."[3] Injustice abounds in this life: "Why do the wicked live on . . . They sing to the tambourine and the lyre,

---

1. C. S. Lewis, *Perelandra* (New York: Scribners, 1996) 131.
2. Shakespeare, *Hamlet,* Act 5, Scene 1.
3. Shakespeare, *Macbeth,* Act 5, Scene 5.

and rejoice to the sound of the pipe" (Job 21:7, 12). "You have exalted the right hand of his foes," the psalmist laments to God about a defeated king, "How long, O Lord? Will you hide yourself forever?" (Ps 89:42, 46). Still, Zophar the Naamathite tells Job "that the exulting of the wicked is short, and joy of the godless is but for a moment" (Job 20:5).

DESPAIR AS BOREDOM

One need only start with the boredom of life. The "aesthetic" voice of Kierkegaard speaks of boredom as the one universal experience of humanity.[4] Aristotle was much too optimistic to say that all humanity seeks to know.[5] "Or is there anyone who would be boring enough to contradict me in this regard?" the voice of the aesthetic continues.[6] In fact, boredom, not money, is the root of all evil. One should only understand how terrible boredom is, and resist it constantly. The gods were bored so they created humanity. Adam was bored so Eve was created, probably with a twinkle in his eye. Kierkegaard concludes that political situations can be solved by "a riot of merriment," avoiding boredom. His solution is "the rotation method," in which like crops being changed, life is constantly seeking new, aesthetic experiences. In fact, this is the essence of the aesthetic. The aesthetic is born out of boredom.

Since we live in a highly aesthetic time in which the aesthetic has practically become our new religion, it is not surprising to read that Karl Barth considers boredom "the signature of modern man."[7] Not just bored with the world, humanity is ultimately bored with itself, weary of itself. Such a weariness reminds me of my high school graduating class of 1972. Despite the tumultuous times, I remember distinctly that what characterized my class was apathy—we did not care—we were weary with ourselves and with all the causes pushed and the promises unfulfilled. We were no longer "interested" in ourselves, as Barth would say. Such people find joy difficult to obtain.

And standing at the end of all of this is the grim specter of death, not only our own death but also the death of our loved ones. Can life have any meaning, we wonder, without our loved ones? Does it really now make

---

4. Kierkegaard, *Either/Or*, part 1, 285–86.
5. Aristotle, *Metaphysics*, bk. 1, ch. 1.
6. Kierkegaard, *Either/Or*, vol. 1, 285.
7. Barth, *CD* III/2, 117.

any sense? The bombastic, macho creator of pulp "yarns" about "Conan the Barbarian," Robert E. Howard, was a burly Texan who ironically shot himself soon after his mother's death.[8] Most of us do not do that. But can we so quickly condemn Howard's act as cowardice or mental imbalance? Is it any wonder that Thoreau classically concludes that "the mass of men lead lives of quiet desperation"?[9]

Despair comes out of purposelessness, the chaos of life. But despair can also come out of order. As Victor Hugo says, "Despair yawns."[10] Despair yawns. Despair is bored, bored with the symmetry, the order, the ordinariness, the routine of life. It does not take a tragedy to bring us to despair. Why is it that we are constantly seeking the new experience? Is it not that we are trying to avoid the despair of boredom?

DESPAIR AS TRAGEDY

Boredom is only interrupted by tragedy. Despair does concern tragedy. And that tragedy often seems immortalized in our memories of the past laid in concrete never to be moved—like the alligator puppet—forever a part of us, defining what it means to be human. The past haunts us:

> Tears, idle fears, I know not what they mean,
> Tears from the depths of some divine despair
> Rise from the heart, and gather to the eyes
> In looking on the happy Autumn—fields
> And thinking of the days that are no more.[11]

The days that are no more may have been days of great joy, of friendships and loves and accomplishments. Or they may have been days of sorrow, of hope destroyed, of bad choices made or of failures of the will. Either way, despair breeds on the tragedy of the past, "the days that are no more." Despair means a loss. Can Jesus deal with our losses? If so, how does he do that?

---

8. Novellene Price Ellis, *One Who Walked Alone: Robert E. Howard, the Final Years* (West Kingston, RI: Donald M. Grant, 1986).

9. Henry David Thoreau, *Walden* (New York: Dutton, 1904) 30.

10. Victor Hugo, *Les Misérables*, trans. Charles E. Wilbour (New York: Carleton, 1863) 84.

11. Alfred Lord Tennyson, "Song (2)" in *The Oxford Dictionary of Quotations*, Third Edition (Oxford: Oxford University, 1980) 542.

Bonhoeffer speaks of how his friends' senses had become dulled by all the sorrows of the war years.[12] Dullness can be created by loss. But the temptation, Bonhoeffer contends, is to try to keep one's senses from being dulled, in effect, trying to bear the suffering and doing that which only Christ can do. Bonhoeffer is appealing to the reality of the vicarious humanity of Christ. "We are not called to burden ourselves with the sorrows of the whole world; in the end, we cannot suffer with people in our own strength because we are unable to redeem."[13] Bluntly, this would be to confuse us with Christ. We are only called to look upon Christ with joy. "Only in such joy toward Christ, the Redeemer, are we saved from having our senses dulled by the presence of human sorrow or from becoming resigned under the experience of suffering."[14]

Eros, Karl Barth claims, is essentially tragic since it involves possession that is always vulnerable to loss.[15] If even the loss has yet to take place, the possibility provides a tragic tension in *eros*, as much as we desire to ignore that. In contrast with this is Christian love, love that is free and spontaneous, the kind of love with which God loves us in Christ. This love is the love of the one who imitates God, existing in fellowship with him, in peace and joy, giving a reason for laughter even in the midst of tears.[16] There is no essential tragedy in that love.

David Bentley Hart has recently provided a damning critique of the emphasis on the "tragic" in modern theology.[17] Hart views Bultmann's preference for personal suffering as more essential to the faith than the beautiful as "a kind of barbarism."[18] Such an emphasis on the "mysticism" of personal suffering in theology eclipses "the need to behold," the need for the beautiful, Hart contends. Why, indeed, glory in the tragic, especially if the goal of the Christian life is to be conformed to the image of his Son, the One, who, indeed, was crucified, but did not remain

---

12. Dietrich Bonhoeffer, "Advent Letter to the Pastors of the Confessing Church," November 29, 1942 in *Dietrich Bonhoeffer*, Writings Selected and with an Introduction by Robert Coles (Maryknoll, NY: Orbis, 2003) 91.

13. Bonhoeffer, "Advent Letter to the Pastors of the Confessing Church," in Robert Coles, *Dietrich Bonhoeffer*, 91.

14. Ibid.

15. Barth, *CD* IV/2, 788.

16. Ibid., 789.

17. David Bentley Hart, *Beauty of the Infinite*, 380–83.

18. Ibid., 23–24.

dead? We have "newness of life" (Rom 6:4) because of his resurrection (a "beautiful" event?).

Hart further criticizes the Kantian tradition in ethics and its emphasis upon disinterest rather than "analogy, vision, and joy."[19] Hart is right to grasp that the *telos* of the Christian life is not despair, but joy. Kantian obligation is famously devoid of joy. Thus, the tragic can easily be a context for the moral dilemma and thus the sum total of human existence, as in the *film noir* genre of Hollywood movies in the forties and fifties.[20] Joy is more connected with desire, a desire for the good that is not simply theoretical. Certainly we can see the vicarious joy of Christ at this juncture: "For the sake of the joy that was set before him (he) endured the cross . . ." (Heb 12:2). "Joy feeds on what it receives," according to Hart. And we may add, with Barth that the one who is truly "the recipient of grace" is Jesus Christ.[21] God "is not only the giver, but also the recipient of grace. He is not only the One who commands, but the One who is called and pledged to obedience."[22] He is the One who is lowly and goes into the far country for us. Ralph Wood also emphasizes that the tragic, while prominent in the theology of someone like Reinhold Niebuhr, is not the essence of the theology of Karl Barth, whose center is the joy of "Jesus is Victor!"[23] According to Barth, paradox is a part of but not the final word for Jesus Christ.

> "Paradox" cannot be our final word in relation to Jesus Christ. Even as it is presented in the New Testament this paradox is not in any sense in conflict with the *doxa* of God. Therefore, although we have not to seek its removal, we have certainly to seek its basis in the *doxa* of God, which means again in the trinitarian life of God.[24]

Hart goes aground, however, with his appeal to the *analogy of being* (*analogia entis*), the classic philosophical-theological understanding that admits similarity but includes a continuity of being; in theology between

---

19. Ibid., 83.

20. *Film Noir Reader*, ed. Alain Silver and James Ursini (New York: Limelight Editions, 1996).

21. Barth, *CD* IV/1, 170.

22. Ibid.

23. Ralph C. Wood, *The Comedy of Redemption: Christian Faith and Comic Vision in Four American Novelists* (Notre Dame, IN: University of Notre Dame Press, 1988).

24. Barth, *CD* IV/2, 348.

God and humanity. But can this continuity of being embrace a solidarity of God with actual hurting, tragic persons? He is right to be concerned with continuity. The "Wholly Other" God, Barth admits, can be "pagan," creating an unbridgeable distance (even for God) between Creator and creature.[25] The continuity, however, is one that can only be created by God, and has been created by God in the incarnation of God in Jesus Christ. What is "tragic" about Hart is his conclusion that love, finally, is pure *eros*, pure desire, without any mention of *agape*, selfless love. Certainly God is not pure *agape* without *eros*. An earlier generation mistakenly thought to isolate *agape* as the distinctive Christian view.[26] But must one go as far as Hart: "Love without eros can be only a subject's victory over the effrontery of the given"?[27] Generosity should not depend on *pathos*, as Hart rightly claims. To ignore *pathos*, however, is to ignore genuine lives of tragedy; in moral dilemmas and fates beyond any of our controls. The vicarious joy of Christ does not sidestep the road of despair in order to too quickly embrace joy. Temporally the way of the cross comes before the reality of the resurrection.

One may also ask Barth and Hart (strange bedfellows that they are) whether the tragic is nonetheless a reality because of our rejection of God's love. Does this not affect God? Issues of the impassibility of God are obvious here, with the implications that God cannot be affected by that which is outside of himself. But is this the God of Jesus Christ? Can he be the God who *rejoices* if he is not also the God who *despairs*?

Ray Anderson notices that we cannot avoid the tragic because we live in human community. "There is something inherently tragic about the form of our present community of human love. We have presence to each other only through the present reality of discontinuity. No other person is ever totally 'at hand' to us."[28] Death and loss of a loved is closely connected to this thought. Even being separated from a loved one through distance or unfortunate events can be tragic. This is the problem of our finitude again. But we must not ignore this present phenomenon of being human for the sake of an abstract and impersonal ("infinite"?) "joy," as Hart proposes.

25. Barth, *CD* IV/1, 186.

26. Anders Nygren *Agape and Eros*, trans. Philip S. Watson (Philadelphia: Westminster, 1953).

27. David Bentley Hart, *Beauty of the Infinite*, 83.

28. Anderson, *On Being Human*, 177.

DESPAIR AND THE TRAGEDY OF DEATH

The great tragedy, of course, is death. The obvious fact of one's eventual demise can bring fear, despair, as well as provide the basis of various "heroic projects" in life as a way to deny our mortality (Ernest Becker's famous thesis in *The Denial of Death*).[29] The child Doug, in Ray Bradbury's story, *Dandelion Wine*, has his "awakening" when he becomes conscious of death. Therefore, you cannot depend on things because they break and people because they die. If this is true, Doug concludes, I, too, must die.[30] What does it mean not to exist? The philosopher Wittgenstein admits his ignorance. We do not know what is means not to exist, so we must be silent about life after death.[31] Of course, in that silence is more fear and therefore more despair. Accepting the absence of the loved one is bizarre. Something tells us that our mother, our father, our wife, our husband, should still be around. The absence becomes as least as powerful as their presence ever was. (Is this a key to understanding the Eucharist?)

Not only is the fear of death an occasion for despair but longing for death also is not unusual for those in despair: "Why is light given to one in misery, and life to the bitter in soul, who long for death, but it does not come, and dig for it more than for hidden treasures, who rejoice exceedingly and are glad when they find the grave?" (Job 3:20–22). The Apocalypse speaks of "those days" when "people will seek death and will not find it; they will long to die, but death will flee from them" (Rev 9:6).

Yet Barth famously argues that though death is the judgment on humanity, dying is not.[32] As a creature, it is no tragedy for there to be an end as well as a beginning. It is natural for human life to runs its course. The promise of eternal life is a gift, not a right. Therefore, the tragedy and despair is found in disease and decrepitude, not in cessation. Ray Anderson concludes that one discovers the spiritual dimension of one's mortality when one is able to look at one's body, even if diseased, and even after prayers for healing have failed, and still say, "This is my body."[33] The

---

29. Ernest Becker, *The Denial of Death* (New York: Free Press, 1973).

30. Ray Bradbury, *Dandelion Wine* (New York: Avon, 1999) 204–10.

31. Ludwig Wittgenstein, *Tractatus Logico-Philosophicus*, trans. C. K. Ogden (Mineola, NY: Dover, 1999) 6.4311, cited in *Real Philosophy: An Anthology of the Universal Search for Meaning*, ed. Jacob Needleman and David Appelbaum (New York: Arcana, 1990) 286.

32. Barth, *CD* III/2, 632.

33. Anderson, *Spiritual Caregiving as Secular Sacrament*, 166–67.

tragedy is not in our finitude. The tragedy is not that we are creaturely. Despair comes in all the events that tragically lead up to death. Anyone who has been with a loved one through prolonged illness leading to death knows what that means.

Nonetheless, is not cessation—ceasing to live—a tragedy, as Becker's *The Denial of Death* reminds us? Barth's distinction between death and dying should not exclude the very real cessation of our existence. It is such a tragedy that, according to Becker, it propels us into all sorts of "heroic" behavior, from cleaning the house to running for president. Tragedy is certainly found in dying, as Barth argues, but it also in the sheer, stark contemplation that there will be a day when my earthly existence will end. Perhaps the key is in the "contemplation" of our upcoming death. We do not know how it will feel to be dead. We do know how our thoughts about our cessation affect us. We know how terrible that is from our experience now when a loved one dies. How bizarre, how weird, how unacceptable is it that the loved one was here yesterday and is no longer here today. Quite possibly, you were able to talk to her yesterday—to ask a question about a memory yesterday—but are prohibited to do so today. Two friends have both related to me the strange feeling soon after a parent's death—of thinking to ask the parent something—but then grimly realizing you cannot call anymore . . . she is not there. Despair, however, is.

Death as absence of the loved one is not unconnected with despair in what is perceived as the absence of God. As mentioned previously, absence is at least as powerful as presence.[34] Whereas Schleiermacher, the father of liberal theology, is well known for defining religion as "the feeling of absolute dependence," contemporary thinkers view "absolute dependence" as too passive. Feelings of abandonment are more basic today than feelings of dependence.[35] Pascal's sentiments are still echoed: "I am terrified by the eternal silence of these infinites spaces."[36] Bob Dylan's classic rock song, "Like a Rolling Stone" expresses the modern malaise well.[37] Christopher

---

34. John Zizioulas, "Human Capacity and Human Incapacity," *Scottish Journal of Theology* 28 (1975) 401–47; *Communion and Otherness* (New York: T. & T. Clark, 2006) 206–49. See also Ray S. Anderson, *Historical Transcendence and the Reality of God* (Grand Rapids: Eerdmans, 1975) 240 n.29.

35. Friedrich Schleiermacher, *On Religion: Speeches to Its Cultured Despisers*, trans. John Oman (New York: Harper and Row, 1958); Colin Greene, *Christology in Cultural Perspective* (Grand Rapids: Eerdmans, 2004) 102.

36. Blaise Pascal, cited by Greene, *Christology in Cultural Perspective*, 102.

37. Bob Dylan, "Like a Rolling Stone." Online: http://bobdylan.com/moderntimes/songs/rolling.html.

Ricks comments on the song: "Its home question: How does it feel? Its home truth: Like a rolling stone."[38] In Martin Scorcese's documentary on Dylan, the singer reflects that from his earliest days in Minnesota, Dylan has always felt that he is searching for "home."[39] He has felt that he was not born in the "right" place. Ecclesiastes is often seen as the quintessential pessimist and agnostic, the man who lives in tragedy and accepts it in a world without the presence of God.[40] For Qoheleth, we cannot tell if God is good or evil (9:1). God is "hiding" (3:10–11) and therefore he is an arbitrary God in an arbitrary universe. In this view, Qoheleth is at home with others who are not sustained by the presence of God, for whom absence and meaninglessness are fundamental experiences. The place that Ecclesiastes has in the canon is certainly curious. It at least says that God takes despair as tragedy seriously. Qoheleth may demonstrate the fallacy of our romantic visions of a natural closeness of God apart from grace. As Kierkegaard puts it so laconically: "To be so close to God as Christianity teaches that man can come to him, dares come to him, and shall come to him in Christ—such a thought never occurred to any man."[41] Despite our plethora of religions (or maybe because of them) we live in terror of the absence of God, as well as our own absence, death.

Perhaps Ecclesiastes' place in the canon is not so unexpected if we read him, with Ray Anderson, as expressing a melancholy that "is inseparable from every mind that looks below the surface and every heart that dares to probe this mystery."[42] Qoheleth has achieved a wisdom by observing the vanity of what poses for success among us. He sees only:

> consequences of bad decisions . . . the emptiness in homes filled with furniture. He sees the futility of over-busy lives. He sees the lack of love between family members. He sees the competiveness of life, the lack of kindness, the lack of concern for the well-being of others. And seeing all of this, he becomes terribly wise, but dreadfully sad.[43]

---

38. Ricks, *Dylan's Vision of Sin*, 185.

39. *No Direction Home: Bob Dylan*, directed by Martin Scorcese, Paramount Pictures, 2005.

40. Jerome T. Walsh, "Despair as a Theological Virtue in the Spirituality of Ecclesiastes," *Biblical Theology Bulletin* 12 (1982) 46–49.

41. Kierkegaard, *Sickness Unto Death*, 125.

42. Anderson, *Exploration into God*, 27.

43. Ibid., 29.

Yet the way has been opened for a wisdom beyond himself. Even in the one contemplating suicide, Barth contends, "in the darkness of his affliction," the word of God can come and speak to him, for "the message of freedom and joy" is that of "God Himself, the true God, the God who is gracious to men in Jesus Christ, who always speaks thus to him," and is distinguished from all other human words and all false gods.[44]

The future is coming and we cannot stop it. Criswell, the talk show prognosticator and charlatan of the 1950s and 60s, begins the classic "bad movie," *Plan Nine From Outer Space*, with the melodramatic intone, "You are interested in the future . . . because the future is where you are going!"[45] That is certainly true (but hardly a profound thought). Yet the jester here speaks the truth: the tragedy of the fear of death. The future is coming upon us, "dark and triumphant," as even the usually cheery Karl Barth puts it.[46] The certainty of death and the uncertainty of life after death are overwhelming; nothing is more definite than death and nothing is more unknown than life after death. Both the reflective person and the unreflective person are, in the end, helpless.[47] The future seizes us; we do not seize the future. How dare we deny this tragedy?

DESPAIR AS EVERYDAYNESS AND THE DENIAL OF WONDER

Despair as tragedy is not simply made manifest by terrible events. Humor, particularly satirical or ironical humor is seen in Walker Percy's novel *The Moviegoer*. His character, Binx Bolling, blithely comments that he is "happy" in the consumer-obsessed America of the late 1950s because he is the model citizen who appears on time for his new auto tag, subscribes to *Consumer Reports*, and actually takes seriously the movie actor's exhortation against being a litterbug.[48] The permanent lettering on the front of the neighborhood movie theater says it well: "Where Happiness Costs So Little." In his world, the movies have more substance than the tragedy he sees around of people who do not care to search. "The search is what everyone would undertake if he were not sunk in the everydayness of his

---

44. Barth, *CD* III/4, 408.

45. *Plan Nine from Outer Space*, directed by Edward D. Wood, Jr., Distributors Corporation of America, 1959.

46. Barth, *CD* III/2, 546.

47. Ibid., 543–44.

48. Percy, *Moviegoer*, 6–7.

own life."[49] The pervasiveness of religion, however, precludes this search. Religion in America too easily becomes part of an "everydayness" that stymies any possibility of a search.[50] Binx's ability to look humorously at this situation keeps him from despair. Why is humor so close, so essential to despair, as paradoxical as that sounds? We are not far from what Kierkegaard calls "unconscious despair." Binx Bolling is not conscious of the despair, which is a despair of tragedy for him, only to be "rescued" by John Wayne killing three men on a dusty street in *Stagecoach*.[51] Beauty in life becomes a cause for despair in Binx: Being with friends or viewing "the beauty of the smoky blue valleys," instead of giving joy, becomes "heartbreaking."[52]

Heartbreaking? Perhaps because this beauty is so frail and fleeting. The lostness of humanity, as we have seen, is revealed in the vicarious faith of Jesus, "a sober realization" of one's "limits and of the frailty and end of all things."[53] But Binx does not think that he owes anything to God. He cannot weep as a sinner. The contrast with the person of faith is striking: "Here the man who must and will weep has not need to be ashamed when faced by the Creator's goodness."[54] What is tragic most of all about Binx is that he cannot weep. The believer can cry, as the lament Psalms constantly remind us. So Binx lives a life seeking to elude misery; misery that will inevitably catch up with him, by fate or old age. Binx may be an example of what Barth means by those who try to elude the misery of life by "a painless mingling of joy and sorrow."[55]

The only alternative for Binx is to live with "wonder." Ray Anderson says frankly that "a joyless life is one that has lost its sense of wonder."[56] Is this a glimmer of hope for Binx? Television helps, not because he likes it, "but it doesn't distract me from the wonder."[57] He is distracted by much. The desire he has for his secretary can easily be embraced as joy, but it ac-

49. Ibid., 13.
50. Ibid., 14.
51. *Stagecoach*, directed by John Ford, United Artists, 1939.
52. Percy, *Moviegoer*, 41–42.
53. Barth, *CD* III/1, 373.
54. Ibid.
55. Ibid.
56. Ray S. Anderson, *Dancing with Wolves While Feeding the Sheep: The Musings of a Maverick Theologian* (Eugene, OR: Wipf & Stock, 2002) 139.
57. Percy, *Moviegoer*, 42.

tually "is like a sorrow in my heart."[58] He is aware enough that her finitude cannot bring him happiness. The tragedy is that she appears so possible to fulfill that desire. That is what the obsession of lust can do. Then we act on it, and it is too late. Despair as tragedy is back, this time disguised as the beautiful blonde. Beautiful yes, but as any *film noir* movie of the forties and fifties reminds us, a trap of despair and tragedy.[59]

The novelist Michael Chabon speaks winsomely about comic books and their influence on him, but not in a patronizing way.[60] For it was the comic book that introduced Chabon to a world of wonder. The contemporary trend to write comic books that are "edgy," "adult," and "dark" betrays the very fascination the medium had for many as children in the past but not for so many today. Few actual children really read comic books today. Chabon contributes suggestions to today's comics writers on how to write so that children will again read comics:

> Let's blow their little minds. A mind is not blown, in spite of whatever Hollywood seems to teach, merely by action sequences, things exploding, thrilling planetscapes, wild bursts of speed. Those are all good things but a mind is blown when something that you always feared but knew to be impossible turns out to be true; when the world turns out to be far vaster, far more marvelous or malevolent than you ever dreamed; when you get proof that everything is connected to everything else, that everything you know is wrong, that you are both the center of the universe and a tiny speck sailing off its nethermost edge.[61]

Chabon is describing wonder, I think; the wonder that despair can so easily lose.

Despair as tragedy can be most devastating, not just in robbing us of the enjoyment of beauty in the world, but most of all in destroying wonder. Is wonder very close to true joy? Does Jesus have a sense of wonder? If he does, it both refuses to ignore despair but also does not settle for "a painless mingling of joy and sorrow."[62] He was the one who was rejected by his own (John 1:10), so despair and tragedy are known at the very beginning

---

58. Ibid., 68.
59. See Silver and Ursini, eds., *Film Noir Reader*.
60. Michael Chabon, "Kids' Stuff," in *Maps and Legends: Reading and Writing Along the Borderlands* (San Francisco: McSweeney's, 2008) 87–95.
61. Chabon, "Kids' Stuff," in *Maps and Legends*, 93–94.
62. Barth, *CD* III/1, 373.

of the Christian story, and certainly climaxing with the death of Jesus.[63] God the Creator is rejected; absurdity cannot be greater. So the reality of the resurrection results in the ascension, where the Son can wonder once again, and we with him. Perhaps sitting at the right hand of the Father only increased his wonder (Acts 2:33; Heb 12:2). There is no mythology here but reality (contra Bultmann). As heaven is that creation of God that is inexpressible, perhaps that is true of its wonder as well. Is joy as wonder finally the only antidote to despair as tragedy, the wonder that only the Son possesses and gives to us? In stark (and tragic) contrast, how easy should it be for the church to be anything but filled with wonder?

UNCONSCIOUS DESPAIR

There is another kind of despair, Kierkegaard contends, that is greater than conscious despair: unconscious despair; a despair one is not aware of or recognizes. In fact, he claims that to limit despair to that which we are aware of is "a very poor understanding of despair."[64] For "not being in despair, not being conscious of being in despair, is precisely a form of despair."[65]

Where is Christ in this? He is the one who brings despair, who announces the "good news" that we are in despair! Plodding through life, we remain ignorant of our meaninglessness, our pride, our self-centeredness, our sin, until Jesus Christ interrupts us. In a vicarious sense, Christ takes our place in the midst of our ignorance about the human condition. He is aware of that despair in his identification with us through his vicarious humanity, and offers it up to the Father through his vicarious faith and obedience.

In a similar way, Kierkegaard views "the physician" as having a vicarious function. We do not ultimately depend upon ourselves to say whether or not we are ill. No, we trust the physician to take our place and make the best diagnosis possible. So also, Kierkegaard says, we should regard "the physician of the soul."[66] For despair is insidious. Its symptoms include "a sense of security and tranquility," as true as it was in the "Christendom" of Kierkegaard's Denmark as it is in my native Wichita,

---

63. Schmemann, *For the Life of the World*, 23–24.
64. Kierkegaard, *Sickness Unto Death*, 23.
65. Ibid.
66. Ibid.

Kansas in the heart of mid-America, with what seems to be a church on every corner.[67] (What would Kierkegaard think of the sixty-three Baptist churches in Waco, Texas, alone?)

What is at stake here, according to Kierkegaard, is "spirit." We may know "school spirit" and "the spirit of entrepreneurship," but we have lost that tension between the finite and the infinite, between necessity and possibility, in relation of our "selves," which is spirit. This is what Christ, in his true humanity, has to give to us in his vicarious life, death, and resurrection. Most will be satisfied with "happiness," but within that facade is the anxiety which Freud and later depth psychology say lies within our subconscious. So also, the suspense films of Alfred Hitchcock repeat the theme that what appears to be normal on the outside is a facade for evil and crime from within. In his film *Rear Window*, Hitchcock tells the story of a bedridden photographer who passes the day by watching through the rear window of his apartment the scenarios of life across the alley through the windows of the adjoining apartments.[68] What appears to be a normal relationship between a couple eventually arouses the photographer's (Jimmy Stewart) attention. She no longer appears in the apartment window. Their dog starts to repeatedly dig in their garden. She has been murdered.

We prefer to live in the "facade," Kierkegaard claims, that is, in the "sensate" world, not acknowledging that we are a synthesis of the finite and the infinite, the necessary and the possible. But this is only to prefer to live in the "basement" instead of the upper stories of the house.[69] This is to deny that we are "spirit."

H. G. Wells, in his classic science fiction novel *The War of the Worlds*, describes the vulnerability of human beings without spirit to the invading Martians.[70] People are described as just trudging to and from work, back to ordinary families, with "no proud dreams and no proud lusts, living in fear only of losing their jobs and in church, of the hereafter. As if hell was built for rabbits! Well, the Martians will just be a godsend to these. Nice roomy cages, fattening food, careful breeding, no worry."[71]

---

67. Ibid., 24.
68. *Rear Window*, directed by Alfred Hitchcock, Paramount Pictures, 1954.
69. Kierkegaard, *Sickness Unto Death*, 43.
70. H. G. Wells, *The War of the Worlds* (New York: New York Review, 1960) 218.
71. Ibid.

Jesus reveals our mediocrity. He does so in the opposition that the "average" man had to him; it was the average man that crucified Christ.[72] Yet can simply a failure to understand Christ be considered a sin? Is the average man really that bad?[73] In fact, is not the average man the normal one and Jesus represents only the religious fanatic? As Barth points out, however, the uniqueness of Jesus is that which distinguishes him from others and this is most of all found in the fact that he "took our place, and the place of all men, that what He is necessarily includes in itself our true being as it is ascribed and given us by God."[74] Thus, the Christian life is to be moved out of our ordinariness. The solidarity of Christ with us is misunderstood if it simply means that Christ becomes "ordinary" or "average" like us. This can only become a form of "cheap" grace. Mediocrity is indeed a sin for humanity, Barth contends, for "it is undeniable in ingratitude to the grace which is shown him."[75] We live with this kind of unconscious despair in an "impossible contradiction" to whom we are really in Christ.[76]

Meaninglessness is a kind of nothing. As Sartre inimically puts it, "Nothing happens while you live."[77] The failings of science, history, rational humanism, and sex to give meaning were evident to Sartre, and have been made even more obvious by postmodernism.[78] Temporality and subjectivity become unreliable foundations. So Camus begins his novel *The Fall* with his famous comments on what future historians will remember about a modern person: "he fornicated and read the newspaper."[79] What appears to be "living" for many, if not most, is for Camus elusive: "Each joy made me desire another. On occasion I danced for nights on end, ever madder about people and life."[80] Is this not the fruit of Kierkegaard's unconscious despair? Is the frenzy of the dance floor really any different

72. Barth, *CD* IV/2, 390.
73. Ibid., 391.
74. Ibid., 392.
75. Ibid., 392–93.
76. Ibid., 393.
77. Jean-Paul Sartre, *Nausea* (New York: New Directions, 1959) 57, cited by C. Stephen Evans, *Existentialism: The Philosophy of Despair and the Quest for Hope* (Grand Rapids: Zondervan, 1984) 47.
78. Evans, *Existentialism*, 51–58; Stanley J. Grenz, *A Primer on Postmodernism* (Grand Rapids: Eerdmans, 1996) 84ff.
79. Albert Camus, *The Fall*, trans. Justin O'Brien (New York: Vintage, 1991) 6–7.
80. Ibid., 30.

from the pedestrian plodding of a typical Presbyterian worship service? And therefore, is the riotous rock worship service of a contemporary church as well as the elaborate liturgical aesthetics of the "high church" both masking a deep despair?

The worst part of despair as the tragedy of the past is not the sense of that which is gone or that which was done. As both Kierkegaard and Walker Percy teach us, the worst kind of despair is not knowing that you are in despair. As another character in Percy's novel, *The Moviegoer*, says, "Losing hope is not so bad. There's something worse: losing hope and hiding it from yourself."[81] The most common kind of despair in the world, according to Kierkegaard, is that despair which is unconscious that it is in despair.[82] It is despair which comes from one having "a very lowly conception of being spirit." If one has no spirit, one does not have a self. This vacuous kind of person is often seen in the deeply religious women of the novels of André Gide.[83] The "everydayness" of this person keeps one from any reflection. This is one who is no longer responsible, not a creature of the Seventh Day, but as bound to brute fate as any mongrel dog. The "search" is not even a desire, even if one were truly "liberal" and free to think economically and politically. This is the person oblivious to the real issues of life, oblivious to asking questions like, Who am I? Why am I here? Does God exist? What should I do? What is love? or What is the future? These are the obvious questions of meaning, of the inquiring, reflective person. Despair is that deep, that devastating; that it can exist, and we do not know that it exists!

Sloth, Karl Barth contends, is a sin, not as any inactivity but as an inactivity that refrains from doing what one really should do, what is really worthwhile.[84] One may be very busy on every committee, yet still be "slothful," in Barth's sense, a sloth that refuses to be concerned and passionate with that which really matters. One wonders in reading some Bible commentaries if the critical commentator is really obsessed with, burdened by, and passionate about the same things that Isaiah or Paul were! Can scholarship become a kind of sloth, then, a kind of unconscious despair? Humanity has been exalted with Christ. To deny this is the sin of sloth, Barth argues: "God Himself has already exalted him.

---

81. Percy, *Moviegoer*, 193.
82. Kierkegaard, *Sickness Unto Death*, 29–41.
83. See as an example, André Gide, *Strait is the Gate* (Cambridge: Bentley, 1980).
84. Barth, *CD* IV/2, "The Sloth of Man," 403–83.

of God which is addressed to him, and leads him, and orders his going, his own dark ways of frivolity or melancholy or despair which he seeks and chooses and follows."[85]

Binx Bolling in Percy's *The Moviegoer* speaks of his scientist friend Harry who has an admirable "flair for research" and will be a success in his field but is not envied by Binx.[86] "For he is no more aware of the mystery which surrounds him than a fish is aware of the water it swims in."[87] Unconscious despair is created when mystery is denied.

Binx's uncle Jules is another example of unconscious despair. The "City of Man" that he lives in is so pleasant that he has no desire for the "City of God."[88] He is a pleasant old time Southerner that lives in a pre-Civil Rights era South in which everything and everyone has a place and everything is pleasant—for him—until he dies of a heart attack.

Here is the unconscious despair of memory; a living in a "golden age" that no longer exists, a sign that one's life is drawing to a close.[89] How sad it is when one has stopped living and is still alive. But how understandable. Memory can be more real than admitting the tragedy of the present and the fear of the future. Yet the unconscious despair does not admit what should be obvious: What is to guarantee that I will continue to be the kind of person I was in the past? "The actual past never returns."[90] But we refuse to admit it; we are in unconscious despair. Whole generations can live with such despair. What is missing is a sense of openness to God being alive and active. If he is, then we are immediately displaced. (We are moving towards the vicarious joy of Christ.) But this should be something to bring us joy; we cannot be dependent upon ourselves anyhow. Unconscious despair is all too unaware of any problem.

There is a kind of existence in the "everydayness" of life that causes unconscious despair for Percy. A mediator is needed to rescue the everydayness from despair. Binx Bolling, in *The Moviegoer*, finds this in the movies. In fact, when he sees a familiar site in a movie, that site—perhaps in his neighborhood—becomes "certified" for him. "It becomes possible

---

85. Barth, *CD* IV/1, 143.
86. Percy, *Moviegoer*, 52.
87. Ibid.
88. Ibid., 31.
89. Barth, *CD* III/2, 512–13.
90. Ibid., 533–34.

for him to live, for a time at least, as a person who is Somewhere and not Anywhere."[91] Why is this needed? Because otherwise, "everydayness" takes over and "seeing, we do not see." There is an unconscious despair of living Anywhere because Anywhere is abstract and generic. We are particular creatures, but that particularity is constantly denied by mass-market culture and religion to the point that we can no longer see that which is the gift of God, including our own particularity. That is why Calvin can speak of the essence of the Christian life as gratitude, seeing and recognizing the gifts of God, in creation, in family, in work, and not taking them for granted.[92] There is a terrible unconscious despair in ingratitude. We do need to see the world through the eyes of Jesus. This is an essential part of his vicarious life.

Keeping life in compartments is another way of living in unconscious despair. From hiding sexual dysfunction to obsessive hobbies, life can become the Hitchcockian facade by neatly separating into personal and professional, religious and secular, visible and hidden. As a coping mechanism it may help us get through the day but ultimately blow up in a bizarre manifestation.[93]

However, is there a cultural or academic snobbery at work here in Kierkegaard and Percy? Is Kierkegaard free of the kind of unconscious despair that cannot imagine a genuine Christian life in an ordinary family, dutifully attending the state church of Denmark? Is that snobbery all too frequent in many college towns and faculty meetings and therefore contains its own unconscious despair: the kind of works righteousness that gives one worth by the academic initials on a business card or office door? What a great despair! But we call this "success."

The unbelief of "the lowly pagan" for Kierkegaard has its own kind of unconscious despair.[94] The pagan sees one's mission well, as well as the fundamentalist: to bear witness of the truth. But he is only negative . . . He exists in relation to what he is against. This is despair. He rejects that there is any foundation but suffers the despair of that nihilism. He

---

91. Percy, *Moviegoer*, 63.

92. Calvin, *The Golden Booklet of the Christian Life*, 87–89; *Institutes*, 3.9.3.

93. Anderson, *Spiritual Caregiving as a Secular Sacrament*, 62. See also on hobbies in Ray S. Anderson, *Everything That Makes Me Happy I Learned When I Grew Up* (Downers Grove, IL: InterVarsity, 1995) 33–34.

94. Søren Kierkegaard, *Christian Discourses and the Life of an Actress*, translated and edited by Howard V. Hong and Edna H. Hong (Princeton: Princeton University Press, 1997) 44–46.

may be conscious of others and their rejection but not conscious of his despair. He is condemned to live "tortured by the thought of being nothing, tortured by the futility of his efforts to become something" but he cannot bring himself to say this.[95] The tragic humor, the irony, is that he really wants to be something. As in the Homeric tale, he is like the one tortured by the king with food within his grasp every time he is hungry only to have it withdrawn.[96] The despairing pagan is one who suffers in "self-contradiction," a form of unconscious despair.

> While he, tortured by being nothing, futilely tries to become something, he really is not only something but is much. It is not the fruits that withdraw themselves from him; it is he himself who withdraws himself even from being what he is. For he is not a human being—and he cannot become a Christian![97]

For the sake of "truth" the despairing pagan withdraws oneself, but to what? "Freedom" has no place to go, and therefore lives in despair, the despair of self-contradiction, unconscious as it may be. Such "freedom" is said to be open to the future, but why be so blithe that we will have a future? "Anticipation is no substitute for the reality anticipated."[98] Unconscious despair can then masquerade as being "relevant" and in tune with the times.[99] Despising the past, one is continually searching for an identity that does not yet exist and may never.[100]

Both belief and unbelief can share a similar kind of despair. When religion becomes superstition (different from mystery) it is dangerously close to unbelief. Both superstition and unbelief are manifestations of rejecting the gospel, Barth contends.[101] Rejecting the gospel stills leaves humanity in its need, a need that will never be fulfilled by the various projects or indulgences of the world. Therefore, a kind of unconscious despair seeps in, a despair that cannot accept joy. A. N. Wilson has cited

---

95. Ibid., 45.

96. Homer, *The Odyssey*, I. Loeb Classical Library, trans. A. T. Murray (Cambridge: Harvard University Press, 1919) 427–29.

97. Kierkegaard, *Christian Discourses*, 46.

98. Barth, *CD* III/2, 513.

99. Ibid., 535.

100. See Jüngel, *God as the Mystery of the World*, 115, on memory and Cartesian doubt.

101. Barth, *CD* IV/3.2, 807–8.

this as typical of many of the nineteenth century critics of religion.[102] The ironic shared attitude of dogmaticism (and sometimes easy movement from one extreme to another) is obvious between the fundamentalist and the unbeliever. Both share in an unconscious despair while rebelling against their suffering. The ignorance on both sides brings neither joy nor peace. Ignorance is that which is lacking, but because it lacks, it does not know that it lacks. Kierkegaard had his "pugnacious proposition": How do we seek for something we do not know?[103] The despair is unconscious, and may be the greatest trap of despair.

Unfortunately, and ironically (and humorously even), it is in the religious person that the unconscious despair is often most apparent. The character of Kate in *The Moviegoer* defines what it means to be a religious person for her:

> What I want is to believe in someone completely and then do what he wants me to do. If God were to tell me, Kate, here is what I want you to do—you get off this train right now and go over to that corner by the Southern Life and Accident Insurance Company and stand there for the rest of your life and speak kindly to people—you think I would not do it? You think I would not be the happiest girl in Jackson, Mississippi? I would.[104]

Kate would be happy, she says. There is no doubt she is right. But happiness will be achieved at a price, the price of her spirit. For her "God" is simply unquestioned authority, an unquestioned authority arbitrarily using Kate. This is the practical theology behind Barth's famous critique of religion. Even our view of "the glory of the Lord" can emphasize "glory" much more than the reality of the Lord. "Glory," like many other values, can simply be given its own apotheosis, which in the end only plays into the hands of Feuerbach's critique of religion as a projection of human wishes and fears, as Barth makes clear.[105]

---

102. A. N. Wilson, *God's Funeral: A Biography of Faith and Doubt in Western Civilization* (New York: Ballantine, 2000). A happier portrait of the modern pagan is presented by Jennifer Michael Hecht, *Doubt: A History* (San Francisco: HarperSanFrancisco, 2003).

103. Søren Kierkegaard, *Philosophical Fragments* in *Philosophical Fragments/Johannes Climacus*, translated and edited by Howard V. Hong and Edna H. Hong (Princeton: Princeton University Press, 1985) 9.

104. Percy, *Moviegoer*, 197.

105. Barth, *CD* II/1, 325–26.

> It is not that we recognize and acknowledge the infinity, justice, wisdom, etc. of God because we already know from other sources what all this means and we apply it to God in an eminent sense, thus fashioning for ourselves an image of God after the pattern of our image of the world, i.e., in the last analysis after our own image.[106]

This is a concern for God's attributes but not God as Lord; "an affirmation which has nothing in common with slavish submission, which contains no fear and therefore no seed of revolt in itself."[107] In "slavish submission," Barth is telling us, is a revolt against God. There is happiness in this, a kind of false security which we mistake for peace and assurance. But there is no spirit.

We can even use Christ to deny that we have a self. This is a kind of "perverse" or "bizarro" vicarious humanity of Christ. "The only profile of my ministry is the dimension of reality and truth in my own life," Ray Anderson writes. "I could assume the righteousness of Christ as a substitute image for my own inner life—and without fear say that when others become like me they are becoming like Christ."[108] Yet this would be a "distortion." "People do not become like who I say that I am—but who I inevitably and existentially am."[109] What I think Anderson is saying here is that religion can falsely try to take the place of our spirit, and that is unconscious despair. In contrast, the vicarious humanity of Christ does not obliterate the self but recreates it.

---

106. Ibid., 333–34.

107. Ibid., 326.

108. Ray S. Anderson, *Soulprints: Personal Reflections on Faith, Hope, and Love* (Huntington Beach, CA: Ray S. Anderson, 1996) 81.

109. Anderson, *Soulprints*, 82.

CHAPTER FIVE

The Resolution of Despair?

Where do we go to find help in our despair? Can despair ever be resolved? The barriers seem insurmountable. When one is emptied of one's spirit, it is increasingly difficult to recognize other spirits, other selves. So, despair is also created by isolation from others. This is a common critique of what is called the "individualism" in Kierkegaard.[1] Sometimes the despair can be stimulated in turn by another's joy and hope. "I can endure my own despair," says William Walsh, "but not another's hope."[2] The happiness of another can present such a stark, ironic contrast to our despair that it becomes like rubbing salt on the wound. Our tendency then is to isolate ourselves from other people. Am I who I am simply in terms of my responsibility? Why is identity connected with relationships?[3] Am I simply to die on the vine of the burden of my responsibility? Most vulnerable are those charged with responsibilities of leadership. Leadership, particularly in the church, is one place that despair is frowned upon. Leaders (especially pastors) are those who do not have or at least have conquered depression, sorrow, and despair! For leaders, the resolution of despair is not just an acute personal issue, but has the existence of their profession at stake.

Fred Shepherd (not his real name) is a Baptist pastor who finally spills his feelings to his friend Tim.[4] In a low, dejected voice, Fred blurts

---

1. See Ray S. Anderson, "Toward a Holistic Psychology: Putting All the Pieces in their Proper Place," *Edification: Journal of the Society for Christian Psychology*, 1:2 (2007) 5–16, with a contrary response by C. Stephen Evans, "Anderson's Encounter with Kierkegaard," 28–29, and a rejoinder by Anderson, "An Edifying Evening Seminar," 41–43.

2. William Walsh in *The Oxford Dictionary of Quotations*, 563.

3. Tom Smail, "Can One Man Die for the People?" in *Atonement Today*, ed. Goldingay, 78.

4. This is a case study provided by James Beasley, a graduate student in ministry at Friends University.

out, "I spend a significant amount of time assisting my members through their struggles. Yet my own hurts are never addressed." Problems with his marriage, his children, and his aging mother all attempt to destroy Fred. And the congregation is so ungrateful at the same time. "When I have sacrificed much of my life for ministry, don't I deserve some break?" cries Fred. Fred's despair is a despair of isolation from others, the isolation, ironically, of one whose responsibility is to love and encourage others.

Bob (not his real name) is a veteran pastor whose wife Alice is pursuing graduate study in ministry.[5] But one December, Bob is told that he has both cancer of the bladder and the prostate. A night without sleep follows. Bob and Alice share both the love of their relationship and the fear for the future. But beyond those emotions is the honest feeling of despair. Bob has been a faithful pastor. They have a good marriage. Why would a God who had been so good to them let this happen? Despair creeps in, the despair of isolation from others, of abandonment by God. For Bob, the "other" is God. Why should God deal this way with one so faithful? Why does life's promise end up crashing to the ground?

What is the answer to despair? There are some pretty easy answers offered, to be sure. Ever try "noble deeds and a hot bath" as "the best cure for depression"?[6] A more serious, pious answer was provided by Jeremy Taylor: "It is impossible for man to despair who remembers that his helper is omnipotent."[7] Both the humorous and the pious rarely perceive the depths that despair can go. Is an omnipotent God really omnipotent if he does not rid me of my despair? Superficial answers are not helpful to despair because often it is the superficiality of life which breeds (unconscious) despair. Sometimes it seems that the only salvation from despair comes when the "golden dreams" of idealism are released:

> But when the days of golden dreams had perished,
> And even Despair was powerless to destroy,
> Then did I learn how existence could be cherished,
> Strengthened, and fed without the aid of joy.[8]

---

5. This is a case study provided by Ellen R. Davis, a graduate student in ministry at Friends University.

6. Dodie Smith in *The Penguin Dictionary of Modern Humorous Quotations*, ed. Metcalf, 73.

7. Jeremy Taylor in *The New Book of Christian Quotations*, ed. Castle, 61.

8. Emily Brontë, "R. Alcona to J. Brenzaida" (March 3, 1845). Online: http://academic.brooklyn.cuny.edu/english/melani/novel_19c/wuthering/poetry.html.

Or perhaps love creates a place in order to displace despair:

> Love seeketh not itself to please,
> Nor for itself hath any care,
> But for another gives its ease,
> And builds a Heaven in Hell's despair.[9]

KNOWLEDGE AS RESOLUTION?

Not all would agree with a place for Kierkegaard's unconscious despair. A common belief is that knowledge of what causes the despair is the first step towards relieving the despair. "Knowing specifically what the despair is about enhances the possibility of discovering resources for coping or overcoming it," claims Mary Louise Bringle.[10] For the philosopher Robert Solomon, despair is an emotion and emotions are "constitutive judgments according to which our reality is given its shape and structure."[11] The solution: "What is needed is constant vigilance and a learned reflective ability to 'catch ourselves' in the midst of every small but significant act of self-degradation."[12] Bringle is wise to respond to Solomon by saying, "Is it not precisely part of the defining dynamism of despair that we do *not* feel like 'talking it out' . . . If we *did* have this energy, we would not be despairing in the first place."[13] Despair creates and feeds upon this weakness.

Despite this caveat, Bringle appeals to cognitive therapy such as that offered by A. T. Beck as a solution for despair, which of necessity must be conscious.[14] The result is that she has to see Kierkegaard's view of unconscious despair as "idiosyncratic," since it "so expands the notion of despair as to rob the term of its specificity as an emotion concept."[15] What

---

9. William Blake, "The Clod and the Pebble," *Poetry and Prose of William Blake*, ed. Geoffrey Keynes (New York: Random House, 1948) 66.

10. Bringle, *Despair*, 118.

11. Robert Solomon, *The Passions: The Myth and Nature of Human Emotion* (Notre Dame: University of Notre Dame, 1983) xix, cited in Bringle, *Despair: Sickness or Sin?* 123.

12. Ibid., 125.

13. Bringle, *Despair*, 126.

14. A. T. Beck, *Depression: Causes and Treatment* (Philadelphia: University of Pennsylvania Press, 1967).

15. Bringle, *Despair*, 133.

Kierkegaard has done, according to Bringle, is conceive of despair "more as a *structure* of existence than as a phenomenon of existence."[16]

But that is precisely the point. The specific contribution of a *theological* view of despair is to go beyond simply the phenomenon and, because of the revelation of Christ's vicarious humanity, be able to say something about the ontology of existence, particularly because of our inability to know this structure apart from grace. As Jesus said, "There is nothing outside a person that by going in can defile, but the things that come out are what defile" (Mark 7:14). So also, an ontological depth is seen in what Bonhoeffer calls "the hidden character of the Christian life" as reflected in Jesus's teaching in the Sermon on the Mount on not parading your righteousness before others (Matt 6:1–8, 16–18).[17] Despair has an ontological, not just phenomenological, existence. The place of Christ is to provide another place of existence, of what now is through Jesus Christ. As Barth suggests, the community does not see in Jesus only what might be, or ought to be, or one day will be; it sees what is, what has come into being in Him and by Him."[18] This does not mean that the human is obliterated, in a kind of grotesque "christomonism," but only that the human "loses the appearance of autonomy and finality."[19]

"WEEPING" AS RESOLUTION?

An ancient tradition in the Christian East speaks of the power of *penthos*, "compunction," or "tears of sorrow." Building on Paul's teaching about the "godly sorrow" that leads to repentance, many ancients in the East viewed *penthos* as the consequence of forgiveness, and as a cure for despair.[20] Much later, John Calvin will teach that, in contrast to the medieval Catholic belief in penitence as a condition to grace, the biblical teaching is that repentance is motivated by and is a consequence of faith and forgiveness.[21] The cure for sadness, according to John Climacus (ca. 570–649),

---

16. Ibid.
17. Bonhoeffer, *Discipleship*, 146–68.
18. Barth, *CD* IV/3.2, 713.
19. Ibid.
20. John Climacus, *Scala Paradisi*, 13: PG 88: 860o; cf. Evagrius, *Pratikos* 27: SCh 563; CS 23; cited in Špidlík, *The Spirituality of the Christian East*, 253.
21. Calvin, *Institutes*, 3.3.4. See also James B. Torrance, *Worship, Community, and the Triune God of Grace*, 54.

John Chrysostom, Gregory of Nyssa, and others, is *penthos*, for genuine, continual tears of sorrow go forth when one acknowledges forgiveness.[22] *Penthos* goes even further than repentance. One monk is said to have spent sixty years of his life never ceasing to weep!

At this point, one wonders if a concept of merit, similar to the medieval Catholic view of penance, has crept in. For Chrysostom, a single tear can wash away the venom of sin.[23] *Penthos* is said to drive away wickedness and bring about joy.[24] St. Anthony is said by Athanasius to have daily sighed over himself, and therefore his countenance became "beautiful."[25] Or, in Ephrem's words, "A face bathed with tears has an undying beauty."[26] This may continue the repentance that is created and motivated by forgiveness, as in Calvin. However, does *penthos* drive away one's despair only to replace it with another, perpetual despair? Does this really resolve despair or end up keeping despair (and guilt) alive? The tradition of "penitential piety" criticized by Wolfhart Pannenberg is alive in the East as well as the West, among Protestants, Catholics, and Orthodox.[27] Perhaps the anthropocentricism of the *penthos* tradition is best revealed when Ephrem says, "The beginning of *penthos* is to know oneself."[28] Part of this, according to Basil, is to refrain from laughter! Yes, there is a spiritual discipline of remembering what one has lost or what one lacked, but not to keep the often terrible pain of that loss or lack alive. "Weeping may linger for the night, but joy comes with the morning," Scripture proclaims (Ps 30:5). The weeping is particularly meaningful, however, on behalf of another, a *vicarious weeping* if you will, a kind of intercessory ministry, as found in Paul's concern for the Corinthians. For many ancients, it is the fear of impending judgment from God that brings about compunction. With Symeon the New Theologian, however, it is the love of God that

---

22. Špidlík, *Spirituality of the Christian East*, 253, 193–94.

23. John Chrysostom, *De paenitentia* 7:5; cited by Špidlík, *Spirituality of the Christian East*, 196.

24. John Climacus, *Scala Paradisi*, 7; cited by Špidlík, *Spirituality of the Christian East*, 196.

25. Athanasius, *Life of Anthony*, 45, 67; cited by Špidlík, *Spirituality of the Christian East*, 196.

26. Ephrem in Špidlík, *Spirituality of the Christian East*, 196.

27. Wolfhart Pannenberg, *Christian Spirituality* (Philadelphia: Westminster, 1983) 13–30.

28. Ephrem in Špidlík, *Spirituality of the Christian East*, 196

causes him to weep.²⁹ So one also cannot follow the ancients who forbid weeping about anything in this world. Jesus did weep for Lazarus (John 11:35).

The prayers of Jesus offer a kind of "vicarious weeping." "Prayer does not mean simply to pour out one's heart," Bonhoeffer argues. "It means rather to find the way to God and to speak with him, whether the heart is full or empty. No man can do that by himself. For that he needs Jesus Christ."³⁰ Neither our robust faith nor our tears of *penthos* are enough. He needs to weep for us. Jesus Christ takes us with him in his prayers, including his prayers of weeping. Judas as an answer to prayer, Ray Anderson contends, stands in for each one of us because he signifies that Jesus continues to pray for us no matter how desperate our condition might be.³¹

Jesus also represents us and takes our place in repentance.³² This is what his baptism is all about. Can we ever weep enough over our sins? Only Christ is able. Even Barth, with his high Christology can say that "in the one Israelite Jesus it was God Himself who as the Son of the Father made Himself the object of this accusation and willed to confess Himself a sinner, and to be regarded and dealt with as such."³³ Our weeping cannot compare with his penitence on our behalf. "What is all our human repentance either in our own name or in that of others compared with this perfect repentance?"³⁴ Barth can even speak of Christ then as "the one great sinner" who is "the one lost sheep, the one lost coin, the lost son (Luke 15:3f.) . . ."³⁵ That is how close he identifies with our despair, sin, brokenness, and death. This is the vicarious despair of Christ.

---

29. Ibid.

30. Bonhoeffer, *Psalms*, 9–10.

31. Anderson, *Judas and Jesus*, 49–50.

32. Barth, *CD* IV/1, 165. Cf. Campbell, *The Nature of the Atonement*, 114–26; R. C. Moberly, *Atonement and Personality* (London: John Murray, 1907) 26–47; C. S. Lewis, "The Perfect Penitent" in *Mere Christianity*, 56–61; Christian D. Kettler, "The Vicarious Repentance of Christ in the Theology of John McLeod Campbell and R. C. Moberly," *Scottish Journal of Theology* 38 (1986) 529–43; Kettler, *Vicarious Humanity of Christ and the Reality of Salvation*, 187–204.

33. Barth, *CD* IV/1, 172.

34. Ibid.

35. Ibid., 259; cf. 261–62.

JESUS THE MAN OF SORROWS

The awareness that Qoheleth (Ecclesiastes) has of the vanity of the world creates a sadness, a sorrow, a weeping that is a protest against the contradictions of life.[36] Qoheleth's spirit is alive in his protest. As Anderson puts it, "the melancholy of the human spirit is really a capacity to sense the deeper things of God's love for us."[37] It is a capacity found in incapacity, and therefore, open to the vicarious humanity of Christ. Just as we are created out of nothing, *ex nihilo*, we need to see the *ex nihilo* in all of theology, and particularly in our human capacity/incapacity.[38] Hilary of Poitiers (ca. 315-367) argues that true faith acknowledges its "incompetence."[39] Qoheleth reveals that to be human is to acknowledge a dissatisfaction with the vanities of life, demanding "more from life than temporal existence offers."[40] This means exploring beyond the phenomena into the ontological, as we have suggested, beyond the surface of human existence into the depth of the mystery of human existence.[41] The passion of Jesus teaches us, David Harned comments, that God is not met in independence but dependence, "not in expressing our own initiatives but in waiting upon the initiatives of others."[42] Like Job, we are to look upon God in the end as our Advocate and Representative.[43] Bonhoeffer speaks of "the God who bears" in Christ, who bears the burdens and sins of humanity, therefore we can let go of the burden of "the self-chosen yoke of their own selves ... Bearing the cross does not bring misery and despair. Rather it provides refreshment and peace for our souls; it is our greatest joy."[44] We have now gone beyond refusing to accept joy if there is grief. Ecclesiastes is among the "wisdom" literature of the Old Testament

---

36. Anderson, *Exploration into God*, 23.

37. Ibid., 25.

38. Ray S. Anderson, *The Soul of Ministry: Forming Leaders for God's People* (Louisville: Westminster John Knox, 1997) 43-51, 112.

39. Hilary of Poitiers, *On the Trinity*, NPNF, series 2, vol. 9, 2.11; cf. Wallis, *Faith of Jesus Christ in Early Christian Traditions*, 209.

40. Anderson, *Exploration into God*, 26.

41. Ibid., 27.

42. David Baily Harned, *Patience: How We Wait Upon the World* (Cambridge, MA: Cowley, 1997) 15.

43. Barth, *CD* III/2, 619; cf. *CD* II/1, 388.

44. Dietrich Bonhoeffer, *Ethics*, ed. Clifford J. Green, trans. Reinhard Krauss, Charles C. West, and Douglas W. Stott, Dietrich Bonhoeffer Works 6 (Minneapolis: Fortress, 2005) 90-91.

because there is wisdom in recognizing one's sadness. We cannot and should not escape it.[45]

But this takes christological courage. Because we are united with the Christ who is both crucified and risen, we are united with both his sorrow and his joy. As Anderson comments, "When we are bound up with Christ in his afflictions, we are simultaneously bound up in his joy."[46] The more we suffer the more God is bound up with us. This was true of the sufferings of Israel in their disobedience and the steadfast love of the Lord.[47] This suffering is not alien to the union of humiliation and exaltation in the incarnation. Here is a communication of the life of God himself. The Son is of one substance with the Father (Nicaea) and therefore the resolution of despair will not be found external but internal to the being of God.[48] Jesus Christ is the witness in his vicarious humanity to this differentiation in God, in which he can be both high and low, in authority and obedience, as Father and Son, and so also be in both joy and despair.[49] God the judge is the judge who is filled with sorrow, for in Christ he bears not only the penalty for sin but also the sorrow in the Father's heart.[50] Jesus has made our suffering his own; our misery has become his misery.[51] The resolution of despair will only be found when our despair is so dramatically taken from us, at an ontological level. So cross and resurrection are not to be seen as polar opposites. As Moltmann says, "The risen Christ is and remains the crucified Christ."[52]

There is pain in God because he is love in himself (the Trinity) and allows himself to be rejected by humanity (John 1:10–11).[53] In an interesting analogy with the act of poetry (and maybe all of the arts), Andrew Rumsey sees the incarnation as well as a "taking in" (humiliation) of the

---

45. Anderson, *Exploration into God*, 40.

46. Ray S. Anderson, "Reconciliation and the Healing of Persons," lecture notes, Fuller Theological Seminary, 1980.

47. T. F. Torrance, *Mediation of Christ*, chapters 1 and 2.

48. T. F. Torrance, *Christian Doctrine of God*, 78.

49. Barth, *CD* IV/2, 351.

50. Barth, *CD* IV/1, 452.

51. Ibid., 184.

52. Jürgen Moltmann, *Theology of Hope*, trans. James W. Leitch (New York: Harper & Row, 1967) 171.

53. Paul Fiddes, *Participation in God: A Pastoral Doctrine of the Trinity* (Louisville: Westminster John Knox, 2000) 165.

world in all of its wonder before there is a "giving out" (exaltation).[54] The taking in of the world by Christ includes taking in its despair before he then "gives out" his joy, with us and for us. What is Gethsemane but Christ "taking in" the burdens of the world, and realizing that they are overwhelming?[55] But he also "gives out" in his prayer as a child to the Father, not demanding but trusting. In Barth's words, "He does not demand. He does not advance any claims. He does not lay upon God any conditions . . . He does not abandon his status as a penitent. He does not cease to allow that God is in the right, even against Himself . . . He prays only as a child to the Father . . ."[56]

Christ's life, death, and resurrection is the light that reveals and overpowers the darkness (John 1:5, 9). Since he has become flesh (John 1:4), he has taken upon our darkness but shines his light "without darkness or shadow."[57] He does this as "the exalted and new true man who is now seated at the right hand of God."[58] Since he takes upon our humanity, we belong to this new, exalted, and true man. The consequence for us is that "man should become light . . . even in the darkness."[59] Even in the darkness! The resolution of despair will come when we can be light in the midst of darkness, even as the eternal Son of God took upon our darkness. The power of the light of Jesus Christ was not overcome by the darkness (John 1:5). Instead, the light illumines the darkness, remarkably, in Barth's words, so that "even in all the sadness which may otherwise engulf us, it effects a clear and invincible joyfulness. For it is always joy to belong to this majestic and true man and to be able to cleave to Him . . . To live in this light which falls from above is always to have joy."[60] But can joy really live with despair? The promise and the challenge of the vicarious joy of Christ is that it can, if it is joy "from above," not just the joys we experienced in the mundane world. It has to be the joy of Jesus. His joy is a joy "from above," the joy of grace.

---

54. Andrew Rumsey, "Through Poetry: Particularity and the Call to Attention" in *Beholding the Glory: Incarnation through the Arts*, ed. Jeremy Begbie (London: Darton, Longman & Todd, 2000) 52.

55. Barth, *CD* IV/1, 266.

56. Ibid., 270.

57. Barth, *CD* IV/2, 310.

58. Ibid.

59. Ibid., 311.

60. Ibid.

There is a place for the vicarious *despair* of Christ as well, a place for participation in the vicarious weeping of Christ, but only as long as it is a response to the grace and love of God, followed by the joy that comes in the morning, the call of Lazarus by Jesus to come forth and be risen from the dead (John 11:43). For this we must depend on the vicarious humanity of Christ.

THE HEART OF JESUS: THE MEDIATOR OF THE HEAD AND THE HANDS

The grace of God in Jesus Christ is an interruption, an address, in the midst of our despair. It comes in the context of solidarity, giving genuine help at the depths of our humanity—including emotions—with a depth of intimacy, and in that way demonstrates what it means for Jesus to be confessed as the Lord who became a servant (Phil 2:5–11). God interrupted Elijah in the midst of his despair over the evil of Jezebel by giving him both physical nourishment and a word "that begins with a question rather than blame": "What are you doing here, Elijah?" (1 Kgs 19:3–20).[61] Anderson suggests that by asking this kind of question not once but twice, God is seeking to address Elijah at the level of his emotions, rather than to simply shame him. So also Jonah pleads for his life to be ended because he cannot accept the grace of God toward the Ninevites. God addresses him with a question as well, "Is it right for you to be angry?" (Jonah 4:2–5). Jonah also is addressed at the level of his emotions.[62] The resolution of despair comes when we are addressed in the whole of our humanity, not just intellectual, moral, or religious, but also emotional. These questions display God's desire for intimacy with the prophets, an intimacy that is fulfilled in the intimacy revealed between the Father and the Son, so that Jesus can even pray, "Now my soul is troubled. And what should I say—'Father, save me from this hour?' No, it is for this reason that I have come to this hour. Father, glorify your name" (John 12:27–28). Anderson comments, "It was the intimate relation of a son to a father that Jesus reached for in His times of greatest stress."[63] Jesus knew who he was because he knew the Father. He could say, "You shall love the Lord your God with all your heart, and with all your soul, and with all your mind" (Matt 22:37) because *he* did. Kate, in *The Moviegoer*, seems at first to be

---

61. Anderson, *Self-Care*, 61.
62. Ibid., 62.
63. Ibid., 63.

similar to Jesus in Gethsemane; she wants God to tell her what to do. In like manner, Jesus decides to obey the Father. The difference, however, is that Kate's soul is not troubled with the hour of suffering; she just wants the authority to tell her what to do. This is the seedling for every kind of authoritarianism that has perennially plagued humanity. Jesus's obedience to Father, in contrast, is in the midst of struggle, sharing in *our* struggle: "Now my soul is troubled . . ."

Furthermore, what is important to Jesus in moral decision making is the intention of the heart, that which is at the center of one's humanity (Matt 5–7, the Sermon on the Mount). [64] But it is not enough simply to have "good intentions" if they cause harm to another.[65] Jesus's "good intentions" are vicarious and efficacious because he knows that which is our good. Jesus is the gift of God's grace because in solidarity with us he communicates a vicarious life, not an intention to be religious, moral, or successful.

In the classic silent science fiction film by Fritz Lang, *Metropolis* (1927), the future is a grim one of workers being exploited by a rich and leisurely class that sits high above the city in penthouse apartments while the drones work in the basements of the futuristic city.[66] The "head" (the managers) has become separated from the "hands" (the workers). Maria, a slave-class madonna implores the workers to pray for a mediator that can bring the heart to mediate between the head and the hands. Freder, the son of the head of Metropolis, becomes that mediator. The Christian symbolism is obvious. It is Jesus's heart, his intentions—the center of his being that brings reconciliation—doing for others, the head and the hands—what they cannot do for themselves. (Ironically, Hitler loved this movie because he saw himself in the role of the mediator!)[67] Are we not in despair because our heads and our hands do not possess the heart of a mediator?

Ray Anderson was fond of telling his story of a dramatic moment for him on the South Dakota farm when his father told him to stick his hand into the soil. He did so and Ray's father looked him in the face, saying, "Son, this soil is part of your life—you take care of it and it will

64. Ibid., 90–91.
65. Ibid., 92.
66. *Metropolis*, directed by Fritz Lang, UFA and Paramount Pictures, 1927.
67. Steve Vineberg, "Heartbreak City," *Christian Century* (September 25–October 8, 2002) 48.

take care of you."[68] Ray first thought this was meant that he would always be bound to the land, always be a farmer. But later reflection brought a greater insight. What Ray's father was saying was not a magical connection to soil, but that wherever Ray put a hand, his heart would be there as well. Anderson took this to mean that one can have a connection between the heart and the hand (shades of *Metropolis*!) wherever one may go. Ray saw that, I believe, because he knew that the mediation of Christ would go with him everywhere, including the prairies of South Dakota, seminary and a pastorate in California, doctoral study in Scotland, and then back to teaching in California, ending with a long career at Fuller Theological Seminary. "No matter what 'soil' my hand was plunged into, if the task was undertaken with my heart," Ray says, "there was a sense of completeness that brought joy and fulfillment."[69] Ray knew that the resolution of despair is found in a very human joy in which Christ's humanity takes on our humanity so that our hands and our heads are never separated from our hearts. Ray Anderson taught that holistic reality by word and by his life.

GRACE TO HELP IN THE EXTREMES OF LIFE AND DEATH

The resolution of despair is found when humanity is genuinely helped by the grace of God. The radical judgment of grace is that which truly helps humanity according to Barth:

> It is just because the New Testament sees and understands man in this light that it cannot oscillate between optimistic, neutral and pessimistic opinions about him ... It measures man by what God has done for him, by what Jesus Christ has accomplished in his place for his justification and deliverance from this burden, for his peace and salvation.[70]

This help begins with God's solidarity with us in Jesus Christ, the Word who became flesh (John 1:14). This help reveals something of God. It is not simply God as "one of the boys" but an "inescapable solidarity" that judges us as well as comforts us: "For he knows his inescapable solidar-

---

68. Ray S. Anderson, *Unspoken Wisdom: Truths My Father Taught Me* (Minneapolis: Augsburg, 1995) 13.

69. Ibid., 18.

70. Barth, *CD* III/2, 605.

ity with all men and indeed all creatures in all their sorrow."[71] Solidarity, however, is not to be a burden that we somehow ought to bear; religiously or ethically. The resolution of despair will be found, in Bonhoeffer's words, when we "joyfully believe that there was, there is, a man to whom no human sorrow and no human sin is strange and who in the profoundest love achieved our redemption."[72] His baptism signifies that even at the beginning of his ministry, Jesus is in solidarity with sinners; taking their despair upon himself, culminating in what Alan Lewis calls his "baptism of hell" on Easter Saturday, his burial and descent into hell.[73] In effect, as Hans Urs von Balthasar puts it, "it is really God who assumes what is radically contrary to the divine."[74] It was only because he had taken upon our fallen human nature that he was truly in solidarity with us, as we are, right now.[75] The cry of abandonment, "My God, my God, why have you forsaken me?" (Matt 27:46) was spoken for us, Athanasius claims, because Christ had become a servant as a human being.[76] This is where God draws closest to our humanity so that we can speak of God as not only suffering "with" but "as" us.[77] The resolution of despair will only take place with this ontological closeness. As I heard James Torrance say many times, "Christ does not heal us as an ordinary doctor might by standing over against us, diagnosing our sickness, prescribing medicine for us to take and then going away, leaving us to getter better as we follow his instructions. No, he becomes the patient!"[78]

What has been accomplished for humanity meets humanity at its most extreme moment: death, and says that death will be taken seriously, indeed, as punishment but not apart from Jesus Christ and his solidarity and vicarious life and death for us because Jesus Christ is the Lord over death. He becomes the "patient" who dies! We cling to Jesus because we see in the Lord over death the gracious God who has elected himself for

71. Barth, *CD* IV/3.1, 365.

72. Bonhoeffer, "Advent Letter to the Pastors of the Confessing Church," in Robert Coles, *Dietrich Bonhoeffer*, 91.

73. Alan E. Lewis, *Between Cross and Resurrection*, 447.

74. Balthasar, *Mysterium Paschale*, 52.

75. T. F. Torrance, *Christian Doctrine of God*, 231–32.

76. Cited by Gérard Rossé, *The Cry of Jesus on the Cross: A Biblical and Theological Study*, trans. Stephen Wentworth Arndt (New York: Paulist, 1987) 76.

77. Fiddes, *Participation in God*, 186.

78. James B. Torrance, *Worship, Community and the Triune God of Grace*, 53; cf. Barth, *CD* IV/2, 485–86.

our sake. We seek refuge in our most extreme moments, whether it is despair, dying, or death. Indeed, "apart from His existence we have no other comfort."[79] Death, especially, leaves us totally embarrassed. This is nothing we can do. Its terror is succinctly summarized by Barth: "To be dead means not to be."[80] That is why the resurrection from the dead is simply an act of grace. The grace of God as the resolution of despair is nothing less than the life, death, and resurrection of Jesus Christ for us, vicariously, in triumphing over death. This is the heart of justification by grace, the *sola* of *sola gratia*, grace alone, which we only find in the vicarious act of Jesus Christ, an act that reaches down into the totality of who we are, including our feelings and emotions, with the feelings and emotions of Jesus Christ. Not only our feelings and emotions, but our minds need to be redeemed, as T. F. Torrance reminds us.[81] The silence of Holy Saturday, Alan Lewis suggests, is appropriate to the all-encompassing nature of death. It happens to the whole person. This means that we can only be passive. Holy Saturday is the act of Christ's solidarity with the dead.[82] Christ takes our place in death and hell.[83] So Ray Anderson can have Jesus saying to Judas, "I have been to the God-forsaken place, Judas; it was on the cross, not in the black hole in your own soul."[84] This is a God who is responsible, who does not simply exhort his creatures to be responsible. Therefore there is freedom to minister because it is God who continues to minister, and we only participate in that ministry. Therefore a pastor need not try to meet every need of every one.[85] Only with solidarity and, dare we say it, in passivity, can we be ready then for the vicarious despair and joy of Christ. Then we can be exalted with Christ in the totality of our being, just as Christ was.[86]

---

79. Barth, *CD* III/2, 610.

80. Barth, *CD* IV/1, 301.

81. T. F. Torrance, *Karl Barth: Biblical and Evangelical Theologian* (Edinburgh: T. & T. Clark, 1990) 231; *The Christian Frame of Mind: Reason, Order and Openness in Theology and Natural Science* (Colorado Springs: Helmers and Howard, 1989).

82. Alan E. Lewis, *Between Cross and Resurrection*, 149.

83. Ibid., 168.

84. Anderson, *Judas and Jesus*, 20.

85. Ray S. Anderson, "Clergy Burnout as a Symptom of Theological Anemia" in *The Shape of Practical Theology: Empowering Ministry with Theological Praxis* (Downers Grove, IL: InterVarsity, 2001) 287–88.

86. Barth, *CD* IV/2, 316.

Here is the answer to the challenge of religious pluralism in a relativistic, postmodern age. Who else has done this for us?[87] The uniqueness of Jesus is not foreign to the New Testament. Barth notes that the cry of the blind men in Matt 9:27–31 is "Have mercy on us, Son of David!"[88] It is not any wonderworker that the men implore in their despair. Their despair is squarely placed upon, and their expectation is solely on, the one who will be the fulfillment of the promise to Israel, the one from the line of David (Acts 2:29–36). Their cry for mercy is specific because their need is specific. Despair should not be met with shrugs that "all is well. We are all one." That is cruel.

Do we risk so much making such exclusive claims about Jesus? No, Barth responds, because it is in him that we find help at the point of our death. There is no restriction here, even in a postmodern, pluralistic society: "We have not really anything to regret or lose. This gathering and concentration is not a restriction but a liberation; it is not an impoverishment but an enrichment."[89] This is a liberation in that we do not have to confuse ourselves with Christ, as Bonhoeffer reminds us, because of the vicarious humanity of Christ.[90] We should not try to burden ourselves with the sorrows of others but to "look with utter joy" to Christ. "Only in such joy toward Christ, the Redeemer, are we saved from having our senses dulled by the pressure of human sorrow or from becoming resigned under the experience of suffering."[91] *Sola gratia* is important in dealing with despair. Only he is able to bear the burdens of the sorrows of the world. That is good news.

Grace does not simply ignore the despair; in fact, it embraces it. Barth stresses that Romans 7 should never be seen apart from Romans 8.[92] The person of Romans 7 is "still surrounded by darkness."[93] That one cries that "the good that would I do not, but the evil which I would not, I do" (Rom 7:19), finally erupting, "Wretched man that I am! Who will

---

87. Barth, *CD* III/2, 615–16; cf. T. F. Torrance, *Karl Barth: Biblical and Evangelical Theologian*, 143.

88. Barth, *CD* IV/2, 235.

89. Barth, *CD* III/2, 615–16.

90. Bonhoeffer, "Advent Letter to the Pastors of the Confessing Church," in Robert Coles, *Dietrich Bonhoeffer*, 91.

91. Ibid.

92. Barth, *CD* IV/1, 581–82.

93. Ibid., 582.

rescue me from this body of death?" (Rom 7:24). This same one is the one who then exclaims, "There is therefore now no condemnation for those who are in Christ Jesus" (Rom 8:1). This one's despair has met the grace of God, justification by grace through faith (Rom 3:24–25). The person of Romans 8 will never forget that one was once (and still is?) the person of Romans 7, as Barth makes plain: "As he bears that deep wound and accepts that bitter pain in penitence, he will hope for the grace of God and in that hope he will be at bottom a cheerful man."[94]

JOY IS THE FRUIT OF GRACE

The climax of this help of grace is in the joy that God will create: "But be glad and rejoice forever in what I am creating; for I am about to create Jerusalem as a joy, and its people as a delight. I will rejoice in Jerusalem, and delight in my people; no more shall the sound of weeping be heard in it or the cry of distress" (Isa 65:18–19). There is an eschatological finality here: "No more . . ." Calvin observes that the joy and the end of weeping will be that which the people will share (vicariously!) with God:

> For by these words he means that he not only will give to men ground for rejoicing, but even will be a partaker with them in that joy. So great is his love toward us, that he delights in our prosperity not less than if he enjoyed it along with us. And hence we obtain no small confirmation of our faith, when we learn that God is moved, and so powerfully moved, by such an affection toward us. If we are in painful and distressed circumstances, he says that he is affected by grief and sorrow; and, on the other hand, if our condition is pleasant and comfortable, he says he takes great pleasure in our prosperity.[95]

The resolution of despair is finally God's business: "Then shall the young women rejoice in the dance, and the young men and the old shall be merry. I will turn their mourning into joy. I will comfort them, give them gladness for sorrow" (Jer 31:13). Note that the resolution of despair is not just the end of despair but to "rejoice in the dance"! The needy come to Jesus because in him they see the coming of the future into the present.[96]

---

94. Ibid., 775.

95. John Calvin, *Calvin's Commentaries: Commentary on the Prophet Isaiah*, vol. 4, trans. William Pringle (Grand Rapids: Baker, 2005) 399–400.

96. Barth, *CD* IV/2, 243.

These are those who have nothing to lose; those who need a physician because they acknowledge that they are sick, the sinners not the righteous (Mark 2:15–17; Matt 9:9–13; Luke 5:27–32). Those who have received this grace from Jesus still live with the occasion to complain, but they remember the grace shown to Lazarus, demons cast out, Satan falling from heaven like lightning, and that their sins are forgiven. "They have seen the signs of the kingdom and its King," Barth continues. "They have seen Jesus as the Saviour of the whole man and the whole cosmos."[97] Their rejoicing in the dance has already begun!

A personal note is in order here. In the preface I mentioned Bob Myers, my first pastor. Bob was such a Christian, joyful in the midst of sorrow. Suffering from acute arthritis most of his life, living with plastic elbows, knees, and knuckles, Bob did not put on a "happy pastor face," denying his pain. But he did communicate a life surrounded by grace. An accomplished Bible teacher, Bob repeatedly reminded many of us "kids" in the Jesus Movement of the early 1970s in Wichita, Kansas, to beware of anyone who adds anything on to "Jesus": "Jesus and baptism," "Jesus and the Spirit," or even "Jesus and the church." The free grace of God was at the heart of Bob Myers' theology. It was Bob who prepared me to see what Karl Barth was driving at; not in a "christomonistic" theology, but a "christocentric" theology that is of necessity a trinitarian theology of the loving triune God, because it is in the incarnation that the rejoicing in the dance has already begun. Bob Myers knew that, lived that, and communicated that to us "Jesus kids."

THE ESCHATOLOGICAL JOY OF GRACE

The eschatology of grace in the midst of despair is demonstrated powerfully in the beatitude, "Blessed are those who mourn, for they will be comforted" (Matt 5:4). This reflects the core of Jesus's ministry as one to the outsiders of society. Those in despair, who mourn, are certainly not held up to be successful! But there will be an eschatological reversal.[98] The power of the resurrection is the power over the dead Jesus, and therefore, over our death. We live with Jesus even now "in the shadow of death, in this discontinuity . . ."[99] Therefore, there is a hope that the despair will

---

97. Ibid., 243–45.
98. Davies and Allison, *Matthew*, vol. 1, 448–49.
99. Barth, *CD* IV/2, 317.

someday end. Having that hope, can we live with both despair and joy? The despairing already have a sense of the future because of this promise, a promise that should not be too quickly "realized." This is for the future, even for another life. But that future speaks to the present because it has already been fulfilled by the despair *and* the joy of Jesus. For Jesus starts his ministry with these words from Isa 61:1–3: "The Spirit of the Lord is upon me, because he has anointed me to bring good news to the poor. He has sent me to proclaim release to the captives and recovery of sight to the blind, to let the oppressed go free, to proclaim the year of the Lord's favor" (Luke 4:18–19). What is amazing is that he sat down and "began to say to them, 'Today this scripture has been fulfilled in your hearing" (Luke 4:21). "Fulfilled"! The grace of God has come for the resolution of despair.

What is lacking of grace sometimes in the *penthos* tradition is discovered by the poet Jane Kenyon in her words about happiness. Happiness is not something you seek, but comes upon you, like "the uncle you never knew about . . . and inquires at every door until he finds you asleep midafternoon as you so often are during the unmerciful hours of your despair."[100] Instead of clawing through weeping and moaning, seeking to earn joy, joy may come as grace when we least expect it (Remember the old "Candid Camera" show of the sixties, when the television camera revealed someone in an embarrassing scenario: "When you least expect it: Smile! You're on Candid Camera!"?). The resolution of despair is a gift of grace. This is the way of the vicarious despair of Jesus, which enables us to participate in his vicarious joy.

What a voice of freedom was sounded when Kierkegaard wrote that all people are in despair, and particularly, those who do not recognize that they are in despair! Not one of us can escape it. So we have no right to be judgmental upon those in despair or to view ourselves as immune from it. All are made level at the foot of the cross, and also at the foot of despair.

Love builds "a Heaven in Hell's despair," says Blake. Is this what is needed? If so, it must not be love as sentimentality, but the love that weeps, for oneself and for others. Where do we find such a love, however? Grace is the movement of God's love, supremely found in Christ. Does Jesus need to weep both on our behalf and in our place, to bring us to the

---

100. Jane Kenyon "Happiness," in *Otherwise: New and Selected Poems* (St. Paul, MN: Graywolf, 1996) 3.

weeping that bears fruit in joy? Is a new place, even a new creation, a new humanity, the answer? Is the "heaven" we need found in the faith of Jesus, the vicarious humanity of Christ? Can we find joy then in the midst of despair? That is the question for Part Two.

PART TWO

Can Joy Live with Despair?
And the Vicarious Joy of Christ

CHAPTER SIX

The Problem of Joy

THE MULTIPLICITY OF JOYS

This is not a particularly dramatic example of despair, but it was significant for me as a child. I remember well the despair and joy of summer. Not involved in athletics or other activities, shy and withdrawn, as a preteenager I was bored during summer. Except that I lived in anticipation of the day when my subscription copies of "The Fantastic Four" and "The Amazing Spider-Man" would arrive in the mail! Although folded with a permanent crease through the middle of the comic (the collector in me cringes!) those comics were messengers of a little joy in the midst of hot, often lonely summers. I lived for those days. Joy came in the midst of despair, even in what seems a trivial sense.

Are we simply describing being happy? There are some kinds of joys that seem to be synonyms with happiness but they seem to either neglect the realm of the emotions that most definitions of joy include or "domesticate" joy into a settled state, as in saying of the aged couple that they had a "happy marriage." Ray Anderson views happiness as something that is acquired through acts of maturity.[1] Thus realizing that life is not fair, free, nor friendly all contribute to happiness, a kind of contented state. Aristotle, of course, finds happiness for humanity only in being true to human uniqueness, the use of the mind, and that, too, assumes bodily health and the totality of one's life. Still, he has a strong distinction between happiness and pleasure.[2] Thomas Aquinas joins joy and happiness

1. Anderson, *Everything That Makes Me Happy I Learned When I Grew Up.*

2. Aristotle, *Nicomachean Ethics*, bk. 10, ch. 6–9. Cf. Daniel Nettle, *Happiness: The Science Behind Your Smile* (Oxford: Oxford University Press, 2005) 17ff. Nicholas White, *A Brief History of Happiness* (Oxford: Blackwell, 2006) 1.

together only in the eschaton in a kind of "perfect happiness," again, a kind of state.³ Augustine agrees with Aristotle that all seek to be happy, but gold, for example, can always be lost once you possess it. "God you will possess as soon as you desire him."⁴ Kant includes the fulfillment of duty along with happiness as "the greatest good."⁵ J. S. Mill represents the modern return to happiness as the avoidance of pain and the achievement of pleasure.⁶ What unites the Greeks and the Enlightenment is the belief that happiness is something that can be achieved by human effort. The pre-socratic Greeks often viewed themselves as pawns of the gods, with lives that were determined by the gods' will. The Enlightenment philosophers were also liberated from the will of God, in this case Christian, and in Kant's case added the ability to fulfill the categorical imperative of duty.⁷ In the theological and Christian view of joy, the joy of Jesus, we are speaking of an action, the action of Jesus's active faith, obedience, worship, and service to the Father. This includes joy. The Gospels do not permit us to speak of Jesus as being "happy." If we speak of the joy of Jesus we certainly run the risk of turning Jesus into a "happy face," Thomas Currie reminds us.⁸ C. S. Lewis speaks of a strong distinction between happiness and joy. "I didn't go to religion to make me happy. I always knew a bottle of Port would do that. If you want a religion to make you feel really comfortable, I certainly don't recommend Christianity."⁹ Lewis apparently had nothing against a bottle of Port but he saw that as something different than joy. So it is with happiness and joy, at least theologically speaking, as we will see from the perspective of the joy of Jesus.

Yet I do not want to quickly "spiritualize" joy. There are many kinds and many definitions and manifestations of joy. Perhaps that is the beginning of the problem of joy. The usually dour Bob Dylan was ecstatic about

---

3. Aquinas, *Summa Theologica*, II of II, Q. 28, Art. 3.

4. *St. Augustine on the Psalms*, vol. 2. Ancient Christian Writers 30, trans. Dame Scholastica Hebgin and Dame Felicitas Corrigan (New York: Newman, 1961) 132.

5. White, *Brief History of Happiness*, 131ff.

6. Ibid., 70–72.

7. See Darren M. McMahon, *Happiness: A History* (New York: Grove, 2006) 60–62, 137.

8. Thomas W. Currie III, *The Joy of Ministry* (Louisville: Westminster John Knox, 2008) 80.

9. C. S. Lewis, "Answers to Questions on Christianity" in *God in the Dock: Essays on Theology and Ethics*, ed. Walter Hooper (Grand Rapids: Eerdmans, 1970) 58.

romantic love in 1970 in the song "New Morning."[10] I enjoyed getting the comic book in the mail. I enjoy a classic "In 'N Out Burger." I enjoy watching the "Wichita Wingnuts" baseball team. The joy of listening to Vin Scully, over fifty years the broadcast voice of the Los Angeles Dodgers, is a small but important joy for me. Friends that share my passions bring me joy. Roger Hill was "desperately seeking posters of movie monsters" according to a column in *Famous Monsters of Filmland* magazine number 22 in 1963, and he still today shares the same joy that I have in Universal monster movies, old comic books, and classic science fiction. But I have heard a church executive comment that he can "enjoy" worship, although we hesitate to use that term! Why is that? Does the manifold nature of joy, instead, testify to the richness of joy, that joy has so many sides and it can be defined in so many ways? Even Michael Polanyi, the philosopher of science, does not hesitate to speak of the moment of discovery in the scientific method as releasing "a great joy."[11] Joy can have its profane and sublime moments.

The joys of childhood are often our most profound joys. Memories of curling up with a copy of the "all Krypton issue" of what seemed to be a huge "80 page Giant" *Superman Annual* still bring me a warm feeling. A charming photo on the cover of the collectors' magazine, *Comic Book Marketplace*, shows three kids lying against a picket fence, obviously in summer, taking in the smell of the green grass while they are gripped by their copies of their "giant" comic books.[12] Summer is filled with rituals, Ray Bradbury reminds us in his stories of growing up in Waukegan, Illinois, *Dandelion Wine*. "The ritual of lemonade or ice-tea making, the ritual of wine, shoes or no shoes, and at last, swiftly following the others, with quiet dignity, the ritual of the front-porch swing."[13] Ray Anderson suggests that "liturgy" and "ritual" are not just pictures of formality but natural rites of reinforcing that which is human.[14] The many-sided natures of these rituals remind us of the multiplicity of joy. But does joy end up meaning everything and therefore nothing?

10. Bob Dylan, "New Morning." Online: http://www.bobdylan.com/#/songs/new-morning.

11. Michael Polanyi, *Personal Knowledge: Towards a Post-Critical Philosophy* (Chicago: University of Chicago Press, 1958) 122.

12. *Comic Book Marketplace*, Gemstone Publishing 35 (May, 1966).

13. Bradbury, *Dandelion Wine*, 31–33.

14. Anderson, *On Being Human*, 181ff.

There is a difference between giddiness, fun, and the joy of Jesus. Alexander Schmemann puts it well: "This world is having fun; nevertheless it's joyless because joy (different from what is called 'fun') can only be from God, only from on high . . . God saved the world through joy."[15] But can we avoid viewing this as a religious, sentimental "joy" that is sweet but without integrity or substance, the kind of joy that does not know sorrow?

JOY IS ORDINARY YET PROFOUND

The Bible is clear that joy can be very ordinary but profound. God "has not left himself without a witness in doing good," Paul argues with the Athenians, "- giving you rains from heaven and fruitful seasons, and filling you with food and your hearts with joy" (Acts 14:17).[16] He will argue much like this with the Romans, that because of creation they are "without excuse" (Rom 1:20). Joy is something God gives, first of all, in creation. Because Paul is proclaiming the grace of God in Jesus Christ he can point to the witness of creation. We know the grace of creation because we know the grace of Jesus Christ, Karl Barth claims:

> When the grace of God is proclaimed to them in Christ, they have to concede that "God has not left Himself without a witness" . . . As they come under the light of this proclamation, the witness awakens and arises and speaks and testifies against them, so that they stand before the God who meets them in this revelation unexcused and inexcusable (Rom 1:20).[17]

The ordinary is celebrated with joy among the ancient Hebrews. The royal wedding is celebrated in Israel with joy and gladness (Ps 45:15). Echoes of Ecclesiastes can be heard here. Qoheleth exhorts his reader to "enjoy life with the wife whom you love, all the days of your vain life that are given you under the sun, because that is your portion in life and in your toil at which you toil under the sun" (Eccl 9:9). In our attempt to be priests, Ray Anderson claims, we often end up as clowns, because

---

15. Alexander Schmemann, *The Journals of Alexander Schmemann, 1973–1983*, ed. Juliana Schmemann (Crestwood, NY: St. Vladimir's Seminary Press, 2002) 137.

16. Jaroslav Pelikan, *Acts*. Brazos Theological Commentary on the Bible (Grand Rapids: Brazos, 2005) 166.

17. Barth, *CD* I/2, 305.

"holiness occurs in the street, not always in the temple."[18] "Liturgical acts" should be found "wherever humanity finds itself, no matter how tattered and torn, no matter how lost and forlorn."[19]

Pleasure is unabashedly sought by Ecclesiastes, although he finds vanity as its result:

> Whatever my eyes desired I did not keep from them; I kept my heart from no pleasure in all my toil, and this was my reward for all my toil. Then I considered all that my hands had done and the toil I had spent in doing it, and again, all was vanity and a chasing after wind, and there was nothing gained under the sun. (Eccl 1:10–11; cf. 5:18–20)

He resigns himself to find enjoyment wherever you can, yet this is from God: "There is nothing better for mortals than to eat and drink, and find enjoyment in their toil. This also, I saw, is from the hand of God; for apart from him who can eat or who can have enjoyment?" (Eccl 2:24–25; cf. 9:7). This is still vanity, however (Eccl 2:22–23, 26). Even if joy is from God, Qoheleth still yearns to find its purpose. Why seek joy in the first place? This may seem self-evident to us but human experience proves that we quickly become bored with what we thought would bring joy. The toy we yearned for at Christmas as a child is discarded after a few days. This can even be true for sex. Ray Anderson paraphrases Qoheleth in this way: "We can anticipate the point at which the greatest sensual pleasure becomes a frightful bore. We can find ourselves carried along by sensuality until we even get bored with sensuality itself."[20] Perhaps the only way is in accepting that the boredom teaches us that something else is being denied: "We become bored, disgusted, heartsick, and we realize that we have gambled away the very meaning of life because we have denied the spirit for the sake of gratifying the flesh."[21] As Aristotle would say, we are trying to fulfill a happiness that cannot satisfy the kind of creatures that human beings are.[22] Maybe we do not know who we are.

---

18. Anderson, *On Being Human*, 191.
19. Ibid.
20. Anderson, *Exploration into God*, 30.
21. Ibid., 31.
22. Aristotle, *Nicomachean Ethics*, bk. 10.

THE DESIRE FOR JOY

We may not know what joy is, but we do want it. We can say this theologically, Barth argues. "The will for life is also the will for joy . . . Even the most primitive of men does not really wish no more. Nor does he merely want to work and to contend for that which is good, true and beautiful. Even at the highest level, he does not merely want 'to love God and man.'"[23] The Christian must see this as an ethical issue. "A person who tries to debar himself from joy is certainly not an obedient person. And the question what it means to will to be happy in obedience is in its place just as serious, and its correct answering is just as important and as little self-evident, as any ethical question."[24] That is not just the "fluff" or the incidental in an otherwise serious life, in contrast to how the aesthete, the ethical person, and, yes, the religious person often take it. But how can we argue this religiously and theologically? Is there a Christian argument for joy? From monks to Puritans (at least extremes or caricatures of) religious people are hardly connected with joy at first thought. The problem of joy may not be that it is irrelevant and a waste of time for only the serious-minded religious person, but that joy seems questionable for the serious artist, the serious intellectual, the serious scientist, the serious professional, and the serious politician (although former vice-president Hubert H. Humphrey did used to speak of "the politics of joy": "Here we are the way politics ought to be in America; the politics of happiness, the politics of purpose and the politics of joy").[25]

David Bentley Hart argues that desire or longing is not an attachment to our being but is being itself.[26] Is this true, though? However our heart may be restless until it knows God (Augustine) our desires now can take on a strange character because of sin. The history of humanity is a tale of desire but desires wrought in what we *think* will bring pleasure, happiness, or joy. "All human life," Barth argues, "is either the quiet and anxious striving or the noisy hunt for this thing, developing into a bitter conflict for it, and finally ending in sad or cynical but always weary resignation when the earth has been ransacked for it in vain and it has not been found."[27] Desire, contra Hart, is not a neutral entity, but one that

23. Barth, *CD* III/4, 375.
24. Ibid.
25. Hubert H. Humphrey, Online: http://www.wisdomquotes.com/000433.html.
26. Hart, *Beauty of the Infinite*, 192.
27. Barth, *CD* IV/1, 460.

is easily perverted and twisted. The problem, Barth concludes, is simply that humanity wants to be its own helper.[28] Life is too tough, however. Drastic help is needed, yes, at the level of our being; something done for us, vicariously. This is true even for our desires and longings, as much as we cherish and protect them.

This is not to mean that God will *destroy* our desires and longings. The patience of God is an extension of his mercy, Barth argues, a patience that is expressed in grace.[29] The grace of the vicarious humanity of Christ is for the creature not against it, including our desires and longings. God "accepts the reality," Barth writes,

> For it as such, He is severe with Himself. He suffers for it. He sacrifices His only Son for it. He does it for the creature as such—which means that God's mercy does not act in such a way to overpower and blot out its object. God does not take the place of the creature in such a way as to annihilate it.[30]

Barth's critics, and critics of Protestantism in general, have often said otherwise of Barth and Protestants. Perhaps it is important to recognize here again that the first act of the incarnation and the atonement is solidarity. No, grace does not destroy nature, for the vicarious act of Christ comes first in solidarity with us, embracing the *Sehnsucht*, the joy as longing of which C. S. Lewis speaks.[31] God allows space and time to humanity, and coming into solidarity with humanity respects that.[32]

Joy as longing, or *Sehnsucht*, communicates the emotional pull of what Lewis means by joy as well as its incompleted nature, yet quite different from happiness or pleasure.[33] In its incomplete nature, joy is always reminding us of something else, perhaps a *witness*, to use Karl Barth's theological sense, in the same way the Bible is a witness to Christ.[34] Why

---

28. Ibid.
29. Barth, *CD* II/1, 411.
30. Ibid.
31. C. S. Lewis, *Surprised by Joy: The Shape of My Early Life* (New York: Harcourt, Brace, and World, 1955) 7, 16–18, 35, 72, 78, 165–66, 180, 219–21, 238. Cf. the discussion of joy as *Sehnsucht* in Corbin Scott Carnell, *Bright Shadow of Reality: C. S. Lewis and the Feeling Intellect* (Grand Rapids: Eerdmans, 1974).
32. Barth, *CD* II/1, 409–11.
33. C. S. Lewis, *Surprised by Joy*, 18.
34. Ibid., 78, 220, 238. Barth, *CD* I/2, 103.

is it that human beings are the only creatures dissatisfied?[35] He describes it pictorially as a longing for Autumn, something that is coming but it is never in our power.[36] So this is true of the joy of Jesus if it is a vicarious joy, a joy that is never in our power.

The incarnation speaks of a desire already given in the midst of the tears of this life. Joy as longing, as we see in C. S. Lewis's thought, always involves dissatisfaction, and therefore, a hint, and maybe more than a hint, of despair. The longing of today will be confirmed and renewed as the desires of Jesus are fulfilled in his joy. What we long for in the darkness is a longing for joy that has already been given in the vicarious joy of Christ. Ray Anderson writes while he was a full-time pastor in the sixties of that joy: "I do not ask that He give me greater joy than the joy I've had through tears—I only ask that He shall wipe the tears away Himself."[37] The joy given through tears is embraced by the joy of Jesus.

A second movement in the incarnation takes place that will purify and cleanse our desires in order to be in conformity with the image of God's Son (Rom 8:29). There is a proper kind of longing that forgoes immediate gratification because it seeks a deeper fulfillment.[38] The joy of Jesus is that kind of longing.

THE CELEBRATION OF JOY

Joy is an agent of celebration. "Let your fountain be blessed," exclaims Proverbs, "and rejoice in the wife of your youth" (Prov 5:18). God "gives the barren woman a home, making her the joyous mother of children" (Ps 113:9). Both youth and living many years are causes for joy (Eccl 11:8–9). The wisdom tradition is aware of both the transitory nature of this kind of joy and also the importance of claiming it as joy. The biblical foundation is laid in Genesis with Adam's exclamation at the creation of Eve: "This at last is bone of my bones and flesh of my flesh . . ." (Gen 2:23) or as Ray Anderson paraphrases it, "At last I have someone in my bed!"[39] Righteous children can make parents rejoice in ancient Israel: "The father of the

---

35. Terry Lindvall, *Surprised by Laughter: The Comic World of C. S. Lewis* (Nashville: Nelson, 1996) 55.

36. C. S. Lewis, *Surprised by Joy*, 16–18.

37. Ray S. Anderson, *Like Living Stones* (Minneapolis: Free Church, 1964) 117.

38. Anderson, *Seasons of Hope*, 68.

39. Anderson, *On Being Human*, 81.

righteous will greatly rejoice; he who begets a wise son will be glad in him. Let your father and mother be glad; let her who bore you rejoice" (Prov 23:24–25; 23:15; 29:3). The royal wedding is cause for rejoicing in ancient Israel: "With joy and gladness they are lead along as they enter the palace of the king" (Ps 45:15). God gives joy to the mother who bears a child: "He gives the barren woman a home, making her the joyous mother of children. Praise the Lord!" (Ps 113:9). Children who are righteous are a source of joy of their parents: "The father of the righteous will greatly rejoice; he who begets a wise son will be glad in him" (Prov 23:24–25). "My child, if your heart is wise, my heart too will be glad. My soul will rejoice when your lips speak what is right" (Prov 23:15–16). "A child who loves wisdom makes a parent glad, but to keep company with prostitutes is to surrender one's substance" (Prov 29:3).

Yet celebration is not a good in itself. It can often express itself as the joy of an ecstasy that is closer to possession than to freedom.[40] Joy is not giddiness but should be an expression of genuine human freedom. This is a part of our confusion about joy. We end up laughing when we should be weeping and weeping when we should be laughing, Barth reminds us.[41] We are out of sync.

Enemies can also rejoice over you: "Do not let my treacherous enemies rejoice over me, or those who hate me without cause wink the eye" (Ps 35:19) so that the innocent person cries to God,

> Vindicate me, O Lord, my God, according to your righteousness, and do not let them rejoice over me. Do not let them say to themselves, "Aha, we have our heart's desire." Do not let them say, "We have swallowed you up." Let all those who rejoice at my calamity be put to shame and confusion; let those who exalt themselves against me be clothed with shame and dishonor. Let those who desire my vindication shout for joy and be glad, and say evermore, "Great is the Lord, who delights in the welfare of his servant." (Ps 35:24–27)

C. S. Lewis remarks that one must be honest about this characteristic protest of innocence by the oppressed psalmists and should not embrace it too quickly.[42] This may express a very distinct difference between Old and New Testament religion that we must not obscure. Yet Lewis argues

---

40. Barth, *CD* IV/2, 93.
41. Ibid., 413.
42. C. S. Lewis, *Reflections on the Psalms*, 9–19.

that there is a distinction "between the conviction that one is in the right and the conviction that one is 'righteous' . . . The question whether the disputed pencil belongs to Tommy or Charles is quite distinct from the question which is the nicer little boy . . ."[43] Still, who makes the decision that the Psalmist is in the right?

GOD AS THE GIVER OF JOY

Who has the right to joy? Ultimately, only God is the giver of joy, only God is the source, and only God is the one who originally and continually rejoices. Here is where the resolution of despair meets our understanding of joy. Biblical joy is founded on the fact that God himself rejoices. And how does God rejoice today? These protests of innocence, that the psalmists' enemies would rejoice over him, are prayers; God is being implored for he is the only one who can bring about this justice, a justice of joy, if you will. "For I pray, 'Only do not let them rejoice over me, those who boast against me when my foot slips'" (Ps 38:16). The Lord will be the vindication: "Do not rejoice over me, O my enemy; when I fall, I shall rise; when I sit in darkness, the Lord will be a light to me" (Mic 7:8). Judgment will come to those who exult falsely: "Though you rejoice, though you exult, O plunderers of my heritage, though you frisk about like a heifer on the grass, and neigh like stallions, your mother shall be utterly shamed, and she who bore you shall be disgraced" (Jer 50:11–12). Ezekiel portrays quite a party, almost like a tent revival meeting, when Ammon rejoices over Israel: "For thus says the Lord God: Because you have clapped your hands and stamped your feet and rejoiced with all the malice within you against the land of Israel, therefore I have stretched out my hand against you, and will hand you over as plunder to the nations" (Ezek 25:6–7). There are dire consequences if one has gloated over the misfortune of Israel: "But you should not have gloated over your brother on the day of his misfortune; you should not have rejoiced over the people of Judah on the day of their ruin; you should not have boasted on the day of distress" (Obad 12). So also it is wisdom not to rejoice when your enemies stumble: "Do not rejoice when your enemies fall, and do not let your heart be glad when they stumble, or else the Lord will see it and be displeased, and turn away his anger from them" (Prov 24:17–18). Joy is a slippery, complicated

---

43. Ibid., 17.

human phenomenon that one must approach with fear and trembling because God, and God's joy, is the foundation for true joy.

We try to help ourselves to joy but miserably fail. We need a helper, in our place, a vicarious help. This is not to deny that we can do many things in life to help ourselves, but, as Barth argues, we need to recognize our limit.[44] We cannot give life when only God can give life. So that is true with joy. Yes, we have our joys, but they are limited, transitory, and vulnerable. To be the arbiter of joy is only humanity trying to be its own lord and judge, a task of which we will always fail.[45]

JOY AS TRANSITORY

There is a kind of joy that is real yet ephemeral; it quickly fades away. This can even be religious, as Jesus tells in the parable of the sower: "As for what was sown on rocky ground, this is the one who hears the word and immediately receives it with joy; yet such a person has no root, but endures only for a while . . ." (Matt 13:20). The problem seems to be that despite the joy, external desires and opposition are mightier: ". . . And when trouble or persecution arises on account of the word, that person immediately falls away" (Matt 13:20). Just as "immediately" the word was received with joy, so "immediately" the believer falls away. Why is joy so vulnerable to "the cares of the world and the lure of wealth" that can "choke the word" so that "it yields nothing" (Matt 13:22)? Why does joy seem to contrast to hearing the word and understanding it (Matt 13:23)? The joy the disciples had in performing exorcisms is said by Jesus not to be compared with the eschatological joy: "The seventy returned with joy, saying, 'Lord, in your name even the demons submit to us!' . . . Nevertheless, do not rejoice at this, that the spirits submit to you, but rejoice that your names are written in heaven" (Luke 10:17, 20; cf. Acts 8:8). Jesus does not want them to rejoice at casting out demons? Can joy then be trusted?

Perhaps our problem is when we restrict joy to a certain pleasure (e.g., sex, wealth, or even eating) and even end up ignoring the richer meanings of joy. Goethe claimed that joy cannot be induced, but only comes by itself.[46] A more modern approach is to seek for joy, even try

---

44. Barth, *CD* IV/1, 459.

45. Ibid.

46. Cited by Verena Kast, *Joy, Inspiration and Hope*, trans. Douglas Whitaker (College Station: Texas A & M University Press, 1991) 75.

to stimulate it among children.⁴⁷ In fact, the claim is that because the modern world has forsaken religious ecstasy, we need to pursue ecstasy anew, particularly in acts of creativity.⁴⁸ Is this enough, however? Does the aesthetic always fulfill our greatest needs? This, of course, will bring us to the question of the joy of Jesus. What was (is) his joy? What is the relation of his joy to the importance that we have seen in the Bible of God's joy? Of course, this depends on how we relate God and Jesus.

THE JOY OF JESUS

The joy of Jesus is our key. "I have said these things to you so that my joy may be in you, and that your joy may be complete" (John 15:11; cf. 17:13). His joy is vicarious, on our behalf and in our place. What are "these things" that he has said so that the disciples should share in Jesus's joy? They might include hearing the voice of the bridegroom, as John the Baptist did, even in the womb (Luke 1:44; John 3:39); the shepherds speaking of the "good news of great joy for all the people: to you is born this day in the city of David a Savior, who is the Messiah, the Lord" (Luke 2:11); the rejoicing of the sower and the reaper over the fruit that is gathered for eternal life (John 4:39); Abraham rejoicing to see Jesus's day (John 8:56); the crowds rejoicing in the triumphal entry of Jesus (Luke 19:37–38) (or else the "stones" will shout out, v. 39); and Jesus rejoicing that he was not there when Lazarus died so that his disciples will believe (John 11:15). Raymond Brown comments,

> Joy is presented as flowing from the obedience and love of which Jesus has spoken. Jesus' own joy springs from his union with the Father which finds expression in obedience and love (John 14:31: "I love the Father and I do exactly as the Father has commanded me"). The obedience and love to which in turn Jesus calls his disciples both constitute and witness their union with him; and it is this union that will be the source of their joy. Thus "my joy," like "my peace" . . . is a salvific gift.⁴⁹

Brown locates the source of Jesus's joy in his obedience to the Father, an obedience that we fail at, so that we need his vicarious help. In the High

---

47. Ibid., 79.

48. Ibid., 109.

49. Raymond E. Brown, S.S., *The Gospel According to John* (xiii–xxi), Anchor Bible 29A (Garden City, NY: Doubleday, 1970) 681.

Priestly Prayer in John 17, the obedient Jesus prays to the Father, "But now I am coming to you, and I speak these things in the world so that they may have my joy made complete in themselves" (John 17:13). Jesus wants us to share in his joy! Edwyn Hoskyns comments,

> The joy of Jesus must, however, be fully reproduced in His disciples, not only in spite of Christian apostasy, but also in spite of the wider and far more general hostility of the world. They succeed to His position in the world, which still remains the theatre of the work of God for the salvation of men. As His joy was to do the work of His Father in the world, so His joy will be fulfilled in them (15:11) when the mission for the glory of the Father and the Son is committed into their hands.[50]

Calvin adds, "He calls it His *joy*, because the disciples had to receive it from Him; or if you want it more briefly, because He is the author, cause and pledge. For in us there is nothing but fear and disquiet; in Christ alone is there peace and joyousness."[51] Christian joy is therefore given to humanity, not earned, as Barth reminds us:

> Men neither appropriated it to themselves, but it came to them in and with the man Jesus. It was given them in Him and by Him . . . It was this objective joy which could and should be reproduced in the joy which they too were permitted and commanded. In the presence of the man Jesus it was already actual for them and could not be resisted or destroyed by anything or anyone—"your joy no man taketh from you." (John 16:22)[52]

The only reason for this joy, Barth adds, "is to be found quite simply in the fact that what met them in this man was the clear, redemptive mercy of God speaking quite unequivocally and authoritatively."[53] Our desperate need cries out for someone else's joy to take our place. The problem of joy is in part the "fear and disquiet" that lives in everyone of us. How then can we be joyful?

The joy of Jesus is found in what he does for the sake of those whom he loves, "who for the sake of the joy that was set before him endured the

---

50. Hoskyns, *Fourth Gospel*, 501.

51. John Calvin, *Calvin's New Testament Commentaries: The Gospel according to St. John 11–21 and the First Epistle of John*, ed. David W. Torrance and Thomas F. Torrance, trans. T. H. L. Parker (Grand Rapids: Eerdmans, 1961) 144.

52. Barth, *CD* IV/2, 182.

53. Ibid.

cross, disregarding its shame, and has taken his seat at the right hand of the throne of God" (Heb 12:2). This joy is not unconnected to his obedience to the Father. Donald Hagner responds to those who say that his joy was an unworthy motive for Jesus by adding that this

> in no way need excludes the motive of obedience to the Father and the procurement of salvation for the world. Indeed, the joy that Jesus was to experience is inseparable from the accomplishment of God's saving purposes, and thus in a fundamental sense it is a shared joy (cf. John 17:13).[54]

His joy, in contrast to our many attempts at joy, is remarkable in that, as Ray Anderson might put it, Jesus's joy was a connection of a heart seeking God to hands that did God's will.

THE JOY OF GOD

The joy of Jesus tells us of the joy of God. God is blessed because he is creator and is enjoined to rejoice in his works: "May the glory of the Lord endure forever; may the Lord rejoice in his works" (Ps 104:31). "The stability of the world depends on this rejoicing of God in his works," Calvin comments, "for did he not give vigour to the earth by his gracious and fatherly regard, as soon as he looked upon it with a severe countenance, he would make it tremble, and would burn up the very mountains."[55] God will rejoice over Israel when Israel is vindicated: "For as a young man marries a young woman, so shall your builder marry you, and as the bridegroom rejoices over the bride, so shall your God rejoice over you" (Isa 62:5). God finds joy when his people obey him:

> Then you shall again obey the Lord, observing all his commandments that I am commanding you today, and the Lord your God will make you abundantly prosperous in all your undertakings, in the fruit of your body, in the fruit of your livestock, and in the fruit of your soil. For the Lord will again take delight in prospering you, just as he delighted in prospering your ancestors, when you obey the Lord your God by observing his commandments and decrees that are written in this book of the law, because you

---

54. Donald A. Hagner, *Hebrews*, A Good News Commentary (San Francisco: Harper & Row, 1983) 197.

55. John Calvin, *Calvin's Commentaries: Commentary on the Book of Psalms*, vol. 4, trans. James Anderson (Grand Rapids: Baker, 2005) 169.

turn to the Lord your God with all your heart and with all your soul. (Deut 30:8–10)

Wisdom, who delights in creation and the human race, is the delight of God, so one is happy if one listens to wisdom: ". . . and I was daily his delight, rejoicing before him always, rejoicing in his inhabited world and delighting in the human race . . . Happy is the one who listens to me . . ." (Prov 8:30–31, 34). In the New Testament, in the parable of the talents, the ones who had invested well enter into the joy of the master: "Well done, good and trustworthy slave; you have been trustworthy in a few things, I will put you in charge of many things; enter into the joy of your master" (Matt 25:21; cf. v. 23).

God's joy is unique since he is the creator and we are the creature. This "supreme disparity between the coming of God and the going of man" needs to be recognized.[56] As such, a bridge, a mediator is needed so that we might participate in God's joy, the bridge of the vicarious humanity of Christ.

Taking upon our humanity, God possesses his own sorrow as well as joy over his creation. As Barth puts it, "the real goodness of the real God is that the contradiction of creation has not remained alien to Himself."[57] Barth can even say then that "His rejoicing and sorrow preceded ours."[58]

THE JOY OF THE BELIEVER AND THE RIGHTEOUS

If God possesses joy, it makes sense that one is exhorted to "rejoice in the Lord" (Phil 3:1; 4:4). Union with Christ is the basis for rejoicing.[59] This may be a strong argument for the deity of Christ, the *homoousion*, the same substance shared by the Father and the Son, the passionate conviction of the Nicene Fathers.[60] This union is known through faith, a faith that brings forth rejoicing: "Although you have not seen him, you love him; and even though you do not see him now, you believe in him and rejoice with an indescribable and glorious joy, for you are receiving the

56. Barth, *CD* III/2, 187.
57. Barth, *CD* III/1, 380.
58. Ibid.
59. Peter T. O'Brien, *The Epistle to the Philippians: A Commentary on the Greek Text*, New International Greek Testament Commentary (Grand Rapids: Eerdmans, 1991) 350.
60. See T. F. Torrance, editor, *The Incarnation: Ecumenical Studies in the Nicene-Constantinopolitan Creed* (Edinburgh: Handsel, 1981).

outcome of your faith, the salvation of your souls" (1 Pet 1:8–9). Trusting in God makes one glad: "Our soul waits for the Lord; he is our help and shield. Our heart is glad in him, because we trust in his holy name" (Ps 33:20–21). When one is delivered by God, there is great rejoicing: "Then my soul shall rejoice in the Lord, exulting in his deliverance" (Ps 35:9). When one is blessed by God, one rejoices, as with Mary: "My soul magnifies the Lord, and my spirit rejoices in God my Savior, for he has looked with favor on the lowliness of his servant. Surely, from now on all generations will call me blessed" (Luke 1:46–48). So Israel is exhorted to rejoice in God: "Let Israel be glad in its Maker; let the children of Zion rejoice in their King . . . Let the faithful exult in glory; let them sing for joy on their couches" (Ps 149: 3, 5). Even the king should rejoice in the Lord: "But the king shall rejoice in God; all who swear by him shall exult, for the mouths of liars shall be stopped" (Ps 63:11). When the people experience judgment, the prayer is that they would be revived again in order to rejoice in the Lord: "Will you not revive us again, so that your people may rejoice in you?" (Ps 85:6).

The righteous in the Bible are said to possess joy. Elihu is convinced that Job is not righteous because of his lack of joy: When the righteous "prays to God, and is accepted by him, he comes into his presence with joy and God repays him for his righteousness" (Job 33:26). Bildad likewise is convinced that if Job is righteous he will be rewarded by God with joy: "See, God will not reject a blameless person, nor take the hand of evildoers. He will yet fill your mouth with laughter, and your lips with shouts of joy" (Job 8:20–21). The righteous are encouraged to be glad in the Lord: "Be glad in the Lord and rejoice, O righteous, and shout for joy, all you upright in heart" (Ps 32:11). "But let the righteous be joyful; let them exult before God; let them be jubilant with joy" (Ps 68:3). "Rejoice in the Lord, O you righteous, and give thanks to his holy name!" (Ps 97:12). "Let those who desire my vindication shout for joy and be glad, and say evermore, 'Great is the Lord, who delights in the welfare of his servant" (Ps 35:27). "Rejoice in the Lord, O you righteous. Praise befits the upright" (Ps 33:1).

But who is truly righteous? Who is truly upright? Paul's letter to the Romans is a ringing indictment of both Jews and Gentiles that "all have sinned and fall short of the glory of God" (Rom 3:23). Do not the Psalms beg for someone to intervene for us, for someone who is perfectly righteous before the Father? And do they not very easily bring shame upon us? Christ is the only one who is righteous. "Certainly this man was innocent [or righteous]" (Luke 23:47). Christ "became for us wisdom from God, and righteousness and sanctification and redemption" (1 Cor 1:30). In the gospel, "the righteousness of God is revealed through faith for faith" (Rom 1:17). "We have an advocate with the Father, Jesus Christ the righteous" (1 John 2:1). No one is ready for the joy of faith, Barth claims, so "a new man is needed, a man who is radically changed in mind and thought and aspiration and will, a man who is adequate for this new thing and open to it."[61] For with the new man there comes a "no" that means that one's "day is over and that he can only perish."[62] The need for the vicarious joy of Christ is great, but accepting it is difficult, for we do not want to die to self. Barth can even speak of this as a "violent . . . assault" upon our self-will."[63] Ironically, with all of our desire for the joy that we so desperately seek to find, we fight against genuine joy, the joy of God seen in the joy of Jesus. Our existence as a sinner has been removed by Christ and therefore the existence that we knew is no more.[64] This is a rather frightening thought. At least we knew the "old man." This "new man" is something new and unknown, and therefore, frightening. Nonexistence is a terrible thought. "To be dead means not to be."[65] There is no longer any place for the will. Yet the Bible is clear that in some way we have "died" with Christ (2 Cor 5:14, 17; Col 2:20; 3:3; Gal 2:20; 6:14; Rom 6:8).[66] Only God is at work but at work in a human way in the vicarious response of Christ.

Our need extends to all of life, from worship to family and social relationships. Righteousness and joy are intermingled in worship: "Let your priests be clothed with righteousness, and let your faithful shout for joy" (Ps 132:9). When justice is done, the righteous rejoice: "When justice is done, it is a joy to the righteous, but dismay to the evildoers" (Prov 21:15). "The righteous will rejoice when they see vengeance done; they will bathe their feet in the blood of the wicked" (Ps 58:10). The future possesses hope for "the meek": "The meek shall obtain fresh joy in the Lord, and the neediest people shall exult in the Holy One of Israel" (Isa 29:19; cf.

61. Barth, *CD* IV/4, 57.
62. Barth, *CD* IV/1, 290.
63. Ibid., 291.
64. Ibid., 292.
65. Ibid., 301.
66. Ibid., 295.

Matt 5:5). In contrast, the unrighteous do not possess joy or create joy for others. Others rejoice in the good fortune of the righteous and the misfortune of the wicked: "When it goes well with the righteous, the city rejoices; and when the wicked perish, there is jubilation" (Prov 11:10). The righteous possesses a light of joy that the wicked does not have: "The light of the righteous rejoices, but the lamp of the wicked goes out" (Prov 13:9). The parents of the fool do not have joy: "The one who begets a fool gets trouble; the parent of a fool has no joy" (Prov 17:21; cf. 23:24).

THE BARRIERS TO JOY

Does joy become more of a problem as we age? This is not to deny the angst that exists in the midst of the otherwise joyful exuberance of youth. But as an adult, it seems harder to find joy in the midst of despair. The aged seminary professor once wearily asked his former student, now a successful minister, "Where's the joy?" It is hard to hear that question, as honest as it is, from someone who from all appearances is very successful in his vocation and admired as a Christian leader. But I suspect that as the years roll on, more of us will be asking that question. The opportunities for despair only increase with age; greater opportunities (and even inevitability) for losing someone we love; greater opportunities for reflecting upon life's missed chances and tragic mistakes. And, if Kierkegaard is correct, the greatest despair is the unconscious despair that catches us unaware, the "soul-sorrow" that Edward Carnell speaks of, founded upon the Kierkegaardian tension between the finite and infinite, the body and soul in the human being.[67]

As adults, we are suspicious of joy as something infantile. Those who live lives of joy are often viewed as naïve. One of the things that was remarkable about the late Tim Russert, the moderator of the political affairs television show, "Meet the Press," was the obvious joy in a life that was surrounded by the cynicism usually associated with politics. Many saw that joy as a result of his Christian faith.

"Ecstasy" does have its roots in ancient religion as the action of one literally "ek-stasis," standing out of himself to make room for a god.[68] Yet modern psychology is more likely to see joy as a repression of deep-seated

---

67. Edward J. Carnell, *Introduction to Christian Apologetics* (Grand Rapids: Eerdmans, 1948) 19–28.

68. Kast, *Joy, Inspiration and Hope*, 6. See also Anderson, "The Ek-static Community" in *Historical Transcendence and the Reality of God*, 238–51.

anxieties.[69] In fact, Verena Kast challenges psychological therapy not to give so much attention to pathologies, but to that which stimulates joy.[70]

Certainly we can too quickly rush to find an experience of joy to mask our pain and anxiety. Kast and other moderns may too quickly rush to embrace joy because of our modern, uncritical embrace of joy as being restricted to pleasure. But Kast may have a point that we also too quickly normalize the pathology, the anger, depression, and aggression, and cannot admit that joy is an essential part of being human. Is this not remarkable when we think of how someone like Tim Russert (as the countless testimonies of those who knew him shows) as the kind of person we most likely want to be around?[71] We find joy in relationships.

There is a more basic problem for joy and that is in the mind, the alienated mind.[72] A false confidence in the flesh (Heb 9:1) refuses to be the new person we are in Christ and still strives to be the creator and engineer of our joy, like when we seek to possess our faith and our obedience to God.[73] This false confidence does not need to take the form of atheism (though it can) but can be very religious and pious. God becomes my helper, the one that gives me what I think is joy. In effect, religion becomes a barrier to joy.[74] We are saying by this, Barth argues, that who else knows my needs but me? I can only be responsible for myself.[75] Our freedom, of course, feels threatened by the free grace of God.[76] But that only reveals that we do not understand freedom. The vicarious joy of Christ definitely questions our ability, but this is a questioning we do not like, but in effect reveals the insidiousness of sin as pride.

THE EXHORTATION TO "REJOICE"

The normal life of the Spirit is indicated by Paul in his list of "the fruit of the Spirit" that includes "joy" along with "love . . . peace, patience, kindness, generosity, faithfulness, gentleness, and self-control" (Gal 5:22–23).

69. Kast, *Joy, Inspiration and Hope*, 14.

70. Ibid., 20.

71. Kast, *Joy, Inspiration and Hope*, 17; Real Clear Politics, "Tim Russert (1950–2008)." Online: www.realclearpolitics/articles/2008/06/tim_russert_19502008.html.

72. T. F. Torrance, *Karl Barth: Biblical and Evangelical Theologian*, 231.

73. James B. Torrance, *Worship, Community and the Triune God of Grace*, 29, 119.

74. Barth, *CD* IV/1, 461.

75. Ibid., 462.

76. Ibid., 464.

These are social relationships, as Ray Anderson observes.[77] Paul is filled with joy when he thinks of his relationships with his churches, regardless of the challenges they face, so that his prayers for them are characterized by joy: "I thank my God every time I remember you, constantly praying with joy in every one of my prayers for all of you because of your sharing in the gospel from the first day until now" (Phil 1:3–5). He calls the Philippians "my joy and crown" (Phil 4:1; cf. 1 John 1:4; 2 John 4, 12; 3 John 3, 4; 1 Thess 2:19, 20; 3:9). Therefore, the Philippians are encouraged to *stand fast* in union with *the Lord*, in spite of the fears and attacks which assail them from without and the encroachment of false doctrine into their church life.[78]

There is almost *a vicarious function* that the Philippians serve (cf. 1 John 1:4; John 15:11). This vicarious function of the church is particularly in the relationship of joy in the midst of despair: "If one member suffers, all suffer together with it; if one member is honored, all rejoice together with it" (1 Cor 12:26). Paul can rejoice when suffering leads to repentance: "Now I rejoice, not because you were grieved, but because your grief led to repentance" (2 Cor 7:9). "I am now rejoicing in my sufferings for your sake, and in my flesh I am completing what is lacking in Christ's afflictions for the sake of his body, that is, the church" (Col 1:24). Whatever Paul means by "what is lacking in Christ's afflictions," the sufferings that he rejoices in are "for your sake," *vicarious*, on their behalf. God comforts the church by one another so that there is rejoicing in the midst of despair:

> For even when we came into Macedonia, our bodies had no rest, but we were afflicted in every way—disputes without and fears within. But God, who consoles the downcast, consoled us by the arrival of Titus, and not only by his coming, but also by the consolation with which he was consoled about you, as he told us of your longing, your mourning, your zeal for me, so that I rejoiced still more. (2 Cor 7:5–7)

In the midst of despair, the fellowship of believers is actually the body of Christ, as Christ continues his vicarious ministry. Paul expects himself to be released from prison in order to minister to the church, fulfilling

---

77. Ray S. Anderson, *An Emergent Theology for Emerging Churches* (Downers Grove, IL: InterVarsity, 2006) 67, 76, 165.

78. Ralph P. Martin, *The Epistle to the Philippians*. Tyndale New Testament Commentaries (Grand Rapids: Eerdmans, 1959) 165.

a vicarious function for the Philippians: "Since I am convinced of this, I know that I will remain and continue with all of you for your progress and joy in faith" (Phil 1:25). Epaphroditus is a source of joy because of his vicarious action, risking his life for the sake of Christ. Paul comments on him: "I am the more eager to send him, therefore, in order that you may rejoice at seeing him again, and that I may be less anxious. Welcome him then in the Lord with all joy, and honor such people, because he came close to death for the work of Christ, risking his life to make up those services that could not give me" (Phil 2:28-30; cf. 2 Cor 7:13-16). The joy of their lives are mutually intertwined: "But even if I am being poured out as a libation over the sacrifice and the offering of your faith, I am glad and rejoice with all of you—and in the same way you also must be glad and rejoice with me" (Phil 2:17-18; cf. 1 Thess 3:9 2 Tim 1:4). "I rejoice in the Lord greatly that now at last you have revived your concern for me; indeed, you were concerned for me, but had not opportunity to show it" (Phil 4:10). "I have indeed received much joy and encouragement from your love, because the hearts of the saints have been refreshed through you, my brother" (Phlm 7). Barth and Banke comment on this verse in Philemon: "Unless the congregation heeds Paul's call to 'rejoice always' (Phil 4:4) the apostle himself cannot find or have joy."[79] If Paul gets to Rome he expects that "I may come to you with joy and be refreshed in your company" (Rom 15:32). Paul desires joy from the Corinthians: "And I wrote as I did, so that when I came, I might not suffer pain from those who should have made me rejoice; for I am confident about all of you, that my joy would be the joy of all of you" (2 Cor 2:3). Paul rejoices at the joy of others (2 Cor 7:13). He rejoices when he sees their commitment to Christ: "For though I am absent in body, yet I am with you in spirit, and I rejoice to see your morale and the firmness of your faith in Christ" (Col 2:5). Hebrews thinks that leaders in the church should experience joy: "Obey your leaders and submit to them, for they are keeping watch over your souls and will give an account. Let them do this with joy and not with sighing—for that would be harmful to you" (Heb 13:17). In the Acts of the Apostles, "rejoice" is an active verb not a passive noun.[80] The Ethiopian eunuch goes on his way rejoicing after his baptism (Acts 8:39). When Barnabas "saw the grace of God, he rejoiced" (a Greek wordplay

---

79. Markus Barth and Helmut Banke, *The Letter to Philemon*, Eerdmans Critical Commentary (Grand Rapids: Eerdmans, 2000) 294-95.

80. Pelikan, *Acts*, 229-30.

between *charin*, "grace," and *ekarē*, "rejoiced") (Acts 11:23).[81] The Gentiles rejoice at news of the mission of Paul and Barnabas to the Gentiles (Acts 13:48) and the jailer and all his household rejoices, like Mary had (Luke 1:47) "that he had become a believer in God" (Acts 16:34). The Johannine community understands joy as communal: "I have said these things to you so that my joy may be in you and that your joy may be complete" (John 15:11). "But now I am coming to you, and I speak these things in the world so that they may have my joy made complete in themselves" (John 17:13). "We are writings these things so that our joy may be complete" (1 John 1:4). "Although I have much to write to you, I would rather not use paper and ink; instead I hope to come to you and talk with you face to face, so that our joy may be complete" (2 John 12). "I have no greater joy than this, to hear that my children are walking in the truth" (3 John 4). There is a primeval root for this joy in one another in the Garden of Eden. After none of the animals satisfy Adam's need for a helper, Eve is created and so Adam exclaims with joy, "This at last is bone of my bones and flesh of my flesh . . . " (Gen 2:23).

Yet Paul can accentuate the problem of joy by simply exhorting the Thessalonians to "Rejoice always" (1 Thess 5:16). "Always"? Really? How is this possible? Is this "categorical imperative" of Paul's just a practical recipe for failure, unless there is the added ingredient of the mediator, the One who can rejoice "always" when we cannot? Indeed, from church splits and schisms to failed marriages and familial spats, community is not always a source of joy!

Still, the vicarious nature of the community's rejoicing with one another, and for one another, may be a clue. There may be someone else's vicarious joy that underlies the possibility of vicarious joy in the community and Paul's daring exhortations. Can they dare to be a vicarious community? Can Paul dare to exhort them to "Rejoice!" because Christ's vicarious joy is the foundation of all such rejoicing?

THE CHILDREN OF JOY

We constantly seem to seek after joy. We know this innately as children. "Truly I tell you," Jesus says, "whoever does not receive the kingdom of God as a little child will never enter it" (Mark 10:15). "Let the little children come to me, and do not stop them; for it is to such as these that the

---

81. Ibid.

kingdom of heaven belongs" (Matt 19:14; Luke 18:15). Is this because joy is at the essence of truly being human? Yet in our cynical postmodern culture, the person of joy is mostly likely to be mocked. Joy is viewed as that which is infantile. That may be one of the insidious tricks of our culture, Ray Bradbury suggests, which demands that we become adults and forget about being children. So even today, Bradbury asks his family to give him toys as gifts: "My basement workshop and my typing office are littered with magic sets, robots, Godzillas, masks, dinosaurs and— leapin' lizards!—an eight-foot-tall Bullwinkle..."[82] There is joy in the toy. How come? Because Bradbury sees in the toy a metaphor of who we are, a compact witness to that which gives us Kierkegaardian passion. That which starts small, however, can develop into that which is great. What is a spacecraft that can take us to Mars but a toy grown large? Bradbury exclaims.[83] Jean Bethke Elshtain speaks of the wonderment that exists among dinosaur paleontologists when they spend hours upon hours searching in dust and rain for creatures that have been extinct for 60 to 75 million years.[84] Who among these paleontologists did not grow up like I did with their beloved miniature toy dinosaur set, pitting the stegosaurus against tyrannosaurus rex? Toys start the joys. Yet our culture says no, and often mocks the kind of joy that children can have. There is a particular problem of joy for adults. Do adults even end up sacrificing the joy of children (and God and Jesus!) for "pleasures," kinds of pseudo-joys? Can the vicarious joy of Christ offer an alternative that is genuinely human in an admittedly very adult world of sorrow and despair?

THE PROBLEM OF BIBLE JOY AS MUSIC, DANCING, SINGING, AND WORSHIP: "HOW COULD WE SING THE LORD'S SONG IN A FOREIGN LAND?"

Nowhere is the problem of joy more accentuated than in the phenomenon of the joy in the Bible of participation in the arts. Bible joy is particularly related to music, dancing, singing, and worship. Because God richly provides for creation (Ps 65:9–11) nature sings for joy: "The pastures of wilderness overflow, the hills gird themselves with joy, the meadows clothe

---

82. Bradbury, *Yestermorrow*, 5.

83. Ibid., 7.

84. Jean Bethke Elshtain, *Who Are We? Critical Reflections and Hopeful Possibilities* (Grand Rapids: Eerdmans, 2004) 141–42.

themselves with flocks, the valleys deck themselves with grain, they shout and sing together for joy" (Ps 65:12–13). All of the earth is exhorted to make "a joyful noise": "Make a joyful noise to God, all the earth" (Ps 66:1; cf. 97:1; 98:4–8; 100:1). Voice and instruments are also to "shout for joy": "Sing aloud to God our strength; shout for joy to the God of Jacob. Raise a song, sound the tambourine, the sweet lyre with the harp. Blow the trumpet at the new moon, at the full moon, on our festal day" (Ps 81:1–3). The festivals of Israel are essential times of worshipping with joy: "Happy are the people who know the festal shout, who walk, O Lord, in the light of your countenance; they exult in your name all day long" (Ps 89:15–16; cf. Lev 23:40). The King James Version classically translates this as "the joyful sound." Augustine preserves the spirit of this "shout":

> All this must surely delight us; but shall we be able to grasp how delighted we are? Or will words suffice to express our gladness: Will any tongue be apt to articulate our joy? . . . Or blessed people, do you think you apprehend what shouting for joy is? You cannot be blessed unless you do understand it. Oh that you may know how to rejoice in something that you cannot put into words, for your joy does not spring from yourself; rather let anyone who would glory, glory in the Lord.[85]

Augustine may be seeing the implication of the arts for theology and worship when he raises the issue of the ineffability of praise and joy before God. We need something else than just propositional statements. Joy cannot be contained in our words, if it is truly joy. Art is not just a matter of imposing on the world or simply expressing feelings but should be a *reception* of the world, as Jeremy Begbie argues.[86] The arts may function in a vicarious way in the same sense friendship does. Dietrich Bonhoeffer expresses this in a letter to his friend Eberhard Bethge: "I have the feeling that to a certain degree you also see things with my eyes, just as I see things here with yours. We thus experience our different fates for each other in a kind of vicarious way."[87] The arts function in *a vicarious way* for us, saying that which we are unable to say. This can only point us to the

---

85. Augustine, *Expositions of the Psalms, 73–98*, translated and notes by Maria Boulding and John E. Rotelle (Hyde Park, NY: New City, 2002) 284.

86. Jeremy S. Begbie, *Voicing Creation's Praise: Towards a Theology of the Arts* (New York: T. & T. Clark, 1991) 226–27.

87. Dietrich Bonhoeffer, *Letters and Papers from Prison*, 191.

Vicarious Person. We need someone else to help us with understanding and experiencing joy. This is the place for the vicarious joy of Christ.

Temple worship in ancient Israel were occasions for joy, especially when it was restored. Jehoida the priest returns the levitical priests to their joyful, singing functions:

> Jehoida assigned the care of the house of the Lord to the levitical priests whom David had organized to be in charge of the house of the Lord, to offer burnt offerings to the Lord, as it is written in the law of Moses, with rejoicing and with singing, according to the order of David. (2 Chr 23:18)

After Joash repairs the temple, "All the leaders and all the people rejoiced and brought their tax and dropped it into the chest until it was full" (2 Chr 24:10). When Hezekiah restores temple worship, it is perceived that this is God's work, and that brings joy: "And Hezekiah and all the people rejoiced because of what God had done for the people; for the thing had come about suddenly" (2 Chr 29:36). In the time of Ezra and Nehemiah, there is joy in those who serve the rebuilt temple:

> On that day men were appointed over the chambers for the stores, the contributions, the first fruits, and the tithes, to gather into them the portions required by the law for the priests and for the Levites from the fields belonging to the towns; for Judah rejoiced over the priest and the Levites who ministered. (Neh 12:44)

Worshipping at the altar includes playing the harp with joy: "Then I will go to the altar of God, to God my exceeding joy; and I will praise you with the harp, O God, my God" (Ps 43:4). A military victory is celebrated when "the women came out of all of the towns of Israel, singing and dancing, to meet King Saul, with tambourines, with songs of joy, and with musical instruments" (1 Sam 18:6). Celebration in the enthronement of Solomon involves "playing on pipes and rejoicing with great joy, so that the earth quaked at their noise" (1 Kgs 1:40). Bringing the ark to Jerusalem, "David also commanded the chiefs of the Levites to appoint their kindred as the singers to play on musical instruments, on harps and lyres and cymbals, to raise loud sounds of joy" (1 Chr 15:16).

Those who cling to God should sing for joy: "But let all who take refuge in you rejoice; let them ever sing for joy" (Ps 5:11; cf. 1 Chr 16:10). Augustine adds that to be glad, to exult, and to sing praise to God (Ps 9:2) is based on "the hidden things of the Son, where the light of your face, O Lord, has been stamped on us."[88] Reflecting upon the Lord in the nighttime, the psalmist's satisfaction with God's help makes him sing for joy: "My soul is satisfied as with a rich feast, and my mouth praises you with joyful lips when I think of you on my bed, and meditate on you in the watches of the night; for you have been my help, and in the shadow of your wings I sing for joy" (Ps 63:5–7). The congregation is urged to be joyful in singing to God: "O come, let us sing to the Lord; let us make a joyful noise to the rock of our salvation! Let us come into his presence with thanksgiving; let us make a joyful noise to him with songs of praise" (Ps 95:1–2). Because God is the source of strength and a shield to the psalmist, he joyfully sings: "The Lord is my strength and my shield; in him my heart trusts; so I am helped, and my heart exults, and with my song I give thanks to him" (Ps 28:7).

Those whom God delivers will sing with joy: "Now my head is lifted up above by enemies all around me, and I will offer in the tent sacrifices with shouts of joy; I will sing and make melody to the Lord" (Ps 27:6). "My lips will shout for joy when I sing praises to you; my soul also, which you have rescued" (Ps 71:23). The heavens and the earth are enjoined to sing with joy because of the comfort that the Lord provides his people: "Sing for joy, O heavens and exult, O earth; break forth, O mountains, into singing! For the Lord has comforted his people, and will have compassion on his suffering ones" (Isa 49:13). The Psalmist implores God: "Consider and answer me, O Lord my God! Give light to my eyes, or I will sleep the sleep of death, and my enemy will say, 'I have prevailed'; my foes will rejoice because I am shaken" (Ps 13:3–4). God's deliverance, however, will cause one to sing with joy: "But I trusted in your steadfast love; my heart shall rejoice in your salvation. I will sing to the Lord, because he has dealt bountifully with me" (Ps 13:5–6). God's deliverance is seen at its foundations in the gift of the child to Sarah that the New Testament views as occasion for rejoicing in the freedom of grace: "Rejoice, you childless one, you who bear no children, burst into song and shout, you who endure no birth pangs; for the children of the desolate woman are more numerous than the children of the one who is married" (Gal 4:27; cf. Isa 54:1; 51:1–3). Thanksgiving sacrifices should be given to the Lord, exhorts the psalmist, as they "tell of his deeds with songs of joy" (Ps 107:22). The righteous, who sing and rejoice, are contrasted with the wicked: "In

---

88. Augustine, *Expositions of the Psalms 1–32*, trans. Maria Boulding and John E. Rotelle (Hyde Park, NY: New City, 2000) 141.

the transgression of the evil there is a snare, but the righteous sing and rejoice" (Prov 29:6).

The foreigners who join themselves to the Lord will be made joyful by God: "These I will bring to my holy mountain, and make them joyful in my house of prayer; their burnt offerings and their sacrifices will be accepted on my altar; for my house shall be called a house of prayer for all peoples" (Isa 56:7; cf. Mark 11:17). Remembrance of glad time pasts include singing with joy to God: "These things I remember, as I pour out my soul: how I went with the throng and led them in procession to the house of God, with glad shouts and songs of thanksgiving" (Ps 42:4). But when judgment comes upon Israel, the joy of the dance ends: "The joy of our hearts has ceased; our dancing has been turned into mourning" (Lam 5:15).

Singing with joy is a feature of the eschatological reality, first of all, in nature: "The wilderness and the dry land shall be glad, the desert shall rejoice and blossom; like the crocus its shall blossom abundantly, and rejoice with joy and singing" (Isa 35:1–2) and in Zion: "And the ransomed of the Lord shall return, and come to Zion with singing; everlasting joy shall be upon their heads; they shall obtain joy and gladness, and sorrow and sighing shall flee away" (Isa 35:10; cf. 51:11). The young and the old will rejoice, as the women particularly will dance with joy: "Then shall the young women rejoice in the dance, and the young men and the old shall be merry, I will turn their mourning into joy, I will comfort them, and give them gladness for sorrow" (Jer 31:13). Both nature and Zion join together in the eschatological rapture of song: "For you shall go out with joy, and be led back in peace; the mountains and the hills before you shall burst into song, and all the trees of the field shall clap their hands" (Isa 55:12). The wicked will be judged as the servants of the Lord will rejoice with song: "My servants shall sing for gladness of heart, but you shall cry out for pain of heart" (Isa 65:14). Singing with joy comes when judgment will no longer be an issue for Israel and her enemies will be defeated: "Sing aloud, O daughter of Zion! Shout, O Israel! Rejoice and exult with all your heart, O daughter Jerusalem! The Lord has taken away the judgments against you, he has turned away your enemies" (Zeph 3:14–15). But why has judgment been averted? God will be in their midst, so Israel is exhorted to rejoice with joy:

> Sing and rejoice, O daughter Zion! Shout aloud, O daughter Jerusalem! For lo, I will come and dwell in your midst, says the

> Lord. Many nations shall join themselves to the Lord on that day, and shall be my people; and you shall know that the Lord of hosts has sent me to you. (Zech 2:10–11)

It was Dietrich Bonhoeffer who so clearly saw the connection between Jesus's worship of the Father and Christian worship and prayer, particularly in the Psalms. Only he can offer the "perfect worship."[89] Jesus Christ is the setting up of our praise, "the normative original of the praise to be ascribed to God by man, the prototype of all doxology as the self-evident response to, and acknowledgment of, the self-demonstration which has come to man from God."[90] Through a correspondence with his vicarious humanity, the Holy Spirit enables us to pray and worship with him. Jesus is "the Bearer and Proclaimer" of the beneficent God, inviting us "to pray with Him."[91] This is so our prayers would be echoes of his, so our worship should become a "liturgical amen" to the worship Christ the high priest offers.[92] He is the *leitourgos,* "the minister in the sanctuary" (Heb 8:2) who is able to fulfill the worship of God that gathers up and replaces the worship of Israel.[93] Calvin, commenting on Hebrews 2:12, can even say that "Christ leads our songs, and is the chief composer of our hymns."[94]

The problem of joy is made acute by the difficulty of prayer. Who has not felt listless in one's prayer and worship life? Joy in worship then seems to be a mockery of ourselves . . . and of God. Since prayer is an essential part of worship, Calvin connects our prayers with the "mouth" of Christ in his *Geneva Catechism* (1541): In answer to the question, "It is not, then, temerity or foolish presumption on our part, if we presume to address God personally, seeing that we have Jesus Christ for our Advocate, and if we set Him before us, that God may for His sake be gracious to us and accept us?" Calvin answers, "No, for we pray as it were by His mouth, since He gives us entrance and audience, and intercedes for us (Rom 8:34)."[95]

---

89. Bonhoeffer, *Psalms*, 41.
90. Barth, *CD* IV/3.1, 48; cf. I/2, 424.
91. Barth, *CD* III/1, 38–39.
92. James B. Torrance, *Worship, Community and the Triune God of Grace*, 14.
93. Ibid., 16.

94. John Calvin, *Calvin's Commentaries: Commentaries on the Epistle of Paul the Apostle to the Hebrews*, trans. John Owen (Grand Rapids: Baker, 2005) 67; cf. James B. Torrance, "The Vicarious Humanity of Christ and the Priesthood of Christ in the Theology of John Calvin" in *Calvinus Ecclesiae Doctor*, ed. Wilhelm H. Neuser (Kampen, Netherlands: Kok, 1979) 70.

95. *Calvin's Geneva Catechism, 1541*, in *School of Faith*, ed. T. F. Torrance, 44.

Karl Barth sees this claim by Calvin as a guarantee of the foundation of prayer in Christ's prayers and Christ continuing to pray:

> And we ourselves pray as though his mouth, inasmuch as he gives us access and audience, and intercedes for us. Thus, fundamentally, our prayer is already made even before we formulate it. When we pray, we can only return to that prayer which was uttered in the person of Jesus Christ and which is constantly repeated because God is not without humankind.[96]

Our prayers are efficacious because "God cannot fail to answer, since it is Jesus Christ who prays."[97] Christ's prayers, worship, and joy are always *before* ours. In fact, would it really be a joy of substance and durability if it depends upon our abilities to sustain it?

These prayers of Christ are an essential part of the "double movement" of the incarnation that finds a parallel double movement in the sending of the Spirit and the response of prayer in the Spirit.[98] No wonder that Paul sees the Spirit as enabling us to pray, interceding for us when we are unable (Rom 8:26).

---

96. Barth, *Prayer*, 14.

97. Ibid.

98. T. F. Torrance, *Christian Doctrine of God*, 152–53; cf. Alan Torrance, *Persons in Communion: Trinitarian Description and Human Participation* (Edinburgh: T. & T. Clark, 1996) 224–25.

CHAPTER SEVEN

Can We Live with Both Joy and Despair?

THE NEED FOR JOY AND THE INEVITABILITY OF DESPAIR

Joy is so human because we seek it so badly at the moment of pain and sorrow. As Ray Anderson comments, therapists will say that the greatest difficulty with people in emotional pain is their desire to get out of the pain too quickly.[1] In Proverbs we find one of the most embarrassing verses in the Bible: "Give strong drink to one who is perishing, and wine to those in bitter distress; let them drink and forget their poverty and remember their misery no more" (Prov 31: 6–7). John Cassian tries to spiritualize wine as the antidote to despair by saying: "To those filled with bitter regret and sadness over their earlier lives give abundantly the joy of spiritual knowledge like 'a wine which gladdens the heart of a man' (Ps 103:5)."[2] However shocking Proverbs' remedy may be to some, Cassian does see the point of how important joy is in the midst of the various trials of life. At times in our lives we may need to be given joy and maybe some wine can be helpful! The broader point is that we cannot do without joy. Yet at what price? Job regrets that there was any joyful cry with his birth: "Yes, let that night be barren; let no joyful cry be heard in it" (Job 3:7). First Peter sees persecution as the source for joy because it is through persecution that faith is tested: "In this you rejoice, even if now for a little while you have had to suffer various trials, so that the genuineness of your faith—being more precious than gold that, though perishable, is tested by fire—may be found to result in praise and glory and honor when Jesus

---

1. Ray S. Anderson, *The Soul of God: A Theological Memoir* (Eugene, OR: Wipf & Stock, 2004) 103.

2. John Cassian, *Conferences*, Conference 9, 117.

Christ is revealed" (1 Pet 1:6–7). In Matthew, Jesus says that when one is persecuted "falsely on my account," one should "rejoice and be glad, for your reward is great in heaven, for in the same way they persecuted the prophets who were before you" (Matt 5:11–12). Luke adds that the rejoicing in persecution should include a "leap for joy" (Luke 6:23)! Is it not difficult enough to be joyful in persecution but one is to "leap for joy" as well? To make a hero of the persecuted is one thing; to be persecuted yourself is another. Is the persecution worth the joy? We might sometimes honestly wonder. A "dark side" of joy exists in the German word, *Schadenfreude*, the joy in some else's despair.[3] This is a "vicarious joy" of the demons, if you will, joy on behalf of others' misfortune. Joy, in other words, is not always to be approached with glad anticipation. Even the Greek god Dionysus, the god of revelry and wine, was approached simultaneously with terror.[4] Sorrow and joy can be found held too closely together.

Despair is inevitable but that does not mean it is only the polar opposite of joy. We know this because God's Word genuinely meets the reality of humanity in Jesus Christ but does not thereby surrender his deity. As joy corresponds to the divine revelation so despair is found in the reality of the human, with all of its temptations to not only claim a place at the table with joy but also to dominate and overcome joy.[5] Does not Jesus reveal that true humanity embraces the ebbs and flows of life, including the joys and the sorrows? Jesus was the man of the resurrection, but he was also the man of the cross. Taking upon our life, he affirms our communal pilgrimage. Ray Anderson sees the importance of embracing all of the "seasons of life": "At any given time we are part of a community where birth and death, joy and sorrow, pain and pleasure, as well as sowing and harvest are taking place. This communal sharing of life replicates all the 'seasons of life' . . . This rhythm of human life is meant to carry the risk of each person's existence."[6] Did not Jesus live this rhythm of life?

Everything human exists with joy and sorrow, G. K. Chesterton writes.[7] The only question is how they are balanced or divided. This is the distinction between the Christian and the pagan, Chesterton claims. Despite the belief that paganism is the religion of joy and Christianity the

3. Kast, *Joy, Inspiration, and Hope*, 85–86.
4. Ibid., 116.
5. Barth, *CD* I/2, 790–91.
6. Anderson, *Seasons of Hope*, 11.
7. G. K. Chesterton, *Orthodoxy* (Garden City, NY: Image, 1959) 158.

religion of sorrow, it is the pagan who gets sadder and sadder because one does not know of life after death. The pagan ends up being joyful over little things but sad over the big things.[8] Joy and despair are inevitable but for the pagan joy has no future. For the Christian, it does.

Yet how does the Christian avoid simply trusting in a cheery optimism that "all will be well"? Does joy have to be naïve? Can the joy of Jesus himself be the criterion for a joy that resists naivete while embracing the inevitability of despair as well?

THE MIXTURE OF JOY AND DESPAIR?

Ancient Israel experienced this mixture joy and sorrow when the new temple was built and for some it only caused them to remember the glory of the original temple:

> And all the people responded with a great shout when they praised the Lord, because the foundation of the house of the Lord was laid. But many of the priests and Levites and heads of families, old people who had seen the first house on its foundations, wept with a loud voice when they saw this house, though many shouted aloud for joy, so that the people could not distinguish the sound of the joyful shout from the sound of the people's weeping, for the people shouted so loudly that the sound was heard far away. (Ezra 3:11–13)

The mixture of joy and sorrow in the cacophony of rejoicing and weeping cannot be distinguished from one another. This indeed summarizes the problem of joy and despair. Yet this may be a great opportunity for us to see the relevance of the vicarious despair and the vicarious joy of Christ. Do either joy or sorrow end up meaning anything if they cannot be distinguished from one another? Or is this simply to be realistic about life? The account of the resurrection of Jesus in the Gospel of Matthew is striking in that Matthew reports that the initial reaction to reports of the resurrected Jesus was one of both fear and joy: "So they left the tomb quickly with fear and great joy, and ran to tell the disciples" (Matt 28:8). Yet Matthew quickly follows with the meeting with Jesus himself: "Suddenly Jesus met them and said, "Greetings!" (*Chairete*, which can also mean "rejoice" or "be glad.") And they came to him, took hold of his

---

8. Ibid., 159.

feet, and worshipped him" (Matt 28:9).⁹ The presence of Jesus, imploring them to rejoice, leads them to worship him. In the midst of the conflict of both fear and joy, Jesus brings joy himself and proves himself to be lord and worthy of being worshipped. Luke reports that joy and unbelief were mixed together when the disciples were met by the resurrected Jesus: "While in their joy they were disbelieving . . ." (Luke 24:41). Calvin suggests that while their joy arose from faith, it became "an obstacle that stopped their faith emerging victorious," a cause to "suspect the intensity of our emotions."[10] A modern commentator, Joseph Fitzmyer, sees Luke using joy as an excuse for the disciples' disbelief (cf. Luke 24:11).[11] But do not both commentators refuse to allow the mystery of fear and joy to stand together? This is a part of the problem of joy living with despair.

The dialectic of sorrow and joy together was a reality not unknown to the early church. Paul speaks of the generosity of the churches of Macedonia toward the church of Jerusalem as coming forth during a time of "a severe ordeal of affliction," when "their abundant joy and their extreme poverty have overflowed in a wealth of generosity on their part" (2 Cor 8:2). The early church had learned to live with joy in the midst of affliction and poverty and that bore fruit in their ministry of generosity to the needy church of Jerusalem. In this, the church saw its utter need as allowing a place for the continuing life and ministry of Christ to work. The churches of Macedonia did not see themselves as taking the place of an absent Christ, a "vicarious humanity of the church," but believing that Christ continues to take their place and act on their behalf as substitute and representative. So Paul can easily transition to a theological foundation for this exhortation to the Corinthians to also contribute to the church of Jerusalem in its need: "I do not say this as a command, but I am testing the genuineness of your love against the earnestness of others. For you know the generous act (*charin*, "grace" in the NIV) of our Lord Jesus Christ, that though he was rich, yet for your sakes he became poor, so that by his poverty you might become rich" (2 Cor 8:9). This, of course is the classic verse concerning "the wonderful exchange" beloved by the *Epistle to Diognetus* among the Apostolic Fathers and John Calvin among

---

9. Hans Conzelmann, "*chairō, chará, synchairō*," TDNT, 9:359–76.

10. Calvin, *Calvin's New Testament Commentaries: A Harmony of the Gospels: Matthew, Mark and Luke*, vol. 3, 243.

11. Joseph A. Fitzmyer, S.J., *The Gospel According to Luke (X–XXIV)*, Anchor Bible 28A (Garden City, NY: Doubleday, 1985) 1576.

the Reformers; the verse that speaks so loudly of the ontological nature of the atonement, the vicarious humanity, not just death, of Christ. He took upon all of our need so that we might partake of his riches, his very life (cf. Phil 2:5–11). Paul is then able to live with the conflicting emotions brought about by his relationship with the Corinthians: "I often boast about you; I have great pride in you; I am filled with consolation; I am overjoyed in all our affliction" (2 Cor 7:4).

So the early church was aware that joy and sorrow may live together, and in this way came to understand the nature of affliction and suffering for the Christian: "My brothers and sisters, whenever you face trials of any kind, consider it nothing but joy, because you know that the testing of your faith produces endurance; and let endurance have its full effect, so that you may be mature and complete, lacking in nothing" (Jas 1:2). Hope is sometimes seen to be the opposite of despair. The moral exhortation to rejoice in hope comes in the midst of the negation of suffering: "Rejoice in hope, be patient in suffering, persevere in prayer" (Rom 12:12). Our rejoicing in hope is an ethical behavior, Barth argues, because hope stands before the negation of what we cannot see: "For in hope we were saved. Now hope that is seen is not hope. For who hopes for what is seen?" (Rom 8:24).

> The sense of present possession, to have and not to need to wait—this is the opposite of hope. To *rejoice in hope* means to know God in hope without seeing Him, and to be satisfied that is should be so. This is what makes of hope an ethical action; for to hope in God turns hope into a joyful act which cannot be brought to naught.[12]

"Without seeing" is rejoicing in hope through the vicarious hope of Jesus. Joy is a problem because God seems to command it. As Barth observes,

> It is astonishing and certainly does not need to be verified by quotations how many references there are in the Old and New Testaments to delight, joy, bliss, exultation, merry-making and rejoicing, and how emphatically these are demanded from the Book of Psalms to the Epistle to the Philippians.[13]

In fact, Barth comments that the command to rejoice arises in the midst of the Bible's "dark places" where it speaks of terror, gloom, judgment,

---

12. Barth, *Epistle to the Romans*, 457.
13. Barth, *CD* III/4, 375.

and darkness, "because God the Creator and Lord of life acts and speaks here, taking the lost cause of man out of his hand, making it His own, intervening majestically, mercifully and wisely for him."[14] "Out of his hand" is another way of speaking of the vicarious joy of Christ, and joy that comes in the midst of terror, gloom, judgment, darkness, and despair. Therefore joy has been qualified, Barth continues. "It has been destroyed on the one hand, and reconstituted and validated, and even raised to the level of a command. Christ is risen. He is truly risen. Joy is now joy before the Lord and in Him."[15]

Yet because it is the joy of the Word who became flesh, it is a very real human joy: "the joy of harvest, wedding, festival and victory; the joy not only on the inner but also of the outer man; the joy in which one may and not drink wine as well as eat bread, sing and play as well as speak, dance as well as pray."[16] His vicarious joy takes our place in death and resurrection so we do not own this joy yet it is very human even as it is given to us by his grace. "Give what you command and command what you will," Augustine famously prayed, and all Pelagians have been offended ever since.[17] God fulfills the command to rejoice in the vicarious rejoicing of the man Jesus.

THE INCARNATION AS THE FOUNDATION FOR JOY AND DESPAIR

Joy and sorrow can only live together for the Christian because the incarnation, the Word who became flesh, comes first into solidarity with our humanity, our humanity that experiences both joy and sorrow. So Christians are to "rejoice with those who rejoice, weep with those who weep" (Rom 12:15). The vicarious humanity of Christ must take our place since our tendency is only to rejoice with those who are joyful when we are joyful or weep with those who are weeping when we are sorrowful. We need to be taken out of ourselves. Joy and sorrow, Barth argues, are not simply "extremes of the biological-erotic emotion."[18] Stoicism and moralism seek to put emotions against each other and ignore the "other." "The unknowableness of the Son of God" reveals that we do not know.

14. Ibid.
15. Ibid.
16. Ibid., 376.
17. Augustine, *Confessions*, 10.29.40.
18. Barth, *Epistle to the Romans*, 459–60.

We must depend on him. We must depend on his vicarious humanity, a humanity that embraces both those who rejoice and those who weep. So Paul can say, "If one member suffers, all suffer together with it; if one member is honored, all rejoice together with it" (1 Cor 12:26). Yet, as John Chrysostom observes, there is a problem of how they all rejoice together, unless "the head is crowned": "But how do they rejoice together you may ask. The head is crowned and the whole person is honored. The mouth speaks and the eyes laugh with happiness, even though the credit does not belong to the beauty of the eyes but to the tongue..."[19] The head, of course, is Christ.

All of salvation history is summed up in Christ, the *totus Christus* who is *Christus Victor*.[20] Christ is not just the summary or end the climax of salvation history, but, in Barth's words, "the establishing and the establishment, truth and verification, the enlightening and the enlightenment, the address and the answer."[21] This must be true also in relation to joy and despair. He is not just the joy who is the answer to our despair, but neither is his joy simply to eternally live in harmony with his despair. His resurrection will not allow that. Baptism is our participation in the death and resurrection, despair and joy, if you will, of Christ. Dying (and despair) will not be given the ontological status of resurrection (and joy). Our "amen" in baptism (by us the individual or the church) is an "amen" to death, and "there is nothing more passive than dying, being buried, being baptized," as James Torrance laconically remarks.[22]

As the *totus Christus*, the total Christ in the entirely of our humanity, he meets us in communion in both a broken form (as the bread is broken) and then in the exalted prayer (the prayer of thanksgiving), as the ascended Lord whose priesthood continues as he continues to be our very human priest in heaven, the significance of the doctrine of the ascension.[23] In this way, there is a "presence-in-absence" (notwithstanding Lutheran objections to the "extra-Calvinisticum"). Christ is there in the bread and cup and in heaven; he is there in our despair (the bread and the cup) and in our joy (heaven). As Gerrit Dawson writes, Christ's ascension

19. John Chrysostom in *The Church's Bible: I Corinthians Interpreted by Early Christian Commentators*, trans. and ed. Judith L. Kovacs (Grand Rapids: Eerdmans, 2005) 209.
20. Barth, *CD* IV/3.1, 216.
21. Ibid.
22. James B. Torrance, *Worship, Community and the Triune God of Grace*, 77.
23. Ibid., 87.

"did not mean the removal of Christ's presence from the earth as if the gift given in the incarnation were withdrawn."[24] The Orthodox theologian John Zizioulas speak of this "presence-in-absence" as a "capacity-in-incapacity" that he connects with human personhood.[25]

The very life, death, and resurrection of Christ of humiliation (death) and exaltation (resurrection and ascension) (Phil 2:5–11) reflects both despair and joy. This antithesis between humiliation and exaltation mirrors a trinitarian reality in God's own being, Barth argues, in which neither one is alien to God.[26] As Barth also comments, "It is not only from a distance that God has reacted against this enemy as against one who has disturbed the peace of the created reality distinct from Himself, but whose evil work did not in any way affect His own life and being . . . God Himself is affected and disturbed and harmed by it."[27] Barth can even say that God "hazards no less than His being as God to encounter it."[28] Therefore, he is not surprised by our despair for the lowliness of despair already exists in the eternal obedience of the Son to the Father. That there exists an "obedience in God" from all eternity is questioned by some, but this does allow Barth to see that the depths of despair are not something that God cannot know or experience.[29] As Alan E. Lewis argues, the descent of Christ into hell is not just to proclaim the gospel to the dead (1 Pet 3:19) but an expression of "the vicarious nature of our Lord's humanity," that there is real failure and real abandonment in the death and burial ("Holy Saturday") of Christ.[30] The brokenness of creation is reflected in the importance of apocalyptic

---

24. Gerrit Scott Dawson, *Jesus Ascended: The Meaning of Christ's Continuing Incarnation* (Phillipsburg, NJ: P & R, 2004) 95.

25. John Zizioulas, *Communion and Otherness: Further Studies in Personhood and the Church*, ed. Paul McPartlan (New York: T. & T. Clark, 2006) 219, previously published in "Human Capacity and Human Incapacity," *Scottish Journal of Theology* 28 (1975) 420; cf. Anderson, *On Being Human*, 177; Anderson, *Historical Transcendence and the Reality of God*, 240 n.29.

26. Barth, *CD* IV/2, 351.

27. Ibid., 401.

28. Ibid.

29. T. F. Torrance, *Karl Barth: Biblical and Evangelical Theologian*, 131–32; and "My Interaction with Karl Barth," in *How Karl Barth Changed My Mind*, ed. Donald K. McKim (Grand Rapids: Eerdmans, 1986) 60–61.

30. Alan E. Lewis, *Between Cross and Resurrection*, 39 n.43.

language in the gospel story.[31] The world of apocalyptic is not a safe world but a world of earthquakes, rivers of blood, and a cross.

In a similar way, the resurrection of Christ does not just attest our longings or human questions but *an actuality of joy* in his resurrection victory.[32] This will be important to remember in assessing C. S. Lewis's embrace of joy as *Sehnsucht,* a "longing." The fearfulness, despair, and sorrow of the disciples, coupled with their joy at seeing the risen Christ, resulted in the triumph of resurrection joy, a joy that they did not and could not anticipate in all of their fondest longings. Their failure to see that did lessen the reality of Easter morning.[33] In all this, there is one Christ, the *totus Christus,* who was humiliated (despair) for the sake of our exaltation (joy) with him.[34]

JOY AND DESPAIR IN THE CHRISTIAN LIFE

The problem of both joy and sorrow involves affirming that which is in the other person, a genuine reality of sorrow. That is why the first movement of the incarnation is the "humanward" movement, from God to humanity. This is the essential precursor to the second movement, the "Godward" movement, from humanity to God, which is more strictly the movement of the vicarious humanity of Christ. But without first the movement of solidarity, atonement and salvation cannot grasp with genuine human emotions of both joy and sorrow and instead end up simply offering a religious category of "sainthood," "mysticism," "deification," "holiness," or "sanctification," all good terms in themselves, but that easily degenerate into the *homo religiosus* that Bonhoeffer warns us about.[35] Yet this movement of solidarity, of Christ sitting at table with sinners and publicans, is so risky, Barth adds that this might "include Jesus Christ among the

---

31. Greene, *Christology in Cultural Perspective,* 351, 377–78. Cf. *The Apocalyptic Jesus: A Debate,* ed. Robert J. Miller (Santa Rosa, CA: Polebridge, 2001); Dale C. Allison, Jr., *Jesus of Nazareth: Millenarian Prophet* (Minneapolis: Fortress, 1998); *Resurrecting Jesus: The Earliest Christian Tradition and Its Interpreters* (New York and London: T. & T. Clark, 2005); *The Historical Christ and the Theological Jesus* (Grand Rapids: Eerdmans, 2009).

32. Barth, *CD* IV/3.2, 835.
33. Barth, *CD* IV/2, 187.
34. Ibid., 356.
35. Bonhoeffer, *Letters and Papers from Prison,* 135.

sinners," as questionable as that might be.³⁶ But is this not the challenge of all pastoral care and Christian comfort? The vicarious joy and sorrow of Christ pushes out of the way our desire to be as God, especially a God of pure transcendence and no immanence. This contrasts with our need for humility, Barth claims in his shorter *Romans* commentary:

> But even so—sharing joy and sorrow with them—he follows a definite course, which is determined by the unity of the Church and her mandate. He will not join in the particular upward impulse and instinct, in the desire to be as God, which is so characteristic of the world which has not yet heard the Gospel. The Christian will always be found where God's grace in Jesus Christ has found him, in the humility of one who knows that, for time and eternity, he owes nothing to his own wisdom and strength in the lowliness of one—in whatever position he may be, in joy or in sorrow, in success or in failure, the majority or in a minority—who has been accepted, whom God has admitted to his way and his work. A Christian can always be found where man's humanity is stressed in contrast to any likeness to God (12:16).³⁷

Our desire to make the "upward impulse and instinct," to be "like God" (Gen 3:5), is graciously displaced by the vicarious humanity of Christ so that to be "participants in the divine nature" (2 Pet 1:4) does not mean "deification" but that the self-giving life of God takes us into his life by adoption as sons and daughters of God (Gal 4:5). As T. F. Torrance comments,

> The Greek Fathers used to speak of that experience as *theopoiesis* or *theosis* which does not mean "divinisation," as is so often supposed, but refers to the utterly staggering act of God in which he gives *himself* to us and *adopts us* into the communion of his divine life and love through Jesus Christ and in his one Spirit, yet is such a way that we are not made divine but are preserved in our humanity.³⁸

We are preserved in our humanity only because God has taken it upon himself to renew and restore it in the vicarious humanity of Christ, starting with our experiences of joy and sorrow. Radical substitution preserves our humanity rather than solely a "humanward" movement of a Word of God that may ironically either destroy our humanity or ignore it, at least

---

36. Barth, *Epistle to the Romans*, 460.
37. Barth, *Shorter Commentary on Romans*, 155–56.
38. T. F. Torrance, *Mediation of Christ*, 64.

leaving it untouched. The substitutionary life, death, and resurrection of Christ removes any possibility of a "harmony of being" or "peaceful co-existence of God" with sin, despair, and brokenness.[39] The quest for sanctification and holiness so often becomes shipwreck on a life of trying to meet conditions rather than the centrality of Christ's life and victory, his refusal to compromise in his own life with anything but God's will, that should be the inspiration for a life lived under grace not law.[40]

Living with both joy and despair does not mean trying for a "synthesis" that does not take joy or despair seriously enough. The temptation is either to ignore and repress despair or to simply live with an uneasy alliance between joy and despair. This is, of course, seen in the life of Jesus. The cross will always be with him, but never apart from the victory of the resurrection. Barth puts it succinctly: "It is not a height far above us, but in our depths, as one of us, that He was and is the new man. If we do not see Him in these depths, we do not see Him at all, and therefore do not see the exaltation that took place in Him. These depths are the place which he has taken from us."[41] Our sanctification is only found in our exaltation with him. Sanctification is not to be separated from substitutionary atonement.

This dialectic of joy and sorrow becomes the very picture of an apostle's existence for Paul: "We are treated as imposters, and yet are true; as unknown, and yet are well known; as dying, and see—we are alive; as punished, and yet not killed; as sorrowful, yet always rejoicing; as poor, yet making many rich; as having nothing, and yet possessing everything" (2 Cor 6:10). Paul is saying that the appearance of an apostle is one thing; its reality is another. He appears to be sorrowful but he is always rejoicing, for he rejoices in hope, realizing his poverty. In realizing his poverty he is utterly dependent on Christ's vicarious faith and hope, and therefore, joy. The problem of joy is not how to get rid of despair in order to be joyful but how to accept the sorrow and the joy together (without sorrow demanding equal billing with joy). We need Christ's vicarious sorrow and joy for this.

So Jesus also connects sorrow and joy (John 16:24) with the goal being that "*my* joy may be in you, and that your joy may be complete" (John 15:22). The "fiery ordeal" that the Christian might encounter, 1 Peter says,

---

39. Barth, *CD* IV/2, 399.
40. Ibid., 400.
41. Ibid., 396.

is a sharing in Christ so that we might "be glad and shout for joy" at his coming: "Beloved do not be surprised at the fiery ordeal that is taking place among you to test you, as though something strange were happening to you. But rejoice insofar as you are sharing Christ's sufferings, so that you may also be glad and shout for joy when his glory is revealed" (1 Pet 4:12–13). Rejoicing in suffering may be a key to that puzzling passage about "completing what is lacking in Christ's afflictions" in Colossians: "I am now rejoicing in my sufferings for your sake, and in my flesh I am completing what is lacking in Christ's afflictions for the sake of his body, that is, the church" (Col 1:24). "For your sake . . ." and "for the sake of his body" Paul says. There is a continuing vicarious function of Christ's afflictions that Paul takes very seriously, as puzzling as this is to us. Perhaps this is because he knows that although Christ has died for our sins once for all that he continues to offer himself in perfect faith and obedience to the Father "for your sake . . ." and "for the sake of his body," language that speaks strongly of a continuing vicarious offering of his life that enables Paul to do the unthinkable: rejoice in suffering. Yet Christ is the one who is communicating his mystical oneness to the church. The reciprocity is based on his vicarious action.[42] Christ continues to live in his body. The key to the problem of joy is in the relationship between the joy of Jesus and our joy and its passageway through sorrow. This is the vicarious sorrow and vicarious joy of Christ.

Joy and sorrow may be mixed together at one point, but there can be a temporal order as well, when the weeping of the night is followed by the joy of the morning when God should be praised because the weeping will not last: "Sing praises to the Lord, O you his faithful ones, and give thanks to his holy name. For his anger is but for a moment; his favor is for a lifetime. Weeping may linger for the night, but joy comes with the morning" (Ps 30:4–5). Weeping and sorrow will not have the last word. Even the sorrowful person will rejoice: "Let me hear joy and gladness; let the bones that you have crushed rejoice" (Ps 51:8). Calvin comments,

> When he speaks of his *bones* as having *broken,* he alludes to the extreme grief and overwhelming distress to which he had been reduced. The joy of the Lord would reanimate his soul; and this joy he describes as to be obtained by *hearing;* for it is the word

---

42. Contra Albert Schweitzer, *The Mysticism of Paul the Apostle*, trans. William Montgomery (New York: Seabury, 1968) 126–27, who says that for Paul Christ not only suffers for "the Elect" but also "the Elect for Christ."

> of God alone which can first and effectually cheer the heart of any sinner... The joy which he desires is that which flows from hearing the word of God, in which he promises to pardon our guilt, and readmit us into his favour.[43]

This experience is not unrelated to experiencing the wrath of God, yet still not apart from grace. As Weiser comments on the psalmist, "It is in this very interaction of judgment and grace that he first experiences God in all his fullness."[44] The exhortation to repent as changing from laughter to lament is clear in the Epistle of James: "Draw near to God, and he will draw near to you. Cleanse your hands, you sinners, and purify your hearts, you double-minded. Lament and mourn and weep. Let your laughter be turned into mourning and your joy into dejection" (Jas 4:8–9). The psalmist has confidence to pray to God for a joy that one has not yet experienced: "Restore to me the joy of your salvation, and sustain in me a willing spirit" (Ps 51:12). Weiser comments,

> Where the soul is not nourished by the power of God, there man cannot rise above a servile obedience nourished by fear. It is the joy of God as the motivating force of man's actions which alone is able to transform ethical obedience into an obedience based on faith. The poet is conscious of this fact when he prays to his God and for help with the new life which he wants to lead.[45]

Weeping can be seen to be the "sowing" and joy the "reaping." There is a priority of sowing before reaping, yet the end result is joy, the psalmist claims: "Restore our fortunes, O Lord, like the watercourses in the Negeb. May those who sow in tears reap with shouts of joy. Those who go out weeping, bearing the seed for sowing, shall come home with shouts of joy, carrying their sheaves" (Ps 126:4–6). Of course, this is the basis for the old hymn, "Bringing in the Sheaves."

The subsequent following of the morning joy over the night of weeping should not cause us to neglect what might be involved in that "weeping." Continuing Christ's afflictions might involve vicariously acting on behalf of others, as one no less than Dietrich Bonhoeffer reminds us, in his words and in his life:

---

43. Calvin, *Calvin's Commentaries: Commentary on the Book of Psalms*, vol. 2, 295.

44. Artur Weiser, *The Psalms: A Commentary*, Old Testament Library (Philadelphia: Westminster, 1962) 406.

45. Ibid., 408.

> It is apparent that in self-renouncing work for the neighbor I give up happiness. We are called vicariously for the other in everyday matters, to give up possessions, honor, even our whole lives... Love demands that we give up our own advantage. This may even include our community with God itself.[46]

One may have to give up happiness and even "community with God"! But there are strong biblical antecedents here: Moses who wishes to be blotted out of the book of life for the sake of the people (Exod 32:32) and Paul, who wishes to be accursed and even separated from Christ for the sake of his people, the Jews (Rom 9:1ff.). Community, Bonhoeffer grimly concludes, is not the ultimate goal of love. I take Bonhoeffer to mean that enjoying the fruits of community is not the ultimate goal of love. For the sake of love you might become separated from your community. This is Paul's obedience to the vicarious humanity of Christ, that Christ would take his place at the end of his own life.

Community, however, is normally the place where joy and despair live together in the church. "Rejoice with those who rejoice, weep with those who weep," the apostle says to the Romans (Rom 12:15). "If one member suffers, all suffer together with it; if one member is honored, all rejoice together with it," Paul teaches the Corinthians (1 Cor 12:26). Those who pray for one another, Bonhoeffer contends, live a single life.[47] The necessity of praying for one another (1 Thess 5:25) expresses a vicarious reality within the church that is the presence of Christ.

The psalmist is aware that one's entire being responds with joy at the deliverance that God brings: "Then my soul shall rejoice in the Lord, exulting in his deliverance. All my bones shall say, O Lord, who is like you? You deliver the weak from those too strong for them, the weak and the needy from those who despoil them" (Ps 35:9–10). As Calvin comments,

> To place the matter in a still stronger light, he assigns to his very bones the office of declaring the divine glory (v. 10). As if not content that his tongue should be employed in this, he applies all the members of this body to the work setting forth the praises of God.[48]

---

46. Bonhoeffer, *Sanctorum Communio*, 184–85.
47. Ibid., 185.
48. Calvin, *Calvin's Commentaries: Commentary on the Book of Psalms*, vol. 4, 581.

The totality of the person is to be filled with joy at God's salvation. After Asa's reforms, the oath to the Lord taken by the people is done with rejoicing that involves the entire person: "All Judah rejoiced over the oath; for they had sworn with all their heart, and had sought him with their whole desire, and he was found by them, and the Lord gave them rest all around" (2 Chr 15:15). Not only the breadth but also the depth of Psalmist is imbibed with joy at the deliverance of God, like after feasting on a glorious meal, and having become fully satiated, reflecting with unbounded pleasure: "My soul is satisfied as with a rich feast, and my mouth praises you with joyful lips when I think of you on my bed, and meditate on you in the watches of the night; for you have been my help, and in the shadow of your wings I sing for joy" (Ps 63:5–7). Joy is that which is expressed to one another especially by the eyes: "The light of the eyes rejoices the heart, and good news refreshes the body (Prov 15:30). As the Old Testament scholar Roland Murphy comments, "The expressiveness of the eyes betrays an inner joy which others can recognize and be affected by."[49] Feasting with joy is the characteristic of settling into the promised land for Deuteronomy: "And you shall eat there in the presence of the Lord your God, you and your households together, rejoicing in all the undertakings in which the Lord your God has blessed you" (Deut 12:7). "Right worship as joyous eating," Walter Brueggemann comments, "is not only a faithful enactment of the goodness of creation. It is also an act of hope, a foretaste of the common abundance when there will be more than enough for all. In Christian extrapolation, this act of joyous eating in the Eucharist is an earnest of 'the Heavenly Banquet.'"[50]

But how rarely is this the believer's experience. Or does it begin as an experience with the experience of Jesus, and then becomes vicarious joy for us? Paul cites Deuteronomy's exhortation to rejoice over the victory of God for his people ("Rejoice, O Gentiles, with his people," Rom 15:10; cf. Deut 32:43) because "Christ has become a servant of the circumcised on behalf of the truth of God in order that he might confirm the promises given to the patriarchs" (Rom 15:8). The people are to rejoice because of the vicarious servanthood of Christ, "on behalf of the truth of God," for

---

49. Roland E. Murphy, *Proverbs*, Word Biblical Commentary 22 (Nashville: Thomas Nelson, 1998) 115.

50. Walter Bruegemann, *Deuteronomy*, Abingdon Old Testament Commentaries (Nashville: Abingdon, 2001) 143–44.

the people. We need Christ to be the vicarious servant in order for us to rejoice. Otherwise, joy can be ephemeral and fleeting.

The whole being must be involved but note how in Isaiah it is the Lord who will "cause" righteousness and praise:

> I will greatly rejoice in the Lord, my whole being will exult in my God; for he has clothed me with the garments of salvation, he has covered me with the robe of righteousness, as a bridegroom decks himself with a garland, and as a bride adorns herself with her jewels. For as the earth brings forth its shoots, and as a garden causes what is sown in it to spring up, so the Lord God will cause righteousness and praise to spring up before all the nations. (Isa 61:10–11)

So, does God "cause" joy? Only if joy affects the whole being, something that is given, as in the vicarious joy of Christ. Augustine reads Ps 30:1 as a proclamation of the humanity of Christ: "I will extol you, O Lord, for you have drawn me up, and did not let my foe rejoice over me."[51] This is "the voice of the Lord himself . . . having stooped to become a man."[52] Jesus prays, argues Augustine, even though one might ask, to whom is God praying? "Is God praying to God? What reason does he have to pray, he who is always blessed, always omnipotent, always unchangeable, eternal, co-eternal with the Father?"[53] The answer is found in John 1:14: "The Word was made flesh and dwelt among us." Both deity and humanity are contained in this verse. "There you have both the majesty to which you pray, and the humanity that can pray for you," the one who intercedes for us (Rom 8:34).[54] The Word became flesh, that is human, Augustine stresses, despite the Apollinarian heresy that denied the humanity of Christ's mind.[55] The deity of Christ is not a stumbling block to his humanity but the foundation of his humanity. Because of the majesty of the Word, "it is not inappropriate for him who became human for your sake to pray for you."[56] For Augustine, the humanity of Christ is real and it is really vicarious, a human being that prays for us, so that our foes might not rejoice over us. The struggle of joy is sometimes in observing the joy

---

51. Augustine, *Expositions of the Psalms 1–32*, 300–304.
52. Ibid., 300.
53. Ibid.
54. Ibid.
55. Ibid., 301–4.
56. Ibid., 304.

of our enemies over us. In contrast to those enemies is the blessing of joy upon those who seek the Lord: "But may all who seek you rejoice and be glad in you; may those who love your salvation say continually, 'Great is the Lord!'" (Ps 40:16; cf. 70:4).

The joy of the kingdom in which God is present means that instead of having joy over our foes we should not rejoice over their falling. This is even true in the Old Testament: "Do not rejoice when your enemies fall, and do not let your heart be glad when they stumble, or else the Lord will see it and be displeased, and turn away his anger from them" (Prov 24:17–18).

The psalms pray for deliverance in the time of death, in the extremity of need: "Be gracious to me, O Lord. See what I suffer from those who hate me; you are the one who lifts me up from the gates of death, so that I may recount all your praises, and, in the gates of daughter Zion, rejoice in your deliverance" (Ps 9:13–14). If God does not rescue the psalmist, then his enemies will rejoice in his plight: "Consider and answer me, O Lord my God! Give light to my eyes, or I will sleep the sleep of death, and my enemy will say, 'I have prevailed'; my foes will rejoice because I am shaken" (Ps 13:3–4). Again, God can give joy because of what his power can do, even to rescue from death. But only God can do this. As Dietrich Bonhoeffer reminds us, "Prayer does not mean simply to pour out one's heart. It means rather to find the way to God and to speak with him, whether the heart is full or empty. For that he needs Jesus Christ."[57] The communion of the saints is not those who are religious but who need Jesus Christ. He is the one for whom "the fear of death does not simply disappear but is certainly outshone by the joy of obedience."[58] Therefore, the church must participate in Christ's substitutionary ministry by praying in the place of those who do not pray, as Christ is praying for them.[59] This is what it means to be in communion with Christ, to truly be the communion of the saints.

Salvation is the source of joy according to the prophets: "With joy you will draw from the wells of salvation" (Isa 12:3). Hannah possesses the joy of bearing Samuel, which she considers to be a "victory": "My heart exults in the Lord; my strength is exalted in my God. My mouth derides my enemies, because I rejoice in my victory" (1 Sam 2:1).

57. Bonhoeffer, *Psalms*, 9–10.
58. Barth, *CD* III/4, 402.
59. Barth, *Prayer*, 23.

JOY AND DESPAIR HERE AND NOW

The relationship of joy and sorrow can have a political and social aspect according to Proverbs: "When the righteous are in authority, the people rejoice; but when the wicked rule, the people groan" (Prov 29:2). Proverbs can also say, "In the transgression of the evil there is a snare, but the righteous sing and rejoice," (Prov 29:6), (a verse for a political party rally?). Whose political party is perceived to be "righteous" and whose is perceived to be "wicked," however, may be problematic, and so the "black and white" morality of Proverbs, as usual, leaves many questions unanswered. Yet there is still a social dimension to joy and sorrow, the problem of joy expressed in the problem of political and social ethics.

The intermingling of joy and sorrow is particularly poignant with the individual. This seems to be an unavoidable phenomenon of being human: "Perfume and incense make the heart glad, but the soul is torn by trouble" (Prov 27:9). There exists in the innermost place of the individual a private sanctuary of both sorrow and joy that no one else really knows, according to this poignant proverb: "The heart knows its own bitterness, and no stranger shares its joy" (Prov 14:10). This is one of the strangest yet most powerful proverbs. Joy and sorrow can be very public, such as in the dedication of the new temple in Ezra. But there can also be something very private about joy and sorrow; a joy and sorrow that nobody knows except God and the self. The vicarious despair and joy of Jesus penetrates to this ontological depth, identifying with us in the depth of joys and sorrows, those joys and sorrows that are not superficial but heart rending. Through Christ's vicarious despair and joy, God respects the deep hurt but also the depths of our greatest joys, hurts and joys that our words cannot express. Jesus gives voice to them. As Roland Murphy comments,

> This psychological observation recognizes that ultimately there are certain feelings, both joyous and sorrowful, that cannot be communicated, no matter how much sympathy and understanding may be present. It does not deny that one can identify to some extent with another's sorrows and joys, but it does imply that such sensitivity has its limits.[60]

Good pastoral practice, in other words, includes realizing the pastor's limitations, the point at which we simply point to the vicarious despair and joy of Christ. But what a freedom this can be for those who minister.

---

60. Murphy, *Proverbs*, 104.

The christological praying of the psalms affects the individual now in the midst of despair. Jesus prays Psalm 31:7, "Into your hand I commit my spirit" from the cross (Luke 23:46). Emilie Griffin calls this "one of the most disturbing sentences in the Scriptures."[61] The context of the entire psalm is trusting in God that results in joy in the midst of despair: "I will exult and rejoice in your steadfast love, because you have seen my affliction; you have taken heed of my adversities, and have not delivered me into the hand of the enemy; you have set my feet in a broad place" (Ps 31:7–8). Yet we are afraid of this psalm often because Jesus prayed it and look at his fate! Griffin remarks,

> We know God asks hard things. We know he did not spare his own Son. We know Jesus prayed, not now and then, but all the time. Isn't this what holds us back—the knowledge of God's omnipotence, his unguessibility, his power, his right to ask an All of us, a perfect gift of self, a perfect act of surrender?[62]

Is there a better description of the need for the vicarious prayers of Christ, Christ's ability to pray before God, an ability that we cannot fathom?

Jesus, however, was "delivered . . . into the hand of the enemy." Despair exists, yet there is a joy that Christ possesses because he alone is able to trust the Father, despite the cross. Peter Craigie comments, "The psalmist prayed for life, for deliverance from death, and that is the psalm's fundamental and legitimate sense. But in the context of resurrection faith, the psalm may also be used as a prayer in death, expressing trust and commitment to the life lying beyond the grave."[63] The uniqueness of Christ is emphasized by Augustine's exegesis: "Let us listen now to something our Lord said on the cross, *Into your hands I commit my spirit* (Luke 23:46). When we hear those words of his in the gospel, and recognize them as part of this psalm, we should not doubt that here in this psalm it is Christ himself who is speaking."[64] Augustine comments on Ps 31:1–2 ("In you O Lord, I seek refuge . . . Incline your ear to me . . ."):

> Christ is speaking here in the prophet; no, I would dare to go further and say simply, Christ is speaking. He is going to say certain

---

61. Emilie Griffin, *Clinging: The Experience of Prayer* (Wichita, KS: Eighth Day, 2003) 3.

62. Ibid.

63. Peter C. Craigie, *Psalms 1–50*, Word Biblical Commentary 19 (Waco, TX: Word, 1983) 263.

64. Augustine, *Expositions of the Psalms 1–32*, 330–31.

things in this psalm that we think inappropriate to Christ, to the excellent dignity of our Head, and especially to the Word who was God with God in the beginning. Some of the things said here may not even seem suitable for him in the form of a servant, that form which he took from the Virgin; and yet it is Christ who is speaking, because in the members of Christ there is Christ.[65]

Augustine is hesitant to ascribe despair to Christ, yet he consents to do so because of Christ's connection with his body: "and yet it is Christ who is speaking, because in the members of Christ there is Christ," a vicarious relationship.

Sin deceives us into thinking that we can rejoice when instead God is calling us to be sorrowful because of our sins. This was true in the history of Israel. "In that day the Lord God of hosts called to weeping and mourning, to baldness and putting on sackcloth; but instead there was joy and festivity, killing oxen and slaughtering sheep, eating meat and drinking wine. 'Let us eat and drink, for tomorrow we die'" (Isa 22:12-13). As Brevard Childs comments, "The miraculous deliverance by God of the city has been basically misunderstood by its superficial inhabitants. Instead of reacting in weeping and mourning, Jerusalem responded with a behavior that flagrantly manifested its continuing disregard for God's will for the nation."[66] As we have seen, James exhorts his readers to repent and turn their laughter and joy into mourning and dejection: "Draw near to God, and he will draw near to you. Cleanse your hands, you sinners, and purify your hearts, you double-minded. Lament and mourn and weep. Let your laughter be turned into mourning and your joy into dejection" (Jas 1:8-9). Grace can be taken for granted and regarded as supplanting judgment. The problem of joy occurs when we try to bypass genuine repentance, even believing that grace and forgiveness negate the place of repentance. Yes, repentance should not be seen as a prelude or condition to grace. The Reformation fought hard for that truth although this is often forgotten by many Protestants. Calvin, among others, strongly emphasizes "evangelical repentance" versus "legal repentance," the repentance that follows and is motivated by grace, faith, and forgiveness.[67] Joy comes

---

65. Ibid., 324.

66. Brevard S. Childs, *Isaiah*, Old Testament Library (Louisville: Westminster John Knox, 2001) 161.

67. Calvin, *Institutes*, 3.3.4; and James B. Torrance, *Worship, Community, and the Triune God of Grace*, 54.

when those whom we love repent. Paul experiences joy when he hears of the Corinthians' repentance:

> For even when we came into Macedonia, our bodies had no rest, but we were afflicted in every way—disputes without and fears within. But God, who consoles the downcast, consoled us by the arrival of Titus, and not only by his coming, but also by the consolation with which he was consoled about you, as he told us of your longing, your mourning, your zeal for me, so that I rejoiced still more . . . Now I rejoice, not because you were grieved, but because your grief led to repentance; for you felt a godly grief, so that you were not harmed in any way by us. For godly grief produces a repentance that leads to salvation and brings no regret, but worldly grief produces death. (2 Cor. 7:5–10)

Here is the problem of joy and despair: We often do not know when we should rejoice and when we should weep. Only the Son in his perfect faith and obedience to the Father really knows when we should rejoice. With his characteristic realism, Ecclesiastes observes that we cannot create a "natural theology" out of experiencing joy or sorrow; we ultimately are in the hands of God: "In the day of prosperity be joyful, and in the day of adversity consider; God has made the one as well as the other, so that mortals may not find out anything that will come after them" (Eccl 7:14). Rejoicing over an athletic or political victory may make an entire city rejoice. That is a nice, yet superficial, joy. Yet the joy before God is something, ultimately, that only the Son knows. Only he can live with both the joy and the sorrow. This is how important the uniqueness of Christ is, particularly in our age of increasingly religious pluralism and skepticism that decries Christian "particularism" and "exclusivism." Much more is at stake than simply the virtue of tolerance, as admirable a virtue that might be. The wretchedness of lives lived in the undulation between joy and despair is at stake.

JOY AS GIFT IN THE MIDST OF DESPAIR

Joy is essential to our humanity but not innate. Joy is given. So "blessedness" is a gift as well, even in the beatitudes of Jesus. The beatitudes are not natural endowments or virtues.[68] Even Mary does not call herself blessed; that is something is to be pronounced about her (Luke 1:48). The

---

68. Barth, *CD* IV/2, 188.

blessedness of the kingdom of God, which is what Jesus is talking about, is something that is given by the one Man who can pronounce this upon our humanity. Despite all appearances in this world, the "blesseds" are pronounced because they are said by him, according to Barth:

> For those who are pronounced blessed it is indeed a matter of their own being, but primarily it is a matter either of the fact that their own being is lit up in a new way by the kingdom of God which has come near to them in Jesus or of the fact that it is ordered by this in a new and very definite manner. Either way, it is quite astounding. Jesus, the kingdom of God, indicates and explains and interprets their being and determines and directs and characterises it. And it is in this fact—this illumination or impression—that they are blessed in spite of all appearances to the contrary. This is what Jesus tells them about themselves. And they are to accept this and put it into practice. But this means that they can and should have the great joy which has come to all people.[69]

"Blessed" is who we are. We may be far beyond simply the pleasure, joy, or happiness of a good glass of wine. But the fact remains: We need joy to be given to us because our humanity needs it. "The meek shall obtain fresh joy in the Lord, and the neediest people shall exult in the Holy One of Israel" (Isa 29:19). Not any kind of joy but "fresh" joy! Those who are righteous will be joyful: "But let the righteous be joyful; let them exult before God; let them be jubilant with joy" (Ps 68:3). "Glory in his holy name; let the hearts of those who seek the Lord rejoice" (Ps 105:3). "For to the one who pleases him God gives wisdom and knowledge and joy; but to the sinner he gives the work of gathering and heaping, only to give to one who pleases God." (Eccl 2:26a). To this, however, Qoheleth still can only resign himself: "This also is vanity and a chasing after wind" (Eccl 2:26b). Joy is still a problem for Qoheleth.

The need for joy is met by the gift of the grace of God. "We ought to find and love God in what he actually gives us," Bonhoeffer writes from prison, and not "try to be more pious than God himself and allow our happiness to be corrupted by presumption and arrogance, and by unbridled religious fantasy which is never satisfied with what God gives."[70] The religious impulse is so often to deny the good things that God gives. "But

---

69. Ibid., 189.
70. Bonhoeffer, *Letters and Papers from Prison*, 168.

to put it plainly, for a man in his wife's arms to be hankering after the other world is, in mild terms, a piece of bad taste, and not God's will."[71]

The people of Israel saw in the new temple a gift of God, so they "celebrated the dedication of the house of God with joy" (Ezra 6:16). With the temple finished, there is a great celebration of joy that is seen as something that God gives and has provided by his providence, even using foreign leaders for the sake of Israel: "With joy they celebrated the festival of unleavened bread seven days; for the Lord had made them joyful, and had turned the heart of the king of Assyria to them, so that he aided them in the work on the house of God, the God of Israel" (Ezra 6:22). When the new city wall of Jerusalem is built, the people saw God as the source of that joy: "They offered great sacrifices that day and rejoiced, for God had made them rejoice with great joy; the women and the children also rejoiced. The joy of Jerusalem was heard far away" (Neh 12:43). "God had made them rejoice"! As coercive or deterministic as that may seem, Nehemiah is not afraid to speak of God actually making the people of Israel joyful. Perhaps this is because he sees joy as something that we cannot stir up but receive; joy is something that is given. This is particularly important when we consider the relationship of the joy of Jesus to our joy. "In your strength the king rejoices, O Lord, and in your help how greatly he exults!" (Ps 21:1). Augustine interprets the king as Jesus Christ: "*O Lord, the king will rejoice in your strength. In your strength, Lord, by which the Word became flesh, the man Christ Jesus will rejoice, and over your salvation he will be exceedingly glad,* for he will exult over that saving deed by which you give life to all things."[72] Like Jesus, the psalmist also testifies that when all his enemies are around him, he will sing to God with joy: "I will offer in his tent sacrifices with shouts of joy; I will sing and make melody to the Lord" (Ps 27:6). "Then I will go to the altar of God, to God my exceeding joy" (Ps 43:4) Why? Because of what God has given by his grace. The temple and Jerusalem particularly make this plain: "Great is the Lord and greatly to be praised in the city of our God, his holy mountain, beautiful in elevation, is the joy of all the earth" (Ps 48:1-2).

Joy is given, but not without tragedy. The challenge of joy is to accept the joy amidst the tragedy. The joy of Jesus, of course, does not merely escape the tragedy of the cross by the resurrection. The joy of the resurrection does not forget the cross: "Let me hear joy and gladness; let the

---

71. Ibid.

72. Augustine, *Expositions of the Psalms 1–32*, 218.

bones that you have crushed rejoice" (Ps 51:8) can certainly be viewed christologically and in a vicarious way, as Calvin does. Christ is the one who joyfully hears the word of God. This joy the psalmist "describes as to be obtained by *hearing*; for it is the word of God alone which can first and effectually cheer the heart of any sinner."[73] Weiser comments on the psalmist: "It is in this very interaction of judgment and grace that he first experiences God in all his fullness."[74] Yet one waits for the eschatological joy that God will give: "Rejoice with Jerusalem, and be glad for her, all you who love her; rejoice with her in joy, all you who mourn over her" (Isa 66:10).

Joy, however, is so quickly sapped from us. Despair, that which we have lost, or will never have, is an all-demanding spouse. Despair is perennial, all-encompassing, and unavoidable. Appearances say that our humanity in its essence is despair. At the very least joy and despair seem to be on equal footing. The reaction among the Israelites when the new temple was built was mixed; for many it was joyful yet it was sorrowful for those who remember the first building, as we have seen (Ezra 3:11–13). Joy and weeping could not be distinguished. They sounded alike. Is this not a poignant way to understand the problem of joy? Can joy be just a childish wish that we need to outgrow along with the toys, a childish wish that tries to ignore the equally powerful sounds of weeping?

Andy, a character in Wendell Berry's short novel, *Remembering*, concludes after reflecting upon his life, the uniqueness and joy of his experience, an ordinary as it may be: "Out of the multitude of possible lives that have surrounded and beckoned to him, like a crowd around a star, he returns new to himself, a mere meteorite, scorched, small, and fallen."[75] Several generations have passed and, in reflecting, he belongs to them all, "whose love has claimed him forever." So that even in his finite, temporal existence, in which there is both despair and sorrow, there is also joy in the gift of what has been given him. "Though he does not hold, he is held. He is grieving and he is full of joy. What is that Egypt but his Promised Land?" The joy and sorrow of Jesus holds together our Egypts and Promised Lands.

---

73. Calvin, *Calvin's Commentaries: Commentary on Book of Psalms*, vol. 2, 295.

74. Weiser, *Psalms*, 406.

75. Wendell Berry, *Remembering*, in *Three Short Novels* (Washington, DC: Counterpoint, 2002) 167.

THE JOY OF GROANING CREATION

Creation "groans," the apostle tells us (Rom 8:22), and the truth of that is not far from any of us. Whether it is through natural disaster of earthquake, fire, flood, or tornaldo, or through humanity's desolating misuse, creation is in despair. Yet there is great cause for joy, beginning with creation. What does the biblical doctrine of creation say? If we are made in the image of God, did God have any other response but joy when, after creation, he saw that it was "very good" (Gen 1:31)? The Lord asks Job pointedly, "Where were you when I laid the foundation of the earth?" (Job 38:4), with the added information that when that happened, "the morning stars sang together and all the heavenly beings shouted for joy" (Job 38:7).

God's creation seems to take on a joy of its own, including shouting and singing: The joy of creation becomes intertwined with the joy of humanity: "For you shall go out with joy, and be led back with peace; the mountains and the hills before will burst into song, and all the trees of the field shall clap their hands" (Isa 55:12). In fact, humanity seems to possess a responsibility to encourage creation to "shout" and "sing" to God: "Let the heavens be glad, and let the earth rejoice; let the sea roar, and all that fills it; let the field exult and everything in it. Then shall all the trees of the field sing for joy before the Lord; for he coming to judge the earth" (Ps 96:11–13). Because the Lord is king, the earth is to rejoice with "a joyful noise," and humanity with its "trumpets and the sound of the horn" joins with the hills singing together for joy" (Ps 98:4–8; cf. 100:1; 97:1). "Then shall the trees of the forest sing for joy before the Lord, for he comes to judge the earth" (1 Chr 16:33). Creation should sing for joy because the Lord has comforted his people: "Sing for joy, O heavens and exult, O earth; break forth, O mountains, into singing! For the Lord has comforted his people, and will have compassion on his suffering ones" (Isa 49:13). In the heavens that "are telling the glory of God" (Ps 19:1), God "has set a tent for the sun, which comes out like a bridegroom from his wedding canopy, and like a strong man runs its course with joy" (Ps 19:4–5). "Do not fear, O soil; be glad and rejoice, for the Lord has done great things" (Joel 2:21). "The gateways of the morning and the evening shout for joy" (Ps 65:8). All of the varieties of nature, including the flocks and the grain, are involved in this joy: "The pastures of the wilderness overflow, the hills gird themselves with joy, the meadows clothe themselves with flocks, the valleys deck themselves with grain, they shout and sing together for joy" (Ps 65:12–13). Singing sheep? Singing wheat? What is going on here? Who sees creation singing for joy? Is there more groaning than singing? Is there a problem of joy living with despair for nature? Is this true?

Humanity is to rejoice because each day is made by God: "This is the day that the Lord has made; let us rejoice and be glad in it" (Ps 118:24). Israel in particular is to rejoice in the Creator: "Let Israel be glad in its Maker; let the children of Zion rejoice in their King" (Ps 149:2). Human beings are to rejoice in the creation of another human being, and particular the male in the creation of the female: "Then the man said, 'This at last is bone of my bones and flesh of my flesh; this one shall be called Woman, for out of Man this one was taken'" (Gen 2:23).

Creation is called upon to rejoice in the latter days: After the victory of "the blood of the Lamb" (Rev 12:11), the call is out to the heavens and the earth, but one is called to rejoice and the other receives woes: "Rejoice then, you heavens and those who dwell in them! But woe to the earth and the sea, for the devil has come down to you with great wrath, because he knows that his time is short!" (Rev 12:12).

Psalm 104 consists of a litany reciting the glories of creation, including the waters that water the earth, the wind, the thunder, the springs that give drink to animals and "wine to gladden the human heart, oil to make the face shine, and bread to strengthen the human heart" (Ps 104:15), ending with the rhapsodic note, "O Lord, how manifold are your works! In wisdom you have made them all; the earth is full of your creatures" (Ps 104:24). The climax is in *God* being implored to rejoice in creation: "May the Lord rejoice in his works" (Ps 104:31). God is asked to rejoice! Joy begins with God, and God's joy in creation. The "singing" sheep and wheat have a friend in God. He will rejoice for them (vicariously!).

Calvin, in a sober and responsible mood, sees a problem with "an excessive joy of life," but we can be delivered from that by seeing life as a gift that demands a response of gratitude.[76] This "excessive joy of life," for Calvin, however, does not preclude "the lawful enjoyment of God's creation," in contrast to the "inhuman philosophy" that would exclude any use of creation "unless it is absolutely necessary."[77]

---

76. Calvin, *Golden Booklet of the True Christian Life*, 73.
77. Ibid., 87.

THE JOY OF THE GOSPEL ... IN THE MIDST OF DESPAIR

Joy is not just a nice by-product of Christianity, but the essence of the gospel. Rooted in the experience of Israel, the joy of the people of God is based on their deliverance from Egypt: "So he brought his people out with joy, his chosen ones with singing" (Ps 105:43). Calvin comments poignantly on the grim picture of that grace:

> The prophet makes mention of *joy* and *gladness,* the more highly to magnify the greatness of God's grace. It was no small matter, that at the very time when the Egyptians were afflicted by a severe and dreadful plague,
> - when the whole kingdom was full of weeping and howling,
> - and when in almost every house there was a dead body,
> - the people who a little before were groaning in great distress, or rather lay almost dead, went forth with joyful hearts.[78]

Moses' father-in-law, "Jethro rejoiced for all the good that the Lord had done to Israel, in delivering them from the Egyptians" (Exod 18:9). Israel will rejoice when they are delivered by the Lord: "O that deliverance for Israel would come from Zion! When the Lord restores the fortunes of the people, Jacob will rejoice; Israel will be glad" (Ps 14:7). The prophetic tradition experiences great joy in proclaiming the prophetic word: "Your words were found, and I ate them, and your words became to me a joy and the delight of my heart; for I am called by your name, O Lord, God of hosts" (Jer 15:16). "Come and see what God has done:" urges the psalmist, "he is awesome in his deeds among mortals. He turned the sea into dry land; they passed through the river on foot. There we rejoiced in him . . ." (Ps 66:5–6). He therefore enjoins God to remember him when he gives joy to the people in their victory: "Remember me, O Lord, when you show favor to your people; help me when you deliver them; that I may see the prosperity of your chosen ones, that I may rejoice in the gladness of your nation, that I may glory in your heritage" (Ps 106:4–5). This will become a common theme in Israel, rejoicing in the deliverance of God: "Let them thank the Lord for his steadfast love, for his wonderful works to humankind. And let them offer thanksgiving sacrifices, and tell of his deeds with songs of joy" (Ps 107:21–22). The steadfast love of God is the source of rejoicing for the Psalmist: "Satisfy us in the morning with your steadfast love, so that we may rejoice and be glad all our days" (Ps

---

78. Calvin, *Calvin's Commentaries: Commentary on the Book of Psalms*, vol. 4, 204.

90:14). Weiser comments, "Just as man is in need of food, so he is in need of God's grace if he is to achieve a joyful affirmation of life; the petition 'Satisfy us in the morning with thy grace' is meant to convey the thought that each day is to be started afresh with that need in mind."[79] The Lord is my help, so the psalmist exults: "The Lord is my strength and my shield; in him my heart trusts; so I am helped, and my heart exults, and with my song I give thanks to him" (Ps 28:7). Out of their oppression by princes, the people will be raised up by God so that "the upright see it and are glad" (Ps 107:42).

Even before the exodus, according to Jesus in the Fourth Gospel, salvation history began with Abraham, telling the Jews "your ancestor Abraham rejoiced that he would see my day; he saw it and was glad" (John 8:56). The other Gospels particularly speak of the joy of Jesus as savior (Luke 1:47; 2:10), the bringer of great joy. How is he different? He is "objective joy," because it is his joy in the Holy Spirit (Luke 10:21), identical with the kingdom of God (Rom 14:17), coming by grace alone, already actualized: "my joy may be in you" (John 15:22), "and no one will take your joy from you" (John 16:22).[80] Jesus's joy is found in what the Father has done in the revelation, not for the wise and intelligent, but for infants: "At the same hour Jesus rejoiced in the Holy Spirit and said, I thank you, Lord of heaven and earth, because you have hidden these things from the wise and the intelligent and have revealed them to infants; yet, Father, for such was your gracious will" (Luke 10:21). Notice that this is rejoicing "in the Holy Spirit," the characteristic Lucan portrayal of Jesus as a man led by the Spirit (Luke 4:1, 14).[81] Joy is not to be disconnected from the Holy Spirit, but first the Spirit in Jesus himself, not just the believer.

The reason for the joy of Jesus "is to be found quite simply in the fact that what met them in this man was the clear, redemptive mercy of God speaking quite unequivocally and authoritatively."[82] The Old Testament promise of joy is fulfilled by nothing less than the joy that belongs to Jesus but is imparted to his disciples. Are we not at the essence of salvation, exposing how superficial our views of salvation often are, as either simply Christ paying the penalty for sin (conservative), or simply as a moral

79. Weiser, *The Psalms*, 602.

80. Barth, *CD* IV/2, 182–83.

81. See James D. G. Dunn, *Jesus and the Spirit: A Study of the Religious and Charismatic Experience of Jesus and the First Christians as Reflected in the New Testament* (Philadelphia: Westminster, 1975).

82. Barth, *CD* IV/2, 182.

example in how to love sacrificially (liberal)? Either of these views can leave out joy (and do). Christian joy must first belong to Jesus, or joy just remains a child's possession or a yearning for the older, naïve time. Who does not have warm memories of an amusement park in one's childhood like the "Kiddieland" in Wichita, Kansas, with my fond remembrances of its "Ghost House"? But I can no longer go to "Kiddieland" (they tore it down anyway!). Our joy must grow up as well, especially if it is able to live with despair.

The joy of the kingdom is the joy that we are commanded to do (Phil 3:1; 4:4), as strange as it may seem.[83] Otherwise it would not be the essence of the kingdom of God, where God rules. Yet it presents the problem of being commanded to rejoice. Is this really possible or even desirable? The angel appearing to Mary does not hesitate to do so (Luke 1:28). The "great joy" of Jesus is brought to the shepherds as something that God has done, not a subjective possibility for religious people (Luke 2:10). As Barth observes, the "great joy" displaces the fear the shepherds possess at the glory of the Lord shining around them (Luke 2:9).[84] Joy takes the place, vicariously, of fear but not first of all the shepherds' joy. All they can bring, even to an appearance of the glory (beauty!) of the Lord, is fear. Joy comes as the kingdom of God comes. John the Baptist (John 3:29) and the disciples (Matt 5:12; Luke 6:23; 10:20) bear witness to this joy as there was joy at the Baptist's birth (Luke 1:14). This joy, however, is first of all, the joy of Jesus: "At the same hour Jesus rejoiced in the Holy Spirit . . ." (Luke 10:21). As Barth remarks, "Men neither appropriated it to themselves nor produced it of themselves, but it came to them in and with the man Jesus. It was given them in Him and by Him."[85] Here is the heart of this entire book.

One of the chief aspects of the problem of joy is how we can possess joy in the midst of despair. Joy must be given to us by the one who does possess joy. The kingdom of God may be hidden, as Barth likes to say, but it is present where Jesus Christ is present, despite the appearances. "We cannot rate it any lower than this when it is a matter of the salvation and life and joy of the kingdom of God, the salvation and life and joy which have appeared and are resolved in Jesus."[86]

83. Ibid.
84. Ibid.
85. Ibid.
86. Ibid., 192.

The joy of the kingdom, however, is not just, in Barth's words, "an empty paradox" or "a dark void," or "a neutral sphere where the promise might just as well mean destruction as salvation or death or life, giving them just as much cause for sadness as joy. Almost and unequivocally its message is one of salvation and life and joy."[87] We should not be satisfied by resolving the problem of joy by simply accepting a little bit of joy and a little bit of sorrow, and be content with that. The joy of Jesus does not permit us to do that. The joy of the kingdom is actualized by the actual joy of the man Jesus. "This man does not only speak, He accomplishes what He says. He makes actual what He declares to be true. He tells in and with the beatitudes that to-day, here and now, He is for those whom He addresses in this way."[88]

The joy that salvation brings is the joy of the kingdom, something very different than living by freedom from religious scruples that can make another stumble (Rom 14:13–23). Karl Barth speaks of this as the constant temptation of "Paulinism," arguing from "the basis of the Reformation."[89] Protestantism can very easily degenerate into a concern for our own autonomy, masquerading as "Christian freedom" in grace. The kingdom of God, manifested as "righteousness and peace and joy in the Holy Spirit" is very different, Paul states (Rom 14:17). It is a joy *for the sake of the other* (vicarious!), which does not allow another to suffer needlessly, even under wrongheaded notions. The problem of joy is often that we pursue our version of joy (including religious, "theological," doctrinally correct joy!), even at the expense of others. The joy that belongs to Jesus is different. "We are servants of Christ *in the Holy Ghost,* never in OUR spirit . . ." Barth adds.[90]

The joy of the presence of the kingdom is found in evangelism and mission. Paul's and Barnabas' report of the conversion of the Gentiles to churches on their way to Jerusalem "brought great joy to the believers" (Acts 15:3). "The entire household" of the centurion in the Philippian jail "rejoiced that he had become a believer in God" (Acts 16:34). The Thessalonians are commended by Paul for receiving the word "with joy inspired by the Holy Spirit" despite persecution (1 Thess 1:6). Even in the midst of persecution, the church in the book of Acts experiences joy

---

87. Ibid.
88. Ibid.
89. Barth, *Epistle to the Romans*, 519–20.
90. Ibid.

as they are involved in proclaiming the gospel: "So they shook the dust off their feet in protest against them, and went to Iconium. And the disciples were filled with joy and with the Holy Spirit" (Acts 13:51–52). Paul strangely does not care that some in Rome are "preaching Christ out of selfish ambition," but is pleased "that Christ is proclaimed in every way, whether out of false motive or true; and in that I rejoice" (Phil 1:18). Christ takes the place (vicariously?) of Paul's own concerns and pride.[91]

But the greatest joy over conversion is the joy in heaven (Luke 15:7) "in the presence of the angels of God over one sinner who repents" (Luke 15:10). The context is, of course, the parables of the lost sheep and the lost coin (Luke 15:1–10) that are told, along with the parable of the prodigal son, because "the Pharisees and the scribes were grumbling and saying, 'This fellow welcomes sinners and eats with them'" (Luke 15:2). The solidarity of Jesus with the disreputable of society and their subsequent conversion is the occasion for the heavenly choir, along with God, to rejoice. As the New Testament scholar Jeremias comments, "Such is the character of God; it is his good pleasure that the lost should be redeemed, because they are his; their wanderings have caused him pain, and he rejoices over their return home. It is the 'redemptive joy' of God, of which Jesus speaks, the joy in forgiving."[92] God himself rejoices; this will be key for us in seeing the place of the vicarious joy of Christ. The one who is God (John 1:1) rejoices. And he rejoices when he finds, a rejoicing that reflects a rejoicing in heaven and among the angels (Luke 15:7, 10; cf. 2:13–15). His joy is a cosmic joy that rejoices over the simple repentance of one on earth. This joy is expressed presently in Jesus's table fellowship with sinners, the occasion for telling these parables (Luke 15:2).

THE PRESENCE OF GOD IN JOY AND DESPAIR

The incarnation of God in Jesus Christ reminds us that, in the Old Testament as well, joy is found in the presence of God: In Jesus we behold the presence of God (John 1:14; 2 Cor 3:18; 1 John 1:1–2). Jerusalem is significant in Old Testament theology because of its profound theology of the presence of God: "Great is the Lord and greatly to be praised in the city of our God. His holy mountain, beautiful in elevation, is the joy of

---

91. O'Brien, *Epistle to the Philippians*, 516.
92. Joachim Jeremias, *The Parables of Jesus*, 2nd ed., trans. S. H. Hooke (New York: Scribners, 1972) 136.

all the earth" (Ps 48:1–2). "Let my tongue cling to the roof of my mouth," the psalmist in exile exclaims, "if I do not remember you, if I do not set Jerusalem above my highest joy" (Ps 137:6). Why is Jerusalem significant for the Christian? Augustine sees Jerusalem as standing for the place of "supreme joy":

> Supreme joy is found where we delight in God, where, free from all anxiety, we live in united fellowship with our brothers and sisters and our true companions in that city. No tempter will molest us there, no one will be able to force us toward any seductive pleasure, nothing will attract us except what is good. All pressure of need will face away, and supreme happiness will dawn upon us.[93]

"Rejoice with Jerusalem," exhorts Isaiah, "and be glad for her, all you who love her; rejoice with her in joy, all you who mourn over her" (Isa 66:10). Jerusalem will be the focus of eschatological joy: "And this city shall be to me a name of joy, a praise and a glory before all the nations of the earth who shall hear of all the good that I do for them" (Jer 33:9). There is great joy when the temple at Jerusalem is rebuilt: "They offered great sacrifices that day and rejoiced, for God had made them rejoice with great joy; the women and the children also rejoiced. The joy of Jerusalem was heard far away" (Neh 12:43). Zion is told to rejoice because the Lord will be in their midst, despite desolation: "Sing and rejoice, O daughter Zion! For lo, I will come and dwell in your midst, says the Lord" (Zech 2:10).

God, Nehemiah reminds us, is the source of the joy and particularly the presence of God. The psalmist says this of the presence of God:

> I keep the Lord always before me; because he is at my right hand, I shall not be moved. Therefore my heart is glad, and my soul rejoices; my body also rests secure. For you do not give me up to Sheol, or let your faithful one see the Pit. You show me the path of life. In your presence there is fullness of joy; in your right hand are pleasures forevermore. (Ps 16:9–11)

Augustine paraphrases this psalm: "You will fill them to the brim with gladness, so that they will look for nothing further when they see you face to face . . . Delight is to be found in your favor and mercy while we are on the journey of this life, which leads to the goal of beholding your face in

---

93. Augustine, *Expositions of the Psalms 121–150*, trans. Maria Boulding, ed. Boniface Ramsey (Hyde Park, NY: New City, 2004) 237.

glory."[94] Calvin allows for there to be a joy in mutually looking upon God in the beatific vision:

> David next adds, that when God is reconciled to us, we have all things which are necessary to perfect happiness. The phrase, *the countenance of God* ["presence" in NRSV] may be understood either of our being beheld by him, or of our beholding him; but I consider both these ideas as included, for his fatherly favour, which he displays in looking upon us with a serene countenance, precedes his joy, and is the first cause of it, and yet this does not cheer us until, on our part, we behold it shining upon us.[95]

A trinitarian relationship between the Father and the Son beholding one another is not hard to see in Calvin's comments. The vicarious joy of the Son has its roots in his beholding of the Father, the roots of the beauty of Jesus Christ that we can participate in. But as Weiser comments, this is only done when God removes the veil: "But God himself will remove the veil from that mystery, and only then will the Psalmist be able to share in the perfect fullness of joy in God's presence and in the blessed communion with him (literally, 'there is satisfaction in the joy in the sight of thy face')."[96] Peter's sermon quotes Psalm 16:8–11 as referring to the resurrected Jesus whom David sees so his heart "was glad, and my tongue rejoiced" (Acts 2:26). He is the one who "will make me full of gladness with your presence" (Acts 2:28). This sermon also speaks of the ascension of Christ and the giving of the Holy Spirit, the continuing presence of Jesus Christ: "Being therefore exalted at the right hand of God, and having received from the Father the promise of the Holy Spirit, he has poured out this that you both see and hear" (Acts 2:33). The trinitarian ministry of Jesus Christ continues.

But why does God wait? the existential sufferer and person in despair exclaims. Why not bring the consummation of all things immediately? Why not destroy the despair and have pure joy right now? Does the joy and despair of Jesus provide any clue to this continual cry?

Despair continues because Jesus too possesses this cry, as we see from the cross. His joy is that he also knows that God does not refuse to live without humanity, giving us time to come to faith and repentance,

---

94. Augustine, *Expositions of the Psalms 1–32*, 184.
95. Calvin, *Calvin's Commentaries, Commentary on the Book of Psalms*, vol. 4, 233.
96. Weiser, *Psalms*, 178.

but also time to be human. The nature of the substitutionary atonement is not to destroy the human. Christ

> came down from God to be its Reconciler and to take the place of man, not in such a way that man is deprived of the meaning and right of his own existence, but rather in such a way that both are restored to him in the relationship to God reconstituted by the intervention of Jesus Christ for him, so that as a man justified before God and sanctified for Him he is lifted up from the ground and set on his feet.[97]

We live with human restrictions and tragedies then. (That is cold comfort, however, for those in extreme pain.) But our despairing humanity will not have the last word, just as it was so for Jesus. We can live in this time of tragedy and frailty with Jesus. He is present, with us.

JOY AND DESPAIR IN THE ESCHATOLOGICAL COMING OF JESUS

Joy is the hallmark of the coming of Jesus: The angel said to the shepherds, "I am bringing you good news of great joy for all the people" (Luke 2:10). Jesus teaches the disciples to keep his commandments and abide in his love, "so that my joy may be in you, and that your joy may be complete" (John 15:10–11; cf. 1 John 1:4). "For the sake of the joy that was set before him," the author of Hebrews proclaims, Jesus "endured the cross, disregarding the shame . . ." (Heb 12:2). The result of the resurrection of Jesus was joy: Afterwards, the disciples returned to Jerusalem "with great joy . . ." (Luke 24:52). Paul views his congregations in the early church as "my joy and my crown" (Phil 4:1), so he exhorts them to "rejoice in the Lord" early in the letter to Philippians (3:1) and could not but help encourage them again later on in the letter to "Rejoice in the Lord always; again I will say, Rejoice" (4:4). There must be a reason why the Philippians need this reminder: it is hard to rejoice in this world. So that even in Philippi among Paul's followers there is the bickering between Euodia and Syntyche (4:2). Paul exhorts the churches to rejoice because they need to, not because he is naïve. He sees that joy is at the heart of the gospel because the gospel comes into our lives of despair, conscious and unconscious.

Yet joy is also an eschatological reality; something that is to come. The problem of joy may also be that we do not yet possess it, at least not

---

97. Barth, *CD* IV/3.1, 331–33.

fully. To the extent that the coming of Jesus fulfills, or at least inaugurates, the eschaton, then a new perspective and yet perhaps a new problem for joy is presented.

Joy is a product of God's eschatological deliverance, a future happening. This may be in terms of deliverance for Israel and Judah: "With joy you will draw water from the wells of salvation" (Isa 12:3). Nature will rejoice and see the glory of God in the future denouement:

> The wilderness and the dry land shall be glad, the desert shall rejoice and blossom; like the crocus it shall blossom abundantly, and rejoice with joy and singing. The glory of Lebanon shall be given to it, the majesty of Carmel and Sharon, they shall see the glory of the Lord, the majesty of our God. (Isa 35:1–2)

"The ransomed of the Lord" will return with joy: "And the ransomed of the Lord shall return, and come to Zion with singing; everlasting joy shall be upon their heads; they shall obtain joy and gladness, and sorrow and sighing shall flee away" (Isa 35:10; cf. 51:11). No longer will Israel be a victim of those who hate her: "Whereas you have been forsaken and hated, with no one passing through, I will make you majestic forever, a joy from age to age" (Isa 60:15). This concerns those freed from the Babylonian exile, so this future is still a this-worldly future, a "majestic" future that includes comfort: "For the Lord will comfort Zion; he will comfort all her wasteplaces, and will make her wilderness like Eden, her desert like the garden of the Lord; joy and gladness will be found in her, thanksgiving and the voice of song" (Isa 51:3). "As a mother comforts her child, so I will comfort you; you shall be comforted in Jerusalem. You shall see, and your heart shall rejoice . . ." (Isa 66:13–14). There will be "a new covenant with the house of Israel and the house of Judah" (Jer 31:31). "Then shall the young women rejoice in the dance, and the young man and the old shall be merry. I will turn their mourning into joy, I will comfort them and give them gladness for sorrow" (Jer 31:13).

The transition from sadness to gladness is prominent. There is joy because God will judge the earth with righteousness:

> Let the heavens be glad, and let the earth rejoice; let the sea roar, and all that fills it; let the field exult, and everything in it. Then shall all the trees of the forest sing for joy before the Lord; for he is coming, for he is coming to judge the earth. He will judge the world with righteousness, and the peoples with his truth. (Ps 96:11–13)

In the future, God is the one who first of all rejoices:

> On that day it shall be said to Jerusalem: Do not fear, O Zion; do not let your hands grow weak. The Lord your God is in your midst, a warrior who gives victory; he will rejoice over you with gladness, he will renew you in his love; he will exult over you with a loud singing as on a day of festival. (Zeph 3:16–18)

There is an advantage to the future coming, although that change may bring gloom. Jesus tells the disciples, "You heard me say to you, 'I am going away, and I am coming to you.' If you loved me, you would rejoice that I am going to the Father, because the Father is greater than I" (John 14:28). Regardless of what Jesus means by "the Father is greater than I," a question of great debate throughout church history, it may be more significant to ask, What does he mean by saying "I am going to the Father"? The Father is his goal, the goal of the vicarious obedience of Christ, and in obeying him the Father is "greater," for the sake of the joy he brings ("you would rejoice that I am going to the Father"). Yet the pain is still there because, in some way, Jesus will be absent. Edwyn Hoskyns comments,

> Great as the joy of the disciples will be when they see the Lord, their joy is not thereby fulfilled. It will be fulfilled only in that intimate fellowship with the Father (1 John 1:4) which is to be effected by the death and resurrection of Jesus. The significance of the death and resurrection is therefore adequately interpreted by the word *I go to the Father* (14:28; 16:10), and the fulfilled joy of the disciples consists in the termination of the ear of their anxious questioning and in the advent of a wholly new and effective economy of prayer—prayer to the Father in the name of Jesus . . . Here then the meaning is that the future joy of the disciples will be a joy in knowledge (John 6:45; 14:20).[98]

But like the pain of the mother bearing a child that gives way to joy, so also for the disciples (John 16:21). "So you have pain now; but I will see you again, and your hearts will rejoice, and no one will take your joy from you" (John 16:22). Leon Morris comments, "It may be significant that He does not speak of their sorrow being replaced by joy, but of turning into it. The very same thing, the cross, that would be to them first a cause of sorrow would later become a source of joy."[99] The prime manifestation

---

98. Hoskyns, *Fourth Gospel*, 488–89.

99. Leon Morris, *The Gospel according to John*, New International Commentary on the New Testament (Grand Rapids: Eerdmans, 1971) 705–8.

of this eschatological fulfillment is to participate in Jesus's prayers to the Father, to ask the Father through Jesus, through his vicarious, mediatory ministry of prayer reflecting his communion with the Father: "On that day you will ask nothing of me. Very truly, I tell you, if you ask anything of the Father in my name, he will give it to you" (John 16:23).

The future eschatological event assumes that there will then be a new quality of the vicarious mediatory ministry of Christ, "of a wholly new and effective economy of prayer—prayer to the Father in the name of Jesus . . . Here then the meaning is that the future joy of the disciples will be a joy in knowledge (John 6:45; 14:20)."[100] And the result of that will be a new fulfilled kind of joy: "Until now you have not asked for anything in my name. Ask and you will receive, so that your joy may be complete" (John 16:24; cf. 17:13). Paul can speak in Romans that having been justified by faith and possessing peace with God through Christ (Rom 5:1), we now "rejoice (NRSV reads "boast") in the hope of the glory of God (Rom 5:2, NIV), although this involves rejoicing in sufferings (Rom 5:3) because of the perseverance, character, and ultimately, hope, that it brings (Rom 5:4). Jesus exhorts the disciples to rejoice because, despite the suffering and persecution, there will be reward in heaven (Matt 5:12; Luke 6:23). Yes, there will be a future reward, but the disciples are exhorted to rejoice in the present. Rejoicing is eschatological because it is the kind of rejoicing that lives in the midst of sufferings, so its greatest fruit can only be hope, the hope that "does not disappoint us, because God has poured out his love into our hearts by the Holy Spirit, whom he has given us" (Rom 5:5).

Hope is the certitude that we live by in the midst of sufferings that, through the gift of the Holy Spirit, connects us with the love of God. Hope created by the Holy Spirit exhibits the character of the Holy Spirit: it comes when he desires, not when we desire.[101] Hope creates gratitude. "The hope for a receiving" is in contrast to "vain and empty pleasure," a kind of "grasping" at something that we think that we can create, "the dangerous cliff of every willed joy."[102] Hope does not have an "audacity" but a reality in connecting us with the love of the triune God, the kind of rejoicing in love for the Father that was made manifest in Jesus himself (Luke 10:21). The future will culminate with the joy of "the marriage of

---

100. Hoskyns, *Fourth Gospel*, 488–89.
101. Barth, *CD* III/4, 379.
102. Ibid., 378.

the Lamb": "Let us rejoice and give him the glory, for the marriage of the Lamb has come, and his bride has made herself ready..." (Rev 19:7). The everlasting is in mind because God is going to create a "new heavens and a new earth":

> For I am about to create new heavens and a new earth; the former things shall not be remembered or come to mind. But be glad and rejoice forever in what I am creating; for I am about to create Jerusalem as a joy, and its people as a delight. I will rejoice in Jerusalem and delight in my people; no more shall the sound of weeping be heard in it, or the cry of distress. (Isa 65:17–19; cf. Rev 21:1)

Isaiah and the Apocalypse are saying that the future will be a time in which we can participate in *God's very own rejoicing:* "I will rejoice in Jerusalem..." "I will rejoice in doing good to them, and I will plant them in this land in faithfulness, with all my heart and all my soul" (Jer 32:41). The way is being paved for the vicarious rejoicing of Jesus, the one who is God and human. As Calvin comments, "So great is his love toward us, that he delights in our prosperity not less than if he enjoyed it along with us. And hence we obtain no small confirmation of our faith, when we learn that God is moved, and so powerfully moved, by such an affection toward us."[103] Calvin adds that this rejoicing includes feeling our sorrow: "If we are in painful and distressed circumstances, he says that he is affected by grief and sorrow..."[104]

The rejoicing by God anticipates the vicarious joy of Christ in which God himself takes our place in our humanity not only in our sorrow but also in our rejoicing, enabling us to rejoice with him. The eschatological goal is that of rejoicing because of God's strength given in Christ: "Now to him who is able to keep you from falling, and to make you stand without blemish in the presence of his glory with rejoicing..." (Jude 24). The rejoicing seems ambiguous here; is it God's rejoicing or our rejoicing? Perhaps both.

Yet joy can also be a present reality, particularly with the advent of Jesus. There is to be future joy, Isaiah tells us, with the righteous reign of the coming king:

---

103. Calvin, *Calvin's Commentaries: Commentary on the Prophet Isaiah*, vol. 4, 399–400.

104. Ibid.

> The people who walked in darkness have seen a great light; those who lived in a land of deep darkness—You have multiplied the nation, you have increased its joy; they rejoice before you as with joy at the harvest, as people exult when dividing plunder. (Isa 9:2–3)

In the Gospel of Matthew, Jesus is seen as fulfilling this prophecy (Matt 4:12–16). In fact, it signifies the beginning of his preaching that the kingdom of heaven is near (Matt 4:17). Matthew does not add the mention of joy in Isa 9:3 but there is no reason to preclude that from his intention to say that there is fulfilled eschatology even in Jesus beginning his ministry, not just restricted to the consummation of the age. The beginning of Jesus's ministry in the Gospel of Luke includes this self-testimony by Jesus in the synagogue: "The spirit of the Lord is upon me, because the Lord has anointed me; he has sent me to bring good news to the oppressed, to bind up the brokenhearted, to proclaim liberty to the captives, and release to the prisoners; to proclaim the year of the Lord's favor . . ." (Isa 61:1–2; cf. Luke 4:18–19). Zechariah speaks of the eschatological presence of God as bringing joy: "Sing and rejoice, O daughter Zion! For lo, I will come and dwell in your midst, says the Lord" (Zech 2:10). Furthermore, the coming King is to be greeted with joy, which the New Testament picks up as speaking of Jesus: "Sing and rejoice, O daughter Zion! Shout aloud, O daughter Jerusalem! Lo, your king comes to you, triumphant and victorious is he, humble and riding on a donkey, on a colt, the foal of a donkey" (Zech 9:9; cf. Matt 21:2–7; John 12:14–15). Zechariah's prophecy speaks of manifestations of joy among the people: "Then the people of Ephraim shall become like warriors, and their hearts shall be glad as with wine. Their children shall see it and rejoice, their hearts shall exult in the Lord" (Zech 10:7). In the prophecy from Joel, so important as an sign of eschatological fulfillment on the day of Pentecost in the Book of Acts (Acts 2:17–21), the people are exhorted to rejoice: "O children of Zion, be glad and rejoice in the Lord your God; for he has given the early rain for your vindication, he has poured down for you abundant rain, the early and the later rain, as before . . ." (Joel 2:23). Isaiah continues to elaborate the transition from sorrow to gladness that is the result of this anointed one and his ministry "to comfort all who mourn; to provide for those who mourn in Zion—to give them a garland instead of ashes, the oil of gladness instead of mourning . . ." (Isa 61:2–3). But Luke makes it clear that this eschatology is fulfilled in the present of Jesus, when Jesus rolls up the scroll and sits down, stating, "Today this scripture has been fulfilled in your hearing" (Luke 4:21). Again, Luke does not continue the Isaian emphasis on joy replacing mourning. But does he need to? There is a joy in Jesus because he himself is the fulfillment, he is the anointed one of Isaiah, a fantastic claim.

How can we experience such joy when the world remains as it is? This, indeed, is the problem of joy living with despair. The Gospel of Luke, however, sees its resolution in nothing less than the joy Jesus brings (Luke 10:21). This joy over Jesus, Jesus tells the Jews in the Fourth Gospel, is even shared already by Abraham: "Your ancestor Abraham rejoiced that he would see my day; he saw it and was glad" (John 8:56). Something about Jesus makes the postmortem Abraham rejoice. This fantastic claim in fact leads Jesus to say, "Before Abraham was, I am" (John 8:58), igniting the Jews to pick up stones to throw at him (John 8:59). There is joy in a present judgment: Because of the conquering of "the blood of the Lamb" (Rev 12:11), some are to rejoice and others are to fear the devil: "Rejoice then, you heavens and those who dwell in them! But woe to the earth and the sea, for the devil has come down to you with great wrath, because he knows that his time is short!" (Rev 12:12). The eternal element of reward is not missing, however: The people will thus "be called priests of the Lord, you shall be named ministers of our God; you shall enjoy the wealth of the nations, and in their riches you shall glory. Because their shame was double, and dishonor was proclaimed as their lot, therefore they shall possess a double portion; everlasting joy shall be theirs" (Isa 61:7; cf. 65:14). The present reality of joy will be an everlasting joy, perhaps even despite appearances and sorrow.

As much as one might find joy in anticipation, one must not forget the joy of fulfillment. Satisfaction is very much a part of joy.[105] Striving is so much of life, so joy comes when there is a rest (the Sabbath?). Because there has been waiting, anticipation, one appreciates the fulfilled joy. The stone-cutting into the sides of my local highway reads, "The Journey is the Reward." Really? Does one possess joy if one never arrives at the destination? Is this simply a postmodern skepticism that there even is a destination? Otherwise, we can very easily live lives of only irony, grimly smiling that life will never turn out like the ideal "Father Knows Best" television family, and finding arrogant pride that at least we are in with the joke that life is. No, joy as rest means that life can smile. "Life smiles

---

105. Barth, *CD* III/4, 376.

at him, not scornfully and ironically (as it can also do) but with friendliness, not as something unknown but in some sense well-known, because he has always meant it to turn out like this and he can now smile at it for once."[106] Barth concludes that this means that joy is gratitude. Gratitude is a kind of rest.

Is this why Hebrews makes a great deal about the Sabbath rest that Jesus, "the apostle and high priest of our confession" (Hebrews' way of speaking of the vicarious ministry of Christ; cf. Heb 4:14–16) brings that Joshua (the Old Testament) was not able to bring (Heb 4:1–11)? He is able to give that rest (Matt 11:28). The problem is that our experiences of joy are either so fleeting (on leave from college to see the girlfriend) or contingent (the girlfriend can always dump you, or even die). How does joy *endure*? is one question in which always the possibility of despair is lurking around the corner. That is why eternal joy in fellowship with God is so important in the Bible. "The desire for duration, even if realized only in a single case, is an essential characteristic of all joy as such."[107] As even Nietzsche can say, "All delight demands eternity."[108]

One can see the accomplished, finished joy of Christ as a manifestation of this, but the fact that he is still coming reminds us of the virtue of anticipatory joy. The problem of joy is that it is both satisfaction and anticipation. Does the vicarious joy of Jesus hold them both together? The church always seems to fall into trouble when it does not maintain both the present and the future of eschatology. Christ's joy is in the midst of that which holds both joy and despair together, not in a tragic paradox or a "neutral sphere where the promise might just as well mean destruction as salvation or death as life, giving them just as much cause for sadness as joy. Always and unequivocally its message is one of salvation and life and joy."[109] This is why that in the beatitudes of Jesus the poor in spirit can inherit the kingdom of heaven, those who mourn will be comforted, the meek will inherit the earth, those who hunger and thirst for righteousness will be filled, the merciful will receive mercy, the pure in heart will see God, the peacemakers will be called the children of God, and those who are persecuted for righteousness' sake will possess the kingdom of heaven (Matt 5:3–11). How important is it that Jesus ends the beatitudes

106. Ibid.
107. Ibid., 377.
108. Friedrich Nietzsche, cited by Barth, *CD* III/4, 377.
109. Barth, *CD* IV/2, 192.

in Matthew with "Rejoice and be glad, for your reward is great in heaven, for in the same way they persecuted the prophets who were before you" (Matt 5:12) and in Luke with "Rejoice in that day and leap for joy, for surely your reward is great in heaven" (Luke 6:23)? Joy is to be the last word, even in the middle of a world of suffering and persecution.

A victory for the Lord's "anointed" is a theme in Psalm 20, a victory that comes "in the day of trouble" (Ps 20:1). God is implored to "help" the anointed, to grant "you your heart's desire, and fulfill all your plans" (Ps 20:2). The result is joy in victory:

> May we shout for joy over your victory, and in the name of our God set up our banners. May the Lord fulfill all your petitions. Now I know that the Lord will help his anointed; he will answer him from his holy heaven with mighty victories by his right hand. (Ps 20:5)

Augustine interprets the anointed as Christ who in his intercessory ministry prays for us so that through his prayers we are victorious: "*He will hear him from his holy heaven*, where he now intercedes for us at the right hand of the Father, and whence he has poured the Holy Spirit down on those who believe in him."[110] Christ prays vicariously for us and his prayers are effective.

The Fourth Gospel is particularly poignant in portraying the priority of sorrow before joy and its resolution by prayer in Jesus's name; very much a vicarious reality of Christ:

> When a woman is in labor, she has pain, because her hour has come. But when her child is born, she no longer remembers the anguish because of the joy of having brought a human being into the world. So you have pain now; but I will see you again, and your hearts will rejoice, and no one will take your joy from you. On that day you will ask nothing of me. Very truly, I tell you, if you ask anything of the Father in my name, he will give it to you. Until now you have not asked for anything in my name. Ask and you will receive, so that your joy may be complete. (John 16:21–24)

"Complete joy" is to pray in Jesus's name, something that only happens after the pain that is akin to a mother's travail during childbirth, but with the same result of joy. The mediation of Christ, praying in his name, is essential for avoiding a deterministic view that the priority of pain leads

---

110. Augustine, *Expositions of the Psalms 1–32*, 216.

to joy. No, this is more descriptive than prescriptive; descriptive of living with the pain but realizing that joy comes because it is first possessed by Jesus: "But I will see you again." Interestingly, the woman no longer "remembers" the pain because the joy is so great. While that may not be true of all childbirths (!), the point is well taken: the joy is going to be greater than the pain. But this remains just a moralism without the mediation of Jesus, the vicarious humanity of Christ.[111] The problem of joy has an eschatological answer in the death and resurrection of Jesus and the new dynamic of prayer *through* Jesus and *with* Jesus.[112] This is living in the vicarious humanity of Christ. George Hunsinger notices the importance of the "perfect" tense for T. F. Torrance in Torrance's doctrine of the sacraments as flowing from Torrance's doctrine of the vicarious humanity of Christ.[113] As Torrance puts it himself,

> Our adoption, sanctification and regeneration have already taken place in Christ, and are fully enclosed in his birth, holy life, death and resurrection undertaken for our sakes, and proceed from them more by way of realization of actualization in us of what has already happened to us in him than as new effect resulting from them: we have been adopted through his incarnational assumption of us into himself, sanctified through the obedient self-offering of Christ in his life and death, and we have been born again in his birth of the Spirit and in his resurrection from the dead.[114]

In other words, our joy and despair have already taken place in Christ and they continue, but only in him and in his perspective.

Sorrow and sighing will one day have an end. "And the ransomed of the Lord shall return, and come to Zion with singing; everlasting joy shall be upon their heads; they shall obtain joy and gladness, and sorrow and sighing shall flee away" (Isa 35:10). John Cassian from the earliest monastic tradition speaks eloquently of the "perpetual and lasting joy":

> For by these tokens the kingdom of God and the kingdom of the devil are distinguished: and in truth if lifting up our mental

---

111. Hoskyns, *Fourth Gospel*, 488–89.

112. James B. Torrance, *Worship, Community and the Triune God of Grace*, 50.

113. George Hunsinger, "The Dimension of Depth: Thomas F. Torrance on the Sacraments," in *The Promise of Trinitarian Theology: Theologians in Dialogue with T. F. Torrance*, ed. Elmer M. Colyer (Lanham, MD: Rowman & Littlefield, 2001) 144.

114. T. F. Torrance, *Theology in Reconciliation: Essays Towards Evangelical and Catholic Unity in East and West* (Grand Rapids: Eerdmans, 1976) 89.

gaze on high we would consider that state in which the heavenly powers live on high, who are truly in the kingdom of God, what should we imagine it to be except perpetual and lasting joy? For what is so specially peculiar and appropriate to true blessedness as constant calm and eternal joy?[115]

Israel will me made "majestic forever, a joy from age to age" even though they "have been forsaken and hated" (Isa 60:15). In "the year of the Lord's favor," those "who mourn in Zion" will be given "a garland instead of ashes, the oil of gladness instead of mourning, the mantle of praise instead of a faint spirit" (Isa 61:2–3). God says through Isaiah, "I will rejoice in Jerusalem, and delight in my people; no more shall the sound of weeping be heard in it, or the cry of distress" when God creates "Jerusalem as a joy" (Isa 65:18–19). "Then shall the young women rejoice in the dance, and the young men and the old shall be merry. I will turn their mourning into joy, I will comfort them, and give them gladness for sorrow" (Jer 31:13). Yet the difficulty remains of seeing the possibility of joy in the midst of the darkest weeping. This is where the vicarious joy of Jesus becomes so important. He rejoices in the midst of the weeping, for us and on our behalf, when we are unable to so do, especially before the consummation of the eschatological victory. His joy and his sorrow eventually relativizes our joy and sorrow (although not without first taking upon them himself in solidarity).

THE RELATIVIZING OF JOY AND DESPAIR

Is there a problem of joy because of the presence of despair? Yes, but in the presence of Jesus, the one who embodies the kingdom of God, is a presence that can say Yes for us, even if we are unable; Yes in affirming the goodness and mercy of God. This reality, therefore, "does not remain future but has already become theirs."[116] Barth hastens to add that this does not rationalize the suffering; there is no place for a "greater good" theodicy. But the reward is "nothing less than the kingdom of God as such, nothing less than Himself."[117] Nothing less than himself! There is an

---

115. John Cassian, *Conferences* 1.13, cited by Steven A. MacKinnon, *Isaiah 1–39*, Ancient Christian Commentary on Scripture: Old Testament 10 (Downers Grove, IL: InterVarsity, 2004) 247.

116. Barth, *CD* IV/2, 192.

117. Ibid.

eschatological future but the joy of that future is a joy that is present. Can we dare say this?

In the end, the present or future reality of eschatology and the kingdom of God is relativized, Paul argues:

> I mean, brothers and sisters, the appointed time has grown short; from now on, let even those who have wives be as though they had none, and those who mourn as though they were not mourning, and those who rejoice as though they were not rejoicing, and those who buy as though they had no possessions, and those who deal with the world as though they had no dealings with it. For the present form of the world is passing away. (1 Cor 7:29–31)

So also, *joy and despair must now lose their place in dominating our lives.* How can this be? Do not rejoicing and mourning have the right to be acknowledged as the center of our humanity? If we ignore rejoicing or mourning in another, are we not rightly accused of becoming at best insensitive or at worst inhuman? How can the Christian live as though there were no rejoicing or mourning and still live with both joy and despair?

At the junction between the present and future reality of the kingdom of God is the resurrection of Jesus. Joy, while sometimes in confliction (Luke 24:41), is the result of encountering the resurrected Jesus: "And they worshipped him, and returned to Jerusalem with great joy" (Luke 24:52). As Calvin comments,

> Briefly, for the fervor of their joy, they broke out into the praises of God and were constantly at the temple, not that they passed night and day there, but they went up to all the assemblies, and at the set and regular hours were there to offer thanksgivings to God. Their joy is contrasted with their fear which previously kept them shut in, hidden, at home.[118]

As Peter preached on the day of Pentecost, "God raised him up, having freed him from death, because it was impossible for him to be held in its power" (Acts 2:24). It is for this reason that Peter can echo the psalmist: "Therefore my heart was glad, and my tongue rejoiced" (Acts 2:26; Ps 16:9). The resurrection of Jesus had already happened. God had already vindicated the one who humbled himself and became obedient unto death (Phil 2:8–9). The stage is set for joy to confront despair.

118. Calvin, *Calvin's New Testament Commentaries: A Harmony of the Gospels: Matthew, Mark and Luke*, vol. 3, 257.

The problem of joy is also the problem of sorrow and despair: How do we live without both joy and despair dominating our lives? But the Christian lives that way because, Paul claims, "the present form of the world is passing away." He knows this because Christ has taken the place of both joy and suffering! The *icon* of the life, death, and resurrection of Jesus is a picture of that. Dare we say joy and suffering are relativized? Or do we have to hold on to our joy and suffering at all costs? Is this just another manifestation of sin? Is this why it is so difficult to apprehend and believe in the vicarious joy, as well as the vicarious despair, of Jesus? Joy and despair will still be there, but it will be the joy and despair of Jesus that we share in. Commenting on 1 Corinthians 7, C. K. Barrett says, "The point is that neither laughter nor tears is the last word; a man should never allow himself to be lost in either."[119] The "last word" is the "last Adam," Jesus Christ (1 Cor 15:45). He has taken the place of our joy and despair. The problem of living with both joy and despair demands this. Christ has taken our place in our joy and mourning (let alone "wives" [!], "possessions," and dealings with "the world"!).

THE COMMAND TO REJOICE IN THE MIDST OF DESPAIR

If we cannot "avoid" joy then maybe Barth's instruction that joy is a command rather than a permission is not as stringent as it first appears.[120] To be created is cause for gratitude before the Creator. Despite the potential for despair, how could it be otherwise? The command of God, Barth argues, is not to be received without joy.[121] "One cannot be obedient to God's command without both joy and seriousness."[122] In fact, Barth is bold enough to say, "The will for life is also the will for joy."[123] The most solemn and serious person cannot deny this. Joy, therefore, should not dismissed as naïve and childish but can even be seen at the center of Christian ethics: "And the question what it means to will to be happy in obedience is in its place just as serious, and its correct answering is just as important and as little self-evident, as any ethical question."[124] "Happy

---

119. Barrett, *First Epistle to the Corinthians*, 178.
120. Barth, *CD* III/1, 371.
121. Barth, *CD* III/4, 277.
122. Ibid.
123. Ibid., 375.
124. Ibid.

in obedience"? Is this possible? Does not the religious or moral person cringe at that paradox? But is that not the reality of Jesus, "who for the sake of the joy that was set before him endured the cross, disregarding its shame, and has taken his seat at the right hand of the throne of God" (Heb 12:2)?

To be redeemed is also cause to receive the command to rejoice. The people wept when they heard anew the commands of the law. Yet Nehemiah and Ezra exhort them to rejoice and to express that joy in feasting:

> And Nehemiah, who was the governor, and Ezra the priest and scribe, and the Levites who taught the people said to all the people, "This day is holy to the Lord your God; do not mourn or weep." For all the people wept when they heard the words of the law. Then he said to them, "Go your way, eat the fat and drink sweet wine and send portions of them to those for whom nothing is prepared, for this day is holy to our Lord; and do not be grieved, for the joy of the Lord is your strength." So the Levites stilled all the people, saying, "Be quiet, for this day is holy; do not be grieved." And all the people went their way to eat and drink and to send portions and to make great rejoicing, because they had understood the words that were declared to them. (Neh 8:9–12)

Notice how the response to conviction over the words of the law is to be joyful when we would expect repentance. For Nehemiah and Ezra there seems to be a seamless relationship between joy and repentance. And the joy that the people are to have is not their own joy, "for the joy of the Lord is your strength" (Neh 8:10). The joy of the Lord is vicarious, rejoicing on behalf and in place of the people when they have been convicted by the words of the law, a precursor to the vicarious joy of Christ. Also, holiness is not simply to bring guilt and despair. "This day is holy to our Lord," therefore "be quiet," "do not mourn or weep," and "do not be grieved" (Neh 8: 9–11). The noise of weeping apparently was replaced with the noise of "great rejoicing" at the feast (Neh 8:12). The people rejoice because they now understand that the words of the law are to bring joy not just condemnation (Neh 8:12).

Not only is there joy in the redeemed keeping the command, but also the one who gives the command rejoices when the command is obeyed: "The father of the righteous will greatly rejoice; he who begets a wise son will be glad in him" (Prov 23:24). The Christian cannot help but think of God the Father's response to the obedient Son: "And a voice from heaven said, "This is my Son, the Beloved, with whom I am well pleased" (Matt 3:17; Mark 1:11; Luke 3:22; cf. Matt 12:18; Matt 17:5; 2 Pet 1:17).

What is "astonishing," Barth observes, is that the command to rejoice comes also in the midst of the Bible's seriousness.[125] Judgment upon the people, the call to repentance, and even the darkness of the day on the cross, all provide the context for the command, nonetheless, to rejoice. How can this be? How can this be done? This is the problem of joy living in the midst of despair. One would assume that in such a world, joy is only a fantasy or a dream. But the good news of Jesus Christ is that joy "arises from these dark places," in Barth's remarkable words, so that it can be commanded, because Christ has been raised from the dead.[126] If this is so, then the meaning of the resurrection involves taking the "dark places" out of our hands: "Because God the Creator and Lord of life acts and speaks here, taking the lost cause of man out of his hand, making it his own, intervening majestically, mercifully and wisely for him."[127] This is done most definitively in the vicarious humanity of Christ, indeed, the vicarious *joy* of Christ. Christ has taken the burden of joy out of our hands, while still maintaining joy as a command.

Joy is just a problem in our world of tears unless there is some way it is related to grace, the grace of God intervening with power yet in identity with our tortured and troubled humanity. From the beginning of the gospel narrative, joy is to replace fear: "Do not be afraid, Mary, for you have found favor with God" (Luke 1:30). The angels say to shepherds, "Do not be afraid—I am bringing you good news of great joy for all the people: to you is born this day in the city of David a Savior, who is the Messiah, the Lord" (Luke 2:10–11). No one who has ever grown up with the animated classic, "A Charlie Brown Christmas," can forget the climax at the school play, when Linus answers Charlie Brown's perplexity about the meaning of Christmas amidst all the commercialism by reading Luke 2:10–11: "That's what Christmas is all about, Charlie Brown," Linus plainly states.[128] The shepherds are told to rejoice, not just to be afraid.[129] Joy takes the place (vicariously?) of fear.

125. Ibid.
126. Ibid.
127. Ibid.
128. *A Charlie Brown Christmas*, directed by Bill Meléndez, United Feature Syndicate and Coca-Cola for CBS, 1965.
129. Barth, *CD* IV/2, 182.

CHAPTER EIGHT

Joy as Gift, Grace, and Gratitude . . . and Its Enemies

Joy as grace is something that is given. God gives joy, says the psalmist: "You have put gladness in my heart more than when their grain and wine abound" (Ps 4:7). Augustine comments, "Joy, therefore, is not to be sought outside oneself, by those who, still heavy in heart, love emptiness and chase falsehood. Rather, it is to be sought within, where the light of God's face is stamped," commenting as well on v. 6: "Let the light of your face shine on us, O Lord!"[1] Calvin adds that the psalmist "rejoices more in the favour of God alone, than earthly men rejoice when they enjoy all earthly good things with the desire of which they are generally inflamed."[2] Notice his contrast between the joy that God gives and the "earthly" joys that are created by inflamed desires.

JESUS GIVES JOY AS GRACE

Jesus gives joy as grace. "I have said these things to you so that my joy may be in you, and that your joy may be complete" (John 15:11; cf. 17:13). "My joy"! The joy that is given as grace is that which belongs to Jesus first of all (cf. Luke 10:21). "Men neither appropriated it to themselves nor produced it of themselves, but it came to them in and with the man Jesus."[3] Joy can be the very ordinary gifts of food, drink, and work. Ecclesiastes is not simply being cynical, but realistic: "This is what I have seen to be good: it is fitting to eat and drink and to find enjoyment in all the toil with which one toils under the sun the few days of the life God gives us;

---

1. Augustine, *Expositions of the Psalms 1–32*, 90.
2. Calvin, *Calvin's Commentaries: Commentary on the Book of Psalms*, vol. 1, 49.
3. Barth, *CD* IV/2, 182.

for this is our lot" (Eccl 5:18). Wealth and possessions are a joy when seen to be a gift of God: "Likewise all to whom God gives wealth and possessions and whom he enables to enjoy them, and to accept their lot and find enjoyment in their toil—this is the gift of God" (Eccl 5:19). In fact, it is these activities that will keep them from despair! "For they will scarcely brood over the days of their lives, because God keeps them occupied with the joys of their hearts" (Eccl 5:20; cf. 9:7). Biblical scholar Roland Murphy comments, "The divine 'pleasure' is manifested in that one is enjoying these gifts that Qoheleth is recommending. However, they are not 'earned,' for humans have no claim on them; they depend on the inscrutable will and generosity of God (Eccl 2:24–26; 3:13)."[4] This is not to say, Barth argues, that there is no place to be "ready" for joy. "It is tempting but over-hasty to say that we cannot will joy but only have it. In reality the truth is—inevitably—that only in fleeting moments do we have joy, namely joy at something, the experience of fulfillment itself and as such. We are poor fools if we rely on this."[5] No, we need to possess a "readiness" for joy. This is the virtue of anticipation. Life is a gift of God's grace, but we always should live in anticipation of it continually being given, "to rejoice in anticipation of something."[6]

But how is the "readiness" of Barth's not a potential or capacity in us to receive grace, something that Barth otherwise would view with abhorrence? We are not meant to "do our part" and work for the coming of the kingdom as part of the bargain.[7] Is there not a need for a "readiness" for joy that God himself provides, humanity's readiness for in the joy of Jesus himself? Or else will we simply be ready for a joy that is coming but we can only recognize it if it fulfills our agendas? Genuine human response is included in God's act of grace, completed in Christ on our behalf.[8] Christ holds the anticipatory and fulfilled joy together through his eschatological presence in the Holy Spirit. Real joy is unpredictable, like the movement of the Spirit.[9]

The gift of joy by grace is one manifestation of substitutionary atonement and the vicarious humanity of Christ. The lordship of God is to speak

4. Roland Murphy, *Ecclesiastes*, Word Biblical Commentary, vol. 23A (Dallas: Word, 1992) 92. Cf. Barth, *CD* III/4, 376.
5. Barth, *CD* III/4, 377.
6. Ibid., 378.
7. Barth, *CD* I/2, 791.
8. Alan J. Torrance, *Persons in Communion*, 318.
9. Barth, *CD* III/4, 379.

of One who is unique. "He is the only one who does what he does."[10] In this simple statement by Barth is the foundation of substitutionary atonement, of God taking our place. Only God can give himself to us as a gift. Contemporary philosophers such as Derrida question whether a gift can ever be given without expecting a response, calling into question what Christians have called "unconditional grace," otherwise the gift becomes pure power, an opportunity to manipulate others.[11] The vicarious joy of Jesus is the reciprocation of the Father's gift, of God's gift that has already been made, a reciprocation that has already been made with no coercion, yet with deep intimacy. We share in his gift of grace but simultaneously have to acknowledge that the gift is no longer in our hands.[12] This is a joy that we share in but we do not possess! Yet it is the only lasting joy. The joy of Jesus is a part of his articulation of reality, his reality as a relationship before the Father, his word of grace.[13]

"God is now not only the electing Creator, but the elect creature. He is not only the giver, but also the recipient of grace."[14] Perhaps nowhere is the vicarious humanity of Christ more clearly pronounced in the theology of Karl Barth than in this statement. Receiving grace involves also Christ's relationship to creation and human beings. Through Christ as the recipient of grace we can see the essence of both creation and humanity as recipients of unconditional, unmerited grace and love.[15] Yet it will be a disturbing experience for human beings, as Barth makes plain: "Free grace is the event of the shattering and destroying of what he is without it and against it."[16] It may even mean that we give up responsibility for others, something near and dear to religious and moral people.[17] Bonhoeffer makes this clear when he discusses the implications of what he calls

10. Barth, *CD* I/2, 382.

11. See the discussion in David Bentley Hart, *Beauty of the Infinite*, 260–68.

12. Barth, *CD* I/2, 383.

13. Alan J. Torrance, *Persons in Communion*, 360.

14. Barth, *CD* IV/1, 170.

15. On creation see Colin E. Gunton, *The Triune Creator: A Historical and Systematic Study* (Grand Rapids: Eerdmans, 1998) 236; on anthropology see Ray S. Anderson, *Something Old, Something New: Marriage and Family Ministry in a Postmodern Culture* (Eugene, OR: Wipf & Stock, 2007) 152.

16. Barth, *CD* IV/2, 402.

17. An obsession over responsibility for others is a distinct characteristic of obsessive-compulsive disorder (OCD) according to the psychiatrist Ian Osborn in his book, *Can Christianity Cure Obsessive-Compulsive Disorder?* (Grand Rapids: Brazos, 2008).

"vicarious representative action" (*Stellvertretung*). A common objection to the atonement is that it is impossible for one to take responsibility for another's good or evil deeds. Bonhoeffer's response is that "we ought to let our sin be taken from us, for we are not able to carry it by ourselves; we ought not to reject this gift of God."[18] Our "responsibility for ourselves" needs to "abandoned"! *Stellvertretung*, vicarious representative action, his term for the vicarious humanity of Christ, demands this. This can certainly be seen in terms of joy. Our joys are temporal, tangential, and fleeting, even as gifts of God. The vicarious joy of Christ is needed.

Joy as a gift reminds us that God's joy is grace not something created by an expression of human freedom. The vicarious humanity of Christ claims that all of our responses should be based on the human response of Christ, and that should include joy. That some would object that this excludes our own response of joy is typical of those who criticize Barth and Torrance, interpreting them as saying that if salvation is all of grace then it has nothing of our humanity in it.[19] But dare we say that our joy is unrelated to God's joy (aptly attested by scripture)? Christian joy is not just our expression but our expression coming from God's gift in the joy of Jesus. This is grounded, of course, in the perichoretic union in the triune God, a joy that exists from all eternity.[20] The Son's "Amen" to the Father is an eternal amen that is now said in our humanity as a gift of grace. In Schmemann's words, "Upon this Amen the fate of the human race is decided. It reveals that the movement toward God has begun."[21]

How does grace affect the one who gives grace? Can we say that God is affected by giving us grace? Certain views of the immutability and impassibility of God would say that God in his serenity cannot be affected by anything else. God is self-contained. But if God truly rejoices, and we see that rejoicing in the joy of Jesus, does not that picture joy as that which affects God when out of his love he gives us grace? In fact, that joy was the basis for one of the chief criticisms of Jesus, saying, "This fellow welcomes sinners and eats with them" (Luke 15:2). Thus, Jesus tells the parables of those who lose something, like a sheep or a coin, and then rejoice when they are found (Luke 15:3–10). Biblical scholars Beyreuther

---

18. Bonhoeffer, *Sanctorum Communio*, 156.

19. T. F. Torrance, "Karl Barth and the Latin Heresy," in *Karl Barth: Biblical and Evangelical Theologian*, 234.

20. James B. Torrance, *Worship, Community and the Triune God of Grace*, 32.

21. Schmemann, *For the Life of the World*, 29.

and Finkenrath remark, "Indeed, the whole of Luke 15 with its parables of the lost sheep, the lost coin and the lost son presents Jesus calling upon men to rejoice with him over the lost returning to the Father (Luke 15:6, 9, 32)."[22] The joy of Jesus, a joy we are unable to have, tells us something about God and something about grace and its effects not only on us but also on God. There is "a divine celebration," even in heaven and with the angels (Luke 15:7, 10).[23] This is truly amazing grace!

Joy comes to the people of Israel when grace is seen as a gift, such as in the ark of the covenant. The ark was the gift of the presence of Yahweh. Bringing the ark to Jerusalem was cause for great joy:

> And the Levites carried the ark of God on their shoulders with the poles, as Moses had commanded according to the word of the Lord. David also commanded the chiefs of the Levites to appoint their kindred as the singers to play on musical instruments, on harps and lyres and cymbals, to raise loud sounds of joy. (1 Chr 15:15–16)

The problem of possessing joy in the midst of the despair of life continues to be a problem for us. Only in Jesus is the kind of joy that lives with despair already made real. Like the kingdom of God coming in his presence, bringing joy, righteousness, and peace, an "objective joy" has been created by Jesus for the disciples. As Barth remarks, "In the presence of the man Jesus it was already actual for them and could not be resisted or destroyed by anything or anyone."[24]

GRACE AND MISERY

Grace enables us to deal with life as misery, yet not always to obliterate it. In Calvin's words, "When we have come to this conclusion that our life in this world is a gift of God's mercy which we ought to remember with gratitude because we owe it to him, it will then be time for us to consider its misery."[25] Calvin recognizes that we cannot wish away misery, sorrow, and pain. Joy is joined with weeping when some compare the new temple with the old (Ezra 3:11–13). The gift of the new temple brings joy to some,

---

22. E. Beyreuther and G. Finkenrath, *NIDNTT*, vol. 2, 358.

23. Joel B. Green, *The Gospel of Luke*, New International Commentary on the New Testament (Grand Rapids: Eerdmans, 1997) 576.

24. Barth, *CD* IV/2, 182.

25. Calvin, *The Golden Booklet of the True Christian Life*, 73.

but to others it reminds them of what used to be. Isaiah speaks of grace found in the midst of the "waste places" that God will give his people, a future comfort that will include "joy and gladness": "For the Lord will comfort Zion; he will comfort all her waste places, and will make her wilderness like Eden, her desert like the garden of the Lord; joy and gladness will be found in her, thanksgiving and the voice of song" (Isa 51:3). The words of God are given to the prophet and they become a joy and delight to him, even like partaking of tasty food: "Your words were found, and I ate them, and your words became to me a joy and the delight of my heart" (Jer 15:16). Joy comes as grace in the gift of the faith of Jesus Christ, a faith that consists in joy before God, a joy it is difficult for us to possess. We desire it, we want it. But when we experience joy it is always so fleeting. When the joy of Jesus comes it is a joy of fulfilled anticipation. Joy is always something out of reach, C. S. Lewis discovered.[26] However, this joy has already been given in Jesus, in the midst of a world in which Christ is still suffering (Col 1:24). "Even in his misery," Barth argues, "man lives as the man for whom Jesus lives. To omit this qualification of man's misery is necessarily to deny Jesus Christ as the Lord who became a servant and the servant who became the Lord and therefore to blaspheme God."[27] Even in the midst of despair and misery "man is not nothing—He is God's man. He is accepted by God. He is recognized as himself a free subject, a subject who has been made free once and for all by his restoration as the faithful covenant partner of God."[28] When grace is given, one is in the presence of God. Even Elihu can say to Job that when one "is accepted by him, he comes into his presence with joy" (Job 33:26). The psalmist sings, "You show me the path of life. In your presence there is fullness of joy; in your right hand are pleasures forevermore" (Ps 16:11). Augustine comments on this verse:

> *You will fill me with joy in beholding your face.* You will fill them to the brim with gladness, so that they will look for nothing further when they see you face to face. Again, because I am among them, *you will fill me* can be the words I use. *Your right hand will be full of delights forever.* Delight is to be found in your favor and

---

26. John Randolph Willis, S.J., *Pleasures Forevermore: The Theology of C. S. Lewis* (Chicago: Loyola University Press, 1983) 7.

27. Barth, *CD* IV/2, 484.

28. Barth, *CD* IV/1, 90.

mercy while we are on the journey of this life, which leads to the goal of beholding your face in glory.[29]

Yet where is this presence in our world of innocent suffering and futility? The problem of living with both joy and despair remains. If grace is a gift, however, perhaps we should begin with the response of gratitude. Gratitude itself, however, is difficult to maintain. Is there Someone who can pave the way for us, who truly and consistently is grateful to God?

JOY AND GRATITUDE

Joy is really the simplest form of gratitude," Barth plainly declares.[30] The psalmist who proclaims to God, " You have put gladness in my heart . . ." (Ps 4:7), sees the result in peace: "I will both lie down and sleep in peace; for you alone, O Lord, make me lie down in safety" (Ps 4:8). Weiser comments, "Lifting up his eyes in gratitude to God who has given him this joyful heart as his most precious possession, the worshipper lies down to spend the night in the peace of God."[31] But in a world of tsunamis, hurricanes, and holocausts, how difficult it is to claim this "safety" and "peace."

The "double movement" of the incarnation can be viewed as a descent (*katabasis*) and ascent (*anabasis*), a descent into our humanity and an ascent to the Father that we join in with Christ (Phil 2:5–11). The second movement involves the vicarious thanksgiving (Eucharist) of Christ, a thanksgiving with joy to the Father. It is *his* thanksgiving, however. We should know this if we know grace and resist Pelagianism.[32] This is just as true for joy, "joyfully giving thanks" (Col 1:11–12), especially in the midst of despair. For Christ is, in Schmemann's words, "the perfect Eucharist; He offered Himself in total obedience, love and thanksgiving to God. God was His very life. And He gave this perfect and eucharistic life to us. In Him God became our life."[33] There is therefore no place left for us to "play" with; even joy is his: "Eucharist is the only full and real response of man to God's creation, redemption and the gift of heaven. But this perfect man who stands before God is *Christ*. In Him alone all that God has given man was fulfilled and brought back to heaven. He alone

---

29. Augustine, *Expositions of the Psalms 1–32*, 184.
30. Barth, *CD* III/4, 376.
31. Weiser, *The Psalms*, 122.
32. T. F. Torrance, *Royal Priesthood*, 39–40.
33. Schmemann, *For the Life of the World*, 34.

is the perfect Eucharistic Being."[34] There must be someone, Schmemann pleads, in a world that rejects God, who can be thankful! This "someone" is Christ, the "new Adam."[35]

This thankful and joyful One has both cosmic and personal implications. "Jesus is the man," Barth writes, "in whose human being and thinking and willing and speaking and acting there takes place the grateful affirmation of the grace of God addressed to the human race and the whole created cosmos—an affirmation which we all owe but none of us makes."[36] Yet his thankfulness and joy is an indictment of our mediocrity, triviality, and sloth as actual sins, like the prisoner who is released from his prison but will not leave his cell! "His shaming is an event."[37]

But does this mean the destruction of our simple and personal joys in life, from a stroll beside a tree-shaded river filled with the quacking of the ducks, to the love of a human mother or father? Is this too absolutist, even too "religious"?

The key may be that Jesus' vicarious humanity is first of all human not religious. The burly old Irish man in Ray Bradbury's story, *Green Shadows, White Whale,* proclaims that "It's an awesome responsibility when the world runs to hand you things. For an instance: sunsets. Everything pink and gold, looking like those melons they ship from Spain. That's a gift, ain't it?"[38] Yet he does not too quickly bring in God. "Well, who do you thank for sunsets? And don't drag the Lord in the bar now! Any remarks to Him are too quiet. I mean someone to grab and slap their back and say thanks for the fine early light thing morn . . ."[39] What if God comes as human so that we have someone to "slap on the back"? Is this not the practical meaning of the incarnation?

Therefore, Christ embraces us as we are, in the humanity that he shares with us, including those personal and funny joys that are little yet give richness to life. Yes, the joy of Christ is in receiving (1 Cor 4:7), not demanding or desiring. Being "born again a pure recipient" does not mean asceticism but "that the great and little things, the external and the internal, which may be good but to which he has no right or claim,

---

34. Ibid., 37.
35. Ibid., 45.
36. Barth, *CD* IV/2, 30.
37. Ibid., 393, 405.
38. Ray Bradbury, *Green Shadows, White Whale* (New York: Avon, 1992) 128.
39. Ibid.

are accepted by him contentedly in the form in which they come."[40] I think Barth is saying here that through Christ's reception by the Father, for example, of thanksgiving and joy, we can bring all the little things in proper perspective, that is, not trying to make them gods or idols. The little joys no longer have to bear the burden of deity! What a relief! Temptations do remain, Barth will admit, "yet no temptation which comes upon a Christian, nor weakness in face of it, can alter the fact that he has been taken out of an existence of desire and demand and set in one of receiving."[41]

Jesus is the one who gives thanks to the Father (Matt 26:27), while we often live lives of ungratefulness. Joy is grace. As Barth comments, "We can create opportunities for it in anticipatory joy, but we cannot create or construct or produce or force it by various plans and measures."[42] Joy is a hope of receiving, the kind of receiving that is epitomized in what the Son receives from the Father (John 16:15; Matt 11:27; Luke 10:22). Joy is "the hope for a receiving and not the covetous glance at a grasping . . . We stand before the dangerous cliff of every willed joy."[43] Barth is under no illusion that our actions of joy can be like standing before a "dangerous cliff." We may desperately demand and covet joy from God and others and not simply receive grace. The need for the vicarious humanity of Christ at this point is very great. We need his perfect faithful and obedient reception from the Father, the reception of him who "did not count equality with God as something to be exploited, but emptied himself . . ." (Phil 2:6–7). Through him and with him we can joyfully give thanks, as Paul prays for the Colossians: "May you be made strong with all the strength that comes from his glorious power, and may you be prepared to endure everything with patience, while joyfully giving thanks to the Father, who has enabled you to share in the inheritance of the saints in light" (Col 1:11–12). "Joyfully giving thanks to the Father" is what it means to live in "the kingdom of his beloved Son, in whom we have redemption, the forgiveness of sins" (Col 1:13).

As grace, joy comes by the Holy Spirit, like the wind, which we do not know from where it comes or where it goes (John 3:8). Genuine celebration, Barth contends, is not planned: "Why are usually the most

---

40. Barth, *CD* IV/3.2, 668.
41. Ibid.
42. Barth, *CD* III/4, 379.
43. Ibid., 378.

successful festivals those which are not foreseen and arranged but which we simply celebrate as they occur, falling as it were from heaven?"[44] As Jesus was open to the will of the Father, so we should be open to different modes of joy, unexpected modes of joy, avoiding the burden and the rut of the usual and expected, that which is not given by grace.[45] No one can pronounce oneself "blessed"; that is something that is given to one as a gift of grace (Luke 1:42, 48; 6:20-23; Matt 5:3-12).[46] The problem of joy becomes most acute when we finally realize that we cannot give ourselves joy or happiness, despite our herculean efforts at pursuing money, power, or prestige. Even Peter's confession of Jesus as the Messiah (Matt 16:16) is immediately qualified by Jesus' answer to him: "Blessed are you Simon son of Jonah! For flesh and blood has not revealed this to you, but my Father in heaven" (Matt 16:17). Peter is "blessed" because of what the Father has revealed to him, not because of his ingenious theology or superior faith.[47] Gratitude can be expressed as well in confession of sin, and with the joy of forgiveness that results, as in Psalm 51.

The psalmist admits one's sin (v. 3) and asks, "purge me with hyssop, and I shall be clean; wash me, and I shall be whiter than snow" (v. 7). The result will be joy and gladness: "Let me hear joy and gladness; let the bones that you have crushed rejoice . . . Restore to me the joy of your salvation and sustain in me a willing spirit" (vv. 8, 12). Weiser comments,

> Where the soul is not nourished by the power of God, there man cannot rise above a servile obedience nourished by fear. It is the joy in God as the motivating force of man's actions which alone is able to transform ethical obedience into an obedience based on faith. The poet is conscious of this fact when he prays to God for joy and for help with the new life which he wants to lead.[48]

Confession of sin, however, is difficult in itself. Who knows if one has confessed sufficiently or is aware of all of one's sins? The Scottish theologian John McLeod Campbell speaks of the vicarious humanity of Christ as including a vicarious *confession* of our sins. His confessions of our sins before the Father was "a peculiar development of the holy sorrow in which He bore the burden of our sins . . . this Amen from the depths

---

44. Ibid., 379.
45. Ibid.
46. Barth, *CD* IV/2, 188.
47. Ibid., 190.
48. Weiser, *Psalms*, 476.

of the humanity of Christ to the divine condemnation of sin."[49] That is what was occurring when Jesus allowed himself to be baptized by John the Baptist, confessing the sins as the representative of all, doing what we are unable to do in its totality.[50] In addition, judgment, the consequences of sin, is also a gift from God resulting in joy that justice has been done: "Let the nations be glad and sing for joy, for you judge the peoples with equity and guide the nations upon the earth" (Ps 67:4). Judgment can be related to joy.[51]

LACK OF JOY: THE GREATEST INDICTMENT

The greatest indictment upon the church, Schmemann contends, is its lack of joy, a charge leveled by Nietzsche, among others.[52] "It is only as joy that the Church was victorious in the world, and it lost the world when it lost that joy."[53] Joy is not to be analyzed or defined, according to Schmemann, but entered into in an experiential sense based on the grace and decision of God: "Enter into the joy of your master" is the invitation to the trustworthy servant (Matt 25:21). Thus, the church is called to enter into through the partaking of the Eucharist. This is faith acting out of its fullness, not merely of a lack.[54] The "real presence" of Christ is the presence of joy, an aesthetic presence, before God's face ("presence" in NRSV): "In your presence there is fullness of joy; in your right hand are pleasures forevermore" (Ps 16:11). Jesus stands before the Father's presence. As Schmemann remarks, "Delight is to be found in your favor and mercy while we are on the journey of this life, which leads to the goal of beholding your face in glory."[55] So often we cannot experience joy in the midst of a loss or a feeling of something we lack. But Jesus Christ is "the perfect Eucharistic Being," in Schmemann's memorable words.[56] Can he be the key to our problem of joy? Does Jesus rejoice, give thanks, when we are unable to? Partaking in the Eucharist is

49. Campbell, *Nature of the Atonement*, 118.

50. T. F. Torrance, "The One Baptism Common to Christ and His Church," in *Theology in Reconciliation*, 85.

51. Weiser, *Psalms*, 476.

52. Schmemann, *For the Life of the World*, 24–26.

53. Ibid., 24.

54. Ibid., 38.

55. Augustine, *Expositions of the Psalms 1–32*, 184.

56. Schmemann, *For the Life of the World*, 38.

only part of the story that begins with Jesus' joy before the Father, as seen in a most telling way in Luke:

> At that same hour Jesus *rejoiced* in the Holy Spirit and said, "I thank you, Father, Lord of heaven and earth, because you have hidden these things from the wise and intelligent and have revealed them to infants." (Luke 10:21)

Christian existence is to reflect the joy of believing that one finds in Jesus. Paul prays this for the Romans: "May the God of hope fill you with all joy and peace in believing, so that you may abound in hope by the power of the Holy Spirit" (Rom 15:13). For Paul, the very nature of prayer for the church at Philippi is "with joy": "I thank my God every time I remember you, constantly praying with joy for all of you, because of your sharing in the gospel from the first day until now" (Phil 1:3–5). The morning is for the believer to be filled with joy: "Satisfy us in the morning with your steadfast love, so that we may rejoice and be glad all our days" (Ps 90:14). This is a petitionary prayer, depending upon God to give this steadfast love and joy as a gift of his grace: "Gladden the soul of your servant, for to you, O Lord, I lift up my soul" (Ps 86:4). As Weiser comments, "Just as man is in need of food, so he is in need of God's grace if he is to achieve a joyful affirmation of life; the petition 'Satisfy us in the morning with thy grace' is meant to convey the thought that each day is to be started afresh with that need in mind."[57]

In contrast to "the works of the flesh," joy is a part of the moral manifestation of the life in the Spirit: The fruit of the Spirit is "love, joy, peace, patience, kindness, generosity, faithfulness, gentleness, and self-control" (Gal 5:22–23). Here joy is not to be seen apart the other various manifestations of the Spirit. Joy is part of the whole person, whose whole humanity has been assumed by the vicarious humanity of Christ. Joy is very much a problem if it is expected by itself. This becomes a telling critique of viewing joy as simply ecstasy or a feeling.[58] The joy of Jesus never exists without love, peace, and other aspects of the fruit of the Spirit.

In the midst of opposition, the believing Jew offers sacrifices in the context of joy: "Now my head is lifted up above my enemies all around

---

57. Weiser, *Psalms*, 602.

58. Contra Barbara Ehrenreich who offers a rather predictable secular critique of religion as that which keeps joy from being ecstasy in *Dancing in the Streets: A History of Collective Joy* (New York: Metropolitan, 2007).

me, and I will offer in his tent sacrifices with shouts of joy; I will sing and make melody to the Lord" (Ps 27:6). But even offering sacrifices does not coerce the grace of God. In the dedication of the new temple, sacrifices are offered because God has provided the joy: "They offered great sacrifices that day and rejoiced, for God had made them rejoice with great joy; the women and children also rejoiced. The joy of Jerusalem was heard far away" (Neh 12:43). Yet giving freely with joy is always commended: "Then the people rejoiced because these had given willingly, for with single mind they had offered freely to the Lord; King David also rejoiced greatly" (1 Chr 29:9).

This joy includes a delight in God's decrees: "I delight in the way of your decrees as much as in all riches . . . I will delight in your statutes; I will not forget your word" (Ps 119:14, 16). "Your decrees are my heritage forever; they are the joy of my heart" (Ps 119:111). God's word brings joy. The prophet finds joy in the words of God: "Your words were found, and I ate them, and your words became to me a joy and the delight of my heart" (Jer 15:16). Even the church at Antioch can delight in the letter with decisions made concerning the Gentiles by the council at Jerusalem: "When its members read it, they rejoiced at the exhortation" (Acts 15:31). Obedience to God's commands is not true obedience without joy, such as in parenthood, according to Barth:

> One cannot assume the burden of obligation without feeling joy in the accompanying honor. Nor can one rejoice in the honour without taking to heart the seriousness of the obligation. The divine command requires all parents, all fathers and mothers, to feel both aspects. One cannot be obedient to God's command without both joy and seriousness.[59]

Joy may be lacking, however, because of the judgment of God. There is no joy when judgment is experienced: "The city of chaos is broken down, every house is shut up so that no one can enter. There is an outcry in the streets for lack of wine; all joy has reached its eventide; the gladness of the earth is banished" (Isa 24:10–11).

> Beat your breasts for the pleasant fields, for the fruitful vine, for the soil of the people growing up in thorns and briers; yes, for all the joyous houses in the jubilant city, for the palace will be forsaken, the populous city deserted; the hill and the watchtow-

---

59. Barth, *CD* III/4, 277.

er will become dens forever, the joy of wild asses, a pasture for flocks... (Isa 32:13–14)

Only the remnant of Israel will possess joy: "My servants shall sing for gladness of heart, but you shall cry out for pain of heart, and shall wail for anguish of spirit" (Isa 65:14). Ironically, the remnant will be mocked by others: "Hear the word of the Lord you who tremble at his word: Your own people who hate you and reject you for my name's sake have said, 'Let the Lord be glorified, so that we may see your joy'; but it is they who shall be put to shame" (Isa 66:5). After the judgment, the shouting that is left is not shouting of joy: "Gladness and joy have been taken away from the fruitful land of Moab; I have stopped the wine from the wine presses; no one treads them with shouts of joy; the shouting is not the shout of joy" (Jer 48:33). Even a city called "the joyful town" (Damascus) can be forsaken: "How the famous city is forsaken, the joyful town!" (Jer 49:25). "The whole earth" will rejoice over judgment on the nations, such as Edom, even as Edom rejoiced over the judgment on Israel: "Thus says the Lord God: As the whole earth rejoices, I will make you desolate. As you rejoiced over the inheritance of the house of Israel, because it was desolate, so I will deal with you" (Ezek 35:14–15). Judgment will come upon Ammon because they rejoiced in Israel's misfortune: "For thus says the Lord God: Because you have clapped your hands and stamped your feet and rejoiced with all the malice within you against the land of Israel, therefore I have stretched out my hand against you, and will hand you over as plunder to the nations" (Ezek 25:6–7). Even the saints, apostles, and prophets will rejoice over the judgment on "Babylon" in the Apocalypse: "Rejoice over her, O heaven, you saints and apostles and prophets! For God has given judgment for you against her" (Rev 18:20). Israel will rejoice in God's judgments on the idolatrous nations: "All worshippers of images are put to shame, those who make their boast in worthless idols; all gods bow down before him. Zion hears and is glad, and the towns of Judah rejoice, because of your judgments, O God" (Ps 97:7–8). The believer has hope that the despair from judgment will give way to joy, and so one prays to God: "Let me hear joy and gladness; let the bones that you have crushed rejoice" (Ps 51:8).

The word of God needs to be heard as the word of joy in the midst of the "bones" that have been "crushed" by God. The God who brought judgment will also bring joy, a joy coming from hearing the word of God according to Calvin:

> When he speaks of his *bones* as having *broken,* he alludes to the extreme grief and overwhelming distress to which he had been reduced. The joy of the Lord would reanimate his soul; and this joy he describes as to be obtained by *hearing;* for it is the word of God alone which can first and effectually cheer the heart of any sinner . . . The joy which he desires is that which flows from hearing the word of God, in which he promises to pardon our guilt, and readmit us into his favour.[60]

But who truly hears the word of God? Or is Jesus Christ both the Word and the one who hears the word, on our behalf and in our place, and therefore also hears the joy? This is despite the fact, interestingly, that his "bones" were not "broken," according to John 19:33, which, according to John 19:36 is a fulfillment of "Scripture": "None of his bones shall be broken," most likely, Psalm 34:20, describing the righteous man: "He keeps all their bones; not one of them is broken." Jesus takes the place of the man with crushed bones even though he is the righteous man whose bones are not broken. Again, we have the "wonderful exchange" (cf. 2 Cor 8:9).

The nations should rejoice that God is the judge: "Let the nations be glad and sing for joy, for you judge the peoples with equity and guide the nations upon the earth" (Ps 67:4). Judgment should, therefore, be a source of joy because God's judgment is righteous.[61] But who is able to make that righteous decision? So who can truly possess joy?

Our lack of joy may be because we refuse the joy that God gives. We may not want God to take our place, particularly in joy. Barth puts it starkly: "If we are not ready to be in the far country we are not ready to allow that the Son of God has come along us. We want to be in hell."[62] We assume we know what joy is. But is that not a great burden?

Joy exists when the righteous are blessed and the wicked perish: "When it goes well with the righteous, the city rejoices; and when the wicked perish, there is jubilation" (Prov 11:10). Jerusalem after judgment will be an object of scorn, no longer remembered for its beauty and joy: "All who pass along the way clap their hands at you; they hiss and wag their heads at daughter Jerusalem; 'Is this the city that was called the perfection of beauty, the joy of all the earth'?" (Lam 2:15). Judgment brings the end of joy in the hearts of the inhabitants: "The joy of our hearts has

---

60. Calvin, *Calvin's Commentaries: Commentary on the Book of Psalms*, vol. 2, 295.
61. Weiser, *Psalms*, 476.
62. Barth, *CD* IV/2, 396.

ceased; our dancing has been turned into mourning" (Lam 5:15). Israel is not to rejoice in its whoring: "Do not rejoice, O Israel! Do not exult as other nations do; for you have played the whore, departing from your God" (Hos 9:1). Because Israel's joy was not in the Lord, it will experience judgment: "Because you did not serve the Lord your God joyfully and with gladness of heart for the abundance of everything, therefore you shall serve your enemies whom the Lord will send against you, in hunger and thirst, in nakedness and lack of everything." (Deut 28:47-48). The enemies of Israel will then be the ones rejoicing: "The Lord has done what he purposed, he has carried out his threat; as he ordained long ago, he has demolished without pity; he has made the enemy rejoice over you, and exalted the might of your foes" (Lam 2:17).

God will find joy in judgment as he did in grace: "And just as the Lord took delight in making you prosperous and numerous, so the Lord will take delight in bringing you to ruin and destruction" (Deut 28:63). As harsh as this may sound to us, Barth reminds us that our idea of grace must expand to include holiness: "If we are concerned about the truth of God who is wholly grace, we cannot and must not cling to our idea of grace as though our understanding of God had not need to grow, as though this idea of ours enabled us to acquire control over God."[63] Holiness is not just a second factor next to grace, however, because "We are merely continuing to speak of God's grace" when we speak of holiness.[64] Yet grace "may bear other names," while maintaining "the unity of the divine being" and not "allowing holiness to appear as a second or third factor in God alongside the primary one."[65]

God will end up going into the despair of judgment with us but not leaving us there; we will be raised up with him in the vicarious joy of Christ (Rom 6:4, 8-10). As Barth remarks, "From the outset, however, the problem is to show the fact and extent that God as gracious is also holy, and again that as holy He is also gracious."[66] The lack of joy that comes from judgment is only the opportunity then for God to be gracious. Therefore, the cross of Jesus Christ should never be viewed apart from his resurrection. This is the perennial problem of medieval obsessions with the quantity of the suffering of Christ, still portrayed in recent times in a film like

63. Barth, *CD* II/1, 358.
64. Ibid., 359.
65. Ibid.
66. Ibid.

Mel Gibson's *The Passion of the Christ*.[67] Grace reveals the opposition of humanity to God, and therefore brings the loss of joy, and with the loss of joy, despair. The problem of joy is that we can so easily lose it. Barth comments, "The revelation of God, just because it is a revelation of His love and grace, means the revelation of His opposition to man, i.e., of His opposition to the opposition in which man exists over against Him."[68] Loss of joy comes from a repudiating of the grace of God; this is the dynamic tension between grace and judgment so that judgment is certainly real, despite liberal theology, but biblical judgment is the judgment of grace, bringing genuine despair, the despair that leads to repentance (2 Cor 7:10). "God is holy because His grace judges and His judgment is gracious."[69] The loss of joy does not mean the loss of grace. Grace exists in judgment.

> If He is not present to us in this tension, He is not present to us at all. If we refuse to recognize and, as is right, to suffer this His opposition to us, we are also repudiating His grace. To believe in God means that we bow to this His opposition to us, accepting, and—despairing of ourselves but not of Him—allowing His good will towards us to be our ground of confidence and hope.[70]

Judgment will come because of the false joy of the nations: "Therefore says the Lord God: 'I am speaking in my hot jealousy against the rest of the nations, and against all Edom who, with wholehearted joy and utter contempt, took my land as their possession . . .'" (Ezek 36:5). The prophets will speak on that day when joy is taken from them:

> And you, mortal, on the day when I take from them their stronghold, their joy and glory, the delight of their eyes and their heart's affection, and also their sons and their daughters . . . On that day your mouth shall be opened to the one who has escaped, and you shall speak and no longer be silent. So you shall be a sign to them; and they shall know that I am the Lord. (Ezek 24:25–27)

When the church reads this, the prophetic office of Jesus Christ is certainly in mind, a prophetic office that is vicarious, on behalf of the prophets and the people of God.

---

67. *The Passion of the Christ*, directed by Mel Gibson, Icon Entertainment, 2004.
68. Barth, *CD* II/1, 362.
69. Ibid., 363.
70. Ibid., 362.

Joy as Gift, Grace, and Gratitude . . . and Its Enemies 199

The Christian life is to be characterized by joy in responding to the gift of God's grace. The people of Israel responded joyfully with offerings for the new temple (1 Chr 29:9). When a battle was won, the people experienced joy because "the Lord had enabled them to rejoice over their enemies" (2 Chr 20:27). The rebuilt temple of Ezra and Nehemiah is cause to celebrate "the dedication of this house of God with joy" (Ezra 6:16).

It is not easy to give thanks in the midst of some forms of despair. Jesus rejoices for us, on our behalf and in our place. He does so by coming into solidarity with us, first of all. The goal of worship may be, in Schmemann's thought, to possess joy by leaving the world in the liturgical experience.[71] But solidarity with sinful humanity is the beginning of the incarnation. The announcement to the shepherds by the angels was already "good news of a great joy" (Luke 2:10). Like the shepherds, we are not "wise and intelligent," so we need to be "surprised by joy," in C. S. Lewis' words.[72] Joy is the happiness that is like the uncle you never knew that shows up while you are sleeping, in Jane Kenyon's poem.[73] Instead of a joy that we envy, which is often the case when we observe the happiness of others, particularly when we are in despair if they possess something we do not or have not suffered a loss that we have suffered, the joy of Jesus is his, first of all, but also something for us to join in (Ps 16:11). Therefore, the Christian life (and particularly the work of the theologian, Karl Barth adds) should be a combination of beauty and joy. Since theology is "a particularly beautiful science . . . The theologian who has no joy in his work is no theologian at all."[74] The joy that Ecclesiastes commends is not a joy of giddied exuberance. Neither hedonistic nor Epicurean, Qoheleth nonetheless is very realistic about accepting what joy can be in a vain and inscrutable world, recognizing that the joy comes from God:

> There is nothing better for mortals than to eat and drink, and find enjoyment in their toil. This also, I saw, is from the hand of God; for apart from him who can eat or who can have enjoyment? For to the one who pleases him God gives wisdom and knowledge and joy; but to the sinner he gives the work of gather-

---

71. Schmemann, *For the Life of the World*, 29.
72. C. S. Lewis, *Surprised by Joy*.
73. Kenyon, "Happiness" in *Otherwise*, 3.
74. Barth, *CD* II/1, 656.

> ing and heaping, only to give to one who pleases God. This also is vanity and a chasing after wind (Eccl 2:24–26).[75]

Even grim Qoheleth embraces joy! But his resignation shows how difficult it seems for him to do so. Yet he still sees the joy as coming from God: "Go, eat your bread with enjoyment, and drink your wine with a merry heart; for God has long ago approved what you do" (Eccl 9:7). "So I commend enjoyment, for there is nothing better for people under the sun than to eat, and drink, and enjoy themselves, for this will go with them in their toil through the days of life that God gives them under the sun" (Eccl 8:15). Yet this counsel can be taken askew by Israel, as how Israel responds to news of Babylon's fall:

> In that day the Lord God of hosts called to weeping and mourning, to baldness and putting on sackcloth; but instead there was joy and festivity, killing oxen and slaughtering sheep, eating meat and drinking wine. "Let us eat and drink for tomorrow we die." The Lord of hosts has revealed himself in my ears: Surely this iniquity will not be forgiven you until you die, says the Lord God of hosts. (Isa 22:12–14)

We can seek joy when we should be repenting.[76] The problem of joy includes the problem of when to be joyful and when to weep and mourn in repentance.

According to Isaiah, salvation should be appropriated with joy: "With joy you will draw water from the wells of salvation" (Isa 12:3). Salvation gives hope for the future: "The meek shall obtain fresh joy in the Lord, and the neediest people shall exult in the Holy One of Israel" (Isa 29:19). Yet judgment can interrupt a complacency of joy that will be replaced by only the joy of animals:

> Beat your breasts for the pleasant fields, for the fruitful vine, for the soil of my people growing up in thorns and briers; yes, for all the joyous houses in the jubilant city. For the palace will be forsaken, the populous city deserted; the hill and the watchtower will become the dens forever, the joy of wild asses, a pasture for flocks. (Isa 32:12–14)

---

75. See Murphy, *Ecclesiastes*, 27.
76. Childs, *Isaiah*, 161.

"My servants shall sing for gladness of heart, but you shall cry out for pain of heart, and shall wail for anguish of spirit" (Isa 65:14). There is hope, however, for those who mourn: "The spirit of the Lord is upon me, because the Lord has anointed me . . . to provide for those who mourn in Zion—to give them a garland instead of ashes, the oil of gladness instead of mourning, the mantle of praise instead of a faint spirit" (Isa 61:1, 3; cf. Luke 4:16–21). The result is a strength given to the redeemed: "They will be called oaks of righteousness, the planting of the Lord, to display his glory" (Isa 61:3).

> For I am about to create a new heavens and a new earth; the former things shall not be remembered or come to mind. But be glad and rejoice forever in what I am creating; for I am about to create Jerusalem as a joy, and its people as a delight. I will rejoice in Jerusalem, and delight in my people; no more shall the sound of weeping be heard in it, or the cry of distress. (Isa 65:17–19; cf. Rev 21:1–5)

THE LURE OF PSEUDO-JOYS

Joy is not giddiness or living with rose-colored glasses and naiveté. Joy is not necessarily happiness, although they are closely related. Yet happiness can easily lack the depth that joy possesses, particularly in the biblical sense of joy. Barth adds to his comment against joyless theologians that "Sulky faces, morose thoughts and boring ways of speaking are intolerable in this science."[77] Our faces, thoughts, and speaking often still live in that despair that no amount of exhortation from Karl Barth is going to change (since, by the way, he is Karl Barth, the great and successful theologian, and I am not!) So we think. The problem of joy remains, not to be solved by moral exhortations or singing "Keep Your Sunny Side Up" or "The Sunny Side of the Street," as wonderful as those old favorites are. Despair has been with us too long and is too honest with us. C. S. Lewis is honest about our condition: "We are half-hearted creatures, fooling about with drink and sex and ambition when infinite joy is offered us, like an ignorant child who wants to go on making mud pies in a slum because he cannot imagine what is meant by the offer of a holiday at the sea. We are far too easily pleased."[78]

77. Barth, *CD* II/1, 656.
78. C. S. Lewis, *The Weight of Glory and Other Addresses* (Grand Rapids: Eerdmans, 1965) 2.

Ed Wood was a hack director of bottom of the barrel science fiction and horror shlock movies of exploitation in the fifties, made most famous by his film, *Plan Nine from Outer Space* (also called *Graverobbers from Outer Space*), often called the worst movie ever made. Ed's life was "celebrated" in Tim Burton's quirky film, *Ed Wood*.[79] Ed may be a good example of one who was "far too easily pleased." Growing up enthusiastic over "B" horror movies of the thirties and forties, Wood took himself and his movies very seriously, despite the atrocious scripts, acting, and sets that consisted of his films. Ed's enthusiasm for his films was legendary. Perhaps it is more than generous to compare Wood to those whom Paul speaks of as having "a zeal for God, but it is not enlightened" (Rom 10:2). He certainly possessed joy, of a kind, and is certainly admirable for his enthusiasm. The only problem was that, frankly, Ed Wood had no talent. Calvin might have seen him as one he criticized for having "an excessive joy of life," that can end in despair.[80] This was true of Ed. His life ended sadly in desperately writing pornographic novels. Augustine claims that it is delight that turns the soul towards or away from the love of God.[81] Perhaps this can be seen in the life of Ed Wood. Unbridled "delight" or joy as giddiness leads to any kind of pleasure.

In a man much more learned than Ed Wood (but at least as controversial!), Friedrich Nietzsche, "Dionysian" joy is that "frenzy" which is the power of all great art and accomplishment. "Apollonian" form and order is inadequate to provide the emotional dynamo that is central to all creativity, in contrast to Jesus the Crucified.[82] The "Dionysian" is "the great pantheistic sharing of joy and sorrow that sanctifies and calls good even the most terrible and questionable qualities of life."[83] Barbara Ehrenrich comically tries to revive pagan ecstasy as justified in a modern dress by commending the hysteria among young girls caused by the Beatles in the sixties! "With his long hair, his hints of violence, and his promise of ecsta-

---

79. See Rudolph Grey, *Nightmare of Ecstasy: The Life and Art of Edward Wood, Jr.* (Portland, OR: Feral, 1994).

80. Calvin, *Golden Booklet of the True Christian Life*, 73.

81. Augustine, *De musica* 6.10.29, *The Fathers of the Church* 26 (1948) 151–379, cited by David Bentley Hart, *Beauty of the Infinite*, 254.

82. Friedrich Nietzsche, *Twilight of the Idols* in *The Portable Nietzsche*, trans. and ed. Walter Kaufmann (New York: Penguin, 1982) 561–62 and *The Will to Power*, trans. Walter Kaufmann and R. J. Hollingdale (New York: Random House, 1967) 539–40. Cf. David Bentley Hart, *Beauty of the Infinite*, 96–97.

83. Nietzsche, *Will to Power*, 539.

sy, Dionysus was the first rock star."[84] Surely joy is more than that. While ecstasy has its roots in a religious sense of "madness," literally ek-stasis, "standing outside of yourself," the chaos created by the Dionysian cult in the ancient world was roundly condemned by the church.[85] Ancient pagan ecstasy was known for producing a state of enthusiasm approaching madness, including lashing themselves with whips and ripping off their clothes with loud cries, culminating in self-castration. Like many moderns, Ehrenreich tends to equate creativity with chaos and religion with repression.

Ed Wood might have affirmed Nietzsche's Dionysian "will to life," but with seedy results. Nonetheless, there is something strangely endearing about Ed and every viewing of *Plan Nine from Outer Space*. Ed was looking for joy. In a way, Ed Wood's joy can be seen to be that kind of joy that admits no despair, but at a great price.

Ed Wood may be a poignant portrait of one that finds joy in folly. "Folly is a joy to one who has no sense" (Prov 15:21). Closely associated is the fool, who is no source of joy for the parents: "The one who begets a fool gets trouble; the parent of a fool has no joy" (Prov 17:21). "Folly is a more dangerous enemy to the good than evil," Dietrich Bonhoeffer writes," for folly cannot be reasoned with. "We shall never again try to convince a fool by reason, for it is both useless and dangerous."[86] The reference to Adolf Hitler and National Socialism is obvious. The failure of the culture of the enlightened, reasonable class of Germany against Hitler was stark, as Bonhoeffer comments in his *Ethics*: "The failure of reasonable people is appalling; they cannot manage to see either the abyss of evil or the abyss of holiness . . . Bitterly disappointed that the world is so unreasonable, they see themselves condemned to ineffectiveness."[87] The only solution is not "instruction" but "liberation," an inward liberation

---

84. Ehrenreich, *Dancing in the Streets*, 40–41.

85. See Abraham Heschel on contrasting ecstasy in the ancient world with prophecy in ancient Israel, in *The Prophets*. vol. 2 (New York: Harper Colophon, 1975) 104–46. On the cult of Dionysus see Hans-Josef Klauck, *The Religious Context of Early Christianity: A Guide to Graeco-Roman Religions*, trans. Brian McNeil (Edinburgh: T. & T. Clark, 2000) 107ff. On the early church see Johannes Quasten, *Music and Worship in Pagan and Christian Antiquity*, trans. Boniface Ramsey (Washington, DC: National Association of Pastoral Musicians, 1983) 36–37, 132.

86. Bonhoeffer, *Letters and Papers from Prison*, 8.

87. Bonhoeffer, *Ethics*, 78.

that precedes an outward liberation.[88] The joy of Jesus is included in that liberation, I think, a joy very different from Nietzschean ecstasy.

More substantive than Wood, yet with the same fannish exuberance, may be seen in the joy of Ray Bradbury, the author of *The Martian Chronicles* and countless other tales of fantasy, and a contemporary of Ed Wood's, whose literary abilities are as evident as Wood's are lacking. Bradbury comments often that his great crime in his age has been to be an optimist. Joy is the stuff of Ray Bradbury's writings, even in his horror and ironic work.[89]

Another false kind of joy is the momentary joy of the godless, as Zophar says in Job, "The joy of the godless is for a moment" (Job 20:5). The nations can do evil with "wholehearted joy": "Therefore thus says the Lord God: I am speaking in my hot jealousy against the rest of the nations, and against all Edom, who, with wholehearted joy and utter contempt, took my land as their possession, because of its pasture, to plunder it" (Ezek 36:5). Israel is not to have that kind of joy: "Do not rejoice, O Israel! Do not exult as other nations do; for you have played the whore, departing from your God" (Hos 9:1). Yet even in the time of Moses there was such revelry in the worship of the golden calf: "At that time they made a calf, offered a sacrifice to the idol, and reveled in the works of their hands" (Acts 7:41; cf. Exod 32:1, 23). There are those who find joy in the suffering of others, as the German word *Schadenfreude* represents.[90] Job asks why are the wicked allowed to possess joy: "Why do the wicked live on, reach old age, and grow mighty with power? . . . They sing to the tambourine and the lyre, and rejoice to the sound of the pipe" (Job 21:7, 12). Job could understand his miseries if he had rejoiced in the wrong thing, "If I have made gold my trust, or called fine gold my confidence; if I have rejoiced because my wealth was great, or because my hand had gotten much . . ." (Job 31:24–25). No, as Paul would say, love "does not rejoice in wrongdoing, but rejoices in the truth" (1 Cor 13:6). This is in bitter contrast with those who would rejoice to die: "Why is light given to one in misery, and life to the bitter in soul, who long for death, but it does not

---

88. Bonhoeffer, *Letters and Papers from Prison*, 9.

89. See Sam Weller, *The Bradbury Chronicles* (New York: William Morrow, 2005); and Calvin Miller, "Ray Bradbury: Hope in a Doubtful Age," in *More Than Words: Contemporary Writers on the Works That Shaped Them*, compiled and introduced by Philip Yancey, ed. James Calvin Schaap (Grand Rapids: Baker, 2002) 252–62.

90. Kast, *Joy, Inspiration, and Hope*, 85f.

come, and dig for it more than for hidden treasures; who rejoice exceedingly, and are glad when they are in the grave?" (Job 3:20–22). Wisdom is needed for help against those "who rejoice in doing evil and delight in the perverseness of evil" (Prov 2:14).

All sorts of material pleasures and joys are brought before us, all making a claim upon us. They certainly do bring joy. We should not deny it. There was certainly joy when Esther saved the Jews from Haman: "For the Jews there was light and gladness, joy and honor" (Esth 8:16). There are all sorts of secular and materialistic joys that are celebrated. So what is the problem? Why are the tabloids full from week to week of fabulously wealthy and successful celebrities burning themselves out at a young age? Ecclesiastes takes the "Hollywood" plunge himself, trying every kind of pleasure (Eccl 2:1–2; 9:7). What he eventually finds is boredom. Ironically, it is often, and tragically, boredom with sensuality, a boredom with God's creation. As Anderson comments, "We realize that we have gambled away the very meaning of life because we have denied the spirit for the sake of gratifying the flesh."[91] Denying the spirit means to begin with triviality and end up with boredom.[92] This can be true for both genuine joys, when we expect of them more than they can give, and "demonic pseudo-joys" that blatantly claim to bring fulfillment.[93] As Zophar in the book of Job reminds us, that according to the conventional piety, "the joy of the godless is but for a moment" (Job 20:5). Idolatry in ancient Israel (and today) presents itself in idols that are made from material sources, crafted by artisans, but "are like scarecrows in a cucumber field, and they cannot speak; they have to be carried, for they cannot walk" (Jer 10:3–5). They are powerless in trying to be God.

In trying to be God we are refusing to admit our limitations. "All evil," Barth claims, "begins with the fact that we will not thankfully accept the limitation of our existence where we should hope in the light of it, and be certain, joyously certain, of the fulfillment of our life in the expectation of its end."[94] It is puzzling, therefore, to read of David Bentley Hart's comment that "In God desire both evokes and is evoked; it is one act that for us can be grasped only by analogy to that constant dynamism within our being that comprises the distinct but inseparable moments of interior

91. Anderson, *Exploration into God*, 30–31.
92. Barth, *CD* III/4, 381.
93. Ibid., 382.
94. Barth, *CD* IV/2, 468.

energy and exterior splendor."[95] Does desire (joy) necessarily come from the "dynamism within our being"? Even though "in him we live and move and have our being" (Acts 17:28), is our problem with joy (and possessing a joy in the midst of despair) a problem that is exacerbated when we forget that God is God and we are not, instead of being open to be *given* joy through the vicarious joy of Christ? The bondage of the will (*servum arbitrium*) is a negation of our true freedom in always recognizing our limitations before God, not a "dynamism within our being." In fact, Barth can speak of the bondage of the will as those who, like in the midst of a joy as ecstasy in the Dionysian tradition, are "possessed."[96] Even Jesus in his humanity expresses human limitations, as Barth remarks: "Thus the man Jesus does not transcend the limits of the humanity common to Him and us, or become alien to us . . . The only difference is that He is it in genuine human freedom."[97]

The freedom of joy is given to us as a gift of grace in the vicarious joy of Christ, in contrast to "the strange and inactive action of the slothful man" who possesses a "tolerant indifference in relation to God."[98] Or perhaps we cling to a cause characterized often by "ceaseless activity" that purports to be humane but in effect ignores the concrete human person.[99] Our joy can become the cause; our freedom has been exchanged with slavery to a cause.[100] Our joy ceases to be the joy of Jesus, for whom even the Sabbath was made for humanity, not humanity for the Sabbath (Mark 2:27). The opposite of the devotee to the cause might be what Barth calls "the dissipated man," the one who wallows in self-pity so inevitably attacks others and is always desperately trying to find new pleasures in order to be fulfilled, often obsessed with the present (especially associated with "dangerous middle age"): *Carpe diem!*[101] This quest, however, ends in a bottomless pit. "There is no infinite to satisfy infinite desires."[102]

---

95. David Bentley Hart, *Beauty of the Infinite*, 269.

96. Barth, *CD* IV/2, 93.

97. Ibid.

98. Ibid., 405.

99. Ibid., 438-39.

100. See Eric Hoffer, *The True Believer: Thoughts on the Nature of Mass Movements* (New York: Time, 1963).

101. Barth, *CD* IV/2, 462-63, 471.

102. Ibid., 463.

Yet joy may be a momentary experience also for the religious. In the parable of the sower, Jesus warns of those who receive the word "immediately . . . with joy," yet because there is no "root," they cannot endure persecution or trouble and become involved in "the cares of the world," or "the lure of wealth" (Mark adds "the desire for other things") (Matt 13:20; cf. Mark 4:13–20; Luke 8:11–15). We may seek for constant joy but it is as problematic as constant sunshine, Barth argues.[103] Much sadness can be created by this constant sunshine, as utopian promises in politics can create expectations that the state can never fulfill. "Our joy has always its proper seat in anticipatory joy . . . The whole of life is provisional. It can only be lived in expectation of eternal life, i.e., in expectation of the revelation of its union with God's eternal life."[104] There is much virtue in viewing joy as a transitory event so that it make us appreciate the whole of life, and reminds us that joy ultimately lies in the hands of God, the source of real pleasure.[105] Do we really know what God only knows, what truly can bring us joy? Barth is even bold enough to say that joy "should not be limited by the suffering of life, because even life's suffering (or what we regard as such) comes from God, the very One who summons us to rejoice. He has given to the cosmos and therefore to our life an aspect of night as well as day . . ."[106]

The cross of Jesus Christ means that God does not avoid despair at all costs, "and our life still proceeds under the shadow of the cross."[107] Barth is clear on this:

> We must not object to the fact that we have to seek the manifestation of God's glory and the glory of our own life in the concealment of this shadow. We must also realize that all the provisional light which we believe we can recognize and enjoy as such really breaks forth from this shadow, that all the little fulfillments in which we may rejoice are only reflections of the great fulfillment which has taken place in the darkness onto which God Himself entered for us in His Son, and that every recognition and experience of these fulfillments is only an advance towards the comprehensive and conclusive revelation of this great fulfillment.[108]

103. Barth, *CD* III/4, 382.
104. Ibid., 384.
105. Ibid., 383.
106. Ibid.
107. Ibid.
108. Ibid.

This is not to be a Stoic or possess a "stiff upper lip," but to possess "the continuation of joy itself even in sorrow."[109]

"The continuation of joy itself even in sorrow"! Barth has indeed hit upon our goal. He rightly sees that Christology is the key. But how is this done? What does this mean? Do we really want this?

---

109. Ibid., 384.

CHAPTER NINE

The Joy That Comes from Struggle

Joy can come from struggle. There is no use in denying this, however much we may wish. The struggle can be trivial or tragic. We live with metaphors of struggle and joy. The struggle of the Brooklyn Dodgers to win a World Series after being continually stymied by the New York Yankees for decades certainly created a greater joy with their win in 1954. More recently, the Boston Red Sox ended a World Series drought that goes back to the beginning of the twentieth century, with the resultant great rejoicing. Comic book historian Gerard Jones comments on the attraction of the new genre of the superhero in comic books of the thirties and forties: "Superheroes turned anxiety into joy. As the world plunged into conflict and disaster almost too huge to comprehend, they grabbed their readers' darkest feelings and bounded into the sky with them."[1] But must we say that there is a necessity for there to be a struggle in order to have joy? Is this perilously close to saying that evil must exist in order for there to be good? The teaching of Genesis 1 that what God creates is good seems to argue against this. Does our experience, however, seem to expect joy only after there is struggle? Are we not far, then, from a kind of "works righteousness," in which the greatness of our joy becomes determined by how hard we have struggled? What, then, happens to grace and faith?

Within this problem, what difference should the vicarious humanity make? Is this a challenge to a doctrine that emphasizes what Christ has *already* done, the *finished* work of Christ in his life of faith and obedience to the Father in the Spirit on our behalf?[2] The reality of God and the reality of the human, Barth reminds us, is a relationship of "polarity

---

1. Gerard Jones, *Men of Tomorrow: Geeks, Gangsters, and the Birth of the Comic Book* (New York: Perseus, 2004) 231.
2. Colyer, *How to Read T. F. Torrance*, 122.

and tension."[3] But we now have "peace with God through our Lord Jesus Christ" (Rom 5:1). Why does the struggle still rage if Christ has "done it all," a question for all theories of the atonement?

THE STRUGGLE WITH STRUGGLE

Joy and struggle, sorrow, and despair can be accepted in a matter of fact way; they just are and we need to accept it rather than fight it: "In the day of prosperity, be joyful, and in the day of adversity consider: God has made the one as well as the other, so that mortals may not find out anything that will come after them" (Eccl 7:14). This is not mere Stoicism, but a trust that God is behind both the joy and the struggle. Yet, it is for the purpose "that mortals may not find out anything that will come after them." This is not to escape the conclusion of the vanity of life's pursuits: "Even those who live many years should rejoice in them all; yet let them remember that the days of darkness will be many. All that comes is vanity" (Eccl 11:8). The purpose is for the sake of our humility, to look beyond ourselves; there is the mystery of God. But is the mystery that we really do not know if God wants our good, that God is ultimately capricious, or is it a positive mystery, a mystery seen in Christ, the man of sorrows, whose goal is for us to participate in his joy?

STRUGGLE AS THE ROAD TO MATURITY

Joy in the midst of suffering seems to have been accepted by the early church. The struggle is accepted because of a perspective that spiritual maturity will come out of it. "My brothers and sisters, whenever you face trials of any kind, consider it nothing but joy [NIV reads, "pure joy"!], because you know that the testing of your faith produces endurance and let endurance have its full effect, so that you may be mature and complete, lacking in nothing" (Jas 1:2–4). Confessing our sins with genuine remorse to the point of changing joy into dejection is said to draw us nearer to God: "Draw near to God, and he will draw near to you. Cleanse your hands, you sinners, and purify your hearts, you double-minded. Lament and mourn and weep. Let your laughter be turned into mourning and your joy into dejection" (Jas 4:8–9). Paul seems to easily accept that conflict in the churches comes with the joy (2 Cor 7:4; 4:7–12). But

---

3. Barth, *CD* I/2, 791.

in our heart of hearts we often ask, Is the testing and the resulting maturity worth it? Do we not need to be convinced that this goal is worth what might be terrible suffering? Many of us would gladly accept being a weaker person in order to avoid the trial.[4] Most of us have encountered the pastoral counsel of those who urge us to see the trial or tragedy from "God's perspective." The problem is, neither we nor they are God.[5]

Trials, according to 1 Peter, are a sharing in the sufferings of Christ. That is the basis for rejoicing: "Beloved, do not be surprised at the fiery ordeal that is taking place among you to test you, as though something strange were happening to you. But rejoice insofar as you are sharing Christ's sufferings, so that you may also be glad and shout for joy when his glory is revealed" (1 Pet 4:12–13). This is not to be unexpected because to be in Christ is to share in Christ. But this must mean that Christ continues to suffer. The vicarious element is not fully here, but there is attention to the identification of our sufferings with Christ as the active Subject who continues to suffer. We do not suffer alone. And the joy before us is eschatological, very plainly in the future. The question is, How does the future affect our present? Or do we just "limp along" until Jesus comes back?

STRUGGLE AS AN ETHIC

Kierkegaard, along with all kinds of martyrology, finds suffering as indication that one is in the right. "For in this way the 'marks' of suffering are the joyous signs that the right way is being followed. But what joy can be greater than to dare to choose the best way, the way to the highest! And again, what joy is so great as this, except the joy of the infinite security of the way!"[6] The obvious question to the Dane is that all sorts of religions and philosophies justify themselves by martyrdom. Grim events in the contemporary world since 9/11 are ready testimony to this. Yet, Kierkegaard's voice needs to be heard because we too quickly (in a Hegelian way?) try to ignore the relationship between suffering and truth because we do not want to suffer. The Christian message does involve a joy in suffering, Kierkegaard contends, when one realizes that one is

---

4. Harold S. Kushner, *When Bad Things Happen to Good People* (New York: Avon, 1981) 26.

5. Ibid., 23.

6. Kierkegaard, *Gospel of Sufferings*, 23.

guilty before God.[7] What suffering does is avoid the rationalizations of the modern person, the excuses and nuances we too quickly offer in the name of reason, and frees one up to know the truth. "Since tribulation is the way, this is the joy that is in it: That it is thereby immediately clear to the sufferer, and he immediately knows as a fact, what is required of him; so that he need not spend time, nor use up any energy, in wondering whether his task might not to be something else."[8] Suffering has a positive place in "clearing" the mind; one at least can focus on what is true for the individual, a preoccupation for Kierkegaard. Conversely, suffering is enlightened by the joy of the "eternal weight of glory" that our temporal sufferings remind us (2 Cor 4:17). This is nothing that reason can teach, Kierkegaard reminds us.[9] "For when is the weight of temporal suffering most terrible upon a man? Is it not when it seems to him to have no meaning, to win nothing, to gain nothing?"[10]

The burden of Kierkegaard is found in embracing suffering and not avoiding it in terms of the truth, but still being confronted by the question of whether or not I am suffering for the right thing. Commenting on Kierkegaard, Ray Anderson writes in an early journal, "If I could have only one truth to guide me through life, it would be the truth of 'the greater suffering.' For all that is good issues from suffering for the right thing. And yet this truth can only be pressed to the heart as paradox."[11] Here we are at the supreme paradox, of Luther, Kierkegaard, and the Christian faith: the crucified God. Suffering brings us to the atonement but not an atonement without joy. We cannot forget Heb 12:2: "Who for the joy that was set before him endured the cross, disregarding its shame, and has taken his seat at the right hand of the throne of God." The cross leads to joy and the ascension of Christ. Anderson concludes: "Now there are those who do not understand this. And they hold that all such talk of suffering is morbid and depressing. I suppose then that they have what they want. But why then do they not have joy?"[12]

---

7. Ibid., 91.

8. Ibid., 97.

9. Ibid., 114, 119–20.

10. Ibid., 119.

11 Anderson, *Soul of God*, 54. Cf. Anderson, *Soulprints*, 91–92.

12. Anderson, *Soul of God*, 54.

STRUGGLE AND THE JOY OF JESUS

"They have not joy"! We remember Nietzsche's damning critique of Christianity. Perhaps they do not possess much joy because they avoid so much suffering. They may have the Kierkegaardian greatest despair of not knowing that you are in despair, but they do not have joy because joy comes to us within the womb of suffering. "No one will understand or share my joy who has not become part of my suffering."[13] This is true most of all christologically. Whether we like it or not, we do not understand the cross without the resurrection, nor the resurrection without the cross.

Our Christology, therefore, is the key to somehow seeing joy in the midst of struggle. Paul prays for the Colossians, "May you be made strong with all the strength that comes from his glorious power, and may you be prepared to endure everything with patience, while joyfully giving thanks to the Father, who has enabled you to share in the inheritance of the saints in the light" (Col 1:12). Paul assumes that there is something to be endured and that "joyfully giving thanks" takes places in its midst. The "joyfully giving thanks," in addition, is particularly to "the Father." Is it significant that Paul names "the Father"? This is the same Father to whom Jesus prays to as the object of thanksgiving in the midst of trials, for "he has rescued us from the power of darkness and transferred us into the kingdom of his beloved Son, in whom we have redemption, the forgiveness of sins" (Col 1:13). We can now join into that Father-Son dialogue of prayer and praise because we "live" in the Son's kingdom, the reality of the vicarious joy and thanksgiving of Christ.

The struggle, however, does not always appear to be good. Ray Anderson suggests that Ecclesiastes' teaching leads to an acceptance of joy within the monotony of life: "This is what I have seen to be good: it is fitting to eat and drink and find enjoyment in all the toil with which one toils under the sun the few days of the life God gives us; for this is our lot" (Eccl 5:18). Anderson comments, "Have you ever suddenly discovered amidst the monotony of your life that you are filled with a strange sense of joy and that this day—today—this moment is worth everything?"[14] When struggle interrupts as anxiety, however, we easily forget about and ignore the joy of everyday life. "Anxiety robs us of the joy of the things

---

13. Ibid., 55.
14. Anderson, *Exploration into God*, 52.

that we possess by anticipating their loss."[15] Anxiety takes the moment and becomes the struggle that constantly reminds us that "This joy can't last!" and therefore brings us into a deeper melancholy. Change can upset everything.

Jesus is said to have "rejoiced in the Holy Spirit" during his earthly ministry (Luke 10:21). The Epistle to the Hebrews, however, speaks of the joy of Jesus as also involving an anticipation of joy, "for the sake of the joy that was set before him [he] endured the cross . . ." (Heb 12:2). Can anticipation of joy be anything more than simply a hoped for dream apart from the anticipation that Jesus had?

STRUGGLE AND DESPAIR

The struggle may be very evident depending upon the source of despair. Evagrius appears to have been the first to view "the noonday demon" as the source of *acedia,* despair or sloth.[16] We expect despair to become a struggle if the source is a demon. But can evil and suffering be easily equated with cosmic struggle between God and Satan? Is a Manichean dualism not far behind? Nonetheless, for Evagrius, after the struggle with the noonday demon comes "a state of deep peace and inexpressible joy."

There is a joy within struggle that the blues music tradition appreciates; a joy in "confessing" your despair or even a sense of elation when the joy actually comes because one has endured the despair. How joyful is the old blues standard, "Sweet Home Chicago," because it is sung by those who have known despair and rejection. This does not, however, legitimate the oppression by others. Exhaustion that comes at the end of a working day is a good kind of joy, despite the difficulty and discipline involved in genuine work. The joy, as is often noted, is that much sweeter. There is an eschatological sense of joy, then, when the toil of this life is at an end: "But they have conquered him by the blood of the Lamb and by the word of their testimony, for they did not cling to life even in the face of death. Rejoice then, you heavens and those who dwell in them!" (Rev 12:11–12). "Let us rejoice and exult and give him the glory, for the marriage of the Lamb has come . . ." (Rev 19:7). John Cassian speaks for centuries of the monastic tradition in his rhapsody concerning the joy

---

15. Ibid., 59.

16. Evagrius of Pontus, *Pratikos* 12, cited by Špidlik, *The Spirituality of the Christian East,* 252–53.

that intense despair ("saving compunction") brings: "Often the fruit of saving compunction emerges as an unspeakable joy and a liveliness of soul. Joy in its immensity becomes unbearable and the soul bursts out in great cries, bringing to a neighboring cell the word of our heart's gladness and of the mightiness of our exultation."[17] For Cassian joy "bursts out" of despair. It is not merely the cure for despair but its vital antecedent, with a largeness that comes out of despair but cannot be contained by it. Apparently this was heard in the adjoining monk's cell! Other times, it is so powerful that it can be expressed in sounds: "Sometimes the soul lies low, hidden in the depths of silence. The stunning onset of sudden light takes all sound of voice away. All its senses are withdrawn into its own depths, or else are let go and with unspeakable groaning it pours out its longings to God."[18] The depths of struggle provide a depth of joy for the monk, sometimes with silence and sometimes with tears. "And sometimes it fills up with such sorrow and grief that it can only shake it off by melting into tears."[19]

Certainly joy is made more acute by the loss of a loved one, when the joy of the past becomes even more joyful than when it happened because one appreciates it more. It will never be again; despair, yes, but also accentuated joy. You know the value of the loved one in a way you never knew before they were gone. Is this behind Jesus's cryptic words to the disciples, "Are you discussing among yourselves what I meant when I said, 'A little while, and you will not longer see me, and again a little while, and you will see me?' Very truly, I tell you, you will weep and mourn, but the world will rejoice; you will have pain, but your pain will turn into joy" (John 16:19–20)? The Spirit will speak into that despair and speak of the Son in a more intense way than he could be known apart from his departure (John 14:15–31). But there is pain before joy.

IS THE STRUGGLE NECESSARY?

Is the tragic essential for the gospel? The Christian conflict may be seen as not just with oneself but with the despair of creation (Rom 8:20–23). H. Richard Niebuhr classically speaks of the Lutheran tradition in this way as "Christ and Culture in Paradox": "Living between time and eternity,

---

17. Cassian, *Conferences* 9, 117.
18. Ibid.
19. Ibid.

between wrath and mercy, between culture and Christ, the true Lutheran finds life both tragic and joyful."[20] This is certainly attractive to us in our most trying moments in which the Christian life is anything but one triumph after another and when personal and corporate sin seem to be still all too prevalent.

David Bentley Hart, however, returns with his loud protest: There is no "pathos" in God. The ancient theologians did not desire "such a miserable, imperfect, shadowy god, but to long rather for a God of superabounding and eternal might, life, joy without any trace of pain, the inexhaustible fountainhead of life and light and beauty . . ."[21] Hart rightly answers the kind of view represented by Nietzsche's commendation of the Dionysian spirit as "the great pantheistic sharing of joy and sorrow that sanctifies and calls good even the most terrible and questionable qualities of life."[22] But does Hart go too far? Such unquestioned hyper-Hegelianism seems to desperately and romantically seek to reconcile even the most vile and disreputable actions in human history: Who wants to justify the Holocaust because it helped to create a homeland for the Jews? But at least Hart can be seen as avoiding the kind of anthropomorphic God suspect in much popular religion, the God very much limited by our desires and imaginations that even a contemporary sympathetic theist (of some sort) like the writer Ray Bradbury discounts: "It's too limiting . . . This universe is all such a great mystery. We just don't know how it was created."[23] Nonetheless, something is missing from Hart.

"Joy without any trace of pain"! How striking. How similar to the kind of decretal Calvinism that Hart would normally eschew, however. Here is a God who is impassible and immutable, but what does that mean for the incarnation? What is the relationship to Jesus, "the man of sorrows and acquainted with grief"? The struggle in the humanity of Jesus according to Scripture was all too real and so was the connection with our struggling humanity.[24] Is that too distant from who God truly is? Is God in solidarity with the truly tragic plight of humanity and creation as

---

20. H. Richard Niebuhr, *Christ and Culture* (San Francisco: HarperSanFrancisco, 2001) 96, 178.

21 David Bentley Hart, *Beauty of the Infinite*, 375.

22. Nietzsche, *Will to Power*, 539.

23. Bradbury quoted in Weller, *The Bradbury Chronicles: The Life of Ray Bradbury*, 8.

24. Trevor Hart, "Through the Arts: Hearing, Seeing and Touching the Truth," in *Beholding the Glory*, ed. Begbie, 17.

well? As Scott Becker, a PhD student at Fuller Seminary, commented on his blog shortly before his death: "The Man of Sorrows and the Prince of Peace—the Crucified and the Risen One—are one and the same."[25] Hart recoils from D. M. Mackinnon's recognition that "revelation is not a charade but in an agony with flesh racked with pain, and human consciousness lost in a sense of the meaninglessness of the world."[26] Bonhoeffer wrestled with the paradox of what others thought of him and what he knew within himself: "Am I then all that which other men tell of? Or am I only what I know of myself, restless and longing and sick, like a bird in a cage . . ."[27] Bonhoeffer was able to face his own pain despite how others view him because Jesus is "the man of sorrows." The persecuted are told by Jesus to rejoice and that they will be rewarded in heaven (Matt 5:12 = Luke 6:22–23). Joy and sorrow live together when the temple is rebuilt and the noise from joy is indistinguishable from those weeping that this is not as great as the earlier one (Ezra 3:12–13). We cannot escape from the fact that not only are our bodies deteriorating, but we also *know* that they are.[28] Ecclesiastes is a skeptic of those whose joy does not encompass sadness.[29] Recognizing the vanity in life is its hope.[30] Accepting that we are both dust and spirit is to realize that this temporal life will not fulfill all human aspirations. "The very conflict of life is evidence that we have eternity in our hearts," Ray Anderson claims.[31] Contra Hart, conflict and tragedy are not to be ignored. Indeed, Karl Barth commends marriage because it includes all of life, joy and sorrow:

> Marriage is "chaste," honourable and truly sexual when it is encompassed by the fellowship of the spirit and of love, but also of work and of the whole of life with all its sorrows and joys, and when this total life experience justifies at the right time and

---

25. Scott Becker, "Con Patienti." Online: http://aufhebung1.blogspot.com/2007/06/con-patienti.html, June 23, 2007.

26. D. M. Mackinnon, *The Resurrection: A Dialogue Arising from Broadcasts by G. W. H. Lampe and D. M. Mackinnon*, ed. William Purcell (London: Mowbray, 1966) 67, 109–110, cited by David Bentley Hart, *Beauty of the Infinite*, 380.

27. Bonhoeffer, *Letters and Papers from Prison*, 347.

28. Anderson, *Exploration into God*, 13.

29. Ibid., 16.

30. Ibid., 19.

31. Ibid., 21.

> place this particular relationship ... To use our earlier phrase, coitus without co-existence is demonic.[32]

This is very different from the actress Penelope Cruz who says that she does not believe in marriage but she does believe in family, love, and children![33] Christologically, joy and sorrow are both lived and expressed in the humanity of Jesus Christ, whose humanity is vicarious at least because it encompasses both the whole of Jesus's life and the whole of our lives.

Is Hart's God ultimately all too remote from despair, and ultimately irrelevant to the life I am actually living right now? Hart has been heard to utter, "I don't have a pastoral bone in my body." This is hardly a commendation of his theology! I am afraid that lacking a pastoral "bone" is all too evident at this point, with "tragic" results for the ministry of the church if his proposal is adopted. Still, no one else than a usual strange theological bedfellow for Hart, Karl Barth, seems to commend a theology of joy without struggle.

JOY AND STRUGGLE FOR KARL BARTH

"Make a joyful noise unto the Lord, all the earth," implores the psalmist (Ps 100:1), yet we do so sometimes with great difficulty. But is our problem that that we are surprised by the difficulty? "Beloved, do not be surprised at the fiery ordeal that is taking place among you to test you, as though something strange were happening to you" (I Pet 4:12); "My brothers and sisters, whenever you face trials of any kind, consider it nothing but joy, because you know that the testing of your faith produces endurance . . ." (Jas 1:2–3). There is almost a matter-of-fact attitude in the New Testament about trials, and the joy that comes out of them. Yet the Christian community is very imperfect and does not like trials. So, as Barth observes, the community comes singing (as joy is so often connected with singing in the Bible), "even though they are weary and heavy-laden because blind and deaf and lame, [they] do come into His presence with real singing, if only in the form of sighs and croaks."[34] Even though we do this so imperfectly, the imperative is still to do this with joy. In fact, Barth adds, this is to be done "without murmuring or complaint."

---

32. Barth, *CD* III/4, 133.
33. Penelope Cruz, *The Wichita Eagle*, July 9, 2009, 1E.
34. Barth, *CD* IV/3.2, 793–94.

Barth's theology of creation is not unconnected with the place of joy apart from despair; just as in creation light is separated from darkness. The separation of the light from the darkness in Gen 1:14–19 is a real separation, Barth contends.[35] It is not "a special, positive work of God." God does not speak the darkness into being. The darkness is simply a pause in which time for a new day is allowed, so that humanity can "live a life which is not merely dreary and vegetative, but which is marked by a wakeful consciousness of time and history."[36] But the darkness has no ontological status. This rhythm, however, makes it possible "for man as a creature to have a history with God."[37] There is no equivalency, however, between light and darkness, just as joy and sorrow are not to be viewed as complementary in an ontological sense. A "wakeful consciousness" for human beings can only be furnished by the positive creation of light.

"Without murmuring or complaint," however? Really? What would Barth say to the psalmist of Psalm 64:1: "Hear my voice, O God, in my complaint; preserve my life from the dread enemy . . ." as well as the many other lament psalms? Daniel Migliore observes that the lament tradition of prayer is "lamentably" (my pun) absent from Barth.[38] Barth does makes the persuasive case that all prayer is petition, a dependence on God's grace, which could include lament as the complaint that, though God is able, he is not coming to my aid. In this sense, the lament is a form of petition. This may avoid the kind of lament emphasis today that turns too quickly into a kind of whining and a justification of our perspectives and agendas before God, often being a manifestation of an ideologically driven theology (e.g., I complain because God or the world is not supporting my capitalism or socialism).

Maybe Barth can do this, but it is difficult for many of us to come to worship with joy. For this, as with everything else, we need Christ, we need his vicarious joy. Barth is close to this when he urges for the basis of the joy of this weary and heavy-laden community in its calling, not its

35. Barth, *CD* III/1, 161–63.
36. Ibid., 162.
37. Ibid., 163.
38. Daniel L. Migliore, "Freedom to Pray: Karl Barth's Theology of Prayer," in Barth, *Prayer*, 111. Cf. Alan Torrance and his commendation of Moltmann in "Christian Experience and Divine Revelation in the Theologies of Friedrich Schleiermacher and Karl Barth," in *Christian Experience in Theology and Life*, ed. I. Howard Marshall (Edinburgh: Rutherford House, 1988) 111 and the critique of the tragic in David Bentley Hart, *Beauty of the Infinite*, 373–93.

experience.³⁹ This joy is that it may be a "likeness" of the kingdom of God to the world. As such, joy possesses the tension of the kingdom of God; being both "present" and "future." Joy is commanded just as the command to respond to the kingdom of God is to "repent" (Matt 4:17). Repentance is part of that serious business of the Bible, including the eschatological judgment.⁴⁰ Joy in the Bible comes in the midst of such seriousness, and therefore takes the form of a command. Otherwise, the nature of this life does not naturally take the form of joy. Yet the joy that God commands in the Bible, in the midst of the frustration, disappointments, and despairs of life, what Barth calls arising "from these dark places," is the joy that in its vicarious expression in the joy of Jesus takes joy out of our hands, in a substitutionary sense.⁴¹ "Because God the Creator and Lord of life acts and speaks here, taking the lost cause of man out of his hand, making it His own, intervening majestically, mercifully and wisely for him."⁴² Barth is neither a Candide nor a Pollyanna, naively praising God and ignoring the devastation around him. Indeed, that is why joy needs to be commanded, because of the chaos around us and in us. Like the nature of religion itself, joy needs *Aufhebung,* destruction and resurrection.⁴³

Joy itself lives between the times. It comes as a fulfillment but a fulfillment that never stays.

> For man has joy when there is in his life great or small fulfillment of his conscious or unconscious desires, cravings and strivings, when an event or change occurs or a state is achieved when he can greet and welcome because openly or secretly he had been waiting for it. Man has joy when for once he has reached his goals or at least one goal.⁴⁴

We like it when finally life smiles on us, when we can truly be thankful.⁴⁵ The problem is that in reaching that goal, it will not last. In fact, "true

---

39. Barth, *CD* IV/3.2, 795.
40. Barth, *CD* III/4, 375.
41. Ibid.
42. Ibid.
43. See Barth, *CD* I/2, "The Revelation of God as the Abolition (*Aufhebung*) of Religion," 280–361.
44. Barth, *CD* III/4, 376.
45. Ibid.

joy" is found only in "the duration of this fulfillment."[46] Is there anyone whose joy, whose gratitude to God, is really lasting? Is this not the joy of Jesus? He is the One who possesses "eternal joy . . . in perfect fellowship with God."[47]

Certainly such joy is a tall order for ordinary Neighborhood Baptist Church! Barth is to be commended for his remarkable ecclesiology that takes seriously the actual congregation on the corner, avoiding the temptation of so many views of the church that never return to earth from their wonderful idealistic rhapsodies about the Body of Christ. However, can Barth place an unbearable burden on the church without a sense that Christ is present, having taken upon despair, so that we might partake in *his* joy, especially if it is to be even a "likeness" to the kingdom of God? A christological indicative is necessary for Barth's realistic ecclesiology in the midst of the imperative of joy. Fortunately, Barth can proceed to say that "joy is now joy before the Lord and in Him. It is joy in His salvation, His grace, His law, His whole action."[48]

The brilliance of Barth's ecclesiology of "sigh and croaks" in the church, however, should not be underestimated. For after speaking of joy as "now joy before the Lord and in Him," Barth hastens to add that "it is now genuine, earthly, human joy."[49] The church does sing with "sighs and croaks," like the farmer in Edna St. Vincent Millay's poem who gets up from the failed crop "with twisted face and pocket full of seeds," as Ray Anderson frequently quotes.[50] The church exists in the world not just with power and potential or even hope ("pocket full of seeds") apart from a "twisted face" that has experienced weariness and failure, and, yes, despair. This is hope in the church, Anderson contends, that is not naïve, but a hope that takes a risk, exposing us to disappointment, frustration and betrayal.[51] Faith may plant the seed, but always with the possibility that the harvest might fail. The struggle is all too real.

46. Ibid., 377.
47. Ibid.
48. Ibid., 375–76.
49. Ibid., 376.
50. Edna St. Vincent Millay, "Sonnet X," in *Collected Poems*, ed. Norma Miller (New York: HarperCollins, 1981) 710, cited by Anderson, *Unspoken Wisdom*, 54, and *The New Age of Soul: Spiritual Wisdom for a New Millennium* (Eugene, OR: Wipf & Stock, 2001) 111.
51. Anderson, *New Age of Soul*, 111.

THE POSSIBILITY OF JOY WITHIN STRUGGLE

Faith may plant the seed of hope, but only God can bring the harvest, Anderson claims.[52] So "spiritual fitness" is not to be judged on the basis of our capacity to carry heavy burdens, but in a faith that loves, expecting nothing but what God will harvest. This is the joy that comes from love, Barth argues, in contrast to an expectation that the joy of love is when it is returned.[53] It is obvious that every parent wants a child's love returned. But the loving parent loves without regard to whether or not that love is returned (certainly not immediately in the case of infants!). Therefore, there is, especially in *eros,* a tragic or melancholy element, "the well-known cycle" of "alteration of possession and loss, intoxication and soberness, enthusiasm and disillusionment."[54] Yet the joy is in the loving first of all, imitating the love of God in order to exist in fellowship with him.

> This is the blessedness of him who loves—unsought, unplanned, undesired—even when his love beats against a stone wall, receiving no answer, or only a more or less hostile answer, from the one whom he loves. He does not love him for the sake of his answer, but because he is made free to do so by God. The peace and joy of the one who is liberated and therefore loves in this way can never suffer disillusionment.[55]

Yet the seeds planted will not necessarily be harvested.

"This is a reason for laughing even when our eyes swim with tears."[56] Laughter happens in the midst of a struggle that is born of joy and love. Another boyhood comic book favorite of mine was *Sgt. Fury and His Howling Commandos.* Amidst the admitted fantastic super-hero exploits of a World War II commando unit, Fury and his group would routinely wisecrack their way through a blaze of German gunfire. In response to some readers' objections that this was taking the tragedy of battle lightly, the creators Stan Lee and Jack Kirby (Kirby was a veteran of battlefield action) responded that in the midst of combat, humor is a great release in order to

---

52. Ibid., 112–13.
53. Barth, *CD* IV/2, 788–89.
54. Ibid., 788.
55. Ibid., 789.
56. Ibid.

break the tension. And, one might add, to share some common humanity communicated in humor in an otherwise inhumane situation.[57]

Response is needed but the only answer seems to be struggle. The parent does desire, desires greatly, a response of love from the child. God also desires that response. Nothing is more obvious from the patience and forbearance of Yahweh with Israel in the Old Testament. But the response that God desires and deserves is never forthcoming from Israel. Here is the need for the vicarious faith and obedience of Christ. A response is needed, from the side of humanity, a response of joy before the Father (Luke 10:21). The Bible is utterly realistic about the struggle of humanity. Bob Dylan's magnificent song, "Mississippi," expresses the struggles that none the less still yearn for joy.[58] The singer can only look back to one mistake, whatever is meant by staying in Mississippi "a day too long." Yet he can still be joyful, even charitable to "all those who've sailed with me." How? Why not be a total cynic? Why not let life devolve into bitterness?

Barth can even speak of a "readiness for joy" that comes from acknowledging life as God's gift of grace. Rejoicing is constantly acknowledging the gift.[59] This is what makes life possible in the midst of the struggle. Does not a gift, however, need a response (Derrida?), a response that we so often do not give back to God? A pause is needed, Barth contends, from the hurriedness of life that is the pause of gratitude.[60] We need Jesus to pause for us in the midst of our "omni-tasking" culture (the vicarious "pausing" of Christ?). This is in contrast to closing ourselves off to joy by solemnity or duty in either worship or ethics. The alternative may end up a life of bitterness. "On the basis of experienced disappointments we can try to establish that our only right is to bitterness."[61] Much of postmodern culture seems to degenerate into an ironic triumph of bitterness. Are we really surprised that the governor of the state of Illinois tried to sell Barack Obama's senate seat to the highest bidder? Nothing and no one can be trusted except our own cynicism. And how can we say otherwise?

57. See Stan Lee, Jack Kirby, and Dick Ayers, *Marvel Masterworks Presents Sgt. Fury and His Howling Commandos: Volume 1 Collecting Sgt. Fury and His Howling Commandos Nos. 1–13* (New York: Marvel, 2006); and Mark Evanier, *Kirby: King of Comics* (New York: Abrams, 2008) 128.

58. Bob Dylan, "Mississippi." Online: http://www.bobdylan.com/#/songs/mississippi.

59. Barth, *CD* III/4, 377–78.

60. Ibid., 378.

61. Ibid.

The true response of joy has to include the whole of life, including the sorrow and the pain.[62] Therefore, momentary joys will be accepted, but without the burden of expecting their duration. Otherwise, they become demonic and oppressive, claiming to bring so much but delivering so little. Ultimately, joy belongs to God; it is not our own, something that is beyond our power to create or sustain.[63] This is an issue of the epistemology of joy. The vicarious joy of Jesus reveals how inadequate our knowledge of joy is, especially when it comes to living with joy in the midst of sorrow and despair. To be "ready" for joy is to be ready for a joy that can encompass sorrow, to see God even in that, despite all the questions of theodicies. The resurrected Christ remains the crucified Christ, Moltmann reminds us.[64] The cosmos "still stands, and our life still proceeds, under the shadow of the cross on which this judgment has been accomplished for the salvation of the world and our own."[65] Barth hastens to warn us, "We must not object to the fact that we have to seek the manifestation of God's glory and the glory of our own life in the concealment of this shadow," because "the great fulfillment" of joy in God's Son brings meaning to the little joys.[66] If this is so, "the real test of our joy of life as a commanded and therefore a true and good joy is that we do not evade the shadow of the cross of Jesus Christ and are not unwilling to be genuinely joyful even as we bear the sorrows laid upon us."[67] This is not "mere resignation" but "the continuation of joy itself even in sorrow."[68] Joy and suffering will melt together:

> It is a matter of the proof of our joy in the fact that our capacity for enjoyment shows itself to be also a capacity for suffering, a readiness to accept with reverence and gratitude and therefore with joy the mystery and wonder of the life given to us by God, its beauty and radiance, and the blessing, refreshment, consolation and encouragement which it radiates as the gift of God, even where it presents itself to us in its alien form.[69]

---

62. Ibid., 382.
63. Ibid., 383.
64. Moltmann, *Theology of Hope*, 171.
65. Barth, *CD* III/4, 383.
66. Ibid.
67. Ibid.
68. Barth, *CD* III/4, 384.
69. Ibid.

How remarkable is it for Barth to speak of an "alien form" of joy! How difficult, in fact, it is to speak of despair and sorrow in this way without saying that God is the author of pain and sorrow! This does not mean "to whine and moan and pity oneself," Kierkegaard teaches, or "to endure with tight lips, or perhaps even find joy in the bitterness of suffering—and not find it only in the hope that the suffering will come to an end in time—but to find it in suffering, as when we say that sorrow is mixed with joy; this is something worth the learning."[70] Yet, do not Kierkegaard and Barth have a point? But in accepting this we need an obedience that is all too difficult for our meager attempts at gratitude. Only in true obedience will it be true joy. "For we then cling even in the former to what God and not we ourselves consider to be our true joy."[71]

Such a melting together of joy and suffering seems impossible. It is only something that can be believed because it cannot be seen, Kierkegaard argues.[72] This is not possible for "the natural man" but "requires the guidance of God," and "the deepest change in a man before he can believe in the mystery of sufferings."[73]

JESUS: THE MAN OF JOY WITHIN STRUGGLE

But where does Kierkegaard's man exist? This man must depend upon another's vicarious life.

> He must first have been deeply moved, and then have been willing to learn from him who alone went out into the world on set purpose to suffer, making the choice, and the demand, that he should suffer. He went out into the world, but he did not go as a young man goes from his father's house, he went out from the Father in heaven, and gave up the glory he had from the foundation of the world, yea, from eternity his choice was free and he came to the world—in order to suffer.[74]

---

70. Kierkegaard, *Gospel of Sufferings*, 29.
71. Barth, *CD* III/4, 384.
72. Kierkegaard, *Gospel of Sufferings*, 32.
73. Ibid., 49.
74. Kierkegaard, *Gospel of Sufferings*, 49.

Jesus himself "learned obedience" (Heb 5:8). "So close is the relation of obedience to the eternal truth, that he, who is the truth, yet learns obedience!"[75]

What does it mean to "learn obedience"? It means to be confronted by struggle in the world and with God. Gethsemane is "the key to our whole doctrine of atonement," the Orthodox theologian Kallistos Ware claims.[76] Jesus is confronted with a choice, a choice that we cannot make: will he trust and obey the Father? The faith of Jesus includes enduring the cross for the joy set before him (Heb 12:2). That "endurance" includes struggle against and the hostility of a sinful world: "Consider him who endured such hostility against himself from sinners, so that you may not grow weary or lose heart" (Heb 12:3)."[77] The effect of Jesus upon people was not always positive. As T. F. Torrance puts it, "The royal presence of Jesus had the effect of dividing them within themselves and among themselves," getting "inside their innermost thoughts."[78] This was a "hardening" that happened with Gentiles, Jews (Rom 1-3), and even believers (Heb 4:12-16), for the word of God is "sharper than any two-edged sword, piercing until it divides soul from spirit, joints from marrow; it is able to judge the thoughts and intentions of the heart" (Heb 4:12).[79] This is the cost of following one who said he came not to bring peace but a sword and to divide members of one's own family from one another (Matt 10:34-36).[80] So much for the "gentle Jesus meek and mild"! Jesus is familiar with struggling humanity, so much that he struggles against humanity itself. "He came to what was his own, and his own people did not accept him" (John 1:11). To follow him is not to avoid suffering, Kallistos Ware reminds us.[81]

Yet is it true, as Ware claims, that Christ did not suffer "instead of" us?[82] Believing in the substitutionary atonement does mean that we avoid all suffering but that Christ has truly taken our place so that not only do we participate in his heavenly goal but we also participate in his suffer-

---

75. Ibid.
76. Ware, *Orthodox Way*, 79.
77. T. F. Torrance, *Incarnation*, 142.
78. Ibid., 143.
79. Ibid., 143-45.
80. Ibid., 145-46.
81. Ware, *Orthodox Way*, 82.
82. Ibid.

ings in the present. His "saving companionship," to use Ware's phrase, is not apart from him graciously moving us out of the way yet always in union with him.[83] There is certainly a uniqueness in that much of what Jesus suffers we will never suffer (the "descent into hell" of the Creed). As Barth remarks, "He alone drinks this cup, not Peter and not Judas... He alone is delivered up 'for us,' in our place."[84] We may have to suffer, even in union with Christ, but never in the unique way that he suffered. This is the importance of Christ's descent into hell, his experience of Holy Saturday, of burial with us (see Alan Lewis and Hans Urs Balthasar), so that we may be raised from the dead.[85] He truly has become "the Rejected of God, for God makes Himself rejected in Him... Whatever God may inflict on them, He certainly does not inflict what He inflicted on Himself by delivering up Jesus Christ."[86] We share in both Christ's humiliation but also his exaltation, the exaltation predicated by his unique faithful response to the Father.

To cry on the cross is not to exclude faith, as some commentators seem to do, wanting to excuse Jesus of such "sin." Calling upon God, especially in anguish, can be an expression of faith.[87] Citing Psalm 22 as a cry of despair that ends in faith does not negate the combination of despair and faith.[88] "My God, my God..." speaks of *his* God, John McLeod Campbell reminds us.[89] Yet are we simply to view Jesus as only "feeling forsaken"? Does the reality of his death and burial, and his solidarity with humanity in their darkest moments permit this? Are we afraid to say with Eberhard Jüngel that "God's identification with the dead Jesus implies a self-differentiation on God's part"?[90] In speaking of the Father and the Son being united in being does not negate the differentiation between

---

83. Ibid.

84. Barth, *CD* II/2, 495.

85. Ibid., 496.

86. Ibid.

87. Raymond E. Brown, *The Death of the Messiah: From Gethsemane to the Grave*, vol. 2 (Garden City, NY: Doubleday, 1994) 1048–50.

88. Contra W. Stacy Johnson, who cannot see despair in Jesus if he possesses faith. See "Jesus' Cry, God's Cry, and Ours," *Lament: Reclaiming Practices in Pulpit, Pew, and Public Square*, ed. Sally A. Brown and Patrick D. Miller (Louisville: Westminster John Knox, 2005) 81.

89. Campbell, *Nature of the Atonement*, 201.

90. Jüngel, *God as the Mystery of the World*, 363.

the persons, as is a tendency in contemporary trinitarian theology.[91] This does not mean that there is a "cleavage" in God himself (Moltmann) because "it must immediately be added that it is an act of God himself who effects his identity with the dead Jesus and as its precondition the differentiation of God and God."[92] This is no play acting on God's part "because love alone is able to involve itself in the complete harshness of death."[93] "God is love" is a meaningful statement because it speaks of love that goes down to death and despair.[94]

There is the response of Jesus, a response that is not just a triumphalistic religious affirmation, but one that comes in the midst of struggle. For that response, as our representative, is the response of struggling humanity: "Because he himself was tested by what he suffered, he is able to help those who are being tested" (Heb 2:18). "For we do not have a high priest who is unable to sympathize with our weaknesses, but we have one who in every respect has been tested as we are, yet without sin" (Heb 4:15). Speaking of Gethsemane, "Although he was a Son, he learned obedience through what he suffered . . ." (Heb 5:8). As a result, like in the penitent thief besides Jesus on the cross (Luke 23:40–43), joy can come in the midst of suffering, for the grace of God brings genuine guilt. The penitent thief does not preach repentance to others but acknowledges his own guilt, "that before God a man always suffers as one who is guilty," and therefore acknowledges as well that God is love, for his cross is beside the cross of Jesus.[95] "He declares the joy that is painful only in the humiliation of the proud."[96] Does Kierkegaard promote a life of *continual* remorse and guilt? Perhaps. But at least his point can be taken that grace creates true guilt. Guilt is not that which triggers grace. And in genuine guilt is genuine joy because it is guilt being beside the cross of Christ.

---

91. This is a problem in W. Stacy Johnson, "Jesus' Cry, God's Cry, and Ours," in Brown and Miller, eds., *Lament*, 88.

92. Jüngel, *God as the Mystery of the World*, 363. Cf. Moltmann, *The Crucified God*, 152: "The cross of the Son divides God from God to the utmost degree of enmity and distinction." Barth usually resists any view that God might "lose" himself (*CD* IV/1, 185) but he can say that God "hazards no less than His being as God" to encounter "the absurdity of sin" (*CD* IV/2, 401). By "hazards" Barth means that God is "affected," but not changed by the world. Cf. Fiddes, *Creative Suffering of God*, 202.

93. Jüngel, *God as the Mystery of the World*, 364.

94. Ibid., 368.

95. Kierkegaard, *Gospel of Sufferings*, 74.

96. Ibid.

Struggling humanity lives in anticipation of joy. Barth adds, "Most joy is anticipatory. Even in the experience of fulfillments, and particularly when this experience is genuine, it usually changes immediately into anticipatory joy, eschatological joy. And to this extent we do right to ask concerning the right will to joy."[97] Again, this is a terrible burden upon Neighborhood Baptist Church, to live in such a dialectic between anticipation and fulfillment. Yet childhood memories of the joy of anticipation before opening the gifts on Christmas morning remind us of the promise of joy. But will growing up cruelly crush those dreams? Do we not end up dreading the Christmas season because loved ones whom we used to share the times with are gone or dreams that we had were never fulfilled? Why is it that depression and suicide are so ripe during the season of the incarnation of God?

One does not love if one is not a cheerful person, Barth adds.[98] If this is so, we desperately need the vicarious joy of Christ. Joy comes in the midst of struggle, but not without the struggle of Christ and the joy of Christ. "Where is the joy?" the seminary professor asked. The joy is in Jesus, his joy. For God takes the risk of unrequited love. And it is genuine risk when those whom he loves and humanity made in his image reject him. The last word is not our rejection, but the perfect response in humanity, the "perfect Amen in humanity to the judgment of God on the sin of man," in the words of the Scottish theologian John McLeod Campbell.[99] This is the perfect Amen of the vicarious humanity of Christ, an Amen of joy, faith, and obedience. The miracle of the incarnation is that God provides both the revelation and the response, and yes, encompasses the sorrow and the joy.[100]

---

97. Barth, *CD* III/4, 377.

98. Barth, *CD* IV/2, 789.

99. Campbell, *Nature of the Atonement*, 118.

100. Ray S. Anderson, "A Theology for Ministry," in *Theological Foundations for Ministry*, ed. Anderson, 11.

CHAPTER TEN

Joy as the Yes of God

JOY AND THE BEING OF GOD

Jesus has said an Amen to the Father. Therefore, there is a Yes in God. But a Yes to what? This depends upon one's doctrine of God. The sovereign, decretal God of much of traditional theism, with its roots in the Aristotelian Unmoved Mover, can say Yes, but only in an arbitrary fashion.[1] The God of panentheism seems more willing to say Yes, but cannot say Yes to himself, only as it is affected by creation.[2] The free God of the Bible, however, the triune God—Father, Son, and Holy Spirit—begins by saying Yes within himself. This is the God who already has his own being, not needing creation to complete it, and is therefore free to give himself to creation.[3] This "absoluteness of God" (what earlier theologians called his *aseity*) "properly understood . . . can signify not only His freedom to transcend all that is other than Himself, but also His freedom to be immanent within it, and at such a depth of immanence as simply does not exist in fellowship between other beings."[4] Therefore, God can have both joy and sorrow in being moved and affected by the world, a *pathos* of God. God cares in a real way.[5] God can have joy as the incarnate Son (the economic Trinity) (Luke 10:21) because he is antecedently in an eternal relationship of joy between the Father and the Son in the Spirit. Joy, therefore, is not first of all a human concoction. Joy is not our job, a kind of Pelagian spiritual response to God. Barth speaks strongly on this:

1. Barth, *CD* II/1, 305.
2. Ibid., 312.
3. Ibid., 309.
4. Ibid., 313.
5. Anderson, *Self-Care*, 57.

> Every relationship into which God enters with that which is not Himself must be interpreted—however much this may disturb or correct our preconceived ideas of connexion and relationship—as eventuating between two utterly unequal partners, the sheer inequality consisting in the fact that no self-determination of the second partner can influence the first, whereas the self-determination of the first, while not canceling the self-determination of the second, is the sovereign predetermination which precedes it absolutely.[6]

What I take Barth to mean here is that the being of God is absolutely prior to any initiative by one of his creatures, and that would include joy. The joy of God in Jesus Christ, who is both divine and human, reveals a joy unlike anything we know. Despite the protestations of the advocates of the analogy of being, the substitutionary atonement affects the totality of our humanity because Christ has taken upon himself the totality of our humanity, effectively representing our joy, but also displacing it with his joy. This is the joy that endures absurd, cruel, and terrible struggles in a world that often makes no sense at all. Ask anyone who has lost a loved one. Their world immediately is different; darker, with a grim, mocking absence that mocks one's will to live. The joy of Jesus, for any confessor of the Nicene Creed, that the Son is of "the same substance" (*homoousios*) with the Father, is the joy of God. That is good news, grounded in the doctrine of the triune God known through the vicarious humanity of Christ, a radical, thorough view of the substitutionary atonement.

Joy is in God himself. This we know from the Son of God who is the joy that responds to the Father in the Spirit, "the faithful answer."[7] It is through Christ that we understand "God as he is in himself."[8] T. F. Torrance stresses that the *homoousion* teaches us "that what God is antecedently, eternally, and inherently in himself he is indeed toward us in the incarnate economy of his saving action in Jesus Christ . . . that what God is toward us in his revealing and saving acts in Jesus Christ he is antecedently and inherently in his eternal being . . ."[9] Karl Rahner's famous "rule" is true at this point: the economic Trinity is the immanent

---

6. Barth, *CD* II/1, 312.
7. T. F. Torrance, *Christian Doctrine of God*, 1.
8. Ibid.
9. Ibid., 97, 107.

Trinity, the immanent Trinity is the economic Trinity.[10] So we may say, can we not, that the joy of Jesus reveals what is manifest eternally in the joy of God? God's being is identical with his act, so the act of the joy of Jesus, just as the love that is in Jesus, reflects the being of God.[11] Torrance, however, adds the caveat that one must have "a significant distinction and delimitation between the economic Trinity and ontological Trinity" or one reads back into God "temporal and causal connections that obtain in our creaturely existence in time space," most notably, gender specifics of "Father" and "Son."[12] These can become a "mythological projection of ideas of our own devising into God, and to prevent us from confounding God known by us with our deficient knowing of him."[13] This is a point that Paul Molnar has stressed in recent years, particularly criticizing anthropocentric tendencies in contemporary trinitarian theology.[14] This is a salutary criticism of that which often passes as trinitarian theology but is really a projection of our own desires for "community" into God. This can also become true of "joy."

How then, however, can we speak of the joy in the man Jesus as being the joy of God? How can we avoid foisting our ideas of joy upon God? Torrance himself is also critical of those who seek any understanding of God from "behind the back" of Jesus.[15] God as Father is the Father in communion with the Son, the Son who responds with joy.[16] If it is Jesus who teaches us to call God "Father," therefore, "Father" must be spoken with the meaning that Jesus has for "Father," that which comes out of this deep communion with the Father. Joy, in other words, is an expression of a communion of love, not just ecstasy, pleasure, or a good feeling. Because Jesus calls upon God as Father, he himself is "the living embodiment of that prayer."[17] To share in that relationship is to be, in the words of John of the Cross, "caught into God's great being; breathing his very air!"[18]

---

10. Rahner, *Trinity*, 21ff.

11. T. F. Torrance, *Christian Doctrine of God*, 165.

12. Ibid., 97, 101.

13. Ibid., 99.

14. Paul D. Molnar, *Divine Freedom and the Doctrine of the Immanent Trinity* (New York: T. & T. Clark, 2002).

15. T. F. Torrance, *Mediation of Christ*, 59–62.

16. James B. Torrance, *Worship, Community and the Triune God of Grace*, 125.

17. Ibid., 84.

18. St. John of the Cross, *Ballad* 4, 61, cited by Fiddes, *Participation in God*, 45.

Torrance responds that Jesus himself is the filter that communicates that which is of God and that which is not and he gives sexual relations or distinctions in gender as an example.[19] I am not sure that Jesus explicitly states that. But he does positively bring and live a life of joy before the Father (Matt 2:10; Luke 10:21). His obedience, doing the will of the Father, is essential to his joy and that is in the entire narrative in the Gospels and commented upon throughout the New Testament. Our ideas of joy join with all of our other ideas when we speak of God in the midst of the Holy of Holies, admitting that all of our language falls short of God's majesty.[20] Joy, however, fits in with worship as sacred epistemology, as Torrance and the Fathers remind us.[21] Worship then leads us to the one true worshipper, in the vicarious humanity of Christ.[22] For Jesus, joy is certainly intertwined with worship. In other words, what the Son positively does in his incarnate life—live a life of joy before the Father—is different from the incidentals of his gender. Therefore, we are to see joy as a part of the essence of God but not the "maleness" of the Son or the Father. Analogy has its limitations so that Torrance can speak of the Father and the Son language as "imageless relations," images that transcend our imaginations and conceptions, as in the *apophatic* tradition of the Eastern Orthodox Church.[23] Yet will this mean that there is indeed a God "behind the back" of Jesus, who God *really* is? Not necessarily, for the joy of Jesus is the joy of God, not as telling us everything about God's joy but telling it truly. As the theologian Cynthia Rigby puts it, we do not know God exhaustively but we do know him *truly*. Therefore, we can have a genuine joy of God through Christ but never exhaust its divine reality. This is an adventure of this life and the next ("the business of heaven" in C. S. Lewis's words).[24]

Torrance, interestingly enough does include the "subjection" of the Son as that which does not reveal the essential being of God because subjection and obedience implies inferiority, a criticism he levels at Karl Barth.[25] But is not the obedience of Jesus an essential part of the gospel narrative?

19. T. F. Torrance, *Christian Doctrine of God*, 107, 157.
20. Ibid., 110.
21. Ibid., 111.
22. Ibid.
23. Ibid., 11, 157.
24. C. S. Lewis, *Letters to Malcolm: Chiefly on Prayer* (New York: Harvest, 1964) 93.
25. T. F. Torrance, *Christian Doctrine of God*, 180; "My Interaction with Karl Barth" in *How Karl Barth Changed My Mind*, ed. Donald K. McKim (Grand Rapids: Eerdmans, 1986) 60–61; *Karl Barth: Biblical and Evangelical Theologian*, 131.

If Jesus does not possess an obedience towards the Father then has there not been a total substitution, taking the place of my disobedience? Like the freedom of Jesus, his obedience should leave the analogy with our ideas and practice behind, vicariously, but stand on its own demonstration, the actuality not possibility of revelation. Therefore, his joy becomes a critique of our joys and we commit a theological error if we attempt to foist our understanding of joy upon God.

The Trinity speaks of God as Father, Son, and Holy Spirit in a relationship of *perichoresis,* a mutual indwelling and movement of community and love.[26] Yet this is not to mean that the Trinity melts together into an amorphous commune. *Perichoresis* does not dissolve but establishes the distinctive persons of the Trinity.[27] It does mean, rather, that there are real distinctives, "individual characteristics," in Torrance's words, in God, but distinctives that cannot be known apart from each other.[28] The reciprocal relations mean distinctives but they also mean genuine love, and I would include, joy. In those distinctives of Father, Son, and Holy Spirit is communion in which the Father is not the Father apart from the Son and the Spirit. So the joy of Jesus towards the Father is a reflection of their eternal relationship. Jesus reveals that love is the essence of God, the love of a relationship between the Father and the Son in the Spirit. In that love we see joy; the joy that the Father has in the Son and the joy that the Son returns to the Father, a "corresponding" joy and love from the Father to the Son that we may now participate in.[29]

Much has been made in contemporary theology of God suffering, "the crucified God" (Moltmann) that can rightly reflect the emotion that is eternally within God, including joy. The Father may suffer but does so differently from the Son, so the joy of the Son is different from the Father.[30] His joy is in response to the Father's love, just as his suffering is a response to the Father's will for him to go to the cross. In fact, Paul Fiddes suggests that the "Yes" of Jesus (and we would include his joy in that) is part of the "wonderful exchange" of our "No" to God.[31]

---

26. T. F. Torrance, *Christian Doctrine of God*, 130.
27. Ibid., 175.
28. Ibid., 132–33, 145.
29. Ibid., 165.
30. Fiddes, *Participation in God*, 184.
31. Ibid. Cf. Hans Urs von Balthasar, *Theo-drama: Theological Dramatic Theory, Vol. IV: The Action*, trans. Graham Harrison (San Francisco: Ignatius, 1994) 329.

The joy of God is in the midst of real abandonment: "My God, my God, why have you forsaken me?" (Matt 27:46). Some reject a real abandonment within God as an impossibility. Jesus only *feels* abandoned.[32] David Bentley Hart will admit that God "both addresses and responds," he is "a reciprocal Thou," but curiously refuses to see this as "another utterance" because of the oneness of God.[33] Any *pathos* for God, according to Hart, is "external to his nature" because God does not possess "shifting emotions within himself."[34] But if the Son does not truly possess despair then he also does not truly possess joy, a joy that can exist in the midst of despair. Does God possess despair eternally? This would give despair an ontologically finality, it seems. This is Hart's concern and it is a genuine concern. But God does not have to possess despair eternally in order to feel it genuinely because his "steadfast love . . . extends to the heavens" (Ps 36:5). His love is enough of a source of his *pathos* towards the Son. The abandonment comes. Jesus really does descend into hell. But there is great joy in God that he will not remain there. So it is with our "hells." We will not remain there. We will be lifted up out of there to be where Jesus is.

THE JOY OF THE WILL OF GOD

The joy of God is found in the doing of the will of God. We know this from Jesus: "Thy will be done . . ." This is in contrast to "a whole monstrous kingdom" of nothingness, including sin, which surrounds us.[35] Delight is found in doing God's will (Ps 119:16). Bonhoeffer can say, "'Delight' is the great word, without which there can be no walking in the way of God."[36] Yet "delight" begins with God. "The Word of God brings fullness of joy to its hearers . . . God's Word is the source of all joy, and the way of his decrees is full of delight, because it is the way which God himself has gone and goes with us."[37] God's Yes in joy is an act of God's freedom.[38] The Yes

---

32. Bishop Hilarion Alfeyev, *The Mystery of Faith*, ed. Jessica Rose (London: Darton, Longman & Todd, 2002) 90,

33. David Bentley Hart, *Beauty of the Infinite*, 168–69,

34. Ibid., 355.

35. Barth, *CD* III/2, 143.

36. Dietrich Bonhoeffer, *Meditating on the Word*, trans. David McI. Gracie (Cambridge, MA: Cowley, 1986) 130.

37. Ibid., 131.

38. Barth, *CD* IV/3.1, 382.

of God is not an automatic, mechanical fiat, so that we can say that everything that happens is the will of God. That is why we must not say that the center of the faith is the doctrine of the sovereignty of God, as important as God's sovereignty is. God's Yes will prevail, there is sovereignty there. But not everything that happens is God's will. We must say with Barth that "nothingness" is that which God did not create, which has no being, cannot be explained but, nonetheless will not prevail.[39] This "menacing frontier" is such a menace that no creaturely being has any hope of conquering. That is why the shout of "Jesus is Victor" is so important.[40] He is victor not simply in sheer power, however. He is victor in taking our side, in his vicarious humanity, doing God's will when we have failed. He is victor in a shout of joy and Yes by a community that shares in the existence of Jesus.[41]

THE JOY OF GOD IN CREATING

The Yes of God is seen in creation. The "very good" of God's response to his creation is an exclamation of joy, said in the midst of God's "joyful Sabbath," the seventh day.[42] There is genuine joy in creating. Here is a joy of God that requires no cooperation with his creature (a clue to the significance of the sovereignty of God's decision in reconciliation and redemption as well, and a critique of all kinds of synergism).[43] In fact, the creation of humanity in God's image is a reflection, Barth boldly suggests, that it is God who is first and foremost of all a Person, a "living Person who knows and wills and speaks."[44] We are not far here from the doctrine of the Trinity: One God, Three Persons. This triune God is the Person who acts, and in acting he is from all eternity never without an answer to his knowing, willing, and speaking: the answer of the obedient Son. As Barth cites Zimmerli: "Nowhere is the real power of a master so fully apparent as in his commandment which is obeyed."[45] God does not wait to create in order to possess an answer to his knowing, willing, and speak-

---

39. Barth, *CD* III/3, "God and Nothingness," 289–368.
40. See Barth, *CD* IV/3.1, "Jesus is Victor," 165–274.
41. Barth, *CD* IV/2, 334.
42. Barth, *CD* III/1, 181.
43. Ibid., 100.
44. Ibid., 110.
45. Zimmerli cited by Barth, *CD* III/1, 111.

ing: This is the trinitarian significance and power of Gen 1:7: "And it was so," "the divine soliloquy," in Barth's words.[46]

At this point we must question the view that we know what a person is. This assumes the importance of a radical theological anthropology of humanity as determined by the divine Word.[47] What joy we possess and experience (and all people do) in this life is derivative of the joy of God the Person. This joy says something extremely significant about humanity: our meaning comes from God's joy, God's rest in which he exclaims, "very good," something it is very difficult at times to see in a "groaning" world (Rom 8:22). Therefore, "even man is not an end in himself," Barth concludes.[48]

> Like health, joy is a social matter . . . but how do I know whether what gives joy to me will do so to them? . . . What is really demanded is that I ask myself from the standpoint of the other what will give him joy, and that I then consider this and put it into effect.[49]

This joy also says that joy is in the presence of the other and as we give to others.[50] In the midst of controversies of whether or not to eat or drink when that would offend a brother or sister, Paul speaks of the social nature of the kingdom of God: "For the kingdom of God is not food and drink but righteousness and peace and joy in the Holy Spirit" (Rom 14:17). Anderson comments on this: "Paul viewed the kingdom of God as not primarily concerned with material things and political realms but rather as a personal and social reality—righteousness and peace and joy—the fruits of the indwelling Spirit."[51] Joy is bound up with righteousness and peace. The Protestant temptation, the early Barth of the *Romans* commentary claims, is that because of individual justification by faith, we can very easily become obsessed with our own autonomy, not "the autonomy of truth," and therefore ignore the other for the sake of "food and drink."[52] God is the one who can ask from the standpoint of the other, for he is "Other" within himself as Father, Son, and Holy Spirit.

46. Barth, *CD* III/1, 111–12.
47. Anderson, *On Being Human*, 33ff.
48. Barth, *CD* III/1, 181.
49. Ibid., 380.
50. Barth, *CD* III/4, 379–80.
51. Anderson, *Emerging Theology for Emerging Churches*, 109.
52. Barth, *Epistle to the Romans*, 519–20.

The source of all of our joys is God, who said that his creation was "very good." God's rest has been "completed at creation" and he has given an "invitation to man to rest with Him."[53] The goal of creation is the participation of humanity, made in God's image, with God's joy that he experiences in himself and in creating, a joy in which God is "satisfied." Barth says it very well: "Not man and not a wisdom or folly, a power or impotence, immanent in the world of man, willed and accomplished in the creature, but God—the God who rejoiced in man as in His own image."[54]

THE JOY OF GOD IN THE HUMAN PERSON

There is genuine joy in the human person because there is joy in God. Can the God of pantheism rejoice, that is, possess an Other over against himself, so that the Other then can rejoice as well, such as Wisdom rejoicing in Proverbs 8:31?[55] The entire person is redeemed by the entire vicarious humanity of Christ. This person is the one who

> can use his senses and understanding to perceive that two and two make four, and to write poetry, and to think, and to make music, and to eat and drink, and to be filled with joy and often with sorrow, and to love and sometimes to hate, and to be young and to grow old, and all within his own experience and activity, affirming it not as half a man but as a whole man, with head uplifted, and the heart free and the conscience at rest.[56]

Note how Barth sees joy and sorrow together in the wholeness of being human. But this wholeness desperately needs to be embraced by God in a way that God takes upon himself the wholeness of human life. The vicarious nature of Christ is not just limited to his death but also includes the entirety of life, the vicarious humanity of Christ. Therefore nothing will escape him. Barth is rhapsodic in speaking of this:

> Therefore nothing will escape Him: no aspect of the great game of creation; no moment of human life; no thinking thought; no word spoken no secret or insignificant enterprise or deed or omission with all of its interaction and effects; no suffering or joy; no sincerity or life; no secret event in heaven or too well-

---

53. Barth, *CD* III/1, 98.
54. Ibid., 99.
55. Barth, *CD* III/3, 86–87.
56. Ibid., 87.

known event on earth; no ray of sunlight; no note which has will not allow anything to perish, but will hold it in the hollow of His hand as He has always done, and does, and will do. He will not be alone in eternity, but with the creature. He will allow it to partake of His own eternal life.[57]

God possesses a joy for humanity that we cannot possess. In fact, we fail miserably when we try to become another's savior, to be the vicarious humanity of Christ for them.[58] There should be no vicarious humanity of *the church*.

The foundation for our joy is in both God's freedom and dependence that we see in Jesus Christ. As a person God expresses his freedom and that to be truly free is to truly be a person. In Barth's famous words, "The doubtful thing is not whether God is person, but whether we are."[59] Yet because we know God through Jesus Christ, we must also say that *dependence* is human because we see this in Christ, the dependence of the Son upon the Father, who receives joy from the Father.[60] The Son receives from the Father and in doing so represents both God and what it means to be made in the image of God.[61]

Receiving as an essential part of the *imago Dei* becomes a judgment upon our reflexive attitudes of self-preservation that deny the ontological status of the social reality of love. This is what is meant for Jesus Christ to be present in and with our humanity, in a "reciprocity of relations," to use Anderson's phrase.[62]

THE SABBATH JOY OF GOD

He is "the God who rejoices," whose joy is the source and foundation for our joy. A kind of "satisfied" joy is what is lacking all too frequently in our experiences of joy, as fleeting and temporal as they are. Sabbath joy, however, is satisfied joy. It is his satisfied, Sabbath joy that becomes our joy, especially made manifest in the joy of Jesus Christ, a participation in

57. Ibid., 90. Cf. Alan J. Torrance, *Persons in Communion*, 35.

58. Daniel J. Price, *Karl Barth's Anthropology in Light of Modern Thought* (Grand Rapids: Eerdmans, 2002) 152.

59. Barth, *CD* I/1, 138–39.

60. Harned, *Patience*, 15.

61. Barth, *CD* IV/1, 272; and Tom Smail, *Like Father, Like Son: The Trinity Imaged in Our Humanity* (Grand Rapids: Eerdmans, 2005) 175.

62. Anderson, *Something Old, Something New*, 96.

his joy that enables us to contemplate the "glory" that is to come with the vision of Jesus, which relativizes the present sufferings (Rom 8:18). Jesus is the one who says, "Come to me, all you that are weary and are carrying heavy burdens, and I will give you rest" (Matt 11:28). This follows immediately the prayer of thanksgiving of the Son to the Father for their mutual knowing based on their mutual being (Matt 11:25–27). Jesus's "yoke" that we are to take is his "rest" (Matt 11:29–30; cf. Heb 4:1–11). As Barth comments, "It is there that He promises rest, a fulfillment which the others can never enjoy, because they do not know of it, because it cannot mean anything to them, His own rest, the rest of His own being in the unity of the obedient Son and the will of the Father and with the Father Himself."[63] His rest is a *vicarious* rest, on our behalf and in our place.

Sabbath rest possesses its external origins in creation. "The goal of creation, and at the same time the beginning of all that follows, is the event of God's Sabbath freedom, Sabbath rest and Sabbath joy, in which man, too, has been summoned to participate."[64] God's joy in the Sabbath means that his joy is foremost, but what he is joyful about is *us*: "It is the work concluded and terminated on the sixth day with the creation of man that is the object of this completing divine rest and joy."[65] God rejoices over Zion as the bridegroom rejoices over the bride (Isa 62:5). God "is himself the source of all joy and delight. Yes, he himself knows joy."[66]

God's word creates delight in doing his decrees (Ps 119:16).[67] Bonhoeffer asks,

> Why is it that my thoughts depart so quickly from God's Word and I find the necessary word is often not there for me in the hour of need? Do I forget to eat and drink and sleep? Why do I forget God's Word? Because I am not yet able to say with the psalmist: 'My delight is in your statutes.' I never forget that in which I delight.[68]

Here begins the foundation for our joy. God is the one who is able to keep us standing and to rejoice in that endurance: "Now to him who is able

---

63. Barth, *CD* IV/1, 179.
64. Barth, *CD* III/1, 98.
65. Ibid., 181.
66. Bonhoeffer, *Meditating on the Word*, 130.
67. Ibid.
68. Ibid., 133.

to keep you from falling, and to make you stand without blemish in the presence of his glory with rejoicing . . ." (Jude 24).

The Sabbath joy of God reveals that our joy is to be found in our limit. This is very hard for us to hear as twenty-first century people who have always been taught that our destinies are limitless. The romanticism of one of my favorite writers, Ray Bradbury, often tends in this direction. But it is no advantage for humanity to pretend to be something it is not. Yes, we are made, incredible as it may seem to say, in the very image of God. But we are not God. There is a difference. The Sabbath rest of God means that God finds joy in creating a limit for himself. The self-limitation of God is extremely important in considering how God is powerful. "A being is free only when it can determine and limit its activity."[69] Decretal Calvinist attempts to deny this are ill advised it seems to me. It is in God's self-limitation that we see one of the greatest expressions of God's sovereignty: his freedom to limit himself, and even to create something with limits. This is an action of the personhood of God, the one true person, and the foundation for our personhood; the one who truly knows, thinks, and speaks. God is not determined by how the world relates to him (panentheism). But he is free to set his own limits. In this self-limitation we have the foundation for humanity as possessing limits because, not in spite of, the fact that humanity was created in the image of God.

God's Sabbath joy also reveals his love.[70] There is no virtue in decrying "anthropomorphizing" God if we are unable to speak of God's love, a very personal action.[71] This action is seen in the very act of creating when God had no necessity to create. We are created out of grace, a movement of God's sheer, undeserved love. Again, God is satisfied with what he has created; it is "very good." This joy means that what he has created he loves; and he will take care of it (providence). And there is limitation here as well. What God has created is not a second God, but a very finite, limited, temporal creature, that will end up doing some very bad and stupid things. But God has chosen to limit himself in creating us; he cannot go back and "uncreate." He can only judge, once with Noah, but one last

---

69. Barth, *CD* III/1, 215.

70. Ibid.

71. See Charles Hughes' insightful criticism of how John Hick can call God "the Real" and still speak of "the Real's" "love" in his essay "Pluralism, Inclusivism, and Christology," in *Jesus: Here and Now*, ed. Marvin Meyer and Charles Hughes (Harrisburg, PA: Trinity, 2001) 162–67.

time in taking the judgment upon himself in Jesus Christ. But in this act of love, God suggests that in his very being is nothing less than love; the revelation of the triune God demonstrates this. So Barth can conclude, "Where is He God more truly, or more perfectly Himself in the whole course of His work of creation, than in this rest on the seventh day?"[72] God is never more God than when he experiences joy. So it is strange to hear David Bentley Hart say, "Joy feeds on what it receives, but rarely on what is establishes."[73] Hart is seeking to distance himself from Kant's emphasis on the moral action as the disinterested action, which acts purely out of duty or obligation, not reward. Yes, God does not love out of pure duty. But surely God's joyful Sabbath rest in the joyful response of Jesus argues for a joy in unconditionally loving creation, even in the fact of creation as an act of grace, as well as God receiving his own Yes in the humanity of Jesus Christ, giving back to God a joy that we have been unable to give to him, yet providing the foundation and impetus for our joy. The double movement of the eternal *perichoresis* between the Father, the Son, and the Holy Spirit, made manifest in the incarnation, is never more important than here. There is a joy in God in both giving unconditionally (the humanward movement) and in receiving the perfect faith, obedience, and service of the Son (the Godward movement).

God's Sabbath rest has happened before and apart from any command for humanity to rest. This is something Sabbatarian legalists of every age fail to understand. God gives himself to creation in simply creating. God belongs to creation in that he has created and already rested. Our rest is found in that already completed rest.[74] We rested with God on the seventh day. He rested in on our behalf and in our place, a vicarious rest, if you will. So, as Barth argues, the history of the covenant exists with creation. Grace is not something secondary but deeply ingrained within creation. "In a world created in this way, with the inclusion of the divine rest on the seventh day, the sphere of grace is not a foreign body."[75] This grace is a vicarious work, for humanity rested with God on the seventh day, "even though it had not as yet any work behind it."[76] Even before our work is God's vicarious joy. The Sabbath points to God's work, not ours.

72. Barth, *CD* III/1, 215.
73. David Bentley Hart, *Beauty of the Infinite*, 83
74. Barth, *CD* III/1, 217.
75. Ibid., 225.
76. Ibid., 217.

The goal of humanity, therefore, is something that has been granted to it, not something to be achieved.[77] This includes the acquisition of joy as well. The joy of God is a joy that we are to receive, not to earn. This is seen ultimately in the vicarious joy of Jesus Christ, for creation cannot overcome nothingness in itself.[78] Creation needs help that is human, from the side of creation, yet perfectly knows and does the will of God. The "negating of the negation" is that which contradicts nothingness and sin by creating a new humanity in the Son. "If now in the vast sphere of human fellowship and history we have to do with the man Jesus, it is because His existence was eternally resolved in the sovereign will of God to save us and all creation . . . It is for this reason that He is the kingdom of God in person."[79] "My food is to do the will of him who sent me and to complete his work" (John 4:34). "I can do nothing on my own. As I hear, I judge; and my judgment is just, because I seek to do not my own will but the will of him who sent me" (John 5:30). "For I have come down from heaven, not to do my own will, but the will of him who sent me" (John 6:38). This is the Godward movement of the vicarious humanity of Christ, a secure clinging to God the Father that we are invited to join in through the Holy Spirit. "On Christ the solid rock I stand, all other ground is sinking sand." This is not meant to be pious tripe but ontological, epistemological, as well as personal reality.

THE JOY OF GOD IN A CREATION WITH LIMITS

The Yes of God is a divine decision taken in Jesus Christ.[80] There is no place for a divine decision apart from Jesus Christ, in disagreement with much of decretal Calvinism.[81] That divine decision is anchored within the

---

77. Ibid., 218.
78. Barth, *CD* III/2, 143.
79. Ibid., 144.
80. Barth, *CD* IV/3.2, 749.
81. James B. Torrance, "The Concept of Federal Theology—Was Calvin a Federal Theologian?" in *Calvinus Sacrae Scripturae Confessor*, ed. Wilhelm Neuser (Grand Rapids: Eerdmans, 1994) 15–40. Cf. James B. Torrance, "Strengths and Weaknesses of the Westminster Theology" in *The Westminster Confession in the Church Today*, ed. A. I. C. Heron (Edinburgh: Saint Andrews, 1982) 127–47; Graham Redding, "Federal Calvinism and the Westminster Tradition, and their Legacy in Reformed Liturgical Developments" in *Prayer and the Priesthood of Christ in the Reformed Tradition* (New York: T. & T. Clark, 2003) 137–88; and Charles Partee, *The Theology of John Calvin* (Louisville: Westminster John Knox, 2008) 5–35.

immanent Trinity, God apart from his "economic" actions towards us. Yet it is a *divine* decision, without our co-operation and whether or not we realize it happening, as much as we desire to hasten to get into the act!

This is a decision to free humanity so that human beings may have joy beyond all that we can comprehend. Such a divine decision in Jesus Christ is the joy of God, the foundation for our joy, even the actuality which creates the possibility of our joy. Seen also in creation, the divine decision in Christ, in God's Sabbath rest, is his joy of responding to his own act. As Bonhoeffer suggests, there is a rhythm in the creation story of alternating between light and darkness that is a rhythm of "both rest and movement, that gives and takes and gives again and takes again and so points forever to God's giving and taking, to God's freedom beyond rest and movement—that is what the day is."[82] Does not this correspond to the double movement of the incarnation—the combination of the humanward and the Godward movements—with the humanward representing the giving of the Word and the Godward the response through the vicarious joy of Christ? We must be careful here in speaking of the relationship between God and creation. God may have joy himself in creation, but is creation itself the joy, as Hart claims?[83] For Hart, creation is "an expression of the superabundant joy and agape of the Trinity," bringing a beauty of "charity" and "awe" and even telling of God. This is "a theological embrace of creation as a divine word precisely in its aesthetic excessiveness, its unforced beauty."[84]

"Aesthetic excessiveness"? However wonderful it is to the eyes of the believing Jew to say "the heavens declare the glory of God . . ." (Ps 19:1) this is not seen from the perspective of "aesthetic excessiveness" but from the revelation of God himself. Hart would do well to listen to Kierkegaard's measured warning about the temptation of remaining solely in the aesthetic mode.[85] "Aesthetic excessiveness" does not necessarily equal God. The wisdom of Ecclesiastes, Ray Anderson suggests, is in his brutal realism that we possess bodies that are decaying. "And the worst of it is, we know it."[86] So suffering is at the core of finite life. Qoheleth is skeptical of

82. Bonhoeffer, *Creation and Fall*, 49.

83. David Bentley Hart, *Beauty of the Infinite*, 255.

84. Ibid., 254.

85. Søren Kierkegaard, *Søren Kierkegaard's Journals and Papers, Volume 1, A-E*, ed. and trans. Howard V. Hong and Edna H. Hong (Bloomington: Indiana University Press, 1967) 368. Cf. Thiessen, *Theological Aesthetics*, 198.

86. Anderson, *Exploration into God*, 13.

those who do not recognize the limits of life and try to find a joy that does not encompass sadness.[87] The aesthetic has a limit, for creation is finite, including human beings. Therefore, we are to enjoy what life has been given us, but what does it means to enjoy life? Is it that self-evident when we routinely read of "celebrities," whom society regards as "successful" whose lives end up badly and sadly? (This was the theme of every episode of the VH1 series "Behind the Music," in which famous rock stars careers were presented in a ever-repeating "dialectic" of aspirations: success, a crash [usually drugs], then redemption, meaning a greater rock and roll career than ever . . . an endlessly silly repetition.)

Creation has its limits. In a fallen world, we need a word from above that brings us joy even in the midst of Roman oppression (Luke 2:10) or our own despair. The double movement of the incarnation is first this word of "good tidings of great joy," but there is also a Godward movement that is joy in the place of humanity, yet for humanity. This is the joy of the Son before the Father (Luke 10:21) that reflects the *perichoresis*, the mutual indwelling between the Father, Son, and the Holy Spirit, what it means for God to be in communion.[88] Here is the "immensity" of joy that John Cassian speaks of that is more than "aesthetic excessiveness," simply restricted to creation, but comes in the context of despair and sorrow, as John Cassian remarks:

> Often the fruit of saving compunction emerges as a unspeakable joy and liveliness of soul. Joy in its immensity become unbearable and the soul bursts out in great cries . . . Sometimes the soul lies low, hidden in the depths of silence . . . And sometimes it fills up with such sorrow and grief that it can only shake it off by melting into tears.[89]

GOD AS THE WITNESS OF JOY IN THE INCARNATION

In Jesus Christ, in his vicarious humanity, God is his own witness (John 8:13–19).[90] Christ is "the direct and perfect witness of the life of God

---

87. Ibid., 16.
88. T. F. Torrance, *Christian Doctrine of God*, 194–201.
89. Cassian, Conference 9 in *Conferences*, 117.
90. Barth, *CD* III/1, 224.

Himself," a witness of both authority and obedience.[91] And this is a witness of joy, his witness of the Father's love. This witness of communion becomes ours as well. "As God knows Jesus, He also knows us."[92] This is demonstrated by the seventh day, in which the covenant of grace is seen to embrace creation as well as reconciliation and redemption. We "enter into the joy of the Lord" through participation by faith in his life, as faith that embraces Christ in the naked, the imprisoned, and poor of the world (Matt 25:51). Zosima, in Dostoevsky's *The Brothers Karamazov*, speaks of the incarnation bringing God's joy to us: "Do not be afraid of him. Awful is his greatness before us, terrible is his loftiness, yet he is boundlessly merciful, he became like us out of love, and he is rejoicing with us, transforming water into wine, that the joy of the guests may not end."[93] Because *God* is rejoicing, Alyosha responds with throwing himself down to the earth, "kissing it, weeping, sobbing, and watering it with his tears, and he vowed ecstatically to love it, to love it, to love it unto the ages."[94] Here is the Orthodox tradition of *penthos*, or compunction, the kind of weeping or crying that in this case is a response to grace not a condition for continual grace.

Certainly the eucharistic life of the church is a part of that, but we cannot say with Schmemann that "we have no other means of entering into that joy."[95] He is right to speak of the Eucharist as a "witness" to the world, and in that witness participates in the joy of God in Christ, most properly in the Eucharist, but wrong to neglect the contingent relationship between Christ and the church. The church is not the Head, only Christ is. As Barth reminds us, the church "has no right to make proposals to men as though they could now help, justify, sanctify and glorify themselves more thoroughly and successfully than hitherto."[96] The church cannot escape the confusion of the world and pretend that is it unaffected by it. So it can only witness to the divine Yes. "The presence of the divine Yes is the new and glorious message which is entrusted to the Christian community and which is commissioned to deliver on earth,"

---

91. Barth, *CD* IV/2, 351.
92. Barth, *CD* III/2, 48.
93. Dostoevsky, *Brothers Karamazov*, 361–62.
94. Ibid., 362.
95. Schmemann, *For the Life of the World*, 25.
96. Barth, *CD* III/4, 507.

and simply to be obedient in doing that.⁹⁷ So the church "does not live by its own triumphs over the world, nor in order to achieve and celebrate such triumphs," such as in numerical growth.⁹⁸ "Its task is simply to see to it that the comfort and exhortation of the divine Yes are declared, and that they are declared as clearly and forcibly and impressively and universally as possible."⁹⁹ Does Schmemann tend to neglect the freedom of God to act towards Christ in the world: "Inasmuch as ye have done it unto one of the least of these my brethren, ye have done it unto me" (Matt 25:40, KJV)?¹⁰⁰ So he can even make the questionable statement that, in the liturgy, because it is a transport to heaven, "We have left 'this world,'" even at the beginning of the liturgy, when one would think that the incarnation demands first of all solidarity with the world.¹⁰¹

Creation, despite its finitude, however, is the "theater" of God's glory (to use Calvin's word) of God's joy as well as sorrow.¹⁰² Kathryn Tanner complains that in Barth's doctrine of the uniqueness of the revelation in Christ God's presence in the rest of creation is neglected.¹⁰³ Despite this criticism, Barth sees the covenant of grace as widely expressed in creation. Tanner ignores that for Barth the uniqueness of Christ reflects back upon creation, and this is to say something important about Christ's vicarious act as in harmony with his being, as well as creation; Christology and soteriology are not to be separated from each other or from creation. Christ's vicarious joy is the fount of joy for creation: "Joy unspeakable, and full of glory," in the words of the old gospel song, a vicarious joy desperately needed if we take seriously the "groans" of creation and ourselves. In fact, without Christ's vicarious joy, we cannot know the joy that God possesses over creation. We, of course, know our own joy over creation, but not God's. God's "wholly other" joy gives creation new meaning.

The double movement of the incarnation, as a reflection of the eternal communion between the Father, the Son, and the Holy Spirit, consists of both sorrow and joy: Sorrow in the humanward movement of embrac-

97. Ibid.
98. Ibid., 508.
99. Ibid.
100. Schmemann, *For the Life of the World*, 26.
101. Ibid.
102. Calvin, *Institutes*, 1.5.8, 1.6.2, 1.14.20, 2.6.1. Cf. Barth, *Dogmatics in Outline*, 58.
103. Kathryn Tanner, "Jesus Christ," in *The Cambridge Companion to Christian Doctrine*, ed. Colin E. Gunton (Cambridge: Cambridge University Press, 1997) 266.

ing our sorrows and plight. This is the eternal Word of God becoming flesh. Joy is in the corresponding Godward movement of the vicarious faith and obedience in the humanity of the Son. God knows of both our joy and sorrow before we are created. "His rejoicing and sorrow preceded ours."[104] These events are not surprises to him. He is still Lord over them. As Lord, his goodness is that "the contradiction of creation has not remained alien to Himself."[105] We are deep into the atonement at this point, a reality of the atonement that is not simply a legal acquittal nor a moral example, but one that reaches into the ontological depths of both the divine and the human. Joy and sorrow, however, are not mutually necessary for God to have joy. They are both embraced under the lordship of Jesus Christ, the one who was crucified, yes, but also raised in triumph from the dead (Rom 1:4). The resurrection is something that happened to Jesus; God raised Jesus from the dead.[106] Jesus is the witness to this act of God, this victory. Such a victory is not simply the triumph of a sovereign Being, proving that he is superior over his creation, but one that expresses the depth of his love, an "eternal mercy" causing the joy and the sorrow "to be internal to Himself, and to find their origin in His own being."[107] Barth's version of supralapsarianism does not allow God's covenant of grace to be an afterthought but the very goal of creation: Creation belongs to God, and that covenant is in his Son. The double movement embraces the contradiction, both the joy and the sorrow, in the incarnation of his Son, Jesus Christ.[108]

There really is a biblical command to rejoice, as there is to weep: to "rejoice with those who rejoice, weep with those who weep" (Rom 12:12). Solidarity is the first movement of the incarnation. Does this mean that despair is caused by God? No, but it does mean that joy and sorrow have their "foundation" in the will of God.[109] They are not "intrinsically right but they are made right" by the double movement of the incarnation.[110] God "uses" them but is not "tied" to them. The key is that the sorrow and the joy both ultimately become God's. Once we lose the vision of

104. Barth, *CD* III/1, 380.
105. Ibid.
106. Barth, *CD* IV/1, 304–5.
107. Barth, *CD* III/1, 380.
108. Ibid., 381–82.
109. Ibid., 376.
110. Ibid.

the sorrow and joy in God, we are left with nothing but self-pity. The alternative is the transformation of joy and sorrow in our participation in the sorrow and joy of God.[111] "Since it is God Himself who here goes His way rejoicing and sorrowing, everything that we think we know about this matter is not just relatively but absolutely transcended."[112] "Indolence and neutrality" no longer have to dominate us and joy and sorrow do not have to be evaded. The apathy of my high school graduating class (that's the way it was in 1972!) is not the only alternative in life.

The Yes of God is powerful; it speaks to our despair firmly and finally. God's decision, his election, is that which drives out despair, the kind of "despair of self," because God does not despair of the creation.[113] Barth can even speak of despair as becoming "unnecessary."[114] This is what the presence of God in Jesus Christ did in the first century, and does today. The joy and the sorrow are embraced by the death and resurrection of Christ: "We live by the death and resurrection of Jesus Christ, by God's own suffering and triumph, sorrow and joy, by His original participation in the twofold nature of our being."[115] Contemporary cynicism snidely discards such a Yes. The degeneration of even humor as satire into mocking is good evidence of this. Yet a pessimist cannot go further than the Christian faith in maintaining the inability of humanity to possess joy in the midst of despair.[116] The few remaining, brave optimists in the contemporary world need to cling to Jesus Christ and his joy.

Often we ask, Why does God wait? Why not the consummation of all things right now, instead of enduring all of the needless suffering and horror of this world? Barth answers that it is because God desires a response.[117] He desires that his grace be met with a response of thanksgiving, grace, and faith. Yet has not that response already been made in the faithful joy of Jesus? We wait, yes, not for a perfect faith in ourselves, but we wait in confidence that the joy of God revealed in Jesus will be shown to have overcome the despair of this world. Therefore, we can wait with joy in the midst of despair.

111. Ibid., 377.
112. Ibid.
113. Barth, *CD* II/2, 29.
114. Ibid.
115. Barth, *CD* III/1, 382.
116. Ibid., 385.
117. Barth, *CD* IV/1, 737.

As Bonhoeffer comments from prison, in a time of insanity, reason, art, and culture rush to Jesus Christ.[118] In an Advent letter written to pastors before his arrest, Bonhoeffer speaks of joy as "something given, free. Joy dwells with God."[119] "Joy dwells with God"! In the midst of his deep travail, Bonhoeffer was still able to see that joy is first of all in God, yet a joy that knows the cross.

> The joy of God has been through the poverty of the crib and the distress of the cross; therefore it is insuperable, irrefutable. It does not deny the distress where it is, but finds God in the midst of it, indeed precisely there; it does not contest the most grievous sin, but finds forgiveness in just this way; it looks death in the face, yet finds life in death itself. We are concerned with this joy which has overcome. It alone is worth believing; it alone helps and heals.[120]

God is in the midst of the joy that does not ignore the despair. Only God in Jesus Christ, and in the Jesus Christ who is joyful when we are not able to be joyful, can we take that despair so seriously, the church boldly claims, because the church lives by the Yes of God, not by its own morality, piety, or truth. "Christian faith lives by the Yes which God Himself has spoken."[121] For in Jesus Christ, there is a finality to God's Yes, and therefore to his joy.[122]

---

118. Bonhoeffer, *Ethics*, 345–46.

119. Bonhoeffer, "Advent Letter to the Pastors of the Confessing Church," in Robert Coles, *Dietrich Bonhoeffer*, 90.

120. Ibid.

121. Barth, *CD* III/1, 385.

122. Barth, *CD* II/2, 31–32.

CHAPTER ELEVEN

Joy as the Yes of Humanity

"While other [apes] sought food and love,
Tarzan sought food and joy."

—Edgar Rice Burroughs, *Jungle Tales of Tarzan*

GOD HEARS HIS OWN WORD OF JOY

In Jesus Christ, the joy of God has become the joy of humanity. God's rest, his rest of accomplishment, is a joy in which he invites humanity to participate. His satisfaction with creation can now become humanity's joyful satisfaction and grateful praise of our creation.[1] Barth's words are memorable: "Not man and not a wisdom or folly, a power or impotence, immanent in the world of man, willed and accomplished in the creature, but God—the God who rejoiced in man as in His own image."[2] We are called to participate, yes, yet not called to rejoice through our own potential or capacity, but in God's already accomplished (creation) and continual (providence) rejoicing, his act of rejoicing.

Joy is certainly a part of a "responsibility in hearing" the Word of God.[3] There is no assumption by God that sinful humanity can hear the Word, but a part of the grace of the incarnation is that God creates the hearing as well. Our perceptions and conception of joy are imperfect and tangential, but in being bound to Christ there is a confession of our imperfections, for a joy in humanity has already been found in the joyful

---

1. Barth, *CD* III/1, 98.
2. Ibid., 99.
3. Anderson, *On Being Human*, 82.

response of the Son to the Father in the Spirit.[4] God's power is not limited to a thundering word from on high but a power that is "on both sides," of both "living speech" and "living hearing."[5] This is the basis for the confidence and joy in the New Testament. But how can God be on the side of "living hearing"? Does God hear his own Word? There is joy in the fact that, indeed, this is so.

George Hunsinger observes that T. F. Torrance's theology of the Eucharist involves a "dimension of depth" in the double movement of God to humanity, and in the eucharistic action of humanity to God in the vicarious offering of Christ, his continual self- offering to God.[6] Is it too much to say that within that eucharistic offering is his eucharistic joy? He is "the perfect Eucharist," in Alexander Schmemann's words, offering "a movement of adoration and praise in which all joy and suffering, all beauty and all frustration, all hunger and all satisfaction are referred to their ultimate End and become finally *meaningful*."[7] In doing so, Christ continually offers a "faithful answer" to the Father.[8] Christ, in his vicarious offering, provides a womb in which humanity can become "accustomed" to both receiving the Word of God and participating in the faith response.[9]

The response of the Son is based on the intra-divine perichoretic relationship between the Father, the Son, and the Holy Spirit. The joy of humanity begins there, where we can speak only with fear and trembling, but which we know because of the incarnation of the Son. The *perichoresis* does not dissolve the distinctions between the persons of the Trinity, but instead establishes them.[10] Through the relationships between the persons there is interaction, such as joy, a delight in one another, if you will, while still being one God. This is another way of saying that God delights in himself, finds joy in himself. In John of the Cross's words, "there

---

4. Karl Barth, *The Knowledge of God and the Service of God according to the Teaching of the Reformation* (Eugene, OR: Wipf & Stock, 2005) 141

5. Barth, *CD* IV/2, 306.

6. George Hunsinger, "The Dimension of Depth" in *The Promise of Trinitarian Theology: Theologians in Dialogue with T. F. Torrance*, ed. Elmer M. Colyer, 151–52.

7. Schmemann, *For the Life of the World*, 35.

8. T. F. Torrance, *Christian Doctrine of God*, 1.

9. Ibid., 78.

10. Ibid., 175.

to be rapt as God is/ seized by the same delight/ for even as father and son/and the third, not less in might . . ."[11]

Hearing God's Word, Jesus responds with prayer, on our behalf in and in our place. We often do not know how or what to pray (Rom 8:26). Prayer is the Son's intercession on our behalf that also involves teaching us to pray and placing that prayer on our lips.[12] Christ's intercession for us (Heb 7:25) is a movement we cannot make on our own.[13] In effect, we can say that he places joy on our lips. Christ does this as our High Priest so that our prayers might be an "echo" of his prayers, a "liturgical amen to the worship of Christ," in James Torrance's words.[14] As priest, Christ is the *leitourgos* (Heb 8:2) the minister in the sanctuary or "worship leader," constantly presenting us before the Father.[15] Discipleship means nothing less than to pray with Jesus.[16] Our confidence and joy in prayer, according to Bonhoeffer, is found in praying with Jesus: "He wants to pray with us and have us pray with him, so that we may be confident and glad that God hears us."[17]

Jesus possesses joy and that joy is unique to him. For as much as he is in solidarity with our humanity, our definition of humanity (including joy) does not limit him. He explains what it truly means to be human.[18] Christ defines Adam, not the other way around.[19] As such, he defines being human as one who does the will of God, so that truly human joy should not be seen apart from its conformity to the will of God.[20] All have participated in the death and resurrection of Christ so there is no place for us to stand, even in our desperate joys.[21] The joy of Jesus speaks of what is fundamental about being human, even as it lives through the inevitability of despair, as seen in the passion of Christ. Melancholy exists but now as

---

11. St. John of the Cross, *Ballad*, 4, 61, cited by Fiddes, *Participation in God*, 45.
12. Barth, *CD* II/2, 126.
13. Schmemann, *For the Life of the World*, 44.
14. James B. Torrance, *Worship, Community and the Triune God of Grace*, 14.
15. Ibid., 29.
16. Barth, *CD* III/1, 39; cf. IV/2, 705.
17. Bonhoeffer, *Psalms*, 11.
18. Barth, *CD* III/2, 59.
19. Karl Barth, *Christ and Adam: Man and Humanity in Romans 5*, trans. T. A. Smail (New York: Macmillan, 1968).
20. Barth, *CD* III/2, 63.
21. Barth, *CD* IV/1, 295, 317.

an interlude, in Chesterton's words.[22] Joy can therefore be "expansive" and "gigantic", while despair can be isolated, "something special and small."[23]

By "gigantic" Chesterton does not mean a big production, an "aesthetic excessiveness," a Disneyland of joy. The joy of Jesus is quiet and perhaps hidden at times by the focus of his true faith, obedience, and service to the Father. Similar to Kierkegaard's "indirect communication," the joy of Jesus is a part of the "God incognito" that is the incarnation, but representing the richest possible joy because of that. That should be the nature of Christian joy as well.

The one who does the will of God reconciles, or is involved in an exchange with, the ones in rebellion, the "wonderful" or "sweet exchange" of the *Epistle to Diognetus* and 2 Cor 8:9.[24] As such, we are exalted with him as we are raised with Christ (Romans 6). "He came down that we might be exalted," according to Gregory Nazianzus.[25] In exaltation is joy, and a unique kind of joy it is. We are not exalted in ourselves but with Christ. "And now His life is our life," Barth concludes. He took upon life "in our depth" and became one us, that is how he is exalted as the New Man.[26] "In Him the Christian life is true—and in Him alone—but in Him as our own Christian life, our thankfulness is true and our penitence, our love to God and man is true, and our service of God is true."[27] The power of the resurrection exalts us in all of our humanity with Christ in all of his humanity.[28] This is something that has already taken place; the exalted Christ is already reigning in joy, as Barth reminds us:

> What option had we but to give our assent not with a sighing Nevertheless, but with a joyful Therefore, to the answer that the power and lordship of the man Jesus are present amongst us, that there is this transition from Him to us, that that power of our participation in His exaltation is at work, that our exaltation in Him has already taken place?[29]

---

22. Chesterton, *Orthodoxy*, 159.
23. Ibid., 160.
24. *Epistle to Diognetus*, 8–9. Cf. T. F. Torrance, *Trinitarian Faith*, 179.
25. Gregory Nazianzus, *Discourse* I, 4, cited by Alfeyev, *Mystery of Faith*, 90.
26. Barth, *CD* IV/2, 386, 396.
27. Barth, *Knowledge of God*, 141–42.
28. Barth, *CD* IV/2, 316.
29. Ibid., 360.

All do not accept this word, but "the situation of all is the situation which is altered by this word."[30] And that would include our joy as well, joy in the midst of despair.

Dynamically connected to our exaltation with Christ is the reality of the ascension of the humanity of Christ. The often-neglected doctrine of the ascension reminds us that our humanity is not left to our own devices but is included even now in the exalted, ascended humanity of the Son sitting at the right hand of God, praying for us (Acts 2:33; Heb 7:25; Col 3:3). T. F. Torrance argues that without a strong sense of the ascended humanity of Christ ministry becomes a Pelagian act based on an adoptionist Christology.[31] In effect, the ascension is the continuing ministry of the vicarious humanity of Christ, a continuing joy of the Son before the Father, if you will.

The writer Ray Bradbury recognizes the need for humanity to be thankful to God for his gifts in his poem, "Joy is the Grace We Say to God."[32] It is not blasphemous to say that there is a grace that goes from us to God. Bradbury instinctively knows this but needs the Christology to give substance to it.

The vicarious response of Christ is a critique of our attempts to locate the crux of salvation in our faith. Alan Lewis criticizes those who make a person's "deathbed state of mind the sole criterion of how he or she would stand" before God.[33] Despair can only be faced, Lewis contends, if we depend upon "the gift of grace outside us and around us. God promises to do what we cannot do and go where we need not go."[34] This certainly includes the difficulty often of joy.

"THE SECRET OF HUMANITY"

The criticism is sometimes levied that the doctrine of the vicarious humanity of Christ does not provide a place for our human response. This is only true if one neglects the doctrine of the Holy Spirit. The Holy Spirit

30. Barth, *CD* IV/1, 317.

31. T. F. Torrance, *Royal Priesthood*, 39–40.

32. Ray Bradbury, *A Chapbook for Burnt-Out Priests, Rabbis, and Ministers* (Baltimore: Cemetery Dance, 2001) 127–28; *I Live By the Invisible: New and Selected Poems* (Clare, Ireland: Salmon, 2002) 54; *They Have Not Yet Seen the Stars: The Collected Poetry of Ray Bradbury* (Lancaster, PA: Stealth, 2002) 257.

33. Alan E. Lewis, *Between Cross and Resurrection*, 430.

34. Ibid., 431.

mirrors the double movement of the incarnation (from God to humanity, from humanity to God) through being given by the Father through the Son (God to humanity) enabling us to respond in faith, participating in the faith of the Son through the Spirit (humanity to God). As T. F. Torrance puts it, "Our receiving of the Spirit, therefore, is not independent of or different from the vicarious receiving of the Spirit by Christ himself but is a sharing in it."[35] Only through the Holy Spirit can we share in the vicarious joy of Christ, the one who "rejoiced in the Holy Spirit" (Luke 10:21). He is the Spirit of Jesus Christ (Rom 8:9) "not, therefore, an alien Spirit, but His own Spirit, in which He is flesh," who "exalts and purifies and sanctifies and dedicates the flesh."[36] The Spirit creates "a new human subject" in Christ but does not destroy the human subject.[37] Alan Torrance suggests that our problem is that we do not include grace in the human response: "The event of grace does not stop where the free human response begins; it includes precisely the human response to the extent that the human response is completed on our behalf in Christ."[38] Important to our understanding of joy is that the grace of the "desire" (also joy) of Jesus is a reality in advance that desires being realized in us.[39] The Holy Spirit's ministry is not only to be the power and presence of Christ sent to us (from God to humanity) but also representing us to God (from humanity to God). The "things of Christ," to use James Torrance's words, are both brought to us in that double movement.[40] The secondary movement, in particular, includes the vicarious joy of Christ.

The Holy Spirit brings us the gift of God's freedom, a freedom to save and reconcile despite our recalcitrance. We might seem threatened by God's action because it would deprive us of freedom, in this case, that we might be deprived of our own joys, maybe even very personal joys. C. S. Lewis often told of his pre-conversion fear that if he became a Christian something very vital to him, some personal joy, would be taken away by God. But the inability of our joys to be sustained and to deal decisively with despair reminds us of our utter need. As Barth remarks, "If God's freedom ended at the very point where we need God most, and if we found

---

35. T. F. Torrance, *Christian Doctrine of God*, 148.
36. Barth, *CD* IV/2, 452.
37. Barth, *CD* IV/1, 89.
38. Alan J. Torrance, *Persons in Communion*, 318–19.
39. Ibid., 319.
40. James B. Torrance, *Worship, Community and the Triune God of Grace*, 88.

ourselves suddenly outside His foreordination and dependent on our own freedom, how could His love find us, or we participate in it?"[41] Substitute "joy" for "freedom" and we can see the need for the vicarious joy of Christ. The truly free act is the action of the Son in response to the Father, a free act of joy and delight in the knowledge of God.[42] "The Holy Spirit," Barth contends, "does not create the ghost of a man standing in decision, but the reality of the man concerning whom decision has already been made in the existence of the man Jesus."[43] There is something very lonely and haunting here in the alternative, "the ghost of a man standing in decision," a loneliness in which there is no joy. Receiving the Spirit, "we know ourselves in Him as those who are elected and created and determined for existence in the truth of His human nature, for an authentically human life."[44] The so-called "free" individual can be the most desolate of beings. The persons who see their joy in Jesus, "those that know this new being as their own" have a vantage point of a reality that brings joy.[45]

Perhaps we can also see the Lord's Supper, the Eucharist, in a different light. The taking of the bread and cup is not simply to be a duty but a joy, a joy of thanksgiving (the meaning of "Eucharist") that is a joy because Christ has already offered himself in joy and thanksgiving to the Father and continues to do so in the Eucharist. As the ancient liturgy of John Chrysostom says, "it is He who offers and it is He who is offered."[46] This is much different than our often perfunctory routines of communion that are done more out of duty than joy. Christ has not left us alone to "drum up" our own joy in the Lord's Supper. He is, indeed, present.

The church finds its true joy in its humility, not in its capacity for religion or joy, in its receiving, not its grasping or coveting.[47] That is why trying to "will" joy is such a dicey proposition. We too often try to demand joy of life and end up with a distortion. Joy is easier to desire than

41. Barth, *CD* II/1, 595. Cf. IV/3.1, 381.
42. Barth, *CD* IV/3.1, 382.
43. Barth, *CD* IV/2, 363.
44. Ibid., 452.
45. Barth, *CD* IV/1, 92.
46. "The Divine Liturgy of St. John Chrysostom," in *Service Book of the Holy Eastern Orthodox Catholic and Apostolic Church according to the Use of the Antiochian Orthodox Christian Archdiocese of North America*, 10th ed., 1997, 105; Schmemann, *For the Life of the World*, 35.
47. Barth, *CD* III/2, 584 and III/4, 378.

to find. As Bonhoeffer remarks, "The one who finds the way of God must first lose all his own riches in order to find in God all manner of riches."[48] Joy includes that which is received; it is a gift of grace people receive, Barth comments,

> not in virtue of their human faithfulness and effort, but in virtue of the new and conclusive act of the Giver Himself proclaimed to them (in and with what they have received) in virtue of His grace and the fact that He is alive for evermore. God's word creates joy and delight in the one who receives it.[49]

"We can create opportunities for it in anticipatory joy, but we cannot create or construct or produce or force it by various plans and measures."[50] Or we can pine away in anticipation of joy, a joy that never comes. Anticipation and fulfillment need to be brought together by One who lives in the tension of a fulfilled yet also anticipated joy, much like the eschatological tension between the kingdom of God as both present and future. The joy of Jesus is the joy that both belongs to Jesus and the joy that is given by Jesus. From the standpoint of the life of Jesus, joy is gratitude to the Father by the one who did not count equality with God a thing to be grasped but "emptied" himself into the form of humanity in order to become "obedient to the point of death—even death on a cross" (Phil 2:6–8). Christ radically re-defines both anticipatory and fulfilled joy.

In God's rejoicing in the vicarious joy of Christ, "the secret of humanity," to use Barth's words, is revealed. Reflecting God's triune being, humanity can "gladly," with joy respond to one another in co-humanity because "this freedom . . . is not merely the crown of humanity, but is root."[51] The joy of God is the root of the joy of humanity.

The resurrection of Christ is that which bears fruit in genuine, human joy "because God the Creator and Lord of life acts and speaks here, taking the lost cause of man out of his hand, making it his own, intervening majestically, mercifully and wisely for him."[52] "Christ is risen!" is a "genuine, earthly, human joy: the joy of harvest, wedding, festival and victory; the joy not only of the inner but also of the outer man, the joy

---

48. Bonhoeffer, *Meditating on the Word*, 130.
49. Barth, *CD* IV/1, 328.
50. Barth, *CD* III/4, 379.
51. Barth, *CD* III/2, 273. Cf. Alan J. Torrance, *Persons in Communion*, 183.
52. Barth, *CD* III/4, 375.

in which we may and must drink wine as well as eat bread, sing and play as well as speak, dance as well as pray."[53] This is "obedient joy." Whose obedience is this but the one "obedient unto death, even death on a cross" (Phil 2:8)?

We are exalted with Christ because Christ lives. We share in his exaltation (Phil 2:5-11). We no longer suffer the unfreedom of needing exaltation by others or by ourselves. Exaltation, our sanctification, is not to be left up to us or accomplished by us.[54] It is wrong to say as Cynthia Rigby does that the human agent "contributes" to reconciliation.[55] Christ does not just create a "place" for us but "takes our place" through his vicarious humanity. He genuinely acts on our behalf and it is only in this acting (including his joy) that through the Spirit we can be free to act in him. This man Jesus with whom we are exalted already possesses joy, the joy and peace of the kingdom of God (Rom 14:17). What does this exaltation mean? Barth makes clear that the joy of the resurrection means an altered state for humanity, despite all appearances: "In Him our conflict with God has been turned into the peace of fellowship. In Him we are no longer below but above; no longer in the far country but home again; no longer servants of God but sons; or no longer lazy and unprofitable, because disobedient, but obedient and profitable servants."[56]

But can this be simply a platonic ideal, a fantasy of the mind, a wistful hope, or can joy be found in the human being that trudges down the pathway of very earthly roads?

JOY IN THE OTHER

True humanity, "the secret of humanity," is concretely found in the joy among one another, a "mutual acceptance," and "common joy" that reflects the freedom of a genuine encounter.[57] The miracle occurs that is the opposite of staying aloof and withdrawn, fearful and mistrustful of one another, the usual fare for humanity. Therefore, joy is found in

---

53. Ibid., 376.

54. Barth, *CD* IV/2, 516.

55. Cynthia L. Rigby, "All God, and Us: Double Agency and Reconciliation in Psalms 22 and 51," in *Psalms and Practice: Worship, Virtue, and Authority*, ed. Stephen Breck Reid (Collegeville, MN: Liturgical, 2001) 203–4.

56. Barth, *CD* IV/2, 363.

57. Barth, *CD* III/2, 271–72.

a vicarious sense of asking, What is joy for the Other? "What is really demanded is that I ask myself from the standpoint of the Other what will give him joy, and that I then consider this and put it into effect."[58] "Being-there-for-others," in Bonhoeffer's phrase, means for Moltmann that when the church is speaking vicariously on the behalf of others it is not to be patronizing but to be an end in itself in which we are genuinely joyful with one another.[59] This also does not mean the obliteration of individuality, for in such joyful mutuality there is the freedom akin to breathing freely, "in which both keep their distance because they are so close, and are so close because they can keep their distance."[60] Human beings relate to one another on the basis of *pathos* (emotions). To do otherwise is to be indifferent, in apathy.[61] Admittedly, we hesitate to relate to others emotionally because we are afraid to make ourselves vulnerable. Perhaps that is part of our ironic indifference to and even fear of joy. Yet what human experience is more meaningful than when, in the midst of the monotony of the day, one becomes joyful in the awareness that "this moment is worth everything?"[62] At that moment, we realize that joy is at the heart of being human.

The delight in God, even in his law, takes place in the inmost self (Rom 7:22). Anderson comments, "Rather than the self being 'annihilated' by the grace of God, it is renewed by its capacity to value for itself the gifts of God and affirmed as a fundamental value in human love."[63] Anderson correctly affirms the very human "delight" in God as being created in the image of God. But Paul's "delight" in the law of God in Romans sees "in my members another law at war with the law of my mind, making me captive to the law of sin that dwells in my members" so that he cries out, "Wretched man that I am! Who will rescue me from this body of death?" (Rom 7:23–24). Is it wise, then, for Anderson to speak of renewing a "capacity" in the self? Paul's own answer to his cry is, "Thanks be to God through Jesus Christ our Lord!" (Rom 7:25). Anderson is right to connect grace with our humanity. How, then, does Jesus Christ create

---

58. Barth, *CD* III/4, 380.

59. Jürgen Moltmann, *Theology and Joy*, trans. Reinhard Ulrich (London: SCM, 1973) 86–87.

60. Barth, *CD* III/2, 272.

61. Anderson, *Self-Care*, 57.

62. Anderson, *Exploration into God*, 52.

63. Anderson, *Self-Care*, 44.

this within our humanity? How does this become *our* humanity? How does this become *our* joy?

There is genuine joy in Adam's response to Eve: "This at last is bone of my bones and flesh of my flesh" (Gen 2:23).[64] Adam finds joy in that which affirms what is truly human: the Other, not just one's individuality. To be human, then, is to be in covenant partnership that expresses joy at what God has given, even "selecting" what God has "elected."[65] This is the Other that can be the object of our love, in Bonhoeffer's poignant suggestion, "at once the embodiment of Adam's limit and the object of Adam's love."[66] Certainly we desire, yearn, to love, often obsessively so. But to be confronted by one's "limit" emphasizes that the Other contributes to our humanity as a gift of God, not something we can demand, a gift that is sacramental in the sense of its potential to transform us. The goal here is not becoming God, but becoming human, realizing one's limit through the Other whom God has given you. Joy in humanity is most concretely and most immediately seen in his exultation of Adam over Eve, this "gladly," as Barth puts it.[67] This joy is in contrast with those Christians whom Bonhoeffer sees "who want to be more spiritual than God himself" and only speak of "battle, renunciation, suffering, and the cross," despising the "earthiness" of the Old Testament and therefore all earthly gifts that God gives. "They want to be schoolmasters in the Holy Spirit and so they lose the full joy of their Christian calling and deny God the thanks they should give for his great friendliness towards us."[68] Immediately we see that there is no natural capacity found in Adam in order to fulfill his humanity.[69] Though God presents all the animals before Adam to name, "the man there was not found a helper as his partner" (Gen 2:21). It is out of Adam's despair and loneliness, Ray Anderson suggests, that God took out Eve, ontologically connected to Adam, but now distinct from him.[70] As we have seen with joy existing in the midst of struggle, Eve comes out of Adam's despair, but not as an answer to the despair. The answer is only in God, but Eve comes as God's gift in the midst of the despair.

64. Bonhoeffer, *Creation and Fall*, 97. Cf. Anderson, *On Being Human*, 81.
65. Anderson, *Something Old, Something New*, 41.
66. Bonhoeffer, *Creation and Fall*, 98.
67. Barth, *CD* III/2, 273, 282–83, 289.
68. Bonhoeffer, *Meditating on the Word*, 110.
69. Anderson, *On Being Human*, 81.
70. Ibid.

Perhaps nowhere do we see the sad irony of sin more than in the puzzlement, and even enmity, between man and woman. The irony certainly is true, particularly in our age of heightened eroticism. What ignites the emotions more than sexual desire? What has the potential for so much conflict as domestic life? But is so much of our frank pursuit of the erotic truly a response of "gladly" to the opposite sex? Is there not at least a hint of threat, a desire to master, to control that which seems to master our emotions and energies? We are always nervous before the opposite sex (this is not limited to the hormone-charged, nervous adolescent). There is so much "interest and curiosity," as well as "reticence and anxiety . . . phantasy, poetry, morality and immorality . . . empty talk and sighing and sniggering on the part of the inexperienced . . ."[71] Inexperienced! Why would Barth say that? Because we do not really know, and perhaps do not want to know this "holy of holies" of the human. What will we find? Will we be disappointed? Yet we are dealing here with "the centre of the human, with the basic form of primal humanity."[72]

Grace reveals that in spite of our "inexperience," because of the resurrection of Christ, we can rejoice in God since we now know the gulf that separates God and humanity, male and female.[73] The gulf does not necessarily have to mean despair but confession of sin. "While I kept silence, my body wasted away through my groaning all day long," cries the psalmist. "For day and night your hand was heavy upon me; my strength was dried up as by the heat of summer. Then I acknowledged my sin to you and I did not hide my iniquity" (Ps 32:3–5). Keeping this silence is what the psalmist really remembers about his sinful past. Remembering this enables one to "live strong and joyful before God as a righteous man," giving him a "joyful certainty" in God's pardon: ". . . and you forgave the guilt of my sin" (Ps 32:5).[74] Confession of sin is that which acknowledges that only God (not even the confession!) can take away that sin (Psalm 51).[75] Without justification, the psalmist is left as only a "sinner."

> What the Psalmist has in mind as the subject matter of his prayer—and obviously not only as the subject matter but also as the presupposition—is, as the continuation shows, his justifica-

---

71. Barth, *CD* III/2, 289.
72. Ibid.
73. Barth, *Epistle to the Romans*, 31.
74. Barth, *CD* IV/1, 577–78.
75. Ibid., 579.

> tion . . . How else, having made that confession of sin, could he go on to say with such confidence—apparently as a supreme and final request: "Make me to hear joy and gladness; that the bones which thou hast broken may rejoice" (v. 8)?[76]

Joy is expected by the justified person, even as one is well aware of one's sin. This is a joy in humanity fulfilled by the vicarious confession of our sins before the Father by the Son, as particularly seen in the baptism of Jesus.

> The man who asks for the forgiveness of his sins and confesses his sins and enters into the light of the situation between God and man as it really is, can and should as such and at once (as this beginner) expect to be satisfied with joy and gladness, and he can and should therefore pray for it, for his new right before God, the new possibility of living before Him.[77]

This person can now cry, "Create in me a clean heart, O God, and put a new and right spirit within me . . . Restore to me the joy of your salvation, and sustain in me a willing spirit" (Ps 51:10, 12).

The joyful response is found in Adam's "gladly" before Eve's creation; a real sense of joy that genuinely completes his humanity. Joy, not serious moralism, is that which should characterize humanity.[78] Perhaps here is a critique of all of our attempts to run from the opposite gender as an attempt to run from our humanity: whether it be homosexual culture or the monastery.[79] Are we really running from joy, the joy that is found in the Thou, the Other, most concretely expressed in the opposite sex? This is a question of joy because to run from our humanity is to not embrace who we are before God in "a placid and cheerful and sure knowledge of the duality of human existence."[80] Do we end up denying our "limit," that is, our creatureliness, for the sake of our futile and quixotic Promethean protests? How threatened I am by this duality . . . not just of male and female (that is its original and most concrete form) but because it points beyond that to my relationship with God and the world: I am not a universe unto myself (contra the Fathers, a "microcosm" of the universe).

76. Ibid., 580.
77. Barth, *CD* IV/1, 580.
78. Barth, *CD* IV/2, 233.
79. Barth, *CD* III/2, 290.
80. Ibid.

I am human, all too human (to borrow from Nietzsche) created as a duality. That humanity does not stand in splendid isolation. Barth expresses it splendidly: "Man would not be man if he were no longer male or female, if his humanity did not consist in this concrete fellow-humanity . . . He has lived in no other way in time, and he can live no other way in eternity. This is something which he cannot lose. For by it there stands or falls his creatureliness."[81]

The command to rejoice is found in our creatureliness as male and female. *Eros* is not just desire unbounded but desire within the command of God. Barth describes the joy in the self-giving and acceptance of the man and the woman in marriage, accepting and giving in all of one's totality, including gender:

> As the desire of love, of true *eros,* desire is legitimate—and this is true of the husband too—when it is preceded by self-giving and thus controlled, not by the need of the other, but by the joy of being his and of willing to belong to him, the confidence of being well-placed with him, the willingness to make common cause with him. Again, this self-giving, as that of love, of genuine *eros,* is legitimate, because free, when it is preceded by understanding, so that it is not a blind surrender to the other, but he is seen in his totality to be partner to whose being in its totality one can honorably give oneself, and whom one may honorably desire in the totality of one's being.[82]

The "totality" of the other can be accepted, including one's difference as male or female, because the biological is not incidental to our humanity, or our joy in marriage. We are to rejoice in marriage because we are male before the female and female before the male. This is not simply a matter of accepting *eros* by itself. That would be to ignore the command of God. Jesus's joy is in accepting that which the Father has given him. He rejoices in the command of God, even though it involves a cross. Jesus portrays that which Barth describes as keeping the command:

> It is he who does not look for holes or spaces between its meshes —for it is not a net with meshes and loopholes, not a mere 'law,' but the command of the living God—through which he or others can escape its demands, and as male or female, outside the

---

81. Ibid., 296.
82. Barth, *CD* III/4, 219.

framework of marriage of within it, can be his own master, lawgiver, judge and teacher.[83]

SABBATH JOY AS HUMAN JOY

This is a crucial question for all Christians: Is there joy in keeping the command of God? The command can only be seen as joyful if it is seen as an expression of the grace of God. This is what is meant by Christ being the Good Shepherd, according to Barth:

> Why rejoices? Because it is the command of the grace of God in Jesus Christ; because in it he does not hear the voice of the stranger but that of the Good Shepherd; because he finds both himself and all men comforted, sustained and carried and therefore claimed and led and guided by the command but that by it there can be life; because he, too, stands in the light of this command.[84]

Christologically, Jesus leads us as he obeys the command; we follow him as he obeys the Father, his vicarious action on our behalf. He can do this because, amazingly, he shares in our creatureliness, in solidarity with our humanity. Yet he does not do so without compassion for our fractured lives. He has been tempted in all ways as we have, except without sin (Heb 4:15). He is present here in a kind of holiness and transcendence that is not moralistic or metaphysical but earthy, dirty, and real; our real, confused, fallen humanity.[85] This is the joy that Bonhoeffer writes of to his fellow pastors in the middle of the Second World War, the joy of the One who was both crucified and raised from the dead, the joy of the One who has overcome, the joy that has risen in the midst of despair and sorrow, even in our confusion over our identities. "It alone is worth believing; it alone helps and heals."[86] In God's joy in our humanity (including our gender, male or female, single or married) we can find joy.

Because the joy of humanity is founded on God's Sabbath joy, expressed in humanity in the vicarious joy of Christ, the Sabbath becomes

---

83. Ibid., 231.
84. Ibid., 231–32.
85. Ibid., 232.
86. Bonhoeffer, "Advent Letter to the Pastors of the Confessing Church," in Robert Coles, *Dietrich Bonhoeffer*, 90.

for humanity a joyful definition that humanity is not determined by one's work. As much as fate or our own choice in workaholic America may desire that, the Sabbath joy represents a prohibition and a limit for humanity.[87] It is not enough, Barth contends, to accept the Sabbath as "recuperation" from work; if so, then work is still the lord of our lives. On the contrary, the Sabbath speaks of humanity belonging to itself. The joy of the Sabbath is an exultation meaning that I am not determined by the workaday world. There is something more essential to who I am. Being "more than these things" is a direct pointer to the vicarious humanity of Christ, for I am "more than these things" because there is One whose humanity is the foundation and substance of my humanity, whose joy is now the foundation and substance of my joy. I am oriented toward a Beyond, if you will: The Cartesian "I am" is no longer found in a solitary, thinking mind, but in the Beyond who is the Thou: Jesus Christ.

Sabbath joy is joy that comes as a gift; something that is given to humanity. It is in this way that the vicarious joy of Christ is a gift given to humanity in contrast to our attempts to generate joy that frustrate and exhaust us. Therefore, our response to this gift of joy can only be gratitude, as it is for Jesus (Matt 11:25; Luke 10:21). This is essential to the Lord's Supper: After breaking and giving the bread, "then he took a cup, and after *giving thanks* he gave it to them . . ." (Matt 26:27; Mark 14:23; Luke 22:19; 1 Cor 11:24). The giving of thanks (*eucharistein*), the blessing of God (*eulogein*), is essential to the Eucharist in the church.[88] In the blessing of the bread, there is a link "between *bread received and shared* and *Jesus given up for God for many*."[89] Barth makes clear that joy as gratitude is different from the coveting that ignores Christ's thanksgiving to the Father and seeks to establish a "grasping" of our own.

> To be joyful means to look out for opportunities for gratitude. To be glad in the sense required is distinguished already from vain and empty pleasure by the fact that it is the hope of a receiving and not the covetous glance at a grasping, at an event to be enacted and established by ourselves, at a condition which we shall construct in some way and with some kind of apparatus.[90]

---

87. Barth, *CD* III/1, 214.

88. Ralph P. Martin, *The Worship of God: Some Theological, Pastoral, and Practical Reflections* (Grand Rapids: Eerdmans, 1982) 28.

89. Alasdair I. C. Heron, *Table and Tradition: Toward an Ecumenical Understanding of the Eucharist* (Philadelphia: Westminster, 1983) 25.

90. Barth, *CD* III/4, 378.

The Sabbath is that which is given, as well, as a check on our "coveting" and "grasping" of life, of trying to create our own, flimsy joy; of ignoring our limit as creatures before God. Ironically, this is in stark contrast to what the incarnate Son did when he voluntarily limited himself in becoming human (Phil 2:6–8).

The Sabbath joy of God enables us to stop amidst the monotony of life and actually be joyful in thanksgiving for being alive, to allow our work to be transformed from drudgery to a proper perspective that does not determine the entirety of our lives. Anderson believes that this is the message of Ecclesiastes: "Likewise all to whom God gives wealth and possessions and whom he enables to enjoy them, and to accept their lot and find enjoyment in their toil—this is the gift of God. For they will scarcely brood over the days to their lives, because God keeps them occupied with the joy of their hearts" (Eccl 5:19–20).[91] The key is how the toil ceases to be drudgery and becomes the "occupation" of joy. Do we just endure the days and even as Christians just endure waiting for something to change, even for eternal life? That is hardly the life of joy. Without the Sabbath, there is no recognition that our humanity is more than just doing a job and bringing home a paycheck. Sabbath joy means that what God has given, not our faithfulness, is what makes the present time a time of joy.

> For all that it is provisional, this time between is made for them a time of joy, in which every moment and every hour means not simply the continuation of that which has been received, not simply an advance in the consequences which can be drawn from it, but also the approach of the making absolute of that which has been received, of its new and definitive form: not in virtue of their human faithfulness and effort, but in virtue of the new and conclusive act of the Giver Himself proclaimed to them (in and with what they have received) in virtue of His grace and the fact that He is alive for evermore.[92]

The kingdom of God has come but it is hidden, Barth contends, so joy has come not just as the continuation of the world as it was before the incarnation, although "the making absolute of what which has been received" is in process. This does not deny the present joy, but only if the workaday world is dethroned as the determinate king of our lives.

91. See Anderson, *Exploration into God*, 52.
92. Barth, *CD* III/4, 328.

AESTHETIC JOY IN GOD

The Sabbath speaks of a different existence that instead of slavery creates freedom and rejoicing in the contemplation of God, a truly aesthetic goal of humanity, "a beholding or vision of God that brings one into union with God," a life of beauty.[93] Much has been made of the importance of aesthetics in contemporary theology (Hans Urs von Balthasar, Jeremy Begbie) and rightly so. Yet contemplation can only truly take place where there is rest: God's rest of Sabbath joy fulfilled in Jesus Christ. Without Christ's joy, there cannot be true contemplation. For he is the one who sees God, who possesses God as "an object of joy."[94] Thus the biblical and aesthetic exhortation is to "taste and see that the Lord is good" (Ps 34:8). The foundation is laid for all those who rejoice, including Mary ("my spirit rejoices in God my Savior" Luke 1:47) and Paul, who can exhort the community to "Rejoice in the Lord always; again I will say, Rejoice" (Phil 4:4). One can "delight . . . in the law of the Lord" (Ps 1:2; 112:1; 119; Rom 7:22). "Take delight in the Lord and he will give you the desires of your heart" (Ps 37:4). The parent will rejoice when the child speaks what is right (Prov 23:16). Those "who take refuge in you rejoice: let them ever sing for joy" (Ps 5:11). "You show me the path of life. In your presence there is fullness of joy" (Ps 16:11). God is the one who gives this joy in the midst of despair: "You have turned my mourning into dancing; and you have taken off my sackcloth and clothed me with joy" (Ps 30:11). "The meek shall obtain fresh joy in the Lord, and the neediest people shall exult in the Holy One of Israel" (Isa 29:19). Worship is the result: "Make a joyful noise to the Lord, all the earth, worship the Lord with gladness; come into his presence with singing" (Ps 100:1–2). Because God radiates joy, he is a God of beauty for whom humor even is not unknown. Therefore God's glory is that which is joyful.[95] Glory, beauty and humor join together in the God of joy. Essentially, this is the triune God whose form of being as Father, Son, and Holy Spirit radiates joy because God himself is in a relationship of "delight," as Jonathan Edwards comments.[96]

---

93. Keith J. Egan, "Contemplation" in *The New Westminster Dictionary of Christian Spirituality*, ed. Philip Sheldrake (Louisville: Westminster John Knox, 2005) 21; and Bonhoeffer, *Creation and Fall*, 63–64. Cf. Kettler, "The Vicarious Beauty of Christ and the Aesthetics of the Atonement," *Theology Today* 64 (2007) 14–24.

94. Barth, *CD* II/1, 654.

95. Ibid., 655.

96. Jonathan Edwards, *The Philosophy of Jonathan Edwards, From His Private Note-*

Barth can add that the Trinity "attracts" and "conquers" through his radiant and beautiful joy. "To this extent the triunity of God is the secret of His beauty. If we deny this, we at once have a God without radiance and without joy (and without humour!); a God without beauty."[97] Beauty, glory, joy, and humor are the substances of participation in the vicarious joy of Christ. They are the goals of the Christian life: ". . . and those whom he justified he also glorified" (Rom 8:30).[98]

Acknowledging the aesthetic is to acknowledge the joy in life. Criticism of the "aesthetic excessiveness" of David Bentley Hart does not mean to deny the place of the aesthetic. Barth speaks of "the will for life" as "also the will for joy, delight, and happiness."[99] The aesthetic slows us down to be grateful, to appreciate that which God has given, to possess the attitude of the Son before the Father in the Spirit. Again, our idols in contemporary America are often found in our work. The aesthetic dethrones those idols; it says that there is something else worthwhile, something else that brings joy in life in beauty, art, and creation. Otherwise, Barth is very frank: we "debar" ourselves from joy, especially under the insidious pretentions of being "spiritual" or "responsible."[100] Barth hastens to add that such a person who debars himself of joy is not really an obedient person! This is certainly true if Jesus possesses joy himself.

We discover the aesthetic joy in the middle of the monotony of life, and in doing so, recognize what Anderson (and Ecclesiastes?) observe as the joy of the sheer giftedness of life, even in the midst of despair. I remember that moment recently during a trip to the Art Institute of Chicago when I viewed in person for the first time one of my favorite paintings, "Nighthawks" by Edward Hopper, the grim picture of a late night urban diner and its lonely inhabitants, seemingly disconnected from each other. I had a print of this above my desk for several years in seminary! This may have been simply a sign of my personal despair (!) but in viewing the original I was reminded of the power of the aesthetic to say, "Yes, this moment, this taking in of artistic talent, a gift from God, even a 'depressing' painting, is good!" I felt some connection with this moment, yet not denying

---

books, cited by Gesa Elsbeth Thiessen, editor, *Theological Aesthetics: A Reader* (Grand Rapids: Eerdmans, 2005) 175.

97. Barth, *CD* II/1, 660–61.
98. Barth, *CD* IV/1, 580.
99. Barth, *CD* III/4, 374–75.
100. Ibid., 375.

the despair and frustrations of life. In some ways, I like to think that in the joy of an aesthetic of despair that joy and despair can live together, again, yet without despair as an equal.

Yet, as C. S. Lewis reminds us, beauty is not joy in itself but that through which joy is found, a *witness* Karl Barth might say, to God's joy.[101] So we do need a mediator to get to God's joy.

JOY IN COMMUNITY

The essential nature of humanity as community is furthered in the act of baptism, for baptism is something that in done unto one, something that is done by the grace of God and by the community, the church. In this way, the church participates in Christ's vicarious act for all that should lead to faith but begins with grace. The baptism of Jesus is a reception from the Father, an obedience to the Father, saying Yes to the Father's will.[102] Barth can say that this Yes is not a sacrament or a means of grace, but can we deny that this is a transforming (sacramental?) event within the one act of revelation and reconciliation, and particularly a part of the act of reconciliation with God in the vicarious response of Christ? This was a joyful moment for Jesus. There is genuine joy, therefore, in our baptism, including that of infants. Barth himself, no friend of infant baptism, can ask, "What is really demanded is that I ask myself from the standpoint of the other what will give him joy, and that I then consider this and put it into effect."[103] In baptism, the church acts in participation with the vicarious faith and obedience of Christ and thus the child is surrounded by grace in the community. So Moltmann can remark, "Being-there-for-others is the fundamental structure of Christ's church which vicariously speaks for men and particularly represents those who have no one to speak for them."[104] He is speaking of social justice here, but is there not a wider application to the entirety of the church's ministry if it is a participation in the continuing vicarious ministry of Christ? Is this not better than to speak as Barth does of baptism as "the first form of the human answer to the divine charge"?[105] What has happened to the vicari-

101. C. S. Lewis, *Weight of Glory*, 4.
102. Barth, *CD* IV/4, 65–66.
103. Barth, *CD* III/4, 380.
104. Moltmann, *Theology and Joy*, 86.
105. Barth, *CD* IV/4, 90.

ous answer of Christ in Barth? Is it not Christ who is "the first form of the human answer"? Barth seems to be too eager to critique infant baptism at this point, but at the expense of the vicarious humanity of Christ. He is unable then to recognize baptism as God acting in the act of the community. Because of that act of the beginning of the Christian life, there follows great rejoicing. (Both pro and anti-infant baptism circles, however, can agree that baptism is the rite of initiation.)[106] The Ethiopian eunuch, after being baptized, "went on his way rejoicing" (Acts 8:39). After the Philippian jailer and his family were baptized, "he and his entire household rejoiced that he had become a believer in God" (Acts 16:34).[107]

Likewise, the joy in the Eucharist is not primarily the community feeding upon Christ, James Torrance argues, but Christ present feeding us in the Spirit through his continual offering to the Father.[108] The continuing priestly ministry of Christ is at the center of the church's life and mission.

The joy of the community of Israel, the joy that the Old Testament so often exhorts Israel to enter into is fulfilled in Jesus Christ, "the one Israelite."[109] Israel is both distinct and in continuity with the church. What Israel has failed to be is fulfilled in Jesus Christ. And Jesus Christ is not without his body, the church, which is a "little witness" to Jesus Christ himself who is "the great witness," the great witness of joy before God in a world that seems so god-forsaken, filled with terror, tragedy, and innocent suffering.[110] Following Christ means "to serve the omnipotent self-witness of Jesus Christ."[111] Christ continues to the great witness, however, because the church often lapses into thinking that we are replacing or continuing Christ's witness. But we have no joy in ourselves.

The church can only be a witness because we are in union with Christ. There is not an identity between Christ and the church but this should in no way de-emphasize the closeness of the church's union with

---

106. R. T. Beckwith, "Infant Baptism: Its Background and Theology," in *NIDNTT*, vol. 1, 154–60.

107. Barth, *CD* IV/4, 82. The NIV reads: "he was filled with joy because he had come to believe in God—he and his whole family." Either way, the fact remains that rejoicing follows baptism.

108. James B. Torrance, *Worship, Community and the Triune God of Grace*, 93.

109. Barth, *CD* IV/2, 823.

110. Ibid., 824.

111. Barth, *CD* IV/3.2, 658.

Christ, so that "the Christian really is where Christ is and Christ where the Christian . . ."[112] The character of the witness is that the witness is not concerned with one's own person. So is the Christian's witness of joy in the midst of despair. We do not point to our own capacities or potentialities for joy, but to Christ's.

The joy of the community is found eschatologically in the reality of the resurrection of Jesus, with whom his body, his community, is resurrected. We are not simply a collection of individual souls that will be resurrected but a community, since, in Anderson's words, "personal communion is a structure of knowing relationships which constitutes the significance of personal human being. This means resurrection of the person (body and soul) as a person-in-relation."[113] The significance of the church as those who are praying together is that of "a single life" in community with God, Bonhoeffer remarks.[114] So much of our earthly despair is in the loss of loved ones. The joy of Jesus is the joy of the one raised from the dead, and that we will be raised with him (Rom 6:5). Resurrection joy is, first of all, Jesus's joy.

THE HUMAN CHARACTER OF JOY

What is remarkable is how *human* the joy of God in Christ is. Whatever 2 Peter 1:4 means by our "participation in the divine nature," it does not mean the obliteration of our humanity. For Jesus's humanity, that which is in solidarity with ours, is that which is risen from the grave. The resurrection of the body is resurrected humanity, but still genuine humanity. That is why it is so sad when materialistic reductionists view humanity as simply a biochemical accident, not recognizing, as Barth wryly remarks that humanity is the only being that is accustomed to laugh and smoke![115] I do not know about the smoking (although both Barth and C. S. Lewis make a strong case for theology with the pipe!) but laughter and humor again turn up as essential to our humanity, and a "red flag" against any theological anthropology that cannot make us smile at times or that which takes itself or the world too seriously.

112. Ibid., 651–52.
113. Anderson, *On Being Human*, 177.
114. Bonhoeffer, *Sanctorum Communio*, 185.
115. Barth, *CD* III/2, 83.

The Bible speaks seriously about the whole person before God, body and soul, because the whole Jesus lived before God, including his life of very human joy. The connections are always inseparable between body and soul. "The whole man is the real man."[116] What the body does affects the soul; What happens to the soul affects the body, because there is one Jesus Christ, one person, as the great christological controversies in the ancient church hammered out, not a dual personality. This wholeness allows for the human joy of Jesus to be taken seriously. Yet the wholeness of the human being in the Bible is like the two natures of Christ; not only are they "not to be separated," but they also are "not to be confused" (Council of Chalcedon): "That he lives and moves, experiences good and ill, is healthy and sick, and in the end dies, is not at all an affair of his as mere body."[117] This raises questions for any theological anthropology that presents itself as "physicalism," even if it calls itself "non-reductive" (Nancey Murphy).[118] Barth's words are instructive: "Rather in all these things there acts and suffers the human subject, and therefore the soul of man, with his experience, his thinking and willing, *his rejoicing* and setbacks, his wants, desires and possessions, and in his temporal limitation."[119] Rejoicing cannot be done by a mere body, Barth seems to be saying. If the soul is the same as the body, then can God bring any joy to humanity? But Scripture testifies that Jesus genuinely possessed joy. True, the saying of Luke 10:21 that Jesus "rejoiced in the Holy Spirit" is, in Barth's words, "strangely isolated."[120] There is little in Scripture that describes the inner life of Jesus, including "meditating, deciding, rejoicing or laughing."[121] Yet Scripture emphasizes that Christ in all ways possessed a genuine human nature (Luke 2:52; Heb 5:8). His rejoicing was real, done on our behalf and in our place as one aspect of the whole man Jesus, soul and body: "The soul is real and important only as *His* shocked and grieved and angered but also loving and *rejoicing* soul; the body, on the other hand, is real and

---

116. Ibid., 431–32.

117. Barth, *CD* III/2, 434.

118. See Nancey Murphy, "Human Nature: Historical, Scientific, and Religious Issues," *Whatever Happened to the Soul? Scientific and Theological Portraits of Human Nature*, ed. Warren S. Brown, Nancey Murphy, and H. Newton Malony (Minneapolis: Fortress, 1998) 1–29.

119. Barth, *CD* III/2, 434 (emphasis mine).

120. Ibid., 329.

121. Ibid.

important only as *His* humiliated but also exalted body."[122] Notice that this includes the "rejoicing" soul. Bodies do not rejoice by themselves (ask any zombie!).[123]

Such a whole existence that includes both body and soul, not to be separated but not to be confused, has profound moral implications. Moral directions may be gleaned in upholding human beings in their ability to express genuine joy. This is not to be based on how tall, thin, athletic, attractive one is (none of which were attributed to Jesus!) and certainly not in the sense that we can or should shape our humanity, but in accepting the joy in embodied existence that is given by God as a good in itself, because it was good in Jesus. This is in contrast to our modern temptation, in Elshtain's words, that "life should be wiped clear of any and all imperfection, inconvenience, and risk."[124] "The man of sorrows" was not the "successful man" (Bonhoeffer) but lived a life of joy that nonetheless was marked by "imperfection, inconvenience, and risk."[125] The culture of cloning, for example, can easily be created by our "narcissistic imaginings of radical sameness," rather than to be conformed to Christ.[126] A challenge exists, however, that we do not interpret our Christology as forcing a "radical sameness" on our visions of anthropology. The Christ who redeems us is the Christ who created us in all our wonderful variety and diversity.

The joy of genuine humanity is revealed in the joy of the risen Christ. Through him we are exalted because when Christ is exalted he does not cease to be human (at the name of Jesus every knee will bow) (Phil 2:5–11).[127] To be exalted in him means to have a share in that which is also quite unlike us, his obedience.[128] Christ reveals that to be in the

---

122. Ibid, 330.

123. The resurgence of popular culture's interest in the fiction of "the walking dead" was recently discussed by National Public Radio, "Zombies: Still Undead, and Suddenly Everywhere." Online: http://www.npr.org/templates/story/story.php?storyId=105510752, July 1, 2009. While zombies are often seen as being popularized by the film *Night of the Living Dead*, directed by George Romero in 1968, they first rose from their graves in the film *White Zombie*, starring Bela Lugosi, in 1932, in famous horror producer Val Lewton's *I Walked with a Zombie* in 1943, and even in 1952's *Zombies of the Stratosphere*, starring a young Leonard Nimoy! Maybe zombies are a metaphor for a despair that never ends and keeps coming back!

124. Elshtain, *Who Are We?* 92, 98–100.

125. Bonhoeffer, *Ethics*, 88–90.

126. Elshtain, *Who Are We?* 103.

127. Barth, *CD* IV/1, 99.

128. Barth, *CD* IV/2, 270.

image of God is to be given the freedom to respond in obedience.[129] God answers for us in Christ, and in that answer is an exaltation of our humanity, certainly a joyful exaltation in the midst of a world of woe.[130] "The glory of our own being, life and activity is still His, and can be valued, and exalted and respected by us only as His."[131] But he is always the risen One who remains the crucified Christ (Moltmann) with holes in his sides even in his resurrected form (John 20:20, 27).[132] The summons to rejoice comes in the midst of the "dark places" of human existence.[133] Joy comes in the midst of despair, even for Jesus. Yet because he is raised from the dead, joy in the midst of despair first belongs to him, and then to us. It is his joy, but it is still human. "Joy is now joy before the Lord and in Him. It is joy in His salvation, His grace, His law, His whole action. But it is now also genuine, earthly, human joy."[134] This includes "the joy of harvest, wedding, festival and victory; the joy not only of the inner but also of the outer man; the joy in which we may and must drink wine as well as eat bread, sing and play as well as speak, dance as well as pray."[135] The time that we have been given as human beings is "allotted time," so that it should be welcomed "with gratitude and joy."[136] This "time between" in which we live is not to be shrugged off as meaningless in light of eternity. The "giftedness" of this present time, "of that which has been received... not in virtue of their human faithfulness and effort," should be the occasion for joy.[137] Bonhoeffer speaks against those Christians who "want to be more spiritual than God himself. They like to talk of battle, renunciation, suffering, and the cross, and it is almost painful for them that the Holy Scripture speaks not only of that, but time and again of the good fortune of the devout, the well-being of the just."[138] The problem is that these Christians are "too constricted" and "too narrow" in being unable to thank God for his earthly gifts, "and so they lose the full joy of their

---

129. Smail, *Like Father, Like Son*, 175.
130. Barth, *CD* IV/1, 15.
131. Ibid.
132. Moltmann, *Theology of Hope*, 171.
133. Barth, *CD* III/4, 375.
134. Ibid., 375–76.
135. Ibid., 376.
136. Barth, *CD* III/2, 555.
137. Barth, *CD* IV/1, 328.
138. Bonhoeffer, *Meditating on the Word*, 110.

Christian calling and deny God the thanks they should give for his great friendliness towards us (Ps 37:36, 24; 34:10, 12; 37:4; Luke 22:35)."[139] In the original Tarzan novels by Edgar Rice Burroughs, the Ape Man finds that what differs him from the apes is joy: "While other [apes] sought food and love, Tarzan sought food and joy."[140]

Faith itself should not be ignored as a very human act that brings comfort, and therefore as an act that demands joy.[141] The pardon of justification is not simply retrospective but prospective (John McLeod Campbell) a pardon that brings forth a life of joy.[142] This is a life of certainty, humility, and penitence.[143] The basis for this certainty is that God is the sovereign who is "on both sides," the one who in Jesus Christ is "living hearing" as well as "living speech."[144]

> The joyfulness of its witnesses rests on the confidence and reliance and hope that they have in this power. And whenever their witness is given to others in such a way that it is received with joyfulness, this other and greater power has been at work. And the joyfulness of the recipients rests also on the confidence and reliance and hope that this sovereign power has awakened in them too.[145]

The joy of Jesus, his "living hearing," is a human hearing that he shares with us and therefore becomes the basis for what is so difficult in our skeptical, cynical, postmodern age: confidence. Without confidence in the truth of the gospel, can we really be said to have joy as Christians? A theology without God being "on both sides" is very tenuous, and lacking a robust Christology, is hardly Christian and in the end unable to stand in our age.

Human joy can now be based on Jesus's joy. Christ taking our place does not mean that we are no longer in the picture. Rather a genuine understanding of substitutionary atonement includes our union with Christ. Even Barth, with his concern for the transcendence and grace of God will

---

139. Ibid.

140. Edgar Rice Burroughs, *Jungle Tales of Tarzan* (New York: Ballantine, 1963) 124; cf. 176.

141. Barth, *CD* III/3, 403.

142. Campbell, *Nature of the Atonement*, 114–50.

143. Barth, *CD* IV/1, 576–77.

144. Barth, *CD* IV/2, 306.

145. Ibid.

admit that "It is a poor theology that persists in the inequality between me and Jesus Christ—a pious cushion which is content to maintain the distinction from Him."[146] We say "too little" if "I myself am so far removed from Him" that I can easily still accuse myself as if nothing had happened. "I am thrown back on myself."[147] There is a "joyful confidence" that comes from relying "on that which has taken place for me."[148] Being in Christ means that he intercedes for us.[149] Jesus gives us the Lord's Prayer so that we may participate in his prayer to the Father, and therefore his truly human joy, especially in times of despair.[150] This is the gift of which the Orthodox theologian Schmemann reminds us we cannot prepare. To say yes is to say joy in gratitude. Therefore, to "feast" is essential in Orthodox piety: "Feast means joy," a joy that dares to exist in the midst of a world of suffering.[151] This is because the joy of Jesus, participating in the feast, is not a break in ordinary life, just as the Sabbath is not, but a "justification of that work, its fruit, its—so to speak—*sacramental transformation into joy* and, therefore, into freedom."[152] The joy of Jesus that is truly human is particularly seen in the Eucharist. Thus "natural" rejoicing, Schmemann claims, is even made "impossible" by the cross of Christ.[153] He uses this as a justification for the liturgical year, but even apart from that he is emphasizing the uniqueness of the human joy that goes beyond any analogy with our experience.

HUMAN JOY AS PERSONAL JOY

The transforming power of joy as gratitude is very different, however, from joy as giddiness or simply emotional exuberance. My first experience of Disneyland was disappointing because I sensed the exuberance there was too forced, too plastic, lacking integrity. It was not *my* joy, but a joy forced upon me. In ironic contrast, the same Walt Disney offered tremendous joy in my childhood through the adventure television

146. Barth, *CD* IV/1, 771.
147. Ibid., 773.
148. Ibid., 774.
149. Barth, *CD* IV/2, 305.
150. Schmemann, *For the Life of the World*, 45.
151. Ibid., 53.
152. Ibid., 54 (emphasis mine).
153. Ibid., 54–55.

shows "Zorro," starring Guy Williams and "The Swamp Fox" with Leslie Nielsen. These became my joy because I chose them to be my heroes. I know this is true because even many of my own age do not remember the Revolutionary War hero, Francis Marion, "The Swamp Fox"! But I remember well trying to find some furry fake animal tail to put in a cocked hat like "The Swamp Fox" and singing, "Swamp Fox, Swamp Fox, Tail on his hat, nobody knows where the Swamp Fox is at!" You may laugh, but you know you have your own joys!

At the heart of such personal joys is the shared experience that Ray Anderson finds in Ecclesiastes' teaching:

> This is what I have seen to be good: it is fitting to eat and drink and find enjoyment in all the toil with which one toils under the sun the few days of the life God gives us; for this is our lot. Likewise all to whom God gives wealth and possessions and whom he enables to enjoy them, and to accept their lot and find enjoyment in their toil—this is the gift of God. For they will scarcely brood over the days of their lives, because God keeps them occupied with the joy of their hearts. (Eccl 5:18–20)

Personal joys are everyday, apparently monotonous experiences, yet they can be transformed with gratitude. Ray Anderson asks us to reflect on what is probably a common experience:

> Have you ever suddenly discovered amidst the monotony of your life that you are filled with a strange sense of joy and that this day—today—this moment is worth everything? You are so happy to be alive and to know yourself, to look around and to be filled with the ecstasy of who you are, that your work is transformed from being mere drudgery into the kind of toil that brings joy to your heart. There is the vigor of joy. There is the reward of something which is done meaningfully and done well.[154]

Gratitude looks at the monotonous with a smile rather than a shrug. But who can do this with any kind of consistency? Even the distinctive human trait of awareness of our own upcoming death is rarely transformed into something other than self-pity. Kierkegaard commends an awareness of "the eleventh hour," that youth find so difficult to grasp.[155] Anderson

---

154. Anderson, *Exploration into God*, 52.

155. Søren Kierkegaard, *Purity of Heart is to Will One Thing*, trans. Douglas V. Steere (New York: Harper Torchbooks, 1956) 41; *Søren Kierkegaard's Journals and Papers Volume 1, A-E*, 94–95, cited by Anderson, *Exploration into God*, 84.

believes that "the eleventh hour" can take joy beyond the exuberance of youth.[156] Perhaps. But I am too busy denying my eschatological existence! There is One, however, who does embrace it, whose mortality does not haunt him. He is the Vicarious One. His joy is unique but it has become human since the Word of God has taken upon the flesh of our very ordinary, monotonous existence.

JOY AND OBEDIENCE

The joy of Jesus is a joy that we do not normally expect, the joy of obedience. This joy does not depend on anything in the world. The grace of God as a gift is that which exposes our sin and provides a bridge from it. Karl Barth waxes eloquently concerning this in his Romans commentary: "Grace is the incomprehensible fact that God is well pleased with a man and that a man can rejoice in God. Grace exists, therefore, only where the Resurrection is reflected. Grace is the gift of Christ, who exposes the gulf which separates God and man and, exposing it, bridges it."[157] Here we see the importance of the vicarious joy of Christ. It is his joy that is not simply the greatest example of our joy, or a perfection, or even a fulfillment of our joy. Our joy may be pointer, a witness, a clue, and even a longing, but only the vicarious joy of Christ can intervene for us in a world of horrendous evils and needless suffering of the innocents. Schmemann puts it well: "It is totally and absolutely a gift, the '*charis*,' the grace. And being pure gift, this joy has transforming power, the only really transforming power in this world."[158] It is as gift that joy demands obedience, so it will be a different kind of joy and a different kind of obedience.

This personal and ordinary joy is nonetheless sharing in the joy of Jesus and therefore is characterized by something we do not usually associate with joy: obedience. "To obey is to rejoice in our honour before and from God. Where we rejoice in it, there we also obey."[159] Yet conversely, obedience is not just a duty but a willing act if it is done with joy. "How can there be this willingness to obey if there is no joy in the fact that God wants the service of man, and therefore no joy in the honour which

---

156. Anderson, *Exploration into God*, 87.
157. Barth, *Epistle to the Romans*, 31.
158. Schmemann, *For the Life of the World*, 55.
159. Barth, *CD* III/4, 650.

God thereby does him?"[160] Because Jesus has joy in going to the cross, we can be obedient as we share in his joy, "looking to Jesus the pioneer and perfecter of our faith" (Heb 12:2). The basis for all of this is that Jesus truly lives. "Jesus Christ lives," Karl Barth says, "is at once the simplest and the most difficult christological statement."[161] That he lives means that he is truly human, and therefore possesses a genuine human joy, a joy that is a human Yes. "He exists in the manner of a man, and therefore like all other created beings, in the freedom and power of such a being as divinely determined and limited, in the relative dependence of a single member in the natural and historical nexus of the created world."[162] He possesses joy as a genuine human being, but this does not negate divine transcendence (and that includes divine joy!) in the midst of his humanity.

> Hence the fact that Jesus lives means concretely that He exists in the manner of the God whose divine transcendence does not find it incongruous but supremely congruous to exist also in the limited manner of the human creature; and conversely He exists in the manner of the man to whom there is given by God that which He cannot take to Himself, namely, to exist also in the sovereign manner of God.[163]

If Jesus lives, this simply means that in sharing with him we do not just sigh but also rejoice. Why is it that "we always have the intrinsically clear knowledge that Jesus lives and that we may live with Him, so that for all our sighing we have a cheerfulness which can never be suppressed, but always keeps breaking in?"[164] Barth's answer is that what we have revealed to us is who God is in himself, the "immanent" Trinity, "concretely as the Father and the Son, and this in the fellowship, the unity, the peace, the love of the Holy Spirit, who is Himself the Spirit of the Father and the Son; as the One who is thrice one in Himself in these three modes of being."[165] Therefore, the very human joy of Jesus that he shares with us (the "economic" joy of Christ) is grounded in the joy that is in God himself as Father, Son, and Holy Spirit (the "immanent" joy of the eternal Son before the Father in the Spirit). Practically this means that our joy

---

160. Ibid.
161. Barth, *CD* IV/3.1, 39.
162. Ibid.
163. Ibid.
164. Barth, *CD* IV/2, 340.
165. Ibid., 341.

does not have to be simply foolishness or giddiness but a grounded joy, a participation through the Spirit in the joy of the Son before the Father. And this trinitarian reality is not simply a "community" of persons that are simply interchanged. For the Holy Spirit has a distinct role as the personal power and presence living within us, not simply to allow the old and new natures to live in peaceful co-existence but to upset that co-existence with the joy of the Spirit, that which is living in the rule of the kingdom of God (Rom 14:17). There is a difference between the one born of the flesh and the one born of the Spirit (John 3:6). The action of the Spirit is not anything one can expect, Jesus says, for it is like the coming of the wind. "The wind blows where it chooses, and you hear the sound of it, but you do not know where it comes from or where it goes. So it is with everyone who is born of the Spirit" (John 3:8). The Spirit does not live peaceably with the old nature. "As the agent of the peace and joy in which man may live, the Holy Spirit inflexibly destroys this balance in which there can never be either peace or joy."[166]

THE JOY AND LAUGHTER OF THE VULNERABLE

Jesus was not known for laughing or his wit, but he did have a hunger for joy, as Anderson puts it; who "for the sake of the joy that was set before him endured the cross, disregarding its shame . . ." (Heb 12:2).[167] Humor reveals in us a hunger for joy. The humorless person no longer hungers for joy but only a mundane existence of Kierkegaard's "everydayness." The humorless person no longer hopes. Jesus was a man of hope. For hope is that which keeps faith from becoming fanaticism and fatalism, as Anderson observes.[168] There is no hope in Islamic terrorism, or in any kind of militant fundamentalism. Their despair, rightfully or wrongfully, has destroyed their hope so they can even turn to suicide bombings in order to express their "faith." Jesus had hope in the Father, so he endured the cross, disregarding the shame. "Bob Hope" was a fine name for a comedian. Laughter is an action of hope and therefore when we laugh we are not far from the kingdom of joy.

The humor of joy is different from the humor of superiority, scorn, and snark. Joy is not just guffawing at "camp" movies from a bygone era

---

166. Ibid., 369.
167. Anderson, *Spiritual Caregiving*, 149.
168. Ibid., 150.

as if through our snickers we are proclaiming our superior culture and intelligence. Sitting at a showing of the classic fifties film version of *The War of the Worlds* I was struck by the response of the audience: snickers, guffaws, giggling at some of the most dramatic parts of the movie.[169] Did the movie take itself too seriously? No, it was meant for entertainment. But I felt both sorry for and angry at the audience that was unable to become children again and be dazzled by George Pal's Martian aliens and the otherworldly moody world created by cinematographer William Cameron Menzies. Was this audience really capable of joy anymore? That may be too hard, but I could not help but think that.

Does our culture of irony and cynicism disallow us from becoming like children in order to enter the kingdom, as Jesus (and Ray Bradbury) argue, for the sake of our humanity? No, we are too busy playing like we are God with our ironically humorous attempts to give meaning to our lives. How dare we pretend that we do longer have the fears that children "gladly" admit, the kind of fears that have been met head on by fantasy literature for generations, from Grimm's Fairy Tales to Superman.[170] The child is amazed at mystery because one is all too aware of how vulnerable one is as a child. My experience as a child of eight in a Chicago hospital room, when my mother was not allowed to stay in the room overnight with me, was a small, yet important moment for me and my realization of my vulnerability. I remember well how as a very young child, reading my first "Superman" comics, and reading that Superman was "invulnerable." (This was a new word for me but I have since learned that this was true of other young "Superman" readers.) And so comic books, instead of retarding by reading as was charged by the great "scare" in the persecution of crime and horror comics in the 1950s, actually increased my vocabulary.[171] How remarkable it is that I took up this word, "invulnerable," perhaps subconsciously recognizing how "vulnerable" I was a child, and therefore even as adults that we are vulnerable as human creatures in a dangerous and frail world. As I age, and the body continues to have its inevitable problems, I am reminded of that again. I am becoming increasingly vulnerable again, like a child. Will I turn then, to find some way to

---

169. *The War of the Worlds*, directed by George Pal, Paramount Pictures, 1953.

170. See Gerard Jones, *Killing Monsters*.

171. See Frederic Wertham, *Seduction of the Innocent* (New York: Rinehart, 1954) and David Haidu, *The Ten-Cent Plague: The Great Comic-Book Scare and How It Changed America* (New York: Farrar, Strauss & Giroux, 2008).

pretend that I am immortal or invulnerable (Does this theology try to do that? I hope not!). What is the alternative?

The "poor in spirit," the vulnerable, are "blessed," Jesus says (Matt 5:3). In taking refuge in God they can sing for joy. "But let all who take refuge in you rejoice; let them ever sing for joy" (Ps 5:11). This is a vicarious act, for the sake of the community. The psalmist continues, "Spread your protection over them, so that those who love your name may exult in you" (Ps 5:11). As Weiser comments, "Since it is the power and the victory of God in which he is primarily interested, the goal for which he strives is at the same time the concern of the whole religious community, too; for its sake he vicariously suffered and for the attainment of it he vicariously prayed."[172] This does not mean, Bonhoeffer reminds us, that we can bear the burden of sorrow for others apart from the burden and joy of God. "How shall we be able to help those who have become joyless and fearful unless we ourselves are supported by courage and joy?"[173] These are those who realize their need, and therefore will not cynically attack others. How cruel it is to laugh at others. Yet humor is an essential part of the joy of humanity; the kind of humor, however, that laughs with, not at, someone else. My annual trek to the mecca of comic book collectors and fans, "Comic-Con International" in San Diego, always includes the presentation by a rotund middle aged cartoonist named Scott Shaw! (yes, with the exclamation point) called "Oddball Comics."[174] Whether it be "Manuel, the Sardine Fisherman" comics, or a crazy Jimmy Olsen comic with Superman's pal as a giant turtle man, this is a riotous response to these old comics and their outrageous themes that is not mocking but endearing and affectionate. I suspect that this is so because us middle-age codgers are laughing with these old comics that we actually bought, and still love. We can have in this a participation in a small part of God's creation and a celebration of simple joys.

There is a humor of the incarnation, a humor that begins with the solidarity of the Word who became flesh. There is a place then for the humor of those set free to be amazed: at God, the world, others, and oneself. The humor of mocking, however, is a joyless humor that is burdened

---

172. Weiser, *Psalms*, 128–29.

173. Bonhoeffer, "Advent Letter to the Pastors of the Confessing Church," in Robert Coles, *Dietrich Bonhoeffer*, 90.

174. See http//www.oddballcomics.com.

with always seeking to justify itself.[175] Understandably, this is all it can do, however. It is left with its own attempts at joy. It desperately needs the vicarious joy of Christ.

THE FRACTURED PLACE OF JOY

We are created for joy but what joy we know is real yet very fractured, tenuous, and transitory. Humanity was created, according to the Fathers, to be "priests" to creation.[176] But Christ the priest of creation intervenes in a vicarious way, not just to fulfill our joy (although he does that as our representative) but also to become the judge of our joy, and to take our place in a wonderful exchange at the point of joy. Just as our sin is no longer our own, our joy is no longer alone—not obliterated—but transformed, "from glory to glory," through Christ the vicarious image and priest of God (2 Cor 3:18).[177] The psalmist prays, "Let me hear joy and gladness; let bones that you have crushed rejoice" (Ps 51:8). Our bones have been crushed. That is what our chapters about despair have been about. We need help so that those bones would rejoice. Christ intercedes with his joy as the joyful vicarious priest of creation in the midst of our humanity.[178] Our fallen nature does not have the last say.[179] We live with him in "cheerfulness" despite the "sighing" of our fractured lives and fractured world.[180] Christ reveals that apart from him we cannot be priests. There is no "natural" capacity to be a priest to creation; our bones have been crushed. Christ does reveal that to be truly human is not necessarily to be in despair, but to be in joy. One can agree with David Bentley Hart that the difference between God and humanity is not based on a "determinate negation" or ontological tragedy but the God who gives the difference that is peace and joy.[181] He gives this difference in rejoicing in our behalf and in our place, in the vicarious joy of Christ.

---

175. See the critique of irony in contemporary culture in Jedediah Purdy, *For Common Things: Irony, Trust, and Commitment in America Today* (New York: Vintage, 1999).

176. Schmemann, *For the Life of the World*, 15.

177. Barth, *CD* IV/1, 234. On Christ the priest see Schmemann, *For the Life of the World*, 93.

178. Barth, *CD* III/2, 435.

179. Barth, *CD* IV/1, 483.

180. Barth, *CD* IV/2, 340.

181. David Bentley Hart, *Beauty of the Infinite*, 177.

Joy as the Yes of Humanity

The joy of Christ reveals the freedom of God over despair and even to use despair. This means that the joy of humanity is a different kind of joy; it is not surprised by the "fiery ordeal." Bonhoeffer is rightly suspicious of a joy that does not admit sorrow. Christian joy "does not deny the distress where it is, but finds God in the midst of it."[182] This is the only joy that has "overcome." "It alone is worth believing; it alone helps and heals."[183] The temptation is for the Christian pastor to try to bear the sorrows himself. "We are not called to burden ourselves with the sorrows of the whole world; in the end we cannot suffer with people in our own strength because we are unable to redeem."[184] Why not, however? Can we not say that Christ is "enabling" us, that he is a "co-worker" with us? This depends upon one's Christology, and for Bonhoeffer, that means everything:

> We are simply called to look with utter joy on the one who really suffered with people and became their redeemer. We may joyfully believe that there was, there is, a man to whom no human sorrow and no human sin is strange and who in the profoundest love achieved our redemption. Only in such joy toward Christ, the Redeemer, are we saved from having our senses dulled by the pressure of human sorrow or from becoming resigned under the experience of suffering.[185]

What we need is both the vicarious sorrow and the vicarious joy of Christ. Like God's righteousness and God's mercy, or other attributes of God, they should not be viewed apart from each another.[186]

We can accept joy as a command because it is a theology of the cross that realizes all too well that situations do not naturally call forth joy.[187] That is why a vicarious, not just analogous, joy is needed. An analogy can only communicate the uniqueness in terms of similarity. A vicarious joy is much deeper. The created world may be filled with joy at times despite the concealment of joy. The new joy of humanity in Christ is not afraid of the Word of God that comes often with silence as well. "For His

---

182. Bonhoeffer, "Advent Letter to the Pastors of the Confessing Church," in Robert Coles, *Dietrich Bonhoeffer*, 90.
183. Ibid.
184. Ibid., 91.
185. Ibid.
186. Barth, "The Mercy and Righteousness of God," *CD* II/1, 368–406.
187. Barth, *CD* III/1, 371.

Word also implies His silence, what He says implies what He does not say; His Yes implies His no; His grace His judgment."[188] And so we wait, perhaps eagerly (Rom 8:19, 23) but still we wait in patience and hope (Rom 8:24).

The command to rejoice is not a burden because it is wrapped up in the faith and obedience of the Son to the Father, a life of response that is not just duty-bound but motivated by both joy and obedience because only the Son knows the Father, that the Father is truly love, despite our frail and often chaotic world of airline crashes, financial, social, and political vulnerability and upheavals, and ultimately the decrepitude of aging that leads us to death. "To obey is to rejoice in our honour before and from God," Barth exhorts us.[189] To want to and to be willing to serve God is joined together in Christ's vicarious joy and obedience with our joy. In fact willingness to obey is not genuine willingness unless it is joy.[190] Like the relationship between God's mercy and righteousness, joy and obedience should not be separated. Barth is so bold to say, "God's righteousness does not really stand alongside his mercy, but that as revealed in its necessary connexion, according to Scripture, with the plight of the poor and the wretched, it is itself God's mercy."[191] The difficulty in keeping together joy and obedience as well is obvious. Our need for Christ's joy in obedience is that great.

To keep the command to rejoice involves human relationships as well, particularly between man and woman, that otherwise would only be a "blind surrender" and not self-giving.[192] Joy involves freedom in relationships, with God and with others, including the different sexes. How much does joy really exist between man and woman in our allegedly liberated, yet fractured, society? Is there really joy in the constant pressure to perform through the right physical appearance, income, or status? Does that obsession simply negate the possibility of freely joining together and therefore genuinely possessing joy in one another? Desire needs to be preceded by self-giving. Barth makes this clear: "As the desire of love, of true *eros,* desire is legitimate—and this is true on the side of the husband too—when it is preceded by self-giving and thus controlled,

---

188. Ibid., 371–72.
189. Barth, *CD* III/4, 650.
190. Ibid.
191. Barth, *CD* II/1, 387.
192. Barth, *CD* III/4, 219.

not by the need of the other, but by the joy of being his and of willing to belong to him ..."[193] Much easier said than done, certainly! Yet did Jesus just *need* the Father? There is certainly "need-love," (Is there a greater motivation for human beings than our need to be loved?) but this often overshadows "gift-love," the love that gives unconditionally.[194] Is not joy limited when it is just based on need? Yes, there is joy in being loved and having our needs/desires met, but do we not err when we see that this is a limited joy without "gift-love"? The command to rejoice is not needed with "need-love." It is, however, with "gift-love," the kind of joy that Jesus will have even going to the cross (Heb 12:2).

Perhaps in the vicarious joy of Jesus we see a bridge between "need-love" and "gift-love" in the joy of *belonging*. Belonging can be demonic, from the institution of slavery to an abusive marriage. The belonging found within the Trinity is different; what we see in the relationship between the Father and the Son. The Son belongs to the Father yet the Son willingly obeys the Father in the Spirit. Genuine belonging means that we embrace the total person, not just physical appearance.[195] Just as the vicarious humanity of Christ embraces the totality of our humanity, the Father embraces the totality of the Son and the Son embraces the totality of the Father, in the Spirit.

Joy is not something that we simply force ourselves to emote. Attempts to do so can be so superficial. The psalmist prays for God to "Create in me a clean heart" (Ps 51:10). Do concerns about protecting the sinlessness of Christ keep us from seeing this as a messianic psalm? But does not the baptism of Jesus, for example, remind us that the first movement of the incarnation was solidarity with sinners (Matt 3:13–17)? Issues of whether or not Jesus took upon fallen human nature come into play here.[196] What is at stake in this argument is the extent of the identification of Jesus with our *actual humanity* as we find ourselves in the

---

193. Ibid.

194. Smedes, *Mere Morality*, 45–46.

195. Barth, *CD* III/4, 219.

196. See Barth's argument that Christ possessed our "fallen" human nature in *CD* I/2, 151ff.; cf. Gerrit Scott Dawson, "Far as the Curse is Found: The Significance of Christ's Assuming a *Fallen* Human Nature in the Torrance Theology," *An Introduction to Torrance Theology*, ed. Gerrit Scott Dawson (London: T. & T. Clark, 2007) 55–74; Harry Johnson, *The Humanity of the Savior* (London: Epworth, 1962); Kettler, *The Vicarious Humanity of Christ and the Reality of Salvation*, 245 n.57 and the critique by Oliver D. Crisp, "Did Christ Have a Fallen Nature?" in *International Journal of Systematic Theology* 6:3 (2004) 270–88.

present. He does not sin but his baptism means that he stands identified with sinners. Therefore, Jesus confesses our sins for us. He also prays for joy in our place and on our behalf. Joy comes in confession of sin, as Barth argues:

> The man who asks for the forgiveness of his sins, and confesses his sins and enters into the light of the situation between God and man as it really is, can and should as such and at once (as this beginner) expect to be satisfied with joy and gladness, and he can and should therefore pray for it, for his new right before God.[197]

This is not just emoting or giddiness. We pray with Jesus for joy: "Do not cast me away from your presence and do not take your holy spirit from me. Restore to me the joy of your salvation, and sustain in me a willing spirit" (Ps 51:11–12).

The prayer for joy, however, is not without admitting the context of despair, especially despair over one's own sins. Paul may emphasize to the Romans that they "have died to the law though the body of Christ, so that you may belong to another, to him who has been raised from the dead in order to bear fruit for God" (Rom 7:4). But in that same famous chapter seven, Paul is wrestling with sin since he knows the law of God (pre or post-conversion?) concluding with a prayer of anguish and the answer in Jesus Christ (the whole of chapter 8): "Wretched man that I am! Who will rescue me from this body of death? Thanks be to God through Jesus Christ" (Rom 7:24–25). The Christian should not forget that the person of Christian joy (Romans 8) is also the person of anguish, sorrow, and despair (Romans 7). "He can only be both at once."[198] Conversely, Christian anguish, sorrow, and despair should never be an excuse for pride, pride in our sufferings, self-pity that defines who we are and forgets about joy. This is a strong admonishment by Barth:

> Has this man really given God the right against himself, has he really accepted His sentence, if he has to accept the fact—and he declares that he has to accept it—that he knows himself to be negated and rejected by God, but cannot make anything of the Yes of God, and does not see anything of the future which is opened up to him, of the right to live which is granted to him? If anyone tries to resist this, if he can and must resist it, then he

---

197. Barth, *CD* IV/1, 580.
198. Ibid., 590–91.

simply shows that it is not the No of God which he maintains that he accepts and to which he maintains that he submits. His vanity still peeps out through the very rents in his garment. The No of God is never without the Yes which follows it.[199]

The vicarious joy of Christ will not allow the No of God to be without the Yes. Is this not the meaning of Romans? "There is therefore now no condemnation for those who are in Christ Jesus. For the law of the Spirit of life in Christ Jesus has set you free from the law of sin and death" (Rom 8:1–2). "Who is to condemn? It is Christ Jesus, who died, yes who was raised, who is at the right hand of God, who indeed intercedes for us" (Rom 8:34).

The frailty of creatureliness speaks loudly of our total need. Our natural joy is real, and it too is a gift of God. But it is frail, temporal, and transient. There can be great despair in the "the frailty and end of all things."[200] Yet that makes sense when one is before the Creator. Jesus stands before the Father: in his baptism, at the transfiguration, at Gethsemane, at the cross, and confesses our lostness to God. We can only weep, even with tears of joy (the truth of the Orthodox tradition of compunction).[201] But with Jesus we do so in the firm knowledge of the goodness of the Father. Therefore, Christian joy is not meant to elude the despair in life, but also cannot accept "a painless mingling of joy and sorrow."[202] Simply experiencing an all too real present darkness does not mean that God has lost his freedom.[203] The eschatological hope is based on the freedom of God to act. Is this not the essence of the Book of Revelation? God is not by nature the God of darkness. We are not simply pawns of a grim, impersonal fate. Yet the darkness is here. We cannot avoid it. Paul is very instructive when he exhorts the Romans to "rejoice with those who rejoice, weep with those who weep" (Rom 12:15). God is on both sides of joy and sorrow. But his final word, the word of the victory of the resurrection is joy. This is expressed in God's eternal covenant of grace with humanity that is

---

199. Ibid., 593–94.

200. Barth, *CD* III/1, 373.

201. Kallistos Ware, "'An Obscure Matter': The Mystery of Tears in Orthodox Spirituality," in *Holy Tears: Weeping in the Religious Imagination*, ed. Kimberly Christine Patton and John Stratton Hawley (Princeton: Princeton University Press, 2005) 247–51.

202. Barth, *CD* III/1, 373.

203. Ibid., 374.

even found in the manifestation of creation.[204] The joy of humanity, then, has its goal, its *telos*, not in sorrow, but joy.

Joy can be weighed down by sorrow if it does not respect what Kierkegaard calls "the eleventh hour."[205] The older person has an advantage over the younger in that one recognizes that one lives in the eleventh hour, only one hour before midnight. Youth needs to hear of the eleventh hour because ignorance of it keeps youth from the joy in which the eternal comes into the moment. Ray Anderson comments, "The eleventh hour is that radical moment when the eternal presses in upon time and demands of its life, demands it in the moment . . ."[206] Otherwise, the occasion for sorrow and despair can obsess the young, such as in a broken love affair, leading perhaps even to taking one's own life. Youth needs to forfeit their youth for the sake of joy! "We would pray for the youth, that they would know the eleventh hour and would be serious as well as joyful."[207] Joy should not be seen as simply the prerogative of the young. "From the perspective of the eleventh hour, there is no such thing as youth and old age."[208] Still, the old need to embrace the eleventh hour and the joy that comes from it as well. Both young and old should live with

> an abandon of joy that would enable them to enter so fully into life that their temporal lives would be filled with eternal meaning. Lived in this way, the passing of time holds no threat to us and we do not have to elevate our exuberance in order to lift the moment, for it is already an "eternal moment," if lived in the eleventh hour.[209]

This is all a part of embracing our creatureliness with joy; that which Jesus did and does in his humanity for us and on our behalf. He knew his own eleventh hour more than any person who ever lived, and for our sake, he responded with joyful obedience before the Father.

Grace is that which reveals to us our frailness and creatureliness but also brings us to God in joy. "Grace is the incomprehensible fact that

---

204. Barth, *CD* III/1, 375.

205. Kierkegaard, *Søren Kierkegaard's Journals and Papers, Volume 1*, 94. Anderson discusses "the eleventh hour" in *Exploration into God*, 84.

206. Anderson, *Exploration into God*, 84.

207. Ibid., 92.

208. Ibid., 85.

209. Ibid., 87.

God is well pleased with a man, and that a man can rejoice in God."[210] This is not to be taken for granted. For we do not want to admit any gulf between God and us. What need does the postmodern person possess for a mediator? Skepticism about genuine knowledge of God and the phenomenon of religious pluralism makes this superfluous. Yet grace as gift reveals that God loves us, a love that is not all joy but joy and despair, telling us that God is well-pleased with us but also of his judgment against sin.[211] "Grace is the gift of Christ who exposes the gulf which separates God and man and, exposing it, bridges it."[212] Despair, yes, in exposing the gulf, but joy in bridging it. The one who keeps the command joyfully (and who does this purely except the faithful and obedient Son?) knows that God's purpose is good.[213]

"Vicarious" can be a hard word. We might not be very happy when someone "takes our place"! We want our joy to remain untouched and only gently sanctified by God. But do we have that option? As Schmemann rightly points out, Christ the priest destroys the dualism between the "natural" and the "supernatural."[214] Yet Christ also displaces our attempts to find a joy in a religion of priests apart from "the sole priesthood of Jesus Christ" (James Torrance).[215] We can too easily reintroduce a dualism in our attempts to separate the clergy from the laity in any way other than simply different gifts. There is not a separate joy of the pastor from the lay person. They are both very creaturely joys and both undergirded by the creaturely joy of Christ our priest. If there is this distinction, then have we not bypassed the true joy, the joy of Christ the vicarious priest? The relationship of joy and obedience goes beyond the utilitarian factor; that we are joyful because we think it will do us some good. Even the devil can be a utilitarian if he thinks obeying God will be good for him! As Ransom, the interplanetary traveler in C. S. Lewis's "space trilogy" says of God on Mars ("Maledil") "Where can you taste the joy of obeying unless He bids you do something for which His bidding is the only reason?"[216] The Green Lady sees that this is true freedom: "Oh, well I

---

210. Barth, *Epistle to the Romans*, 31.
211. See Barth on judgment and punishment, *CD* II/1, 386–96.
212. Barth, *Epistle to the Romans*, 31.
213. Barth, *CD* III/4, 232.
214. Schmemann, *For the Life of the World*, 129.
215. James Torrance, *Worship, Community, and the Triune God of Grace*, 43–67.
216. C. S. Lewis, *Perelandra*, 118.

see it! We cannot walk out of Maledil's will; but He has given us a way to walk out of *our* will."²¹⁷ We can walk now in the will of the Son, the will of obedient joy given for our sakes.

A JOY NOT OF OUR OWN

In Christ there is revealed the joy of humanity, a Yes to God that we cannot say on our own. a joy we do not possess in ourselves. This is a Yes, but not a Yes that alternates with a No. That would speak of our essence, since we are still liable to sin, as a divided nature, divided into "spiritual" and "sinful" natures, as is common in evangelical piety. The humanity of Christ does not allow us to be settled with that division, as much as empirical evidence seems to argue for it. We are not "to understand ourselves alternately or simultaneously in abstract subjectivity and concrete objectivity, apart from Christ and in Him, without Him and with Him, looking at ourselves and looking at Him."²¹⁸ This is the joy that comes to us in the midst of the monotony, a joy that does not easily vacillate with despair but purely gives thanks to God for the moment. This is the truth of Anderson's wistful rhetorical question, "Have you ever suddenly discovered amidst the monotony of your life that you are filled with a strange sense of joy and that this day—today—this moment is worth everything?"²¹⁹ As wonderful as this experience is, it can be very transitory. The vicarious joy of Christ intervenes with a joy that displaces and embraces our joy with the joy of the eternal Son before the Father. This is a joy which has "a greater joyfulness in God than in his own," when joy lives in the realm of the good and the right, a part of the faithful obedience of the Son.²²⁰ This is "the joyfulness always to give precedence to God in the determination of the form of his own honour and always to accept and maintain it as the right one."²²¹

Before God, this joy is always something new, "not following the familiar lines of self-understanding," but Jesus's understanding of joy that takes the place of our understanding of joy.²²² The Christian is a "new

---

217. Ibid.
218. Barth, *CD* IV/2, 272.
219. Anderson, *Exploration into God*, 52.
220. Barth, *CD* III/4, 672.
221. Ibid.
222. Ibid.

creation" because of that. Despite all the problems that Paul had with the Corinthian church, he could still call them "a new creation" (2 Cor 5:17)! For in Christ, as Paul said to Corinth, "every one of God's promises is a 'Yes'" (2 Cor 1:20). Thus, in the midst of our despair and sin, a Yes can penetrate, the Yes of Jesus Christ, as the Yes of joy. This Yes is nothing less than the joy of "Christ is risen."[223] Therefore, to be truly human then is not to doubt but to rejoice.[224]

The penitential psalms are not to be understood, Barth argues, as a "preparation" for grace but the prayer and reaching that comes ("Create in me a clean heart, O God . . ." in Ps 51:10) because the gift has *already* been given.[225] The *ordo salutis* (the way of salvation) must not be seen as steps to salvation, e.g., in "And those whom he justified he also glorified" (Rom 8:30). Just as justification is based on Christ the Justified One, so also glorification should be based on Christ the Glorified One. So Christ is the completion of the psalmist's plea, "Let me hear joy and gladness; let the bones that you have crushed rejoice" (Ps 51:8). Barth makes it clear that there is no "prevenient grace":

> Note that instead of any intervening and preparatory operations to make it possible we have at once the new creation of a clean heart, i.e., of the man who has already turned to God from himself and his sin; at once the gift of a new and right or constant spirit, the spirit with which man can only look forward and not backward, the willing spirit, by which the joy of God's salvation is created and continually renewed . . .[226]

Joy is not to be restricted to the consummation of all things. Yet how can we, in our present struggles, embrace that reality? Someone needs to embrace it first for us, even one who has the confidence to confess our sin when we are unable to even understand or accept what they are.[227] Only the eternal Son who has become incarnate, being baptized for us, confessing our sins on our behalf can do this (Matt 3:13–17). In the waters of the Jordan we were baptized with him and thus began his ministry of reconciliation through his life, death, and resurrection, in which our

---

223. Barth, *CD* IV/2, 355.
224. Barth, *CD* III/1, 350.
225. Barth, *CD* IV/1, 580.
226. Ibid.
227. Ibid.

justification and our glorification come together in his justification and his resurrection (Rom 4:25).

Yet is this an "overly realized" eschatology of joy, a joy that really has no place for the consummation of all things, as the critics of Barth often accuse him? True, this can be a temptation. But an "overly futurized" eschatology can also restrict joy only to the future. Can we say this if Christian joy is based on the joy of the One who has already been raised from the dead? Apocalyptic eschatology should be careful not to divorce itself from actual history.[228]

Still, a theology of the joy and despair of Jesus will look forward with him to the consummation of all things. Joy is, as C. S. Lewis puts it, "the serious business of heaven."[229] What is the joy of heaven? It is a joy that Jesus already possesses, sitting at the hand of the Father, but a joy that will someday be ours. Our culture is hardly obsessed with images of heaven. Perhaps that is why our joys are so transitory. Both heaven and earth are creations of God. The earth, however, is the creation conceivable to us; "heaven is the creation inconceivable to man," Barth argues.[230] We have returned to the old hymn then, "Joy Unspeakable and full of glory . . ." Paul speaks of Jesus as "the man of heaven" (1 Cor 15:48). In fact this is the Jesus who is the goal of the believer: "Just as we have borne the image of the man of dust, we will also bear the image of the man of heaven" (1 Cor 15:49). To bear the image of the man of heaven is our goal; our goal is to share in his heavenly joy. There is a truth in the fairy tale, J. R. R. Tolkien writes, of the joy of the happy ending, the *eucatastrophe*, the "turn" in the fairy story.[231] If one rejects this, one is heading for "sadness or wrath." Within *eucatastrophe*, despair is not denied, for there would be no need for a happy ending without the *dyscatastrophe*, of sorrow and failure.[232]

But in the meantime we live in a world of war and disease, so hope that we have must be wistful and realistic. In Bob Dylan's song of the Civil War, "'Cross the Green Mountain," the paradox of courage and valor in the midst of the insanity of warfare ascends into an eschatological dream. We weep with Jesus in the midst of the goodness of life yet its transitory

---

228. T. F. Torrance, *Incarnation*, 303.

229. C. S. Lewis *Letters to Malcolm*, 93.

230. Barth, *Dogmatics in Outline*, 59.

231. J. R. R. Tolkien, "On Fairy Stories," in *Essays Presented to Charles Williams*, ed. C.S. Lewis (Grand Rapids: Eerdmans, 1966) 83.

232. Ibid., 81.

and fragile state. Yet, his joy includes the joy of "a far better land."[233] This is "the joy set before him . . ." (Heb 12:2).

The result of joy is that one can love in imitation of God, the God who loves but whose love is sometimes not returned.[234] Again, our humanity regains its "secret," that there is the freedom that brings joy in mutuality and loving freely, not as a duty. This is the continual love of the humanity of Jesus, a love that is not just duty-bound, but looks towards joy. Was joy then a reward for Jesus, so that we too should love in order to possess joy? No, then love would cease to be free. Joy is a reward as a by-product, a fruit of free love, not its motivation. Perhaps I hesitate to say this because I do not believe that God actually loves *me*. The vicarious joy of Christ, however, involves his taking upon the humanity of all, because God loves "the world" (John 3:16). Therefore, love can bring joy even when love is not reciprocated, as with God and Israel . . . and God and us, at times. "He does not love him for the sake of the answer, but because he is made free to do so by God. The peace and joy of the one who is liberated and therefore loves in this way can never suffer disillusionment."[235] Freedom comes from a love that is already fulfilled. Otherwise, disillusionment is always a possibility, as it is found the various forms of theology that view the love of God as conditional upon certain performances. You do whatever you can to appease God in order to avoid that disillusionment. But the Christian gospel promises love without disillusionment, so different from romantic love of every age. This can be because Jesus has already provided the joyful reciprocation, his perfect love for the Father, in which we then can participate. This is entering into the joy of the Master (Matt 25:23).

The joy of our humanity exists because of the joy of God in Jesus Christ. God's joy has become our joy, but not through bypassing suffering. The cross will not allow that. The true majesty of God is found in the cross. The joy of Jesus is the joy of the one who was crucified, so there is never any question of a "giddy" joy of religiosity devoid of the cruel realities of this life. Jesus will not permit that, and particularly if Christian joy proceeds from his vicarious joy. "There is a joy which knows nothing of sorrow, need and anxiety of the heart," Bonhoeffer observes, but "it has

---

233. Bob Dylan, "'Cross the Green Mountain." Online: http//www.lyricstime.com/bob-dylan-cross-the-green-mountain-lyrics.html.

234. Barth, *CD* IV/2, 788–89.

235. Ibid., 789.

no duration, and it can only drug one for the moment."²³⁶ The God of the cross possesses joy, because it "has been through the poverty of the crib and the distress of the cross . . . It does not deny the distress where it is, but finds God in the midst of it."²³⁷ At death, "the old grief," Zosima says in *The Brothers Karamazov*, "by a great mystery of human life, gradually passes into quiet, tender joy . . ."²³⁸ This is the joy that has "overcome," that "finds life in death itself . . . It alone is worth believing; it alone helps and heals . . . The risen one bears the marks of the cross upon his body."²³⁹ The tears of the spiritual person, says John the Solitary, comes not from sorrow for sin but by considering God's majesty.²⁴⁰ That majesty is found in the cross. Rejoicing in afflictions can be so much whistling in the dark unless it is grounded in the joy of the suffering Jesus and our participation in his continual suffering.²⁴¹ Only then can we with any kind of integrity glory in our afflictions. For the last word is joy.

---

236. Bonhoeffer, "Advent Letter to the Pastors of the Confessing Church," in Robert Coles, *Dietrich Bonhoeffer*, 90.

237. Ibid.

238. Dostoevsky, *Brothers Karamazov*, 292.

239. Bonhoeffer, "Advent Letter to the Pastors of the Confessing Church," in Robert Coles, *Dietrich Bonhoeffer*, 90.

240. John the Solitary, cited by Špidlik, *Spirituality of the Christian East*, 195.

241. Barth, *CD* IV/3.2, 642.

Subject Index

Acedia ("the noonday demon"), 14, 214. *See also* Sin, Sloth
Acts, Book of, 55, 125, 163, 172
Aesthetics, 42, 61, 63, 77, 91n54, 110, 116, 127, 128, 128n86, 216n24, 244, 245, 250, 268–70. *See also* Creativity
Agape, 67, 67n26, 244. *See also* Love.
Analogy of being *(analogia entis),* 66, 231
Anxiety, 22, 75, 123, 165, 209, 213, 214, 162
Atonement, xi, xiii, xxin56, 12, 16n59, 32, 39n80, 52n37, xiiin17, 83n3, 88n, 111, 138, 142, 210, 212, 227n89, 248, 268n93, 276n142. *See also* Jesus Christ, Representative Atonement, Substitutionary Atonement, Salvation

Baptism, 21, 99, 140, 270, 271, 271n106, 107
Beauty, xiin9, xxin56, 26, 41, 42, 54, 56n52, 65, 65n17, 66, 67n27, 72, 73, 87, 110n26, 140, 156, 162, 164, 165, 166, 184n11, 196, 199n82, 202n81, 82, 206n95, 216n21, 217n26, 219n38, 224, 235n33, 242n73, 244, 252, 268, 269, 284n181. *See also* Jesus Christ, Beauty of.
Belief, believer, believing. *See* Faith.
Bible, the, xvi, xxi, 33, 45, 47, 54, 77, 108, 112, 116, 121, 127–33, 173, 181, 216, 220, 223, 230, 273, 286
Blessed, blessing, blessedness, 154, 155, 224. *See also* Joy

Bliss, 138. *See also* Joy

Calvinism, xix, 216, 243, 243n81
Christian life, the, xvi, 37, 44n2, 58, 65, 66, 76, 79n92, 86, 142–50, 186n25, 193, 199, 202n79, 254, 269, 271, 272, 275
Christianity, 17, 20, 70, 106, 106n9, 122, 184n17, 203n85, 211, 212, 213, 276
Christology, xi, xvii, xxiv, 8, 20, 29, 39, 54, 61, 69n35, 88, 90, 142n31, 152, 157, 208, 213, 218, 241n71, 247, 255, 265, 273, 276, 280, 285. *See also* Jesus Christ
Church, the, xvii, xx, xxi, xxiii, 10, 12, 18, 21, 22, 23, 28, 30, 35, 47, 55, 56, 58–60, 74, 75, 77, 99, 107, 124, 124n77, 137, 141n25, 143, 145, 153, 163, 167, 192, 194, 202n81, 203, 203n85, 210, 218, 221, 237n51, 243n81, 246, 247, 250, 251, 260, 266, 270, 271. *See also* Community, Christian, Vicarious Reality
Comic books, xxiii, 3, 4, 31, 73, 105, 106, 209, 208n1, 222, 223n57, 282, 283
Community, Christian, xiiin18, xviiin43, xi, 15, 18, 21, 27, 28n36, 28n43, 37n75, 58–61, 59n74, 86, 86n21, 95n78, 122n68, 126, 123n73, 132n92, 140n23, 147, 150, 153n67, 176n112, 185n20, 218, 219, 236, 246, 253n14, 256n40, 270–72, 291n215. *See also* Church, the

Subject Index

Confidence, 123, 146, 198, 204, 249, 252, 253, 263, 264, 276, 277, 293
Compunction *(penthos)*, 49, 86, 87, 88, 100, 215, 245, 246, 289
Confession, xi, 210, 214, 251, 262, 263
Covenant, 168, 186, 187, 242, 246, 247, 248, 261, 289
Creation, xi, xii, xiii, 4, 13, 21n4, 23, 25, 35, 39n81, 44, 45, 74, 95, 101, 108, 119, 127, 128n86, 141, 158, 159, 184, 188, 189, 205, 207, 215, 216, 219, 224, 230, 236–38, 240, 242, 244, 245, 246, 247, 248, 251, 268n93, 269, 283, 284, 285, 290, 294. *See also* Nature
Creation out of nothing (*ex nihilo*), 89, 241
Creativity, 116, 202, 203. *See also* Aesthetics
Culture, xxiii, 7, 69n35, 69n36, 127, 142n31, 203, 215, 216, 216n20, 223, 250, 250, 282, 294

Dance, 48, 98, 127–33, 139, 168, 177, 197, 259, 268
Darkness, xxii, 4, 8n22, 12, 21, 44, 45, 55, 71, 91, 98, 112, 114, 139, 172, 181, 207. *See also* Sin
Dejection, 146, 153, 210. *See also* Despair
Delight, x, 48, 98, 113, 118, 119, 120, 138, 165, 171, 174, 177, 187, 192, 194, 202, 205, 235, 240, 252, 253, 257, 260, 268. *See also* Joy
Deliverance. *See* Salvation
Depression, ix, x, xxi, 8–13, 20, 21, 24, 83, 84, 85n14. *See also* Despair
Descent into Hell. *See* Jesus Christ, Burial (Holy Saturday)
Desire, xi, 6, 11, 15, 23, 33, 39, 42, 46, 51, 52, 54, 65, 66, 67, 73, 77, 78, 92, 106, 109, 110, 111, 112–15, 121, 125, 134, 143, 146, 148, 170, 174, 175, 182, 187, 190, 196, 205, 206, 207, 216, 220, 223, 232, 244, 249, 256, 257, 261, 262, 264, 266, 268, 273, 286, 287. *See also* Eros, Joy
Despair, ix, x, xiii, xviii, xxi, xxii, xxiv, xxv, 3, 4, 5, 6, 7, 8, 9, 13, 14, 15, 16, 18, 19, 19 n. 73, 20, 21, 22, 23, 24, 25, 26, 27, 28, 29, 30, 31, 32, 33, 34, 36, 38, 40, 44, 45, 46, 47, 51, 56, 58, 62, 66, 69, 70n40, 72, 73, 74, 76.n77, 77, 78, 81, 83, 84, 85, 85n10, 11, 13, 15, 86, 87, 90, 91, 92, 96, 97, 98, 100, 101, 105, 112, 124, 134–81, 183, 198, 202, 207, 210, 215, 218, 219, 220, 225, 228, 245, 249, 250, 253, 254, 255, 261, 262, 269, 270, 272, 275, 277, 284, 285, 288, 289, 291, 292, 293, 294. *See also* Gloom, Dejection, Lament, Depression, Mourning, Sadness, Pain, Sighing, Melancholy, Misery, Sorrow, Grief, Jesus Christ, Despair of, Jesus Christ, Vicarious Despair of, Weeping
And joy: a mixture? 136–39, 292–96
And joy: can we live with both? 134–81
Attachment of, 4–8
Boredom, 63–64, 109, 201, 205, 213, 268. *See also* Monotony
Comforted, 50
Command to rejoice in the midst of, 179–81
Conscious, 20, 22, 74, 167
Death, 68–71
Educative, 51–52,
Eschatology, 167–77
Everydayness and the denial of wonder, 71–74, 281
From God, 44–61
In weakness, 36
Inevitability of, 134–36
Knowledge as resolution? 85–86
Meaninglessness, xxi, 6, 62–82, 217
Not to will to be oneself, 20
Of the eternal or over oneself, 23, 41
Over one's weakness, 36, 39, 40
Over something, 20–43

Over the earthly or our something earthly: lack or loss, 23, 39, 64, 65, 67, 87, 192, 214, 215
Over the eternal, 36–43
Resolution of, xxi, 83–101
Soul-sorrow, 122
Sources of, 3–19
Struggle, 214–15
To will to be oneself: defiance, 20, 43
Tragedy, xxi, 22, 40, 42, 64–71, 72, 73, 80, 122, 156, 167, 215–18, 219n38, 271
Unconscious, x, xxi, 20, 72, 74–82, 122, 167, 213
Vicarious, xxi. *See also* Jesus Christ, Vicarious Despair of
Weeping as resolution? 86–88
Devil, the (the Adversary, the Tempter, Satan), xi, 11n32, 21, 45, 159, 165, 173, 176, 214
Discipleship, 17, 17n62, 59, 59n71, 86n17, 253
Doubt, xxi, 13, 14, 17, 22, 36, 80n100, 81n102, 204n89, 293

Earth, earthly, earthiness, xi, 21, 48, 118, 122, 130, 141, 156, 158, 161, 164, 165, 168, 171, 173, 174, 193, 195, 196, 201, 239, 261, 268, 275, 294
Ecclesiastes, 24, 30, 44, 49, 62, 70, 89, 108, 109, 154, 182, 199, 205, 213, 217, 244, 267, 269, 278
Ecstasy, 32, 106, 113, 116, 122, 193, 193n58, 202, 202n79, 203, 203n85, 204, 206, 232, 278. *See also* Joy
Election, xii, 48, 60, 95, 184, 249, 257, 261 *See also* Jesus Christ, Election of
"Eleventh hour, the" (Kierkegaard), 278, 279, 290
Emotions, emote, emoting, x, xxiii, 6, 8, 12, 32, 85, 85n11, 92, 96, 105, 111, 134, 137, 138, 139, 202, 234, 260, 262, 277, 287, 288
Enemies, 25, 38, 63, 113, 114, 130, 131, 149, 150, 152, 156, 182, 193, 197, 199, 203, 219
Enjoyment, 25, 44, 107, 109, 147, 159, 182, 183, 199, 200, 224, 245, 278. *See also* Joy
Eros, erotic, 40, 65, 67, 67n26, 222, 262, 264, 286. *See also* Desire, Love
Eschatology. 48, 52, 56, 99–101, 106, 167–77, 178, 258. *See also* Joy, Eschatology
Esther, 205
Ethics, xiv, xxivn58, 41, 61, 66, 89n44, 93, 95, 105n2, 106n9, 109n22, 110, 138, 146, 179, 180, 191, 193, 201, 203, 203n95, 211–14, 223, 242, 250, 250n118, 262, 263, 264–76, 274, 274n125, 287, 287n194
Eucharist, the (The Lord's Supper, Communion), xvi, 68, 140, 148, 188, 192, 246, 246, 252, 257, 266, 266n89, 271, 277
Existentialism, 7, 76n77, 76n78
Exult, exultation, 128, 129, 131, 147, 150, 152, 156, 158, 161, 168, 169, 172, 197, 200, 204, 214, 215, 261, 266, 268. *See also* Joy
Ezekiel, 114
Ezra, 151, 180, 199
Faith, xi, xv, xvi, xvii, xviii, xix, xx, xxi, xxii, 24, 29, 31, 43, 44, 49, 50, 51, 52, 53, 54, 60, 61n84, 66n23, 72, 81n102, 82n108, 86, 89, 98, 119, 121, 123, 125, 132n95, 138, 146, 153, 166, 170, 171, 191, 192, 193, 209, 210, 218, 235n32, 246, 249, 250, 252, 254n24, 25, 255, 270, 271, 271n107, 276, 280, 285, 294

Feelings, 5, 6, 8, 85, 96, 128, 151, 192, 193, 232
Film noir, xxiii, 66, 66n20, 73, 73n59
1 Corinthians, 179
1 Peter, 134
Flesh, xvi, 14, 50, 109, 124, 191, 193, 205, 217, 256, 281

300 Subject Index

Forgiveness, 11, 13, 86, 87, 99, 153, 190, 191, 200, 213, 250, 262, 263, 288
Fun, 108

Genesis, 112
Giddiness, 108, 113, 201, 202, 277, 281, 288, 295. *See also* Joy
Glad, gladness, x, 49, 108, 113, 114, 120, 125, 128, 129, 131, 135, 136, 145, 151, 156, 157, 158, 160, 165, 168, 169, 172, 173, 175, 176, 177, 178, 180, 182, 187, 188, 191, 192, 193, 194, 195, 197, 201, 205, 211, 205, 211, 253, 258, 261, 263, 268, 282, 288. *See also* Joy
Gloom, 169. *See also* Despair
Glorification, 293, 294
God, xi, xiv, xv, xvii, xviii, xx, xxi, xxiii, xxivn58, xvn28, 4, 5, 8, 8n20, 11, 12, 13, 16, 19, 21n5, 22, 23, 25, 28, 24, 31, 33, 39, 39n78, 40n84, 40, 43, 46, 46n30, 47, 49, 50, 50n23, 51, 52, 53, 56, 56n53, 57, 58, 65, 67, 69n34, 70n42, 72, 76, 77, 81, 81n102, 82, 88, 89, 89n36, 90, 90n45, 48, 53, 95, 95n75, 77, 106n9, 108, 109, 109n20, 114–115, 116, 120, 122n68, 124, 128, 129, 130, 133, 133n98, 134n1, 141n25, 143, 146, 149, 151, 152, 154, 164, 166, 170, 171, 180, 182, 183, 184, 185, 186, 187, 190, 199, 200, 202, 206, 205, 205n9, 206, 209, 210, 211, 212n11, 12, 213n14, 217n28, 219, 220n43, 222, 226, 227n90, 228n92, 93, 230–50, 251, 252n8, 263, 255, 256, 256n35, 258, 259n55, 260, 260n62, 261, 263, 266, 271, 271n107, 273, 278n154, 155, 279n156, 280, 282, 285, 286, 288, 289, 290, 290, 290n205, 206, 291, 292 n. 219, 295
  Absence of, 37, 45–46, 69, 70
  Action of, 42, 54, 58, 143, 236, 271, 275, 289

Advocate, 89
Attributes of, 82, 285
Anthropomorphic, xxiii, 216, 241
Being and act, 232
Beauty of. *See* Beauty
Creator, xi, xiv, 6, 16, 49, 54, 61, 63, 72, 74, 98, 118, 139, 159, 179, 181, 184, 184n15, 209, 220, 236–38, 241, 251, 258, 289
Decrees of, 118, 194, 235, 240
Despair of, 67, 235. *See also* God, Sorrow of
Father, xi, xii, xiin12, xiii, xiv, xv, xvii, xviii, xix, 10, 15, 16, 17, 18, 28, 29, 34, 39, 41, 46, 47, 52, 58, 74, 88, 90, 91, 92, 93, 116, 117, 121, 132, 141, 145, 154, 161, 166, 169, 170, 175, 180, 184, 186, 188, 190, 191, 192, 193, 209, 213, 223, 225, 226, 227, 230, 231, 232, 234, 237, 239, 240, 242, 243, 245, 247, 252, 253, 254, 255, 256, 257, 263, 265, 268, 270, 271, 275n129, 277, 280, 281, 286, 287, 289, 290, 292, 294, 295
Freedom of, xiin12, 16, 54, 57, 230, 232n14, 235, 239, 240, 241, 244, 247, 256, 285, 289
Gifts of, 79, 93, 255, 256, 261, 269, 279, 289, 291, 293
Glory of, xx, 81, 117, 118, 168, 170, 244, 268
Goodness of, xxiii, xxv, 6, 72, 119, 177, 248, 289
Grace of, xxiii, xxiiin18, xxiv, 10, 33, 37n75, 38, 39, 47, 50, 51, 53, 78, 86n21, 92, 93, 94, 95, 95n78, 98, 99, 100, 108, 123, 123n73, 125, 140n22, 143, 153n67, 155, 157, 161, 176n112, 182–208, 219, 228, 253n14, 256n40, 260, 265, 270, 271n108, 275, 276, 279, 286, 291n215. *See also* Grace
Imitation of, 65, 295
Immanence of, 143
Immutability of, 185, 216
Impassibility of, 67, 185, 216, 235. *See also* God, Suffering of

Subject Index

Joy as the Yes of, 230–50
Joy of, xxii, xxv, 12, 54, 98, 115, 116, 118–19, 121, 230–50. *See also* God, Rejoices
Judgment of, 60, 87, 90, 94, 114, 131, 138, 146, 153, 157, 158, 168, 181, 192, 194, 195, 196, 197, 220, 224, 241, 242, 286, 291, 291n211
Kingdom of, 57, 99, 126, 150, 155, 158, 161, 162, 163, 172, 174, 176, 177, 183, 186, 220, 237, 243, 258, 259, 267, 281, 282
Knowledge of, xix, xxiv, 16, 35, 41, 42, 252n4, 254n27, 257, 291
Lord, 60, 82, 139, 161, 169, 181, 183, 193, 201, 204, 220, 248, 258, 268, 275
Love of, 6, 28, 34, 42, 54, 55, 65, 87, 89, 90, 92, 100, 110, 169, 170, 171, 198, 202, 222, 228, 234, 241, 241n71, 242, 246, 254, 257, 286, 291, 295. *See also* Love
Mercy of, 111, 117, 161, 165, 177, 181, 188, 192, 216, 220, 248, 258, 285, 285n182, 286
Participation in. *See* Jesus Christ, Participation in
Presence of, 45, 69, 70, 164–67, 172, 218, 249, 268, 288
Providence of, xi, xxin56, 16, 44, 46, 46n10, 156, 241, 251
Rejoices, 67, 114, 119, 159, 164, 169, 171, 185, 197, 216, 224, 230–50, 251–55, 258, 283. *See also* God, Joy of
Rest of (Sabbath), 238–44, 251, 268
Righteousness of, xi, 113, 120, 168, 285, 285n182, 286
Sorrow of, 119, 171, 248. *See also* God, Despair of
Sovereignty of, 54, 236, 248, 276, 280
Suffering of, 45, 90, 216, 228n92, 234, 235, 249. *See also* God, impassibility of
Transcendence of, 143, 265, 276, 280
Trinity, xii, xiin12, xiiin18, xvn26, xvn28, xviii, 28, 28n43, 37n75, 47, 56, 66, 86n21, 89n39, 90, 90n53, 95n78, 99, 123n73, 133n98, 140n22, 141, 153n67, 166, 170, 176n112, 176n113, 183n8, 184 n. 13, 15, 185, 185n20, 228, 130, 131, 132, 132n10, 14, 16, 236, 237, 239n61, 242, 244, 247, 252, 252n6, 253n14, 254n24, 256n38, 40, 258, 258n51, 268, 269, 271n108, 280, 281, 287, 291n215. *See also Perichoresis*
Will of, xi, 15, 44, 57, 58, 60, 61, 153, 161, 183, 233, 235–36, 240, 243, 248, 253, 270
Witness of joy in the incarnation, 245–50
Word of, xi, xiii, xiv, xv, 53, 71, 146, 157, 194, 195, 196, 226, 235, 237, 240, 251–55, 258, 285, 286. *See also* Jesus Christ, Word of God
Wrath of, 47, 48, 146, 216, 294
Gospel, the, xxi, 124, 142, 143, 152, 160–64, 167, 181, 193, 295
Gospels, the, 10, 26, 161, 233
Grace, xii, xvii, xx, xxiii, xxiv, 17, 36, 37, 37n76, 46–48, 47n14, 49, 66, 70, 76, 86, 91, 94–98, 99–101, 111, 137, 146, 153, 161, 163, 181, 182–208, 209, 223, 241, 242, 246, 247, 248, 249, 251, 255, 256, 258, 262, 267, 270, 289, 290, 291, 293. *See also* God, grace of
Gratitude, xiv, 42, 44, 159, 170, 174, 179, 188–92, 221, 223, 224, 225, 258, 266, 275, 278. *See also* Joy, Fulfilled, Thanksgiving, Jesus Christ, Vicarious Thanksgiving
Grief, 29, 31, 32, 40, 48, 49, 50, 51, 53, 53n42, 44, 89, 99, 124, 145, 154, 196, 215, 216, 245, 296. *See also* Despair, Sorrow
Guilt, xvii, 29, 37, 38, 50, 56, 59, 59n74, 87, 146, 180, 196, 212, 228, 229, 262

Happiness, x, xxv, 9n25, 26, 71, 73, 75, 79n93, 81, 82, 83, 100, 100n100, 105, 105 n. 1, 2, 106n5, 7, 109, 110, 119, 128, 140, 147, 155, 165, 166, 179, 191, 199, 199n73, 201, 169. *See also* Joy
Hearing, x, xiii, xv, 115, 116, 145, 156, 196, 243, 251, 252
Heaven, xi, xv, 21, 46, 48, 74, 85, 100, 101, 115, 127, 140, 161, 170, 175, 177, 180, 186, 188, 191, 193, 195, 225, 226, 233, 238, 253, 247, 294
Hebrews, Epistle to the, xiii, 54, 125, 167, 214
Hell, 85, 43, 56, 57, 76, 95, 96, 100, 101, 141, 196, 227, 235
Hobbies, 79, 79n93
Holiness, 109, 142, 144, 180, 197, 203, 265. *See also* Sanctification
Holy Spirit, the, xviii, 10, 28, 34, 35, 47, 51, 54, 99, 100, 123, 132, 133, 143, 161, 162, 163, 164, 166, 170, 173, 175, 176, 183, 190, 193, 209, 214, 215, 230, 231, 234, 237, 242, 243, 245, 247, 252, 255, 256, 257, 259, 261, 268, 269, 271, 273, 280, 281, 287, 288, 289
Homo religiosus, 142
Homosexuality, 263
Hope, xiv, xx, 19, 38, 39, 41, 44, 50, 57, 61n84, 64, 76n77, 77, 82n108, 83, 90n52, 98, 99, 100, 112n38, 115, 122n68, 123, 135n3, 6, 144, 148, 170, 190, 201, 204n89, 90, 214, 221, 222, 224n64, 225, 275n132, 281, 286, 289, 294
Humans, xi, xii, xiv, xivn25, xvi, xvin38, xix, xxiv, xxv, 4, 5, 5n7, 6n11, 13, 9, 9 n. 27, 10, 11, 12, 14, 15, 16, 20, 21, 22, 22n10, 23, 24, 25, 27n34, 28, 29, 30, 32, 33, 33n59, 37, 39, 40, 40n82, 45, 46, 46n11, 47, 53, 59, 61, 63, 67, 67n28, 69n34, 70, 74, 76, 77, 77n84, 78, 80, 82, 86, 88, 89, 90, 92, 100, 101, 105, 107n14, 109n18, 110, 111, 112n39, 115, 117, 119, 123, 127, 133, 134, 135, 139, 141n25, 148, 149, 151, 154, 155, 157, 158, 159, 161, 167, 175, 178, 179, 184, 184n15, 187, 188, 193, 206, 209, 216, 217, 218, 219, 223, 225, 229, 237n47, 238–39, 239n58, 61, 244, 251, 251n3, 252, 253, 253n19, 254, 255, 256, 257, 258, 261, 263, 272, 273n118, 275, 276, 277, 279, 284, 287, 288, 289, 290, 291, 295
Adam and Eve, 46, 47, 63, 112, 126, 159, 253, 253n19, 261, 263
Autonomy and/or freedom of, xix, xx, xxi, 15, 16, 21, 22, 24, 27, 42, 71, 80, 86, 96, 101, 113, 123, 130, 151, 163, 185, 206, 219n39, 257, 258, 259, 260, 268, 275, 286, 292, 293, 295
Bitterness of, 25, 223, 225
Bondage of the will *(servum arbitrium)*, 206
Brokenness, alienation, and lostness of, 8, 21, 39, 46–48, 49, 52, 54, 59, 72, 134–36, 136–38, 144, 181, 189, 190, 199, 201, 210, 211, 218, 226, 228, 251, 258, 285, 289
Co-humanity, 46, 258
"Collective person" (Bonhoeffer), 28
Creatureliness, 21, 67, 68, 69, 73, 75, 112, 118, 122, 184, 205, 206, 217, 231, 241, 245, 257, 264, 265, 267, 280, 281–84, 289, 290, 291
Death, 12, 17, 21, 27, 29, 31, 32, 38, 39, 42, 63, 64, 67, 68–71, 87, 95, 96, 97, 98, 100, 121, 130, 135, 136, 140, 150, 152, 154, 155, 160, 163, 174, 178, 186, 228, 274, 274n123, 288, 296,
Fall, the, 16, 21n4, 39n81, 46, 47, 50, 52, 245, 268n93, 284
Heart, 24, 39, 42, 48, 49, 51, 52, 53, 61, 62, 64, 70, 72, 73, 88, 92–94, 108, 109, 110, 113, 114, 118, 119, 120, 125, 130, 131, 134, 146, 148, 150, 151, 153, 155, 156, 157, 159,

160, 161, 165, 166, 168, 169, 170, 171, 172, 174, 175, 178, 182, 183, 187, 188, 194, 195, 196, 197, 198, 200, 201, 204, 210, 211, 215, 217, 223, 226, 238, 260, 263, 267, 268, 278, 278n155, 287, 293, 296

Image of God, 158, 238, 241, 260, 275

Individual, 28, 83, 151, 212, 260, 261

Marriage, 3, 14n49, 40, 84, 105, 126, 171, 184n15, 215, 217, 218, 264, 265, 287

Needs, xiv, 8, 11, 12, 23, 32, 121, 123, 138, 155, 161, 165, 193, 200, 256, 268, 283, 287, 289, 291, 295

New and exalted, xviii, xx, 96, 121, 123, 142, 254, 257, 259, 275, 293

Other, the, 27, 32, 237, 259–70

Response of faith and obedience, xv, xviii, xix, xx, 255–59, 263, 270

Self, the, 6, 14, 15, 20, 27, 43, 75, 77, 82, 83, 151, 249, 260

Sexuality, 46, 47, 76, 79, 109, 115, 159, 217, 233, 262, 286

Sons and daughters of God, xv, 143

Soul, 3, 14, 15, 18, 22, 24, 37n76, 39, 44, 49, 49n20, 51, 68, 75, 82n109, 89, 89n38, 92, 93, 96, 113, 119, 120, 122, 125, 130, 131, 134n1, 145, 146, 147, 148, 151, 171, 191, 196, 202, 204, 212n1, 11, 12, 215, 221n51, 222 n51, 226, 245, 272, 273, 273n118, 274,

Spirit, xxiv, 20, 21, 28, 29, 33, 36, 51, 75, 77, 81, 82, 83, 89, 109, 115, 120, 123, 125, 146, 152, 163, 174, 177, 191, 195, 201, 205, 217, 218, 226, 256, 263, 268, 283, 288, 293

Vicarious living. *See* Vicarious reality

Humor, xxv, 71, 72, 80, 81, 222, 223, 249, 268, 269, 272, 281, 283

Imagination, 25, 40, 289n201

Intentionality, 15, 16, 17, 27

Intercession, xiv, 37, 87, 132, 133, 149, 175, 253, 277, 284, 289. *See also* Prayer, Jesus Christ, Prayers of

Intimacy, 15, 40, 92, 184

Irony, xx, 18, 47, 71, 80, 81, 83, 84, 93, 121, 143, 173, 174, 195, 204, 205, 224, 260, 262, 267, 277, 282, 284n175

Isaiah, 165, 171, 172, 173, 187, 200

James, Epistle of, 146, 153

Jesus Christ, x, xii, xiii, xiv, xvi, xviii, xix, xxin56, xxiv, 6, 7, 8, 10, 11, 12, 16, 16n59, 17, 21, 26, 32, 33, 36, 46, 49, 50, 51, 52, 54, 56, 58, 59, 60, 61, 65, 70, 71, 73 76, 77, 79, 82, 86, 88, 88n31, 32, 91, 93, 97, 98, 100, 108, 115, 116–21, 125, 134, 135, 136, 140, 142, 142n31, 153, 155, 156, 162, 166, 167, 169, 170, 172, 172, 174, 187, 210, 215, 216, 216n20, 233, 235, 236n40, 239, 243, 244, 246, 247, 247n103, 250, 251, 253, 253n19, 260, 264, 266, 271, 272, 280, 283, 285, 287, 287n296, 288, 289, 292. *See also* Atonement, Christology, Salvation

Advocate, 121, 132

Apostle, 174

Ascension, xii, 74, 140, 141, 141n24, 166, 212, 255

Baptism of, xii, 8, 56, 88, 95, 192, 263, 270, 288, 289, 293

Bearer and proclaimer, 132

Bearing sin, 8, 89

Beauty of, 166. *See also* Beauty

Beatitudes of, 154

Burial of (Holy Saturday), 56, 56n52, 57, 95, 96, 141, 227, 235

Confession by, xi, xii, xiii, 8, 88, 91, 288, 289, 293

Cross of, 15, 16, 17, 18, 22, 26, 37, 38, 41, 45, 49, 50, 54, 56, 56n52, 53, 54, 55, 57, 59, 60, 61, 65, 66, 67, 76, 89, 90, 95n73, 76, 96, 96n82, 101, 118, 135, 141n30, 142, 144, 152, 156, 166, 167,

Jesus Christ, Cross of (*continued*)
169, 180, 181, 197, 202, 207, 212, 213, 214, 217, 224, 226, 227, 228, 228n93, 229, 234, 248, 250, 255n33, 258, 259, 261, 264, 275, 277, 280, 281, 285, 287, 289, 295, 296. *See also* Jesus Christ, Death of

Cry of abandonment, 38, 46, 50, 56, 58, 95, 95n76, 166, 227, 227n88, 228n91, 235

Death of (vicarious), 55, 56, 58, 66, 74, 75, 91, 96, 99, 140, 141, 144, 169, 176, 178, 179, 227, 227n87, 249, 253, 293

Deity of, xv, xix, 135, 149, 171, 231

Despair of, xix, xxi, 9, 15, 22, 38, 39, 58, 61, 89–92, 100, 166, 227n88. *See also* Jesus Christ, Sorrow of, Vicarious Despair of

"Double movement" of the incarnation, xv, 133, 188, 242, 244, 245, 247, 248, 252, 256, 276

Election of, 8, 57

Exaltation of, 90, 91, 141, 142, 166, 227, 255, 256, 259, 274

Faith of (vicarious), xi, xii, xv, xvi, xviii, xix, 10, 11, 15, 16, 17, 31, 39, 51, 54, 58, 60, 61, 66, 74, 88, 89n39, 101, 106, 144, 145, 152, 154, 187, 190, 209, 223, 226, 227, 227n88, 229, 242, 248, 249, 254, 256, 270, 286, 291, 292

Faithful answer, 252

Fallen human nature, 95, 265, 287n196

Freedom of, xiii, 57, 58, 225, 226, 234, 280

Gethsemane, 55, 58, 91, 93, 226, 227n87, 228, 289

Glory of, 117, 293

Good Shepherd, the, 265

Grace of, 28, 139. *See also* God, Grace of

Head (of the church), xiii, 58, 140, 153

Hearing of (the word of God), 21, 157, 196, 253, 276

Heart of, 92–94

High Priest, xv, 132, 174, 228, 253. *See also* Jesus Christ, Priesthood of

Historical Jesus, xi

Homoousios, 90, 119, 231

Humanity of, xv, xviii, xix, 8, 10, 11, 22, 117, 149, 156, 161, 163, 171, 182, 186, 189, 192, 206, 216, 218, 231, 242, 243, 248, 255, 256, 257, 272, 273, 280, 287n196, 290, 292, 295

Humiliation of, 99, 141, 142, 227, 258, 274

Humility of, 33

Imitation of, xv, 14, 17, 23, 82

Incarnation of, xv, 6, 31, 38, 51, 54, 67, 90, 91n54, 111, 112, 119n60, 139–42, 164, 176, 188, 189, 199, 216, 226n77, 229, 242, 245–50, 251, 254, 267, 283, 293, 294n228

Joy of, xix, 15, 25, 35, 36, 38, 49, 52, 54, 60, 90, 91, 100, 106, 116–18, 156, 157, 161, 162, 163, 166, 174, 182–86, 189, 192, 204, 210, 213–14, 220, 221, 225–29, 231, 232, 245, 246, 249, 251, 253, 254, 255, 259, 264, 268, 270, 273, 276, 277, 280, 281, 285. *See also* Jesus Christ, Vicarious joy of

King, 172, 213

Lamb of God, 171, 173, 214

Last Adam, xii, 179

Logos, xiin12

Loneliness of, 55

Lord, xiii, 16, 33, 58, 92, 95, 116, 137, 169, 181, 187, 210, 260

Love of, xvii, 51, 92, 116, 188

Man of heaven, the, 294

Mediator, xn2, xiv, xix, xvn31, 51, 90n47, 92–94, 119, 126, 143n38, 170, 175, 176, 232n15, 270, 291

Messiah, 57, 116, 181, 191, 227n87

Ministry of. *See* Ministry

New Adam, xvi, xvii, 91, 189

Obedience of (vicarious), xiii, xv, xvii, 10, 11, 17, 57, 74, 90, 93, 106, 116, 117, 118, 141, 145, 154,

169, 176, 178, 180, 185, 188, 190, 191, 209, 223, 226, 228, 229, 230–50, 253, 254, 265, 270, 274, 279–81, 286, 287, 290, 291, 292
Participation in, xix, 17, 18, 21, 32, 34, 69n34, 100, 135, 140, 145, 166, 170, 188, 199, 210, 226, 232, 234, 238, 239, 245, 246, 247, 249, 251, 253, 254, 257, 269, 270, 279, 280, 281, 295, 296
Passion of, 54, 58, 89, 253
"Perfect Eucharistic Being" (Schmemann), 188, 189, 192, 252
"Perfect penitent, the" (C. S. Lewis), xixn52, 88n32
Prayers of (vicarious), 26, 29, 32, 35, 55, 57, 57n61, 58, 88, 91, 117, 133, 149, 170, 175, 176, 213, 232, 253, 255, 277, 283, 288. See also Prayer
Presence of, 141, 147, 192, 226, 249, 257, 268, 271. See also Eucharist
Priesthood of, xvii, 57, 132n94, 140, 253, 271, 284, 284n177, 191. See also Jesus Christ, High Priest
Rejected of God, 60, 227
Resurrection (vicarious), xii, 17, 55, 56, 56n52, 56n55, 57, 66, 67, 74, 75, 90, 91, 95n73, 96, 96n82, 99, 135, 136, 139, 140, 141, 141n30, 142, 142 n. 31, 144, 152, 156, 166, 167, 169, 176, 178, 179, 181, 197, 213, 217, 224, 248, 253, 254, 255n33, 258, 262, 265, 272, 274, 275, 279, 288, 289, 293, 296
Righteousness of, 22, 50, 82, 121
Sanctification, 121, 256
Savior, 99, 116, 161, 181, 287n196
Servant, 16, 33, 92, 95, 153, 187
Solidarity with humanity, 29, 32, 53, 74, 76, 88, 92, 93, 94, 95, 96, 111, 139, 142, 164, 177, 185, 199, 216, 227, 247, 248, 253, 265, 283, 288
Son, xi, xiin12, xiii, xiv, xv, xvi, xviii, 15, 16, 17, 18, 28, 39, 46, 47, 49, 53, 65, 74, 88, 90, 92, 129, 141, 154, 166, 180, 181, 190, 213, 227, 228, 228n92, 230, 232, 234, 237, 239, 242, 245, 247, 248, 252, 253, 255, 256, 263, 267, 268, 269, 275n129, 280, 286, 287, 291, 292, 293
Son of God, xiv, xvi, 17, 32, 51, 58, 91, 112, 139, 152, 207, 224, 231
Son of Man, 48
Sorrow of, 157, 210, 216, 217. See also Jesus Christ, Vicarious sorrow of
Stellvertretung ("deputyship" or "vicarious representative action" in Dietrich Bonhoeffer), xvii
Suffering by, 8, 15, 17, 18, 57, 59, 60, 90, 187, 197, 211, 226, 228, 283, 296. See also Suffering
Transfiguration of, 289
Union with, xv, 17, 18, 50, 54, 59, 60, 90, 116, 119, 124, 227, 271, 272, 276, 277
Uniqueness of, 76, 97, 152, 154, 227, 247, 227, 247, 253
Vicarious act of, 111, 247, 257, 259, 265, 270, 283
Vicarious answer of, 270, 271
Vicarious confession of sins, 191, 263
Vicarious death of, x, 17, 50, 95, 138, 139, 141. See also Jesus Christ, Death of
Vicarious despair of, xxi, 52–58, 88, 92, 96, 136, 151, 179, 227. See also Jesus Christ, Despair of, Vicarious Sorrow of, Sorrow of
Vicarious hope of, 138, 144
Vicarious humanity of, x, xn2, xi, xv, xvi, xvii, xixn52, xxi, xxin56, xxv, 7, 11, 14, 17, 20, 21, 22, 28, 34, 35, 36, 50, 51, 53, 55, 56, 58, 65, 74, 82, 86, 88n32, 89, 92, 93, 97, 101, 119, 132n94, 138, 139, 140, 141, 142, 143, 147, 157, 170, 176, 181, 183, 184, 189, 190, 193, 198, 200, 229, 231, 233, 235, 236, 238, 243, 245, 255, 259, 266, 271, 279, 291
Vicarious image of God, 284

Jesus Christ (*continued*)
Vicarious joy of, xxi, xxii, 54, 67, 78, 96, 100, 112, 121, 123, 126, 129, 133, 136, 139, 143, 144, 145, 149, 151, 164, 166, 171, 174, 179, 180, 181, 184, 197, 206, 213, 219, 229, 233, 243, 244, 247, 256, 257, 258, 265, 269, 279, 284, 285, 287, 289, 292, 295. *See also* Jesus Christ, Joy of
Vicarious life of, 8, 17, 22, 75, 79, 91, 95, 96, 162, 176, 179, 209, 218, 225, 233, 246, 259, 280, 293
Vicarious offering of, 252, 257, 271
Vicarious "pausing" of, 223
Vicarious reality. *See* Vicarous reality
Vicarious repentance of, 56. *See also* "Perfect penitent, the,"
Vicarious response of, 43, 121, 228, 229, 242, 252, 255, 257, 270, 286
Vicarious rest of, 240
Vicarious service, 106, 148, 149, 242, 254
Vicarious sorrow of, 143, 145, 229, 274, 285. *See also* Jesus Christ, Sorrow of, Sorrow
Vicarious thanksgiving of, 188, 189, 192, 213, 240, 257, 266. *See also* Thanksgiving, Eucharist, Gratitude
Vicarious weeping of, 29, 37, 92. *See also* Weeping
Vicarious work of, 17, 50
Vicarious worship of, 106, 132, 133, 233, 253. *See also* Worship
Witness, xiii, 90, 271
"Wonderful" or "sweet exchange" (*Epistle to Diognetus*), 24, 38, 137, 196, 234, 254
Word of God, xiii, xiv, xv, xvi, 53, 94, 135, 139, 149, 153, 156, 196, 248, 279, 283
Joel, Book of, 172
John, Gospel of, 161, 173, 175
Joy (Rejoice, Rejoicing), ix, x, xiv, xvii, xviii, xxi, xxii, xxiii, xxv, 12, 16, 17, 18, 23, 25, 25n25, 27, 30, 32, 33, 34, 40, 41, 42, 46, 48, 49, 52, 53, 55, 60, 61, 63, 65,72, 73, 80, 81, 83, 84, 87, 89, 90, 91, 92, 95, 97, 100, 101, 105–33, 134–81, 182–208, 209–29, 230–20, 251–96. *See also* Blessed, Blessedness, Bliss, Desire, Enjoyment, Fun, Ecstasy, Exult, Giddiness, Glad, Gladness, Happiness, Merry, Merry-making, Pleasure, Shout, Shouting
Actuality of, 142
Aesthetic joy in God, 268–70
And despair: a mixture? 136–39
And despair: can we live with both? 134–81
And despair here and now, 151–53
And despair: relativizing of, 177–79
And laughter of the vulnerable, 281–84
And obedience, 279–81
Anticipated. *See* Eschatological
Apollonian, 202
As the Yes of God, 230–50
As the Yes of Humanity, 252–96
Barriers to, 122–23
Believer, 119–22
Bible: Joy as Music, Dancing, Singing and Worship, 127–33. *See also* Music and Song
Celebration of, 112–14, 129, 156, 186, 190, 283
Children of, 126–27
Command to rejoice, 123–26, 138, 139, 162, 179–81, 220, 224, 248, 285, 286, 287
Desire for, 110–14
Dionysian, 202
Ecstasy. *See* Ecstasy
Entered into (experiential) (Schmemann), 192
Epistemology of, 170, 224
Eschatological (anticipated), 25, 34, 35, 40, 60, 98, 99–101, 115, 131, 157, 165, 167–77, 178, 187, 190, 200, 207, 211, 214, 215, 220,

221, 229, 233, 258, 272, 279, 289, 294, 295
Eucharistic, 252. *See also* Eucharist
Feasting, 148, 161, 180, 182, 187, 193, 200, 237, 238, 251, 268, 275, 276, 277
Folly, 203
Fractured place of, 284–92
Fruit of grace, 98–99
Fulfilled, 173, 174, 176, 177, 178, 183, 187, 207, 220, 221, 224, 240, 250, 252, 254, 271
Gift, grace, and gratitude ... and its enemies, 25, 182–208, 224
Gift in the midst of despair, 154–57, 266
God as the giver, 114–15
Groaning creation, 158–59
Human character of joy, 272–77
Human joy as personal joy, 277–79
In community, 270–72
In the other, 259–70
Lack of, the greatest indictment, 192–201
Longing, 33, 35, 49, 68, 111, 111n31, 112, 142, 154, 215, 279
Loss of, 198
Need for and the inevitability of despair, 134–36
Not of our own, 292–96
Of belonging, 287
Of God in a creation with limits, 243–45
Of the gospel ... in the midst of despair, 160–64
Of the will of God, 235–36
Ordinary, 108–9, 182, 183, 199, 213, 214
Problem of, 105–33, 153, 154, 157, 162, 163, 167, 173, 174, 176, 177, 179, 181, 186, 188, 191, 192, 192, 193, 198, 200, 201, 206
Pseudo-joys, xii, 127, 201–8
Readiness for, 183, 223
Sabbath joy as human joy, 265–67
Sabbath joy of God, 239–43
That comes from struggle, 209–29

Transitory, 115–16, 201–8, 224, 284–92, 294
Justification, 50, 94, 96, 98, 167, 170, 262, 263, 269, 279, 293

Knowledge, 63, 81, 107n11, 139, 155, 170, 199, 233, 246, 289

Lament, 17, 23, 24, 37, 63, 72, 146, 153, 210, 219, 227n89, 228n92 *See also* Despair
Lamentations, 48
Laughter, xxv, 32, 42, 65, 87, 112n35, 120, 146, 153, 179, 210, 222, 272, 273, 281–84
Law, 37, 42, 118, 129, 144, 180, 221, 260, 264, 265, 268, 275, 288, 289
Loneliness, 13, 31, 36, 46, 55, 257, 261
Lord's Supper, the. *See* Eucharist
Love, xiii, xv, xx, 6, 40, 42, 48, 65, 67, 68, 70, 77, 82n108, 85, 95, 100, 119, 137, 147, 152, 157, 162, 165, 179, 184, 193, 204, 217, 222, 229, 232, 234, 238, 239, 246, 251, 260, 261, 283, 285, 287, 290, 295. *See also* Agape, Eros
Luke, Gospel of Luke, xviii, 135, 137, 172, 173, 175

Matthew, Gospel of, 135, 136, 172, 175
Medication, x, 9, 10
Melancholy, x, 7, 14, 21, 40, 42, 48, 70, 78, 89, 214, 222, 253. *See also* Despair
Memory, 40, 41, 42, 64, 78, 80n100
Merry, merry-making, 131, 168, 177, 200. *See also* Joy
Ministry, xvii, xxi, xxin56, 6, 10, 12, 82, 84, 84n5, 83n4, 87, 89n38, 95, 96, 100, 106n8, 137, 151, 163, 170, 172, 174, 175, 229n100, 255, 270, 271, 293. *See also* Vicarious Reality (and Ministry)
Misery, 11, 15, 18, 23, 25, 26, 29, 49, 68, 72, 89, 90, 134, 186–88, 204. *See also* Despair
Modernity, 63, 116, 123, 203, 212

Subject Index

Monotony, 213, 260, 267, 269, 278, 292
Mourn, Mourning, 34, 124, 131, 146, 153, 154, 157, 165, 168, 172, 173, 174, 177, 178, 179, 180, 197, 200, 201, 210, 215, 268. *See also* Despair
Music and song, singing, xxi, xxv, 107, 127–33, 139, 156, 158, 159, 160, 168, 169, 172, 176, 186, 187, 192, 194, 196, 203n85, 204, 214, 218, 223, 238, 259, 268, 294. *See also* Joy, Bible: Music, Dancing, Singing, and Worship
Mythology, 45, 74

Necessity, 21, 38, 46, 59, 159, 209, 215–18
Nehemiah, Book of, 156, 165

Obedience, xv, xix, 43, 50, 61, 66, 110, 118, 123, 146, 179, 191, 194, 225, 246, 247, 252, 259, 269, 286, 291. *See also,* Jesus Christ, Obedience of
Ontological, ontology, 22, 36, 43, 46, 51, 86, 89, 90, 95, 138, 148, 151, 219, 232, 235, 239, 243, 248, 261, 284

Pain, x, 6, 7, 21, 31, 36, 45, 53, 58, 98, 123, 134, 167, 169, 175, 176, 186, 195, 201, 215, 216, 217, 224, 225, 228. *See also* Despair
Pastors, clergy, pastoral care, xvii, 10, 11, 12, 13, 35, 36, 65n12, 65n13, 83, 84, 95n72, 96, 96n85, 97, 99, 143, 151, 211, 218, 265, 265n86, 266n88, 283n173, 285n182, 285, 285n182, 291, 296n236, 239
Patience, 41, 60, 89n42, 123, 138, 190, 193, 213, 286
Peace, 5, 18, 36, 38, 41, 42, 52, 58, 61, 65, 81, 82, 89, 94, 116, 117, 123, 131, 141, 144, 158, 163, 170, 174, 186, 188, 193, 210, 214, 217, 222, 226, 237, 259, 280, 281, 284, 295
Pelagianism, 139, 188, 230, 255

Penal substitution, xix, 12, 35, 60, 90, 95, 161
Penitence. *See* Repentance
Penthos. See Compunction
Perichoresis, 234, 242, 245, 252. *See also* God, Trinity
Philippians, Epistle to the, 138
Pleasure, 99, 105, 106, 109, 110, 111, 115, 123, 127, 135, 145, 155, 164, 165, 170, 183, 187, 187n26, 192, 202, 205, 207, 232, 266. *See also* Joy
Pluralism, 97, 154, 241n71, 291
Postmodernism, 76, 76n78, 97, 127, 173, 223, 276, 291
Praise, xvii, 32, 39, 52, 113, 120, 128, 128n86, 129, 130, 132, 134, 136, 145, 147, 148, 149, 150, 156, 164, 165, 177, 178, 201, 213, 251, 252. *See also* Worship
Prayer, xiii, xiv, xivn23, 24, xviii, 6, 16, 28, 35, 41, 45, 58, 59, 88, 114, 120, 131, 132, 133, 133n96, 138, 139, 140, 146, 147, 150, 152, 152n61, 169, 175, 176, 190, 191, 193, 219, 219n38, 233, 253, 259, 262, 263, 288, 293. *See also* Jesus Christ, Prayers of
Pride, 13, 15, 49, 74, 123, 138, 164, 173, 288. *See also* Sin
Proverbs, 112, 134, 151, 238
Psalms, xiii, 17, 25, 26, 31, 32n53, 39, 45, 47, 58, 63, 72, 113, 114, 130, 132, 138, 146, 147, 148, 150, 152, 218, 262, 283, 287, 293

Reconciliation, xv, 18, 22n10, 90n16, 93, 176n114, 192,n50, 236, 246, 259, 259 n. 55, 270, 293
Redemption, 65, 66n23, 95, 121, 164, 180, 201, 245, 285
Rejoice, rejoicing. *See* Joy
Religion, xix, xxi, 10, 14, 24, 38, 39, 48, 55, 61, 63, 69, 69n35, 70, 72, 76, 77, 79, 81, 82, 93, 95, 108, 110, 113, 115, 116, 123, 155, 162, 163, 180, 189, 193n58, 207, 211, 220, 220n43, 257, 283, 291, 295

Repentance (penitence), xix, 49–51, 56, 86, 88, 88n32, 98, 124, 146, 153, 154, 164, 166, 180, 181, 198, 200, 220, 228, 254, 276, 293

Representative atonement (on our behalf), xv, xix, 11, 18, 21, 11, 50, 56, 58, 88, 100, 116, 137, 180, 192, 196, 199, 209, 240, 242, 245, 253, 256, 259, 265, 273, 284, 288, 290, 293. *See also* Atonement

Revelation, Book of (the Apocalypse), 21, 56, 171, 195, 289

Revelation (doctrine of), xv, xvi, xii, xxv, 20, 28, 52, 86, 108, 135, 161, 207, 217, 219n39, 220n44, 229, 234, 242, 244, 247, 270

Righteous, the, 112, 113, 114, 119–122, 130, 131, 151, 155, 161, 196, 262

Sadness, 6, 9,n26, 21, 26, 30, 51, 70, 86, 89, 90, 110, 163, 174, 207, 217, 245, 294. *See also* Despair

Salvation (deliverance), xii, xv, xvii, xix, xxin56, 16n59, 18, 50, 61, 65, 84, 88n32, 94, 116, 117, 118, 120, 130, 140, 142, 146, 148, 149, 150, 156, 160, 161, 162, 163, 168, 169, 174, 200, 224, 243, 247, 255, 263, 275, 287n196, 288, 293. *See also* Holiness

Schadenfreude, 135, 204

Secularism, 81n102, 135, 136, 193n58, 202, 203, 203n85

Shame, 10, 36, 47, 47n14, 52, 60, 61, 92, 113, 118, 167, 173, 180, 195, 212, 281

Shout, shouting, 45, 113, 116, 120, 121, 128, 130, 131, 136, 156, 158, 159, 172, 175, 194, 195, 211, 136. *See also* Joy

Sickness, xxi, 5n4, 5n7, 11, 12, 13, 20, 60, 70n41, 75n69, 77n82, 85n10, 11, 95, 99

Sighing, 21, 125, 131, 168, 176, 254, 262, 280. *See also* Despair

Silence, 37, 38, 49, 51, 54, 70, 96, 215, 245, 262, 285, 286

Sin, sinners, xi, xii, xv, xvi, xix, xxi, 7n18, 9, 10, 11, 11n32, 12, 13, 14, 17, 19, 20, 21, 24, 29, 36, 37, 40, 43, 44, 46–48, 48n17, 52, 56, 58, 59, 62, 70n38, 72, 74, 76, 77, 86, 87, 88, 90, 95, 99, 110, 121, 123, 143, 144, 146, 153, 155, 164, 179, 190, 191, 192, 196, 199, 210, 213, 216, 226, 228n92, 235, 243, 251, 260, 262, 263, 285, 287, 288, 291, 293. *See also* Darkness, Pride, Sloth, Wicked

Sloth, 14, 77, 77n84, 189, 206. *See also* Acedia, Sin

Sorrow, ix, x, xxv, 5, 9n26, 12, 17, 18, 24, 25, 29, 39, 31, 32, 33, 36, 41, 42, 44, 49, 50, 51, 53, 61, 64, 65, 72, 73, 83, 86, 87, 89–92, 95, 97, 98, 108, 119, 127, 131, 134, 135, 136, 138, 139, 142, 143, 144, 151, 154, 168, 169, 171, 172, 173, 175, 176, 177, 179, 186, 191, 202, 208, 209, 215, 216, 217, 218, 224, 225, 238, 245, 247, 248, 265, 283, 285, 288, 289, 290, 295. *See also* Despair, Jesus Christ, Sorrow of, Vicarious Sorrow of,

Struggle, xxii, 93, 209–29

Substitutionary atonement (in our place), xi, xiii, xv, xvi, xix, 11, 21, 22, 22n10, 23, 24, 25, 56, 58, 59, 60, 74, 76, 83n3, 88, 96, 100, 116, 117, 137, 139, 143, 144, 167, 179, 180, 181, 183, 184, 196, 199, 220, 226, 227, 231, 234, 240, 242, 245, 253, 259, 273, 276, 284, 291, 292. *See also* Atonement

Suffering *(pathos)*, xvii, xxin56, 56, 12, 17, 18, 19, 36, 37, 38, 41, 44, 54, 55n51, 61, 65, 81, 90, 93, 97, 124, 138, 145, 150, 158, 166, 170, 177, 179, 187, 204, 207, 210, 211, 211 n.6, 212, 214, 216, 224, 225, 225n70, 72, 74, 226, 227, 228n95, 240, 244, 252, 259, 261, 271, 273, 275, 277, 279, 285, 295. *See also* God, Suffering of, Jesus Christ, Suffering of

Subject Index

Thanksgiving, xvii, 120, 130, 131, 140, 161, 168, 178, 187, 189, 190, 199, 213, 200, 220, 249, 254, 255, 257, 266, 267, 276. *See also* Eucharist, Gratitude, Jesus Christ, Vicarious Thanksgiving of,
Theodicy, 177, 224, 279
Therapists, 13, 134
Toys, 25, 109, 127
Tragedy. *See* Despair, Tragedy

Vicarious. *See* Jesus Christ, Vicarious Humanity of, Substitutionary Atonement
"Vicarious humanity of the church," 137, 239
Vicarious reality (and ministry), 34, 51, 59, 59n74, 87, 115, 116, 124, 125, 128, 145, 146, 147, 163, 164, 175, 180, 181, 185, 260, 270. *See also* Church, the

Weeping, 6, 19–51, 55, 58–61, 64, 65, 86, 87, 88, 89, 92, 98, 100, 101, 112, 113, 136, 139, 145, 146, 153, 157, 160, 171, 177, 179, 180, 181, 186, 200, 201, 215, 217, 222, 245, 246, 289, 289n201, 296. *See also* Despair
Wicked or unrighteous, 122, 130, 131, 151, 196, 204
Witness, xxi, xxii, xxv, 15, 29, 32, 43, 80, 108, 111, 116, 127, 162, 245–50, 270, 271, 272, 276, 279
Wonder, 71–74, 127, 224
Worship, xiii, xiiin18, xx, 28n43, 37, 37n75, 77, 86n21, 95n87, 121, 127–33, 123n73, 132n92, 132, 137, 140n22, 153n67, 176n112, 178, 185n20, 188, 195, 199, 203n85, 204, 218, 223, 233, 253n14, 256n40, 259n55, 266, 268, 271n108, 291n215. *See also* Jesus Christ, Vicarious Worship of, Praise

Zombies, 274, 274n123

Name Index

Adams, Robert M., 31n52
Alfeyev, Bishop Hilarion, 235n32, 254n25
Affleck, Ben, 27
Alexander the Great, 62
Aldworth, A. S., 55n51
Allen, Woody, 4
Allison, Dale, xi, xin3, 58, 58n69, 142n31
Andersen, Francis I., 23n16
Anderson, Ray S., xi, xin18, xiv, xivn25, xxin, 56, xxiii, xxiv, xxv, 5, 5n6, 5n7, 5n8, 6, 6n11, 6n13, 9, 9n27, 10, 10n28, 10n29, 14, 14n50, 15, 15n53, 30, 30n46., 37, 37n76, 39n,78, 40, 40n82, 46n11, 49, 50n23, 61, 61n84, 67, 67n28, 68, 68n33, 69n34, 70, 70n42, 72, 72n56, 79n93, 82, 82n108, 82n109, 83n1, 88, 88n31, 89, 89n36, 89n38, 89n40, 90, 90n45, 90n46, 92, 92n61, 93, 94, 94n68, 96, 96n84, 96n85, 105, 105n1, 107, 107n14, 108, 109, 109n18, 109n20, 112, 112n37, 112n38, 112n39, 118, 118n55, 122n68, 124, 124n77, 134, 134n1, 135, 135n6, 141n25, 184n15, 205, 205n91, 212, 212n11, 212n12, 213, 213n14, 217, 217n28, 221, 221n50, 221n51, 222, 222n100, 230n5, 237, 237n47, 237n51, 239, 239n62, 244, 244n86251n3, 260, 260n61, 260n62, 260n63, 261, 261n64, 261n65, 261n69, 267, 267n91, 269, 272, 272n113, 278, 278n154, 278n155, 279n156, 281, 281n167, 290, 290n205, 290n206, 292, 292n219
Appelbaum, David, 68n31
Aquinas, Thomas, 19, 19n73, 34, 105, 106n3
Aristotle, 63, 63n5, 105, 105n2, 106, 109, 109n22
Arndt, Stephen Wentworth, 95n76
Aslan, 30
Athanasius, xiv, xivn26, xvi, xxi, 87, 87n25, 95
Augustine, 10, 10n31, 25, 34, 34n61, 106, 106n4, 110, 128, 128n85, 129, 130n88, 139, 139n17, 149, 149n51, 152, 152n64, 153, 156, 156n72, 165, 165n93, 166n94, 175, 175n110, 182, 182n1, 187, 188n29, 192n55, 202, 202n81

Balthasar, Hans Urs von, 56n52, 95, 95n74, 227, 234n31, 268
Banke, Helmut, 125, 125n79
Bareman, Kristen, xxv
Barth, Karl, xiii, xiiin13, xiiin14, xiiin15, xiv, xivn23, xivn24, xvn27, xvi, xvin33, xvin36, xviii, xviiin45, xviiin48, xix, xixn49, xx, xxn54, xxi, xxii, xxiin57, xxiv, xxivn58, xxivn59, xxv, xxvn60, xxvn62, xxvn63, xxvi, 5n9, 8, 8n21, 11, 11n33, 12, 12n36, 15, 16, 16n54, 16n57, 16n58, 21, 21n6, 22n9, 23, 23n17, 24, 25, 25n24, 25n27, 32, 32n54, 32n55, 33, 33n58, 35, 35n66, 37n73, 38, 38n77, 40, 40n83, 40n85, 41, 41n88, 41n90, 42, 42n91, 42n93, 44, 47, 47n12, 47n13, 47n15, 49, 49n18, 49n21,

Barth, Karl (*continued*)
50, 50n24, 51, 51n34, 52, 52n36, 52n39, 53, 53n43, 53n45, 53n46, 54, 54n48, 54n49, 57, 57n60, 57n61, 57n62, 58, 58n68, 59, 59n70, 60, 60n75, 60n77, 60n80, 61, 61n82, 63, 63n7, 65, 65n15, 66, 66n21, 66n24, 67, 67n25, 68, 68n32, 69, 71, 71n44, 71n46, 72, 72n53, 73n62, 76, 76n72, 77, 77n84, 78n85, 78n89, 80, 80n98, 80n101, 81, 81n105, 82, 86, 86n18, 88, 88n32, 88n33, 89n43, 90n49, 90n50, 91, 91n55, 91n57, 94, 94n70, 95n71, 95n78, 96, 96n79, 96n80, 96n81, 96n86, 97, 97n87, 97n88, 97n89, 97n92, 98, 98n96, 99, 99n99, 108, 108n17, 110, 110n23, 110n27, 111, 111n29, 111n32, 111n34, 113, 113n40, 115, 115n44, 117, 117n52, 119, 119n56, 119n57, 121, 121n61, 121n62, 123, 123n72, 123n74, 125, 125n79, 132n90, 132n91, 133, 133n96, 135n5, 138, 138n12, 138n13, 139, 139n18, 140, 140n20, 141, 141n26, 141n29, 142, 142n32, 142n33, 143, 143n36, 143n37, 144, 144n39, 150n58, 150n59, 154n68, 155, 161n80, 161n82, 162, 163, 163n89, 167n97, 170n101, 173n105, 174, 174n108, 174n109, 177, 177n116, 179, 179n120, 179n121, 181, 181n129, 182n3, 183, 183n4, 183n5, 183n7, 183n9, 184, 184n10, 184n12, 184n14, 184n16, 185, 185n19, 186, 186n24, 187, 187n27, 187n29, 188, 188n30, 189, 189n36, 190, 190n40, 190n42, 191n46, 194, 194n59, 196, 196n62, 197, 197n63, 198, 198n68, 199, 199n74, 201, 201n77, 205, 205n92, 205n94, 206, 206n96, 206n101, 207, 207n103, 208, 209, 210n3, 217, 218, 218n32, 218n34, 219, 219n35, 219n38, 220, 220n39, 220n40, 220n43, 220n44, 221, 222, 222n53, 223, 223n59, 224, 224n65, 224n68, 225, 225n71, 227, 227n84, 228n92, 229, 229n97, 229n98, 230, 230n1, 231, 231n6, 233, 233n25, 235n35, 235n38, 236, 236n39, 236n40, 236n41, 236n42, 236n45, 237, 237n46, 237n48, 237n50, 237n52, 238, 238n53, 238n55, 238, 238n58, 238n59, 238n61, 240, 240n63, 240n64, 241n69, 242, 242n72, 242n74, 243n78, 243n80, 245n90, 246, 246n91, 246n92, 246n96, 247, 247n102, 248, 248n104, 248n106, 248n107, 249, 249n113, 249n115, 249n117, 250n121, 250n122, 251, 251n1, 252n4, 252n5, 253n12, 253n16, 253n18, 253n19, 253n20, 253n21, 254, 254n26, 254n27, 254n28, 255n30, 256, 256n36, 256n37, 257, 257n41, 257n42, 257n43, 257n45, 257n47, 258, 258n49, 258n50, 258n51, 258n52, 259, 259n54, 259n56, 259n57, 260n58, 260n60, 261, 261n67, 262, 262n71, 262n73, 262n74, 263n77, 263n78, 263n79, 264, 264n82, 265, 266, 266n87, 266n90, 267, 267n92, 268n94, 269, 269n97, 269n98, 269n99, 270, 270n102, 270n103, 270n105, 271, 271n107, 271n109, 271n111, 272, 272n115, 273, 273n117, 273n119, 274n127, 274n128, 275n130, 275n133, 275n136, 275n137, 276, 276n141, 276n143, 276n144, 277n146, 277n149, 279, 279n157, 279n159, 280, 280n161, 280n164, 284n177, 284n178, 284n179, 284n180, 285n186, 285n187, 286, 286n189, 286n191, 286n192, 287n195, 287n196, 288, 288n197, 289n200, 289n202, 290n204, 291n210, 291n213, 292n218, 292n220, 293, 293n223, 293n224, 293n225, 294, 294n230, 295n234, 296n241
Barth, Markus, 125, 125n79
Barrett, C. K., 31n49, 34, 35n63, 179, 179n119
Barthell, Joe, xxv
Baxter, Christina, 16n59
Beardslee, Michael, xxv

Beasley, James, 83n4
Beck, A. T., 85, 85n14
Becker, Ernest, 68, 68n29, 69
Becker, Scott, 36n68, 217, 217n25
Beckstrom, Karen, 14n45
Beckwith, R. T., 271n106
Begbie, Jeremy, 91n54, 128, 128n86, 216n24, 268
Begley, Sharon, 9n25
Belew, Greg, xxv
Benedetti, Gaetano, 19n73
Bernanos, Georges, 6, 6n12, 51, 51n33, 52, 52n35, 53
Berkeley, Theodore, 44n1
Berry, Wendell, 13, 13n41, 35, 35n64, 157, 157n75
Bethge, Eberhard, 34n60, 128
Beyreuther, E., 185, 186n22
Blake, William, 85n9, 100
Bolling, Binx, 42, 71, 72, 78
Bonhoeffer, Dietrich, xiii, xii n19, xvii, xviii, xviii n43, xviii n44, xxi, 9n27, 17, 17n62, 21, 21n4, 23, 28, 28n36, 33, 34n60, 39, 39n81, 40, 40n86, 58, 59, 59n71, 59n74, 65, 65n12, 65n13, 86, 86n17, 88, 88n30, 89, 89n44, 95, 95n72, 97, 97n90, 128, 128n87, 132, 132n89, 142, 142n35, 146, 147, 147n46, 150, 150n57, 155, 155n70, 184, 185, 185n18, 203, 203n86, 203n87, 204n88, 217, 217n27, 235, 235n36, 240, 240n66, 244, 244n82, 250, 250n118, 250n119, 253, 253n17, 258, 258n48, 260, 261, 261n64, 261n66, 261n68, 265, 265n86, 268n93, 272, 272n114, 274, 274n125, 275, 275n138, 283, 283n173, 285, 285n182, 295, 296n236, 296n239
Boulding, Maria, 128n85, 130n88, 165n93
Bowden, John, xxv n60, 56n54,
Bradbury, Ray, 3, 25, 25n26, 68, 68n30, 107, 107n13, 127, 127n82, 189, 189n38, 204, 204n89, 216, 216n23, 241, 255, 255n32, 282
Bringle, Mary Louise, 8, 36n72, 85, 85n10, 85n11, 85n13, 85n15, 86

Brontë, Emily, 84n8
Brown, Charlie, 181, 181n128
Brown, Colin, xxvi, 228n91,
Brown, Raymond, 116, 116n49, 227n87,
Brown, Sally A., 227n88
Brown, Warren S., 273n118
Bromiley, Geoffrey W., v, xi, xix, xxv, xxvi, 19n73
Bruce, F. F., 35n65
Brueggemann, Walter, 148, 148n50
Bultmann, Rudolf, 65, 75
Burroughs, Edgar Rice, xxiii, 251, 276, 276n140
Busch, Eberhard, xxv n60, xxv n62,
Burroughs, Edgar Rice, xxiii, 251, 276, 276n140
Burton, Robert, 8
Burton, Tim, 202

Calvin, John, xiv, xiv n23, xxvi, 29, 29n44, 34, 34n62, 39n79, 44, 44n2, 46, 46n9, 49, 49n22, 79, 79n92, 86, 86n21, 87, 98, 98n95, 117, 117n51, 118, 118n55, 132, 132n94, 132n95, 133, 137, 137n10, 145, 146n43, 147, 147n48, 153, 153n67, 157, 157n73, 159, 159n76, 160, 160n78, 166, 166n95, 171, 171n103, 178, 178n118, 182, 182n2, 186, 186n25, 195, 196n60, 202, 202n80, 204n89, 216, 243n81, 247, 247n102
Campbell, John McLeod, 39, 39n80, 52, 52n37, 88n32, 191, 192n49, 227, 227n89, 229, 229n99, 276, 276n142
Camus, Albert, 76, 76n79
Carnell, Corbin Scott, 11n31
Carnell, Edward J., 122, 12n67
Cassian, John, 49, 49n19, 134, 134n2, 176, 177n115, 214, 215, 215n17, 245, 245n89
Chabon, Michael, 73, 73n60, 73n61
Chadwick, Henry, 10n31
Chandler, Raymond, xxiii
Chaney, Lon, 11
Chesterton, G. K., 26, 26n29, 135, 135n7, 254, 254n22

Name Index

Childs, Brevard, 153, 153n66, 200n76
Chrysostum, John, 14m 14n47, 87, 17n23, 140, 140n17, 257, 257n46
Clément, Olivier, 44n1, 51n32
Climacus, John, 86, 86n20, 87n24
Clines, David J. A., 23n16, 45n6
Coles, Robert, 65n12, 65n13, 95n72, 97n90, 250n119, 265n86, 283n173, 285n182, 296n236, 296n239
Collier, Charlie, xxv
Colyer, Elmer M., xi, 176n113, 209n2, 252n6
Coulter, Allen, 27n32
Craigie, Peter, 152, 152n63
Crisp, Oliver P., 287n196
Criswell, 71
Crow, Jayber, 35, 35n64
Cruz, Penelope, 218, 218n33
Currie, Thomas W. III, 106, 106n8
Curtis, C. Michael, 40n84

Davis, Ellen R., 84n5
Dawson, Gerrit, 140, 141n24, 287n196
DeGruchy, John, 21n4
D'Elia, John A., 24n23
Derrida, Jacques, 184, 223
Diadochus, 51, 51n32
Dillon, Marcia, xxv
Dionysus, 135, 203. 203m/85
Disney, Walt, 277
Disraeli, Benjamin, 14, 14n45
Doerge, Halden, xxv
Donceel, Joseph, xiin12
Dostoevsky, Fyodor, ix, ix n1, 3, 6, 6n10, 246, 246n93, 296n238
Dubus, Andre, 40, 40n84
Dunn, James D. G., 161n81
Dylan, Bob, ix, xxiii, 5, 5n5, 7, 7n15, 26, 26n30, 27n31, 48, 69, 69n37, 70n39, 106, 107n10, 223, 223m.58, 294, 295n233

Edwards, Jonathan, 268, 268n96
Egan, Keith J., 268m/93
Ehrenreich, Barbara, 193n58, 203, 203n84
Elder, Will, 31n52
Ellis, Novellene Price, 64n8

Elshtain, Jean Bethke, 127, 127n84, 274, 274n124, 274n126
Evagrius, 14, 14n48, 86n20, 214, 214n16
Evanier, Mark, 223n57
Evans, C. Stephen, 76n77, 76n78, 83n1

Fahlbusch, Erwin, 19n73
Fariña, Richard, 3, 3n1
Ferrie, W., 55n51
Feuerbach, Ludwig, 81
Fiddes, Paul, 45, 45n7, 90n53, 95n77, 228n92, 234n30
Finkenrath, G., 186, 186n22
Fitzmyer, Joseph A., 137, 137n11
Foley, Grover, xxiv n59
Ford, John, 72n51
Ford, Paul D., 25n25
Fowler, James, 36, 36n72
Frankenstein, 43, 43n97
Fraser, John W., 34n62
Friedrich, Gerhard, xxvi,
Frost, David, 3, 3n2,
Fuller, Reginald H., 34n60

Gator, Alexander (Alley) K., 4
Gibson, Mel, 198, 198n67
Gide, André, 77, 77n83
Godsey, John D., 17n62
Goldingay, John, 16n59, 83n3
Green, Barbara, 17n62
Green, Clifford J., xviii n43, 89n44
Green, Joel B., 186n23
Greene, Colin, 69n35
Grenz, Stanley J., 76n78
Grey, Rudolph, 202n79
Griffin, Emilie, 152, 152n61
Groening, Matt, 4
Guder, Darrell L., 56n53
Gunton, Colin E., xiii n17, 184n15, 247n103
Guthrie, Woody, 26
Gythiel, Anthony P., 14n47

Haidu, David, 282n171
Hanger, Donald, 118, 118n54
Harned, David Baily, 89, 89n42, 239n60

Harris, Murray J., 31n50, 46, 46n8
Harrison, Graham, 235n31
Hart, David Bentley, xii, xiin9, xiin12, xxi, 56n52, 65, 65n17, 66, 67, 67n27, 110, 110n26, 184n11, 202n81, 202n82, 205, 206n95, 216, 216n21, 217, 217n26, 218, 219n38, 235, 235n33, 242, 242n73, 244, 244n83, 269, 284, 284n181
Hart, Trevor, 22n10, 216n24
Hauerwas, Stanley, 11, 11n32, 55n50
Hawley, John Stratton, 289n201
Hays, Richard B., xvin35
Hecht, Jennifer Michael, 81n102
Heron, Aladair I. C., 243n81, 266n89
Heschel, Abraham, 203n85
Hick, John, 241n71
Hill, Roger, 107
Hippocrates, 8
Hitchcock, Alfred, 75, 75n68, 79
Hitler, Adolf, 93, 203
Hobbs, Ray, 24
Hoffer, Eric, 206n100
Hollaway, Wilma, xxv
Holly, Buddy, 26
Homer, 80, 80n96
Hong, Edna, 5, 13n44, 41n89, 79n94, 81n103, 244n85,
Hong, Howard, 5, 13n44, 41n89, 79n94, 81n103, 244n85,
Hope, Bob, 281
Hopper, Edward, 269
Horowitz, Allan V., 9n26
Hoskyns, Edward Clement, 29n45, 117, 117n50, 169, 169n98, 170n100, 176n111
Howard, Robert E., 64, 64n8
Hughes, Charles, 241n71
Hugo, Victor, 11, 11n35, 64, 64n10
Hummerstone, Jeremy, 44n1
Humphrey, Hubert H., 110, 110n25
Hunsinger, George, 176, 176n133, 252, 252n6

Irenaeus, xxi, xii

Jeremias, Joachim, 164, 164n92

Johansson, Scarlet, 26
Johnson, Harry, 287n196
Johnson, W. Stacy, 227n88, 228n91
Jones, Gerard, 31n51, 209, 209n1, 282n170
Jones, Indiana, 26, 26n28
Jüngel, Eberhard, 56, 56n53, 80n100, 227, 227n90, 228n92, 228n93

Kashner, Sam, 27n32
Kast, Verena, 115n46, 122n68, 123, 123n69, 123n71, 135n3, 204n90
Kastor, Frank S., 25n25
Keillor, Garrison, 12, 12n39, 13
Kelly, Geffrey B., 17n62
Kenyon, Jane, 100, 100n100, 1899, 199n73
Kierkegaard, Søren, x, xxi, xxiii, 4, 5, 5n4, 5n7, 7, 13, 13n44, 14, 20, 20n1, 21, 21n8, 22, 22n11, 36, 36n69, 41, 41n89, 43, 43n94, 55, 55n51, 63, 63n4, 63n6, 70, 70n41, 72, 74, 74n64, 75, 75n69, 76, 77, 77n82, 79, 79n94, 80n97, 81, 81n103, 83, 83n1, 85, 86, 101, 122, 127, 211, 211n6, 212, 213, 225, 225n70, 225n72, 225n4, 228, 228n95, 244, 244n85, 254, 278, 278n155, 281, 290, 290n205
Kimble, Richard, 30
Kirby, Jack, 222, 223n57
Kittel, Gerhard, xxvi,
Klauck, Hans-Josef, 203n85
Kovacs, Judith L., 34n61, 140n19
Kramer, Peter, 8, 9n24
Krauss, Reinhard, xviii n43, 17n62, 89n44
Kushner, Harold S., 211n4
Kuske, Martin, 17, 62

Ladd, George Eldon, 24
Lang, Fritz, 93, 93n66
Lee, Stan, 222, 223n57
Leibniz, Gottfried, 5,
Lewis, Alan, 56, 56n52, 56n55, 95, 95n73, 96, 96n82, 141, 141n30, 227, 255, 255n33

316   Name Index

Lewis, C. S., xix, xix n52, xx, 25, 25n25, 30, 30n48, 31, 32, 32n53, 33, 43, 43n98, 53, 53n42, 53n44, 62, 62n1, 88n32, 106, 106n9, 111, 111n31, 111n33, 112, 112n35, 112n36, 113, 113n42, 142, 187, 187n26, 199, 199n72, 201, 201n78, 233, 233n24, 256, 270, 270n101, 272, 291, 291n16, 294, 291n229, 294n231
Lewton, Val, 274n123
Lindvall, Terry, 122n35
Liu, Catherine, 11n35
Lugosi, Bela, 274n123
Luibheid, Colin, 49n19
Lukens, Nancy, xviii n43
Luther, Martin, xvii, 50, 212

Mackey, Ryan, xxv
Mackinnon, D. M., 217, 217n26
MacKinnon, Steven A., 177n115
Macmurray, John, 27, 27n34
Malmud, Bernard, 24n22
Malony, H. Newton, 7n16, 273n118
Marion, Francis, 278
Maris, Derek, xxv
Martin, Ralph P., 17n60, 35n65, 124n78, 266n88
McCreight, Katheryn Greene, 8
McKee, Elise Anne, 29n44
McKim, Donald K., 141n29, 233n25
McMahon, Darren M., 106n7
McNeil, Brian, 203n85
Meadow, Mary Jo, 7n16, 7n17
Meléndez, Bill, 181n128
Menzies, William Cameron, 282
Meredith, William, 7, 7n14
Merton, Thomas, 13, 13n40
Meyer, Marvin, 241n71
Migliore, Daniel, 219, 219n38
Mill, J. S., 106
Millay, Edna St. Vincent, 221, 221n50
Miller, Calvin, 204n89
Miller, Norma, 221n50
Miller, Patrick D., 227n88, 228n91
Miller, Robert J., xi n3, 142n31
Molnar, Paul D., 232, 232n14
Moltmann, Jürgen, 56, 56n54, 90, 90n52, 219n38, 224, 224n64, 228, 228n92, 234, 260, 260n59, 270, 270n104, 275, 275n132
Montgomery, William, 145n42
Morris, Leon, 169, 169n99
Morris, Pamela, 6n12
Mozart, xxv, xxv n63
Murphy, Nancey, 273, 273n118
Murphy, Roland, 148, 148n49, 151, 151n60, 183, 183n4, 200n75
Murray, A. F., 80n96
Murray, John, 88n32
Myers, Robert W., x, 99, xxv

Nazianzus, Gregory, 254, 254n25
Needleman, Jacob, 68n31
Nelson, Rick, xxiii
Neuser, Wilhelm, 132n94, 243n81
Nichols, Aidan, 56n52
Niebuhr, Reinhold, xvi, xvi n38, 66
Niebuhr, H. Richard, 215, 216n20
Nielsen, Leslie, 278
Nietzsche, Friedrich, xxi, 174, 174n108, 192, 202, 202n82, 202n83, 203, 213, 216, 216n22, 264
Nimoy, Leonard, 274n123
Norris, Kathleen, 14, 14n49
Nygren, Anders, 67n26

Oates, Joyce Carol, 7n18
Obama, Barack, 223
O'Brien, Justin, 76n79
O'Brien, Peter T., 119n59, 164n91
O'Conner, Richard, 8n23
Ogden, C. K., 68n31
Olsen, Jimmy, 283
Oman, John, 69n35
Osborn, Ian, 9n24, 184n17

Pal, George, 282, 282n169
Pannenberg, Wolfhart, 87, 87n27
Partee, Charles, 243n81
Pascal, Blaise, 69, 69n36
Patton, Kimberly Christine, 289n201
Peers, E. Allison, 49n20
Pelikan, Jaroslav, 108n16, 125n80
Percy, Walker, 42, 42n92, 71, 77
Petersen, Leigh Anne, xxv
Pevear, Richard, ix n1, 6n10

Name Index

Pilate, Pontius, xii
Polanyi, Michael, 107, 107n11
Pott, Clarence K., xxv n 63
Powell, Randy, xxv
Price, Daniel J., 239n58
Purves, Andrew, xvii, xvii n41, xvii n42

Quasten, Johannes, 203n85

Rahner, Karl, xii, xiin12, 231, 232n10
Ramm, Bernanrd, xxv n61
Ramsey, Boniface, 165n93, 203n85
Redding, Graham, 243n81
Reeves, George, 27
Reid, Stephen Breck, 259n55
Ricks, Christopher, 48, 48n17, 70, 70n38
Rigby, Cynthia, xxiv, 233, 259, 259n55
Romero, George, 274n123
Rose, Jesica, 235n32
Rossé, Gérard, 95n76
Rumsey, Andrew, 90, 91n54
Russert, Tim, 122, 123, 123n71
Rüter, Martin, 21n4

Sanders, John, 46, 46n10, 55
Sartre, Jean-Paul, 76, 76n77
Schaap, James Calvin, 204n89
Schleiermacher, Friedrich, 69, 69n35, 219n38,
Schmemann, Alexander, xvii, xvii n39, xxi, 74n63, 108, 108n15, 185, 185n21, 188, 188n33, 189, 192, 192n52, 192n56, 199, 199n71, 246, 246n95, 247, 247n100, 252, 252n7, 253n13, 257n46, 277, 277n150, 279, 279n158, 284n176, 284n177, 291, 291n214
Schmemann, Juliana, 108n15
Schoenberger, Nancy, 27n32
Schweitzer, Contra Albert, 145n42
Scorcese, Martin, 70, 70n39
Scully, Vin, 107
Shakespeare, William, 62, 62n2, 62n3
Shaw, Scott, 283
Sheldrake, Philip, 268n93
Shelley, Mary, 43n97
Shepherd, Fred, 83, 84

Shults, F. LeRon, 33, 33n59
Silver, Alain, 66n20, 73n59
Simon and Garfunkel, 14
Simon, Paul, 14n46
Smail, T. A., 253n19, 46n9
Smail, Tim, 83n3, 239n61, 275n129
Smedes, Lewis, xxiv, xxiv n58, 13n43, 47n14
Smith, Dodie, 84n6
Solomon, Robert, 85, 85n11
Soosten, Joachim von, xviii n43, xviii n44
Speidell, Todd, xxi n56, xxii, 9n27
Špidlik, Tomáš, 14n47, 14n48, 86n20, 87n22, 87n23, 87n24, 78n25, 87n26, 87n28, 214n16, 196n240
Spielberg, Steven, 26n28
Starke, Ekkehard, 19n73
Steere, Douglas V., 278n155
Stewart, Jimmy, 75
Superman, 27, 27n32, 33, 107, 282, 283
Stott, Douglas W., xviii n 43, 89n44

Tanner, Kathryn, 247, 247n103
Tate, Marvin E., 48n16
Taylor, Jeremy, 84, 84n7
Tennyson, Alfred Lord, 64n11
Thiessen, Gesa Elsbeth, 244n85, 269
Thimell, Daniel, 22n10
Thomson, G. T., 51n34.
Thoreau, Henry David, 64, 64n9
Tillich, Paul, xxiv
Tödt, Ilse, 17n62, 21n4
Tolkien, J. R. R., 294, 294n231
Torrance, Alan J., 133n98, 183n8, 184n13, 219n38, 239n57, 256, 256n38, 258n51, 287n196
Torrance, David W., xi, xvin35, 34n62, 39n79, 46n9, 117n51, 287n196
Torrance, James B., v, x, xi, xiii, xiiin18, xvin35, xviin42, xxv, 22n10, 28n43, 37, 37n75, 86n21, 95, 95n78, 123n73, 132n92, 132n94, 140, 140n22, 153n67, 176n112, 185n20, 232n16, 243n81, 253, 253n14, 256, 256n40, 271, 271n108, 287n196, 291, 291n215

Name Index

Torrance, Thomas F., v, x, xn2, xi, xin5, xii, xiin6, xivn23, xv, xvn28, xvn31, xvi, xvin32, xvin34, xvin35, xix, xixn50, xx, xxn53, xxivn58, xxv, xxvi, 8n20, 21n5, 22, 22n10, 34n62, 39n79, 46n9, 52n38, 90n47, 90n48, 95n75, 96, 96n81, 97n87, 177n51, 119n60, 123n72, 132n95, 133n98, 141n29, 143, 143n38, 176, 176n113, 176n114, 185, 185n19, 188n32, 192n50, 209n2, 226, 226n77, 231, 231n7, 232, 232n11, 232n15, 233, 233n19, 233n25, 234, 234n26, 245n88, 252, 252n6, 252n8, 254n24, 255, 255n31, 256, 256n35, 287n196, 294n228

Ulrich, Reinhard, 260n59
Ursini, James, 66n20, 73n59

Van Andel, Henry J., 44n2
Vedantam, Shankar, 9n25
Vineberg, Steve, 67, 96
Volokhonsky, Larissa, ix n1, 6n10
Voltaire, 31, 31n52

Wade, Audrey, xxv
Wakefield, Jerome C., 9n26
Walker, Robert T., xi
Wallis, Ian G., 17n61, 89n39
Walsh, Jerome T., 70
Walsh, William, 83, 83n2

Ware, Kallistos, 60, 60n79, 226, 226n76, 2276n81, 227, 289n201
Warren, Barney E., ix
Watson, Philip S., 67n26
Wayne, John, 72
Weil, Simone, 7, 7n16, 7n17
Weiser, Artur, 146, 146n44, 157, 157n74, 161, 161n79, 160, 166n96, 188, 188n31, 191, 191n48, 192n51, 193, 193n57, 196n61, 283, 283n172
Weller, Sam, 204n89, 216n23
Wells, H. G., 75, 75n70
Wertham, Frederic, 282n171
West, Charles C., xviii n43, 89n44
Whitaker, Douglas, 115n46
Wilbour, Charles E., 64n10
Williams, Guy, 278
Williams, Hank, 26
Willis, John Randolph, 187n26
Wilson, A. N., 80, 81n102
Wilson, R. A., 56n54
Wirt, Sherwood, 14n45
Wittgenstein, Ludwig, 68, 68n31
Wood, Edward D., 71n45, 202, 202n79, 203, 204
Wood, Ralph C., 26n29, 66, 66n23
Worsley, Wallace, 11n35

Yancey, Philip, 204n89

Zimmerli, 236, 236n45
Zizioulas, John, 69n34, 141, 141n25

Scripture Index

GENESIS
1	54, 209
1:7	237
1:14–19	219
2:21	261
2:23	261
3:7	47
4:13	47

EXODUS
3:6	53
18:9	160
32:1	204
32:23	204
32:32	147

LEVITICUS
23:40	128

DEUTERONOMY
12:7	148
28:47–48	197
28:63	197
30:8–10	119
32:43	148

JUDGES
6:22	53

1 SAMUEL
2:1	150
18:6	129

1 KINGS
1:40	129
19:3–20	92
19:4	38
19:11	38
19:11–12	38
19:18	38

1 CHRONICLES
1:30	121
15:15–16	186
15:16	129
16:10	129
16:33	158
29.9	194, 199

2 CHRONICLES
15:15	148
20:27	199
23:18	129
24:10	129
29:36	129

EZRA
3:11–13	136, 157, 186
3:12–13	217
6:16	156, 199
6:22	156

NEHEMIAH
8:9–11	180
8:9–12	180
8:10	180
8:12	180

Scripture Index

NEHEMIAH (*continued*)
12:43	156, 165, 194
12:44	129

ESTHER
8:16	205

JOB
1	45
3:3–4	45
3:7	23, 45, 134
3:11	23
3:20–22	68, 205
7:16	23
7:19	23
8:20–21	120
20:5	63, 204, 205
21:7	63, 204
21:12	63, 204
31:24–25	204
33:26	120, 187
38:4	158
38:7	158

PSALMS
1:2	268
4:7	182, 188
4:8	188
5:11	129, 268, 283
6:5	31
9:2	129
9:13–14	150
13:3–4	130, 150
13:5–6	130
14:7	160
16:8–11	166
16:9	178
16:9–11	165
16:11	187, 192, 199, 268
19:1	158, 244
19:4–5	158
20	175
20:1	175
20:2	175
20:5	175
21:1	156
22	227
22:1	38, 58
27:6	130, 156, 194
28:7	130, 161
30:1	149
30:4–5	145
30:5	87
30:11	268
31:1–2	152
31:7	152
31:7–8	152
32:3–5	262
32:5	262
32:11	120
33:1	120
33:20–21	120
34:8	268
34:10	276
34:12	276
34:20	196
35:9	120
35:9–10	147
35:19	113
35:24–27	113
35:27	120
36:5	235
37:4	268, 276
37:24	276
37:36	276
38:16	114
39:12–13	58
40:16	150
41:9	28
42:3	37
42:4	131
43:1–2	39
43:4	129, 156
43:5	39
45:15	108, 113
48:1–2	156, 165
51	191, 262
51:3	191
51:7	191
51:8	145, 157, 191, 195, 284, 293
51:10	263, 287, 293

51:11–12	288	104:15	159
51:12	146, 191, 263	104:24	159
58:10	121	104:31	118, 159
63:5–7	130, 148	105:3	155
63:11	120	105:43	160
64:1	219	106:4–5	160
65:8	158	107:21–22	160
65:9–11	127	107:22	130
65:12–13	128, 159	107:42	161
66:1	128	112:1	268
66:5–6	160	113:9	113
67:4	192, 196	118:24	159
68:3	120, 155	119	268
70:4	150	119:11	194
71:23	130	119:14	194
77	48	119:16	194, 235, 240
77:1–2	45	119:28	24
77:3	45	123:2–3	54
79:1	48	126:4–6	146
79:5	48	132:9	121
81:1–3	128	137:6	165
85:6	120	139:9	112
86:4	193	149:2	159
88:3	39	149:3	120
88:10–12	31	149:5	120
89:15–16	128		
89:42	63	PROVERBS	
89:46	63	2:14	205
89:47	31	5:18	112
90:14	161, 193	6:23	54
95:1–2	130	8:30–31	119
96:11–13	158, 168	8:31	239
97:1	128, 158	8:34	119
97:7–8	195	11:10	122, 196
97:12	120	13:19	122
98:4–8	158	14:10	151
100:1	128, 158, 218	15:21	203
100:1–2	268	15:30	148
102	45	17:21	122, 203
102:1–2	26	21:15	121
102:1–3	45	23:15	113
102:3	25	23:15–16	113
102:5	25	23:16	268
102:11–12	45	23:24	122, 180
102:12	25, 45	23:24–25	113
103:5	134	24:17–18	114, 150
104	159		

PROVERBS (continued)

27:9	151
29:2	151
29:3	113
29:6	131, 151
31:6–7	134

ECCLESIASTES

1:10–11	109
2:1–2	205
2:20–21	62
2:21	24, 25
2:22–23	109
2:24–25	109
2:24–26	183, 200
2:26	109, 155
3:1	44
3:4	44
3:10–11	70
3:13	183
5:18	183, 213
5:18–20	109, 278
5:19	183
5:19–20	267
5:20	24, 183
7:14	154, 210
8:15	200
9:1	70
9:7	109, 200, 205
9:9	108
11:8	210
11:8–9	112

ISAIAH

6:5	53
9:2–3	172
9:3	173
12:3	151, 168, 200
22:12–13	153
22:12–14	200
24:10–11	194
29:19	121, 155, 200, 268
32:12–14	200
32:13–14	195
35:1–2	131, 168
35:10	131, 168, 176
38:18	32
49:13	130, 158
51:1–3	130
51:3	168, 187
51:11	131, 168
53	12, 59
53:3	30, 59, 61
53:3–4	60
53:4	12
53:9	56
54:1	130
55:12	131, 158
56:7	131
60:15	168, 177
61:1	201
61:1–2	172
61:1–3	100
61:2–3	172, 177
61:3	201
61:7	173
61:10–11	149
62:5	118, 240
65:14	131, 173, 195, 201
65:17–19	171, 201
65:18–19	98, 177
66:5	195
66:10	157, 165
66:13–14	168

JEREMIAH

10:3–5	205
15:16	160, 187, 194
31:13	98, 131, 168, 177
31:31	168
32:41	171
33:9	165
48:33	195
49:25	195
50:11–12	114

LAMENTATIONS

2:15	196
2:17	197
3:31–32	48
5:15	48, 131, 197

EZEKIEL

2:8–3:3	56
24:15–16	48
24:23	48
24:25–26	198
25:6–7	114, 195
35:14–15	195
36:5	198, 204

HOSEA

7:14	40
9:1	197, 204

JOEL

2:21	159
2:23	173

AMOS

9:10	48

OBADIAH

12	115

JONAH

4:2–5	92
4:8	38

MICAH

7:8	114

ZEPHANIAH

3:13–14	131
3:16–18	169

ZECHARIAH

2:10	48, 165, 172
2:10–11	132
9:9	172
10:7	172

2 MACCABEES

6:12–17	54

MATTHEW

2:10	233
3:13–17	xii, 287, 293
3:17	181
4:1–11	22
4:4	xi
4:12–16	172
4:17	172, 220
4:19	10
5-7	93
5:3	283
5:3–11	174
5:3–12	191
5:4	99
5:5	122
5:11–12	135
5:12	162, 170, 174, 217
6:1–8, 16–18	86
6:10	60
6:25	22
8:17	12
9:1–8	11
9:9–13	99
9:27–31	97
10:34–36	226
11:24	174
11:25	266
11:25–27	240
11:27	190
11:28	240
11:29–30	240
12:18	181
13:20	115, 207
13:22	115
13:23	115
15:21	119
16:16	191
16:17	191
17:5	181
17:20	17
19:14	127
20:20	55
21:2–7	172
21:21–22	17
22:37	92
24:30	48
25:21	192

MATTHEW (continued)

25:23	295
25:40	247
25:51	246
26:26–39	55
26:27	190, 266
26:36	32
26:37	55
26:69–75	37
26:75	29
27:3–5	37
27:46	38, 46, 58, 95, 235
28:8	136
28:9	137

MARK

1:9–11	xii
1:11	181
1:40	12
2:1–12	11
2:15–17	99
2:17	12
2:27	206
4:13–20	207
7:14	86
9:24	17
9:28–29	16
10:15	126
10:47	12
10:48	12
11:17	131
11:22	17
14:23	266
14:32	32
14:72	29
15:34	38
15:39	58

LUKE

1:14	162
1:28	162
1:30	181
1:42	191
1:44	116
1:46–48	120
1:47	126, 161, 268
1:48	154, 191
2:9	162
2:10	161, 162, 167, 199, 245
2:10–11	181
2:11	116
2:13–15	164
2:52	273
3:21–22	xii
3:22	181
4:1	161
4:1–13	22
4:14	161
4:16–21	201
4:18–19	100, 172
4:21	100, 173
5:8	47, 53
5:17–26	11
5:27–32	99
6:20–23	191
6:22–23	217
6:23	135, 162, 170, 175
8:11–15	207
10:17	115
10:20	115, 162
10:21	xviii, 161, 162, 170, 173, 182, 193, 214, 230, 223, 230, 233, 245, 256, 266, 273
10:22	190
12:50	56
13:1	11
15	186
15:1–10	164
15:2	164, 185
15:3	88
15:3–10	185
15:6	186
15:7	164, 186
15:10	164, 186
17:5–6	17
18:9	47
18:15	127
19:37–38	116
20:13	53
22:19	266
22:26	29
22:35	276

Scripture Index   325

22:40	32	12:27	32
22:44	55	12:27–28	92
22:45	31	12:49	xi
22:61–62	47	14:15–31	215
23:40–43	228	14:19	xi
23:46	152	14:20	169, 170
23:47	121	14:28	169
24:41	137, 178	14:31	116
24:52	168, 178	15:10–11	167
		15:11	116, 121, 126, 182
		15:22	144, 161

JOHN

1:1	164	16:6	53
1:1–2	164	16:15	190
1:4	91	16:19–20	215
1:5	91	16:21	169
1:5, 9	91	16:21–24	175
1:10	73	16:22	117, 161, 169
1:10–11	90	16:23	170
1:11	22, 226	16:24	144, 170
1:14	94, 149, 164	17	117
1:29–34	xii	17:8	53
3:6	281	17:13	116, 117, 118, 126, 170, 182
3:8	xviii, 190, 281	19:33	196
3:16	295	19:36	196
3:29	162	20:11–18	26
3:39	116	20:13	26
4:34	243	20:15	26
4:39	116	20:16	26
5:19–20	xi	20:20, 27	275
5:30	xi, 243	20:21	53
6:28	xi	21:17	47
6:38	243		
6:45	169, 170		
7:17	xi		

ACTS

8:13–19	245	2:17–21	172
8:42	xi	2:24	178
8:56	116, 161, 173	2:26	166, 178
8:58	170	2:28	166
8:59	170	2:29–36	97
9:2–3	11	2:33	47, 166, 255
11:4	20	3:20	53
11:15	116	5:41	55
11:33	29	7:41	204
11:35	29, 85	8:8	116
11:41–43	29	8:32–33	59
11:43	92	8:39	125, 271
12:14–15	170	11:23	126

ACTS (continued)

13:48	126
13:51–52	164
14:17	108
15:3	163
15:31	194
16:34	126, 163, 271
17:28	206

ROMANS

1–3	226
1:4	248
1:15	51
1:17	121
1:18–32	49
1:20	108
3:23	120
3:24–25	98
4:25	294
5:1	170, 210
5:2	170
5:3	41, 170
5:4	170
5:5	170
5:13	193
6	254
6:3	56
6:4	66, 197
6:5	272
6:8	121
6:8–10	197
7	97, 288
7:4	288
7:19	97
7:22	260, 268
7:23–24	260
7:24	98
7:24–25	288
7:25	260
8	97, 288
8:1	98
8:1–2	289
8:9	256
8:18	240
8:19	286
8:20–23	215
8:22	158, 237
8:22–23	36
8:23	6, 13, 52, 286
8:24	138
8:26	36, 133, 253
8:29	60, 112
8:30	269, 293
8:34	132, 149, 289
9:1	147
10:2	202
12:12	41, 138, 248
12:15	30, 32, 140, 147, 289
14:13–23	163
14:17	161, 163, 237, 259, 281
15:8	148
15:10	148
15:32	125
16:26	51

1 CORINTHIANS

1:30	121
4:7	189
7	179
7:29–31	34, 178
7:31	34
11:24	266
12:14	30
12:26	30, 124, 140, 147
12:27	31
13:6	205
13:13	xxv
15:3	58
15:45	34, 179
15:48	294
15:49	294

2 CORINTHIANS

1:20	293
2:3	125
3:18	164, 284
4:7–12	210
4:17	212
5:2	35
5:6	46
5:14	121
5:17	121, 293

5:19	24	4:1	124, 167
6:8–10	41	4:2	167
6:10	54, 144	4:4	119, 125, 162, 167, 268
7:4	138, 210	4:6	22
7:5–7	27, 124	4:10	125
7:5–10	154		
7:9	50, 124		
7:10	18, 50, 198		
7:13	125		
7:13–16	125		
8:2	137		
8:9	xvi, 137, 196, 254		

COLOSSIANS

1:11–12	188, 190
1:12	213
1:13	190, 213
1:15	xiii
1:20	xiii
1:24	59, 124, 145, 187
2:5	125
2:20	121
3:3	52, 53, 58, 121, 255

GALATIANS

1:4	57
2:20	51, 57, 121
2:20–21	xvi
3:1–4:11	xvi
4:5	143
4:27	131
5:22–23	123, 194
6:14	121

1 THESSALONIANS

1:6	164
2:19, 20	124
3:9	124, 125
5:16	126
5:25	147

EPHESIANS

4:30	52
5:2	xiii, 57

1 TIMOTHY

2.6	57
6:13	xii

PHILIPPIANS

1:3–5	124, 193
1:18	164
1:21	xvi
1:23	46
1:25	125
2:2–4	33
2:5–11	xx, 33, 92, 138, 141, 188, 259, 274
2:6–7	190
2:6–8	258, 267
2:7	xv, 57
2:8	259
2:8–9	178
2:17–18	125
2:28–30	125
3:1	119, 162, 167
3:20	46

2 TIMOTHY

1:4	125

PHILEMON

7	125

HEBREWS

2:12	132
2:18	228
4:1–11	174, 240
4:12	226
4:12–16	226
4:14–16	174
4:15	228, 265
5:7	6, 55
5:8	226, 228, 273

HEBREWS (continued)

7:25	253, 255
7:27	57
8:2	xiii, 132, 253
9:1	123
12:2	54, 60, 66, 74, 118, 167, 180, 212, 214, 226, 280, 281, 287, 295
12:3	226
12:7	54
13:17	125

JAMES

1:2	138
1:2–3	217
1:2–4	210
1:8–9	153
1:12	52
1:13	52
1:14	52
4:8–9	146, 210

1 PETER

1:6–7	52, 135
1:8–9	120
3:19	141
4:12	218
4:12–13	145, 211

2 PETER

1:4	143, 272
1:17	181

1 JOHN

1:1–2	164
1:4	124, 126, 167, 169
2:1	121

2 JOHN

4	121
12	121, 126

3 JOHN

3	124
4	124, 126

JUDE

24	171, 241

REVELATION

1:7	48
5:3–4	21
6:8–18	56
9:6	68
10:9	55
12:11	159, 173
12:11–12	214
12:12	159, 173
18:20	195
19:7	214
19:17	171
21:1	171
21:1–5	201

www.ingramcontent.com/pod-product-compliance
Lightning Source LLC
Chambersburg PA
CBHW020109010526
44115CB00008B/758